Popular Culture and Industrialism

1865–1890

Documents in American Civilization Series

General Editors:
HENNIG COHEN AND JOHN WILLIAM WARD

Statement by the General Editors

The Anchor Series, "Documents in American Civilization," provides primary materials for the study of the history of the United States and for the understanding of American culture. In the belief that neither history nor culture can be properly studied without consideration of a variety of sources, the editors have adopted the interdisciplinary approach in the selection of documents. In our sense, a "document" is any idea, institution, or man-made object that provides a clue to the way in which subjective experience is organized at a specific moment in time.

The purpose of the series is twofold: to show the pervasiveness of those themes which are central to particular moments in history; and to underline the significance of cultural documents in their total historical context—and thus to illuminate problems or themes that characterize American society.

HENNIG COHEN is Professor of English at the University of Pennsylvania and editor of *American Quarterly*. He is also editor of *Selected Poems of Herman Melville* (Anchor Books, A375) and co-editor of *Folklore in America*.

JOHN WILLIAM WARD is Professor of History and American Studies at Amherst College. He is the author of *Andrew Jackson: Symbol for an Age* and editor of *Society, Manners, and Politics in the United States* by Michael Chevalier.

HENRY NASH SMITH was born in Dallas, Texas, where he received his A.B. from Southern Methodist University in 1925. He has an A.M. (1929) and Ph.D. (1940) from Harvard. Since 1953 he has been Professor of English at the University of California (Berkeley) where he was Chairman of the Department of English from 1957–60. Mr. Smith was a visiting lecturer on American literature at Harvard from 1945–46 and a fellow of the Huntington Library from 1946–47. He is the author of several books pertaining to the American scene, among them, *Virgin Land: The American West as Symbol and Myth* (for which he was awarded the Bancroft Prize in American History and the Dunning Prize of the American Historical Association); *Mark Twain: The Development of a Writer*; and *Mark Twain's Fable of Progress: Political and Economic Ideas in "A Connecticut Yankee"*; and he is co-editor with William M. Gibson of *Mark Twain–Howells Letters, 1872–1910*.

POPULAR CULTURE AND INDUSTRIALISM 1865–1890

Edited with an Introduction by
Henry Nash Smith

Anchor Books
Doubleday & Company, Inc.
Garden City, New York

Grateful acknowledgment is made for permission to reprint the following copyrighted material.

HARPER & ROW, PUBLISHERS, INCORPORATED. Letter from Mark Twain to Andrew Lang, in London, 1889, from *Mark Twain's Letters*, Vol. II, arranged by Albert Bigelow Paine. Copyright, 1917, by Mark Twain Company; renewed 1945 by Clara Clemens Samossoud. Reprinted by permission of the publisher.

HARVARD LIBRARY BULLETIN. Speech by Mark Twain, from "That Hideous Mistake of Poor Clemens's," by Henry Nash Smith. Published in *Harvard Library Bulletin*, IX, Spring 1955. Reprinted by permission of the publisher.

The Anchor Books edition is the first publication
of *Popular Culture and Industrialism, 1865–1890*.

A hardcover edition is available from
the New York University Press.

Anchor Books edition: 1967

Introduction

I

The phrase "popular culture" is intended to indicate what is left out of the present anthology rather than to define precisely what is included. Since I am concerned here with the commonplace and the ordinary rather than with distinguished achievement, I have passed by the writers who are fixtures in standard anthologies. Mark Twain appears three times in the table of contents and Whitman once, but they figure as spokesmen for widely held views rather than as artists in their own right. Similarly, I have made no effort to represent the work of major thinkers such as those included in Perry Miller's anthology *American Thought: Civil War to World War I* (New York, 1954)—the pioneers in theology and philosophy and social theory who were, as Miller says, carrying forward "one of the most radical revolutions in the history of the American mind" under the impact of post-Hegelian idealism and Charles Darwin's theory of organic evolution.

In other words, this book deals with the beliefs and attitudes that most Americans took for granted, with the accepted patterns of thought and feeling. As a consequence, the materials I have collected consist in large part of pseudo-ideas and stereotypes rather than challenging intellectual discoveries. The most widely read fiction, then as now, was a kind of pseudo-art from which original insights and subtleties of technique were excluded on principle. The popular culture of the post-Civil War period was not strikingly different in content from that of earlier periods, but it had undergone an unprecedented quantitative transformation. The significant event was the development of mass media of communication on something like a modern scale. Several factors contributed to this change: the cost of producing printed matter was lowered by the introduction of steam-powered presses; the spread of free public schools conferred a kind of half-literacy on large segments of the population that had previously been unable to read at all, or had read only with difficulty; trunkline railways connecting the principal cities facilitated the nationwide distribution of books and magazines. A national market for such commodities came into being, and a new large-scale industry was created to supply the demand.

In surveying this mass-produced art and public discourse, the historian must guard against concluding too hastily that industrialization had degraded American taste. Perhaps the steam presses merely reduced to print and thus preserved for our inspection crudities of a sort that in previous generations had been propagated orally. The avalanche of cheap reading matter, however, undoubtedly made for a standardization of both taste and opinion, and in fiction as well as in the reporting of news, the pressures of competition among producers stimulated feats of sensationalism hardly conceivable in a pre-industrial age.

Even so, popular culture embodied some awareness of the transformation of American society. In the decades following the war, the public at large gradually began to recognize that a nation supposedly agrarian was in fact irrevocably committed to an urban-industrial way of life. The old simplicities were gone, or going. The increased scale of business enterprise was producing a new dominant type, the multimillionaire financier or captain of industry, and a new environment, the metropolis with its garish palaces and its portentous slums. The sectional tensions of the pre-Civil War period were being supplanted by conflicts between big business and the vast but largely unorganized labor force. Even in the sphere of religion, the processes of urbanization gave rise to a new kind of revivalism. These are the principal phenomena illustrated by the documents brought together here.

II

The obvious place to find materials for such an anthology is the daily and weekly press. But the problem of selection is staggering. Even a rudimentary "content analysis" of American newspapers and popular magazines for a twenty-five-year period would be an overwhelming task. Of course there are monographic studies, on which I have relied heavily. (Those I have used most extensively are cited in footnotes or listed among the *Suggested Readings* at the end of the book.) Ultimately, however, I have had to make some arbitrary choices. I have drawn on monthly magazines and on widely read books, but I have relied mainly on one metropolitan newspaper—the New York *Herald*—and one nationally circulated journal, *Harper's Weekly*, which, as the reader will notice, has provided most of the illustrations. I believe these are highly representative publications; the fact that both were edited in New York merely emphasizes the fact that New York was the center of mass-circulation journalism. In addition, I have included a number of excerpts from the four volumes of verbatim transcripts of testimony before the Senate Committee on Education and Labor which held hearings on "the relation between labor and capital" in New York, New England, and several parts of the South in 1882–83. The Committee allowed scores of witnesses to talk at length about almost every aspect of contemporary society, with results of great interest for a cultural historian.

Given the complexity of the topic and the limitations of space, I have welcomed several major simplifications dictated by the over-all plan of the series to which this anthology belongs. Separate volumes are to deal with the South, the West, and Industrial America. I have therefore virtually ignored the regions in selecting materials, and have given relatively little space to the actual processes of industrialization. I have emphasized urban rather than rural conditions because in this period the city was the focus of the emergent mass culture; and among cities I have limited the materials almost entirely to New York. Then as now, New York was more conspicuous than typical, but by 1890 it had assumed very nearly its present position as the cultural capital of the nation.

On the theory that it is better to document a few topics with reasonable fullness than many topics more scantily, I have decided not to include a section on morals, although the section on popular literature contains some specimens of the vigorous contemporary debate concerning the morality of sensation fiction. And from a projected section on religion I have kept only a couple of sermons illustrating the popular style of oral discourse and a group of documents bearing on urban revivalism.

III

The Civil War killed a half-million men, left tens of thousands of veterans with empty sleeves or wooden legs, and devastated many of the former states of the Confederacy. Sectional bitterness was kept alive for a decade after Lee's surrender at Appomattox by military occupation of greater or smaller portions of the South. For at least another decade Republican politicians tried to exploit the emotions generated by the conflict in Bloody Shirt oratory. Hawthorne, Melville, and Whitman had recognized the war as a tragic experience for the nation. But these writers reached only a small audience. Generally speaking, public discourse during the post-war decades reveals surprisingly few traces of the agony that both North and South had undergone during the 1860s. Several factors contributed to this apparently rapid psychological recovery. Although there was much bitterness in the defeated South, the demands of economic recovery left relatively little energy for recrimination. The victorious North inevitably dominated the principal channels of communication such as magazines and publishing houses. As Paul Buck has pointed out in *The Road to Reunion* (Boston,

1937), during the 1880s the national magazines were filled with local-color fiction celebrating a largely legendary Old South, but the nostalgia of this writing was quite shallow. It allowed Northern readers to share in an easy sentimentalism comparable to that expressed in the popular songs of Stephen Foster. Thus Thomas W. Higginson, a New England abolitionist who had commanded a regiment of freed Negroes mustered into the Union army, could shed tears over Thomas Nelson Page's "Marse Chan," which exploits the pathos of slave-owning aristocrats ruined by the war. The New South leaders who emerged in the 1870s and 1880s advocated a program of industrialization and diversified agriculture intended to assimilate the region to the national pattern. In the mid-1870s political leaders of the two sections were able to strike a more or less clandestine bargain that readmitted the Southern states to full status in the Union while turning over the problem of the freed slaves to local authorities. Despite ceremonial tributes to the dead on Decoration Days and Memorial Days, both sections evaded full recognition of the tragic import of the war. Only later, in the twentieth century, would William Faulkner and other Southern writers make articulate the enduring traumas it had inflicted on the South and the nation. The hardened resistance of conservatives both North and South to the civil rights movement of the mid-twentieth century shows that the refusal to confront the race issue as tragedy has had inevitably pathological consequences.

The remarkable resilience of both Northern and Southern public opinion in the post-Civil War period was due in large part to the pace of economic expansion, but it was also fostered by habits of thought established during the early decades of the Republic. The eyes of Americans had always been fixed on the future rather than the past. The belief of the Founding Fathers that they were creating a new nation free of the ills entailed on the Old World by centuries of bloodshed, bigotry, and tyranny lay deeper in the American tradition than the sectional controversies leading to the Civil War. The idea of progress as the controlling force in history, with America at the forefront of advance toward a millennial fulfillment, was the true secular theology of this country in the nineteenth century. Faith in progress had been direly threatened by the war but the triumph of union brought as a rebound an intensified confidence in the Manifest Destiny of the nation. Having survived its supreme test, the country was stronger than ever. It had created a military power greater than had ever been seen on the continent of Europe, and its soldiers had demonstrated martial virtues and capacities equal to those of the most warlike nations of the Old World. There is a good deal of understandable although not very attractive arrogance in American public rhetoric of the post-Civil War decades—even in such a dignified utterance as Lowell's Commemoration Ode for the war dead of Harvard.

With the end of hostilities, however, the main emphasis in national self-congratulation began to turn from military to economic achievement. Henry Ward Beecher, as always, uttered the sentiments of a vast public when he declared from the pulpit in 1872:

> So the crushing power, the organized physical force, that men now form into armies, and by which they sweep fellow nations, is to be directed against nature —against the soil, against the rock, against metal. We are to pierce mountains; we are to tunnel hills; we are to cut ways for industry; we are to rear up fleets; and we are to battle storms. We are to be warriors still, but warriors for peace; warriors against the forces of nature that resist us, until we subdue the nations to the blessed condition of industry, as well as social and civil conquest. And the ratio of civilization will be found to be just in proportion to the difference that exists between the use of physical force for managing men, and the use of physical force for controlling nature.

The higher instincts, then, when civilized, become engineer's forces, and not military forces.[1]

Beecher's use of the idea that civilization is a war against nature is characteristic of the muddle resulting from what might be called the domestication of American romanticism. On most occasions Beecher maintained the transcendental doctrine of nature as the garment of God. Not only in the little essays on gardening and landscape which often appeared in his weekly column in the *New York Ledger*, but in his novel *Norwood*, serialized in the same paper, he normally resorted to this idea as a reputable means of softening the acerbities of Calvinism. Josiah G. Holland, the most popular lay moralist of the mid-nineteenth century, preached a similarly gelatinous gospel. The protagonist of Holland's novel *Arthur Bonnicastle* (1873), for example, maintains that

All the things we see are types of things we do not see—visible expressions of the things and thoughts of God. All the phenomena of nature—the persistent radiance of the sun and moon—the coming, going, and unloading, and the grace and glory of the clouds —the changes of the seasons and of the all-enveloping atmosphere, are revelations to our senses and our souls of those operations and influences which act upon our spiritual natures.[2]

Spokesmen for the popular culture continued to give perfunctory assent to such propositions, in equally flaccid language, but in practice most nineteenth-century Americans regarded nature as a storehouse of raw materials awaiting exploitation. After the war this industrial view was more and more often made explicit. In *The Machine in the Garden* (New York, 1964) Leo Marx has traced

[1] Henry Ward Beecher, *The Sermons of Henry Ward Beecher in Plymouth Church Brooklyn from Verbatim Reports by T. J. Ellinwood*. "Plymouth Pulpit," Ninth Series (New York, 1874), pp. 225–26 (23 November 1872).

[2] *Arthur Bonnicastle: An American Novel* (New York, 1918), p. 371.

from the 1790s onward a continuous development of the notion that the American national destiny was inseparably bound up with technological advance. By the 1880s this belief had become an axiom. And in 1891 Senator Platt of Connecticut could declare that the "subtle influence exercised upon the character of man" by the contemplation of nature as landscape was of little moment in comparison with "the greater and subtler molding influence" of technological mastery—man's "subjection of the forces of nature to become his ministering spirits" in the form of steam and electricity (Document 5).

The blend of nationalism and jubilation over economic progress that pervaded American popular culture in the post-Civil War period is well expressed in the voluminous writings of Edward A. Atkinson, a Boston textile manufacturer who made a specialty of statistical studies. According to tables which he compiled in 1886, the growth in economic power of the United States during the twenty years following the Civil War could be represented as follows:

	1865	1885
Miles of railway in operation	33,908	125,379
Tons moved one mile by six railway systems in the Middle West ("the food-providers"), in millions	573	6,500
Production of pig-iron, in tons	931,582	4,529,869
Total fire-insurance risks reported by the Insurance Commissioner for the State of New York, in millions of dollars	2,564	10,517

On the basis of these and similar statistics, Atkinson proclaimed an orthodox version of the national faith. It is significant that for him the war has become not a national tragedy but a powerful stimulus to industrialization:

It is sometimes held, and perhaps with truth, that in

the very struggles which ensued between the dates 1861 and 1865, in the effort to eliminate from our organic law the elements of injustice and wrong by which it had been perverted, that [sic] the imagination of the people of both sections was first aroused and their knowledge of each other was greatly extended. A knowledge of the vast extent of the land and its resources also became common to all. Thus great enterprises became possible which might otherwise have been deferred for half a century or more. The great railway constructor, the manufacturer, and the merchant of to-day engage in affairs as an ordinary matter of business, which to their predecessors, or even to themselves in their early manhood, would have been deemed impossible of accomplishment in a whole lifetime. Before the war, one line of railway to the Pacific was the vision of a half-cracked enthusiast; to-day the opening of a fifth or sixth line would call only for a descriptive paragraph in a newspaper.

. . . may it not be held that the alternate periods of activity and depression which have affected the industries of this country since the end of the civil war, have been mere fluctuations or ebbs and flows in the great rising tide of material progress, ending in an adjustment to ever new and better conditions of life? Is it not true that while the rich may have become relatively no poorer, the poor have been steadily growing richer, not so much in the accumulation of personal wealth as in the power of commanding the service of capital in ever-increasing measure at a less proportionate charge? Can it be denied that labor as distinguished from capital has been and is securing to its own use an increasing share of an increasing product, or its equivalent in money?[3]

[3] Edward A. Atkinson, "The Relative Strength and Weakness of Nations," an address read before the American Association for the Advancement of Science in 1886, reprinted in *The Industrial Progress of the Nation. Consumption Limited, Production Unlimited* (New York, 1890), pp. 58–66 (statistics), 71–72, 79.

IV

The unshakable confidence in the future that pervades Atkinson's discourse was shared by nearly all observers who reflected upon the highly encouraging statistics concerning economic development. Yet there was an articulate minority protest which became stronger year by year. In 1879 Henry George declared in *Progress and Poverty* that "discovery upon discovery, and invention after invention, have neither lessened the toil of those who most need respite, nor brought plenty to the poor."[4] The influential Protestant minister Josiah Strong declared in 1885 that the tendency of technological advance "under our present industrial system, is to separate classes more widely, and to render them hereditary." Wages, maintained Strong, had not risen so fast as the general standard of living. "Moreover, our labor system, together with mechanical invention, is steadily developing an unemployed class, which furnishes ready recruits to the criminal, intemperate, socialistic and revolutionary classes."[5]

Although the effect of industrialization on wages in this period is a complex problem for the historian, it now seems likely that the over-all tendency of real wages during the post-Civil War decades was upward. Nevertheless, the growth of slums in the major cities led many contemporary observers to agree with George and Strong that the condition of the working class was growing worse rather than better. The theme was, to be sure, not new. Even before the Civil War, pioneers in social welfare such as Theodore Parker had called attention to the misery and degradation of dwellers in Boston slums, especially recent immigrants. But it was only in the 1870s that urban poverty came to seem, in Charles L. Brace's term, actually dangerous.[6] Another major problem became conspicuous

[4] *Progress and Poverty* (New York, 1929), p. 5.
[5] *Our Country: Its Possible Future and Its Present Crisis* (New York, 1885), pp. 94–95, 98.
[6] *The Dangerous Classes of New York, and Twenty Years' Work among Them,* New York, 1872.

during the same decade. In 1877 occurred the first nation-wide strike in American history, which led to a blockade of traffic on all the main railways and was brought to an end only after pitched battles between strikers and militia or regular troops. This was but the beginning of a series of bloody outbreaks of industrial warfare extending into the twentieth century. The power of state and federal governments was habitually exerted on behalf of business against the workers, and public opinion was generally hostile to them. Given the complacency of popular culture, it is not surprising that from the outset such disturbances were regarded as the work of foreign agitators. Both urban slums and militant labor unionism were considered exotic growths foreign to the American way of life. In the 1880s these problems of an industrial society began to haunt the popular mind.

V

Periodization in history—especially when the period is as short as twenty-five years—can hardly be anything but an arbitrary ordering of the past for the intellectual convenience of a later day. Yet the World's Columbian Exposition which opened in Chicago in 1893 does provide something like a mark of punctuation in American cultural history. The most remarkable feature of the fair was the fact that it was a product of the West, overwhelming evidence that the Garden of the World in the interior of the continent had become an industrialized region capable of creating the enormous ugly mass of Chicago and a dozen other urban centers from Cleveland to Minneapolis and Kansas City. These cities belonged to the new age of steam and steel rather than to the frontier or agrarian past. Americans from the East—Henry Adams and William Dean Howells among them—were deeply impressed by the crude energy of the Black City that provided the material basis for the dreamlike White City conjured into existence on the shore of Lake Michigan.

At the same time, Easterners were disposed to take the

Columbian Exposition at Chicago's evaluation and to consider it evidence of artistic maturity in a region supposedly too primitive for esthetic ambitions. From the standpoint of the mid-twentieth century, the fair demonstrated the bankruptcy of the American Genteel Tradition. Louis Sullivan's Transportation Building embodied an original conception, but most of the architectural show pieces of the fair were constructed of lath and plaster in a pseudo-classical style that was embarrassingly unrelated to American experience. On the other hand, the financing and building of these structures in less than three years gave evidence of the administrative talent that had made possible the almost incredibly rapid construction of the American industrial plant—the American trait that Atkinson had called "the habit of combination and organization engendered by long practice. . . ."[7] The Exposition, with all its committee squabbles and near escapes from financial collapse, was a technical triumph at the same time that it was, in an equally representative fashion, an esthetic failure.

The name of Chicago calls up yet other indications that American society was entering upon a new phase. At a meeting of the American Historical Association held in conjunction with the fair, Frederick Jackson Turner read his now celebrated paper on "The Significance of the Frontier in American History," in which he used data from the census of 1890 to proclaim the end of the frontier era. Historians have subsequently shown that the number of homestead entries in the West actually increased for a time after 1890, but the exact date is a minor matter in comparison with Turner's recognition that the future of American society would be radically different from its past. The machine had entered the Garden of the World in the American hinterland; and by 1890 this new force was beginning to be perceived as an ambiguous portent.

The process was accelerated by an event occurring in Chicago that was recognized then and later as symbolic.

[7] *The Industrial Progress of the Nation,* p. 77.

This was the Haymarket bombing of 1886. Theodore Dreiser describes the incident from the point of view of his financial Titan Frank Cowperwood. The bombing, says Dreiser,

> had brought to the fore, once and for all, as by a flash of lightning, the whole problem of mass against class, and had given it such an airing as in view of the cheerful, optimistic, almost inconsequential American mind had not previously been possible. It changed, quite as an eruption might, the whole face of the commercial landscape. Man thought thereafter somewhat more accurately of national and civic things. What was anarchism? What socialism? What rights had the rank and file, anyhow, in economic and governmental development? Such were interesting questions, and following the bomb—which acted as a great stone cast in the water—these ripple-rings of thought were still widening and emanating until they took in such supposedly remote and impregnable quarters as editorial offices, banks and financial institutions generally, and the haunts of political dignitaries and their jobs.[8]

The shock lay in the grim intimation of class warfare waged by violence. The crudity and intensity of the emotions aroused by the bombing are revealed in the cartoons by Thomas Nast reproduced as Documents 58 and 59. Although the actual criminal who threw the bomb was never identified, the trial of the men accused of conspiracy to murder because of their incendiary speeches took on a ritual character in the national press. It released a fury of vindictiveness expressing the uncertainties and fears engendered by a threat to the comfortable belief that continuous progress need entail no clash of interests within American society. The nation had enjoyed a kind of nationalistic euphoria as the wounds of the Civil War were healed. Within a generation after Appomattox, however,

[8] *The Titan* (New York, 1914), pp. 186–87.

the "slumberous combustibles" of class war that Melville's expatriate Southerner Ungar had described in 1876[9] had begun to trouble even "the cheerful, optimistic, almost inconsequential American mind." This dawning recognition threw into relief the besetting dilemma of American popular culture: its inability to reconcile traditional values with its dawning perception of social fact. The cult of ideality, a degraded heritage from transcendentalism, achieved its consummation in the transient splendors of the Columbian Exposition. But what was the relation of the White City to the Black City where industrialization had produced, along with wealth, the dirt and crime of the slums? From the standpoint of popular culture, the question answered itself: esthetic value, like social justice, was unreal by definition; the realm of ideals was a dreamland. This implicit theoretical position did less than justice to the actual character of the American people, who had resources of energy and imagination and good will that transcended their ideology and would manifest themselves in due time. But as of 1890, the popular culture was more of a handicap than an aid to the full development of the nation's human resources.

The reader should be warned that many of the selections in this anthology have been condensed. Omitted passages are indicated by the conventional ellipsis. Author's footnotes have in some instances been silently dropped. Some two dozen typographical errors in the texts involving spelling and punctuation have been silently corrected.

[9] *Clarel*, Part IV, Canto xxi.

Acknowledgments

I wish to thank Arthur E. Gordon for his help in translating quotations from Latin poets and Herschel B. Chipp for identifying the mediums used in a number of drawings and engravings reproduced here as documents. Mayne Smith and Mrs. Andrea Corvasce gave me valuable advice about choosing and interpreting the tunes of Gospel Hymns. I also take pleasure in acknowledging the collaboration of Evan Alderson and Miss Louise Dunlap, who worked with me as research assistants but offered suggestions of more than routine importance. My greatest debts, however, are to Mrs. Susan C. Trotman for her painstaking editorial scrutiny of the typescript and to Hennig Cohen for his subtle and perceptive aid in interpreting the documents in the anthology, especially the illustrations. As in the past, I am grateful to the Senate Committee on Research of the Berkeley Division of the University of California for the grant of funds in support of this project.

Contents

Introduction   vii

PART I. NATIONALISM, PROGRESS, TECHNOLOGY   1

1. Oration, *William M. Evarts*   3
2. The American Soldier, *Carl H. Conrads*   19
   (PLATE 1)   *in group following page*   132
3. The Century Vase, *George Wilkinson and
   Thomas J. Fairpoint*   21
   (PLATE 2)   *in group following page*   132
4. Inaugural Address, *Robert H. Thurston*   23
5. Invention and Advancement, *Orville H. Platt*   33
6. Testimony before the Senate Committee on
   Education and Labor, *Carroll D. Wright*   51
7. Causes of American Nervousness,
   George M. Beard   57
8. Our Centennial—President Grant and Dom
   Pedro Starting the Corliss Engine,
   Theodore R. Davis   71
   (PLATE 3)   *in group following page*   132
9. Edison in his Workshop, *Anonymous*   73
10. Interior of a Southern Cotton Press by Night,
    J. O. Davidson   78
    (PLATE 4)   *in group following page*   132

PART II. THE TITANS   81

11. The Vanderbilts, *William A. Croffut*   83
12. The Vanderbilt Monument, *Albert de Groot
    and Ernest Plassman*   91
    (PLATE 5)   *in group following page*   132

13. The Vanderbilt Monument, *Anonymous*   92
14. The Vanderbilt Memorial, *Anonymous*   96
15. Cornelius Vanderbilt, *Anonymous*   102
16. A Railroad Eulogy, *Anonymous*   125
17. Testimony before the Senate Committee on
        Education and Labor, *Jay Gould*   130
18. The Genesis of a Money-Maker,
        Henry F. Keenan   140
19. The Rich, *James W. Buel*   150
20. B. P. Hutchinson ("Old Hutch"), the Great
        Chicago Grain Operator,
        Arthur J. Goodman   159
        (PLATE 6)   *in group following page*   132

PART III. THE CITY: DIVES AND LAZARUS   163

21. New York, *Mary L. Booth*   165
22. Testimony before the Senate Committee on
        Education and Labor, *Edward H. Ludlow*   168
23. Perils.—The City, *Josiah Strong*   171
24. A Blockade on Broadway, *Taylor and Meeker*   179
        (PLATE 7)   *in group following page*   132
25. The Great Fancy Dress Ball,
        William A. Croffut   181
26. The World of Fashion, *Ward McAllister*   186
27. The Drive—Central Park—Four O'Clock,
        Gray Parker   193
        (PLATE 8)   *in group following page*   132
28. Rich and Poor, *Sol Eytinge, Jun.*   194
        (PLATE 9)   *in group following page*   132
29. The Prolétaires of New York, *Charles L. Brace*   195
30. Under-Ground Life, *Anonymous*   202
        (PLATE 10)   *in group following page*   132
31. Station-House Lodgers, *Winslow Homer*   205
        (PLATE 11)   *in group following page*   132
32. Prostitution, *Edward Crapsey*   210
33. The Common Herd, *Jacob A. Riis*   217

34. Among the Tenement-Houses During the
      Heated Term—Just before Daybreak,
      Sol Eytinge, Jun.   227
          (PLATE 12)   *in group following page*   132

PART IV. RACIAL STEREOTYPES   229

35. Way Down upon the Swanee Ribber,
      R. N. Brooke   231
          (PLATE 13)   *in group following page*   132
36. Colored Rule in a Reconstructed (?) State,
      Thomas Nast   233
          (PLATE 14)   *in group following page*   132
37. Their Pride, *Thomas Hovenden*   234
          (PLATE 15)   *in group following page*   132
38. The Greek Slave, *Thomas Nast*   235
          (PLATE 16)   *in group following page*   132
39. The Unconditional Surrender—July 11th,
      Thomas Nast   237
          (PLATE 17)   *in group following page*   132
40. The Usual Irish Way of Doing Things,
      Thomas Nast   239
          (PLATE 18)   *in group following page*   132
41. Sectarian Bitterness, *Thomas Nast*   240
          (PLATE 19)   *in group following page*   132

PART V. IMMIGRANTS   241

42. Perils.—Immigration, *Josiah Strong*   243
43. Land, Ho!—Scene on Board an Emigrant Ship,
      Anonymous   249
          (PLATE 20)   *in group following page*   372
44. The Modern Ship of the Plains,
      R. F. Zogbaum   250
          (PLATE 21)   *in group following page*   372
45. Immigrants Waiting to Be Distributed in the
      Coal Regions of Pennsylvania,
      W. A. Rogers   251
          (PLATE 22)   *in group following page*   372

46. A Question of Labor, *W. A. Rogers*   252
        (PLATE 23)   *in group following page*   372

PART VI. PROTEST   253

47. Testimony before the Senate Committee on
        Education and Labor, *Henry George*   258
48. Testimony, *Louis F. Post*   267
49. Testimony, *John Morrison*   272
50. Testimony, *Samuel Gompers*   290
51. A Riot on Forty-Second Street, Near Broad-
        way, *Graham and Durkin*   296
        (PLATE 24)   *in group following page*   372
52. Testimony, *Edward King*   297
53. Testimony, *Karl Daniel Adolf Douai*   302
54. Testimony, *R. Heber Newton*   315
55. The Strike, *Robert Koehler*   330
        (PLATE 25)   *in group following page*   372
56. The Great Strike—Scenes of Riot in Chicago,
        C. and A. T. Sears   332
        (PLATE 26)   *in group following page*   372
57. The Anarchist Riot in Chicago—A Dynamite
        Bomb Exploding among the Police,
        Thure de Thulstrup   335
        (PLATE 27)   *in group following page*   372
58. Equal to the Anarchists, *Thomas Nast*   338
        (PLATE 28)   *in group following page*   372
59. Liberty is Not Anarchy, *Thomas Nast*   338
        (PLATE 29)   *in group following page*   372

PART VII. THE CONSERVATIVE POSITION   339

60. Views, *Dexter A. Hawkins*   344
61. Testimony before the Senate Committee on
        Education and Labor, *Edward A. Atkinson*   353
62. Testimony, *Danford Knowlton*   361
63. Testimony, *Jay Gould*   365
64. The Workingman's Mite, *Thomas Nast*   375
        (PLATE 30)   *in group following page*   372

65. Seed That Bears Fruit, *Thomas Nast*   376

PART VIII. THE ARTS IN POPULAR CULTURE   379

A. IDEALITY, REVERENCE, AND THE MAN OF LET-
    TERS   379

66. The Bryant Vase, *James H. Whitehouse*   381
        (PLATE 31)   *in group following page*   372
67. Memorable Ghosts, *Rebecca Harding Davis*   383
68. Speech at the Whittier Birthday Dinner,
        Samuel L. Clemens (Mark Twain)   389
69. Mark Twain's Mistake at the Whittier Dinner,
        Anonymous   396
70. Letter to Andrew Lang, *Samuel L. Clemens*
        (Mark Twain)   398

B. STORY-PAPER FICTION   403

71. Story-Paper Literature, *W. H. Bishop*   407
72. Half-Dime Novels and Story Papers,
        Anthony Comstock   422

C. ORAL DISCOURSE AS A POPULAR ART   428

73. How to Tell a Story, *Samuel L. Clemens*
        (Mark Twain)   431
74. Sensation versus Stagnation,
        T. De Witt Talmage   438

D. PAINTING, CHROMOLITHOGRAPHS, SCULPTURE   448

75. Across the Continent, *F. E. Palmer*   451
        (PLATE 32)   *in group following page*   372
76. The Spirit of '76, *Archibald M. Willard*   453
        (PLATE 33)   *in group following page*   372
77. Custer's Last Rally, *John Mulvany*   456
        (PLATE 34)   *in group following page*   372
78. Mulvany's "Custer's Last Rally",
        Walt Whitman   458

79. Weighing the Baby, *John Rogers*   461
        (PLATE 35)   *in group following page*   372
80. Checkers up at the Farm, *John Rogers*   461
        (PLATE 36)   *in group following page*   372

PART IX. RELIGIOUS REVIVALISM   465

81. The Revivalists in Brooklyn—Opening Service
        of Messrs. Moody and Sankey in the
        Rink, *Anonymous*   470
        (PLATE 37)   *in group following page*   372
82. Mr. Moody's Work, *Anonymous*   471
83. The Prodigal Son, *Dwight L. Moody*   476
84. The Gospel Sowers, *Charles Nordhoff*   487
85. Moody and Sankey, *Arthur G. Sedgwick*   498

FIVE GOSPEL HYMNS   505

86. The Ninety and Nine, *Ira D. Sankey*   508
87. Almost Persuaded, *Philip P. Bliss*   510
88. Whosoever Will, *Philip P. Bliss*   513
89. (a). We're Marching to Zion, *Robert Lowry*   515
    (b). Shirland, *Samuel Stanley*   515
90. Sweet Hour of Prayer, *William B. Bradbury*   518

Suggested Readings   521

PART I

Nationalism, Progress, Technology

DOCUMENT 1

Oration

SOURCE: William M. Evarts, "Oration" (Centennial Ceremonies, 4 July 1876), in United States Centennial Commission, *International Exhibition, 1876*, 11 vols., Vol. II, *Reports of the President, Secretary, and Executive Committee* (Washington, D.C., 1880), pp. 67–76.

During the nineteenth century, public ceremonies on the Fourth of July commemorating the Declaration of Independence evolved into a ritual patterned on a Protestant church service, in which the reading of Scripture was replaced by the reading of the Declaration, and the equivalent of the sermon was an address by the most imposing orator of the community. The celebration of the one-hundredth anniversary of the Declaration arranged by the Commission in charge of the United States International Exhibition in Philadelphia was the apotheosis of this conspicuous item in American folkways. It took place in Independence Square. The program began with an orchestral "Grand Overture, 'The Great Republic,' founded on the National Air, 'Hail Columbia.'" Then followed a prayer; a hymn composed for the occasion by Oliver Wendell Holmes to a familiar religious tune; the reading of the Declaration from the original manuscript by Richard Henry Lee of Virginia, descendant of one of the signers; further music; the recitation of a "National Ode" by the author, Bayard Taylor; and then, as the climax, the "Oration" by William M. Evarts of New York, a celebrated lawyer and a power in the Republican party who was sometimes compared to Daniel Webster for his impressive gifts as a public speaker. "Upon the conclusion of the oration," according to the official report, "the Hallelujah Chorus from Handel's *Messiah* was rendered by the orchestra and chorus. Then followed the Doxology, *The One Hundredth Psalm,* sung by all present; and with this the formal ceremonies were brought to a close."

Evarts' discourse has in ample measure the weight and dignity demanded by the occasion. Although the unusual number of Latin quotations reveals an old-fashioned elegance of taste, the speech is in effect anonymous—a statement of the basic tenets of the national faith. After a survey of the background of the Declaration and an analysis of the Constitution (omitted from this selection), Evarts exhibits the progress of the nation during its first century in a fashion that suggests he is really answering European critics of the early nineteenth century such as Tocqueville. In asserting that our history is a "natural growth" expressing God's will, he invokes a conception of nature that stands midway between the conception embodied in the reference to "the Laws of Nature and of Nature's God" in the Declaration, and the Darwinian idea of natural selection that was already under debate among sophisticated scientists and philosophers. He believes that the abolition of slavery has removed the only serious threat to the harmonious growth of a united American nation. His thought, in other words, is anchored in the pre-Civil War intellectual world. His comments on the material development of the country are equally archaic. The "power" that he ascribes to the United States is essentially agrarian. Its bases are territorial expansion and increase of population. Wealth is the fruit of "industry, persistency, thrift as the habits of the people." The fact that he makes no concrete reference to economic activity shows how deeply buried is his assumption that agriculture is the mainstay of the nation.

And now, after a century of growth, of trial, of experience, of observation, and of demonstration, we are met, on the spot and on the date of the great Declaration, to compare our age with that of our fathers, our structure with their foundation, our intervening history and present condition with their faith and prophecy. That "respect to the opinion of mankind," in attention to which our statesmen framed the Declaration of Independence, we, too, acknowledge as a sentiment most fit to influence us in our commemorative gratulations to-day.

To this opinion of mankind, then, how shall we answer the questioning of this day? How have the vigor and success of the century's warfare comported with the sounding phrase of the great manifesto? Has the new nation been able to hold its territory on the eastern rim of the continent, or has covetous Europe driven in its boundaries, or internal dissensions dismembered its integrity? Have its numbers kept pace with natural increase, or have the mother-countries received back to the shelter of firmer institutions the repentant tide of emigration? or have the woes of unstable society distressed and reduced the shrunken population? Has the free suffrage, as a quicksand, loosened the foundations of power and undermined the pillars of the State? Has the free press, with illimitable sweep, blown down the props and buttresses of order and authority in government, driven before its wind the barriers which fence in society, and unroofed the homes which once were castles against the intrusion of a King? Has freedom in religion ended in freedom from religion? and independence by law run into independence of law? Have free schools, by too much learning, made the people mad? Have manners declined, letters languished, art faded, wealth decayed, public spirit withered? Have other nations shunned the evil example, and held aloof from its infection? Or have reflection and hard fortune dispelled the illusion under which this people "burned incense to vanity, and stumbled in their ways from the ancient paths"? Have they, fleeing from the double destruction which attends folly and arrogance, restored the throne, rebuilt the altar, relaid the foundations of society, and again taken shelter in the old protections against the perils, shocks, and changes in human affairs, which

"Divert and crack, rend and deracinate
The unity and married calm of States
Quite from their fixture?"

Who can recount in an hour what has been done in a century on so wide a field and in all its multitudinous aspects? Yet I may not avoid insisting upon some decisive lineaments of the material, social, and political development of our country which the record of the hundred years displays, and thus present to "the opinion of mankind," for its generous judgment, our nation as it is to-day, —our land, our people, and our laws.

And, first, we notice the wide territory to which we have steadily pushed on our limits. Lines of climate mark our boundaries north and south, and two oceans east and west. The space between, speaking by and large, covers the whole temperate zone of the continent, and in area measures near tenfold the possessions of the thirteen colonies; the natural features, the climate, the productions, the influences of the outward world, are all implied in the immensity of this domain, for they embrace all that the goodness and the power of God have planned for so large a share of the habitable globe. The steps of the successive acquisitions, the impulses which assisted, and the motives which retarded the expansion of our territory; the play of the competing elements in our civilization and their incessant struggle each to outrun the other; the irrepressible conflict thus nursed in the bosom of the State; the lesson in humility and patience, "in charity for all and malice toward none," which the study of the manifest designs of Providence so plainly teach us,—these may well detain us for a moment's illustration.

And this calls attention to that ingredient in the population of this country which came, not from the culminated pride of Europe, but from the abject despondency of Africa. A race discriminated from all the converging streams of immigration which I have named by ineffaceable distinctions of nature; which was brought hither by a forced migration and into slavery, while all others came by choice and for greater liberty; a race unrepresented in the Congress which issued the Declaration of Independence, but now, in the persons of four million of our countrymen raised, by the power of the great truths then declared, as it were from the dead, and rejoicing in one country and the same constituted liberties with ourselves.

In August, 1620, a Dutch slave-ship landed her freight in Virginia, completing her voyage soon after that of the "Mayflower" commenced. Both ships were on the ocean at the same time, both sought our shores, and planted their seeds of liberty and slavery to grow together on this chosen field until the harvest. Until the separation from England the several colonies attracted each their own emigration, and from the sparseness of the population, both in the Northern and Southern colonies, and the policy of England in introducing African slavery, wherever it might, in all of them, the institution of slavery did not raise a definite and firm line of division between the tides of population which set in upon New England and Virginia from the Old World, and from them later, as from new points of departure, were diffused over the continent. The material interests of slavery had not become very strong, and in its moral aspects no sharp division of sentiment had yet shown itself. But when unity and independence of government were accepted by the colonies, we shall look in vain for any adequate barrier against the natural attraction of the softer climate and rich productions of the South, which could keep the Northern population in their harder climate and on their less grateful soil, except the repugnancy of the two systems of free and slave labor to commixture. Out of this grew the impatient, and apparently premature, invasion of the Western wilds, pushing constantly onward, in parallel lines, the outposts of the two rival interests. What greater enterprise did for the Northern people in stimulating this movement was more than supplied to the Southern by the pressing necessity for new lands, which the requirements of the system of slave cultivation imposed. Under the operation of these causes the political divisions of the country built up a wall of partition running east and west, with the novel consequences of the "Border States" of the country being ranged, not on our foreign boundaries, but on this middle line, drawn between the free and slave States. The successive acquisitions of territory by the Louisiana purchase, by the annexation of Texas, and by the treaty with Mexico, were all in the interest of the Southern policy, and, as such, all suspected or resisted by the rival interest in the North. On the other hand, all schemes or tendencies toward the enlargement of our territory on the north were discouraged and defeated by the South. At length, with the immense influx of foreign immigration, reinforcing the flow of population, the streams of free labor shot across the continent. The end was reached. The bounds of our habitation were secured. The Pacific possessions became ours, and the discovered gold rapidly peopled them from the hives of free labor. The rival energies and ambitions which had fed the thirst for territory had served their purpose in completing and assuring the domain of the nation. The partition-wall of slavery was thrown down; the line of Border States obliterated; those who had battled for territory, as an extension and perpetuation of slavery, and those who fought against its enlargement, as a disparagement and a danger to liberty, were alike confounded.

Those who feared undue and precipitate expansion of our possessions, as loosening the ties of union, and those who desired it, as a step toward dissolution, have suffered a common discomfiture. The immense social and political forces which the existence of slavery in this country, and the invincible repugnance to it of the vital principles of our State, together, generated, have had their play upon the passions and the interests of this people, have formed the basis of parties, divided sects, agitated and invigorated the popular mind, inspired the eloquence, inflamed the zeal, informed the understandings, and fired the hearts of three generations. At last the dread debate escaped all bounds of reason, and the nation in arms solved, by the appeal of war, what was too hard for civil wisdom. With our territory unmutilated, our Constitution uncorrupted, a united people, in the last years of the century, crowns with new glory the immortal truths of the Declaration of Independence by the emancipation of a race.

I find, then, in the method and the results of the century's progress of the nation in this amplification of its domain, sure promise of the duration of the body politic, whose growth to these vast proportions has, as yet, but laid out the ground-plan of the structure. For I find the vital forces of the free society and the people's government, here founded, have by their own vigor made this a natural growth. Strength and symmetry have knit together the great frame as its bulk increased, and the spirit of the nation animates the whole:

>   —"*totamque, infusa per artus,*
> *Mens agitat molem, et magno se corpore miscet.*"*

We turn now from the survey of this vast territory, which the closing century has consolidated and confirmed as the ample home for a nation, to exhibit the greatness in numbers, the spirit, the character, the port and mien of the people that dwell in this secure habitation. That in these years our population has steadily advanced, till it counts forty millions, instead of three millions, bears witness, not to be disparaged or gainsaid, to the general congruity of our social and civil institutions with the happiness and prosperity of man. But if we consider further the variety and magnitude of foreign elements to which we have been hospitable, and their ready fusion with the earlier stocks, we have new evidence of strength and vivid force in our population, which we may not refuse to admire. The disposition and capacity thus shown give warrant of a powerful society. "All nations," says Lord Bacon, "that are liberal of naturalization are fit for empire."

Wealth in its mass, and still more in its tenure and diffusion, is a measure of the condition of a people which touches both its energy and morality. Wealth has no source but labor. "Life has given nothing valuable to man without great labor." This is as true now as when Horace

---

* The quotation is from the *Æneid*, Book vi, lines 726 f. Anchises is speaking to Æneas. The lines may be translated: ". . . and mind, permeating the members, moves the whole mass and mingles with its mighty frame."

wrote it. The prodigious growth of wealth in this country is not only, therefore, a signal mark of prosperity, but proves industry, persistency, thrift as the habits of the people. Accumulation of wealth, too, requires and imports security, as well as unfettered activity; and thus it is a fair criterion of sobriety and justice in a people, certainly, when the laws and their execution rest wholly in their hands. A careless observation of the crimes and frauds which attack property, in the actual condition of our society, and the imperfection of our means for their prevention and redress, leads sometimes to an unfavorable comparison between the present and the past in this country, as respects the probity of the people. No doubt covetousness has not ceased in the world, and thieves still break through and steal. But the better test upon this point is the vast profusion of our wealth and the infinite trust shown by the manner in which it is invested. It is not too much to say that in our times, and conspicuously in our country, a large share of every man's property is in other men's keeping and management, unwatched and beyond personal control. This confidence of man in man is ever increasing, measured by our practical conduct, and refutes these disparagements of the general morality.

Knowledge, intellectual activity, the mastery of nature, the discipline of life—all that makes up the education of a people—are developed and diffused through the masses of our population, in so ample and generous a distribution as to make this the conspicuous trait in our national character, as the faithful provision and extension of the means and opportunities of this education are the cherished institution of the country. Learning, literature, science, art, are cultivated, in their widest range and highest reach, by a larger and larger number of our people, not, to their praise be it said, as a personal distinction or a selfish possession, but, mainly, as a generous leaven, to quicken and expand the healthful fermentation of the general mind, and lift the level of popular instruction. So far from breeding a distempered spirit in the people, this becomes the main prop of authority, the great instinct of obedience. "It is by education," says Aristotle, "I have learned to do by choice what other men do by constraint of fear."

The "breed and disposition" of a people, in regard of courage, public spirit, and patriotism, are, however, the test of the working of their institutions, which the world most values, and upon which the public safety most depends. It has been made a reproach of democratic arrangements of society and government that the sentiment of honor, and of pride in public duty, decayed in them. It has been professed that the fluctuating currents and the trivial perturbations of their public life discouraged strenuous endeavor and lasting devotion in the public service. It has been charged that, as a consequence, the distinct service of the State suffered, office and magistracy were belittled, social sympathies cooled, love of country drooped, and selfish affections absorbed the powers of the citizens, and ate into the heart of the commonwealth.

The experience of our country rejects these speculations as misplaced and these fears as illusory. They belong to a condition of society above which we have long since been lifted, and toward which the very scheme of our national life prohibits a decline. They are drawn from the examples of history, which lodged power formally in the people, but left them ignorant and abject, unfurnished with the means of exercising it in their own right and for their own benefit. In a democracy wielded by the arts, and to the ends of a patrician class, the less worthy members of that class, no doubt, throve by the disdain which noble characters must always feel for methods of deception and insincerity, and crowded them from the authentic service of the State. But, through the period whose years we count to-day, the greatest lesson of all is the preponderance of public over private, of social over selfish, tendencies and purposes in the whole body of the people, and the persistent fidelity to the genius and spirit of popular institutions, of the educated classes, the liberal professions, and the great men of the country. These qualities transfuse and blend the hues and virtues of the manifold rays of advanced civilization into a sunlight of public spirit and

fervid patriotism, which warms and irradiates the life of
the nation. Excess of publicity as the animating spirit and
stimulus of society more probably than its lack will excite
our solicitudes in the future. Even the public discontents
take on this color, and the mind and heart of the whole
people ache with anxieties and throb with griefs which
have no meaner scope than the honor and the safety of
the nation.

Our estimate of the condition of this people at the close
of the century—as bearing on the value and efficiency of
the principles on which the government was founded, in
maintaining and securing the permanent well-being of a
nation—would, indeed, be incomplete if we failed to measure the power and purity of the religious elements which
pervade and elevate our society. One might as well expect
our land to keep its climate, its fertility, its salubrity, and
its beauty were the globe loosened from the law which
holds it in an orbit, where we feel the tempered radiance
of the sun, as to count upon the preservation of the delights and glories of liberty for a people cast loose from
religion, whereby man is bound in harmony with the moral
government of the world.

It is quite certain that the present day shows no such
solemn absorption in the exalted themes of contemplative
piety as marked the prevalent thought of the people a
hundred years ago; nor so hopeful an enthusiasm for the
speedy renovation of the world as burst upon us in the
marvelous and wide system of vehement religious zeal,
and practical good works, in the early part of the nineteenth century. But these fires are less splendid only
because they are more potent, and diffuse their heat in
well-formed habits and manifold agencies of beneficent activity. They traverse and permeate society in every direction. They travel with the outposts of civilization and
outrun the caucus, the convention, and the suffrage.

The Church, throughout this land, upheld by no political establishment, rests all the firmer on the rock on
which its founder built it. The great mass of our countrymen to-day find in the Bible—the Bible in their worship,

the Bible in their schools, the Bible in their households—the sufficient lessons of the fear of God and the love of man, which make them obedient servants to the free Constitution of their country, in all civil duties, and ready with their lives to sustain it on the fields of war. And now at the end of a hundred years the Christian faith collects its worshipers throughout our land, as at the beginning. What, half a century ago, was hopefully prophesied for our far future, goes on to its fulfillment: "As the sun rises on a Sabbath morning and travels westward from Newfoundland to the Oregon, he will behold the countless millions assembling, as if by a common impulse, in the temples with which every valley, mountain, and plain will be adorned. The morning psalm and the evening anthem will commence with the multitudes on the Atlantic coast, be sustained by the loud chorus of ten thousand times ten thousand in the Valley of the Mississippi, and be prolonged by the thousands of thousands on the shores of the Pacific."

What remains but to search the spirit of the laws of the land as framed by and modeled to the popular government to which our fortunes were committed by the Declaration of Independence? I do not mean to examine the particular legislation, State or general, by which the affairs of the people have been managed, sometimes wisely and well, at others feebly and ill, nor even the fundamental arrangement of political authority, or the critical treatment of great junctures in our policy and history. The hour and the occasion concur to preclude so intimate an inquiry. The chief concern in this regard, to us and to the rest of the world, is whether the proud trust, the profound radicalism, the wide benevolence which spoke in the "Declaration," and were infused into the "Constitution," at the first, have been in good faith adhered to by the people, and whether now these principles supply the living forces which sustain and direct government and society.

He who doubts needs but to look around to find all things full of the original spirit and testifying to its wisdom and strength. We have taken no steps backward, nor have we needed to seek other paths in our progress than those in which our feet were planted at the beginning. Weighty and manifold have been our obligations to the great nations of the earth, to their scholars, their philosophers, their men of genius and of science; to their skill, their taste, their invention; to their wealth, their arts, their industry. But in the institutions and methods of government; in civil prudence, courage, or policy; in statesmanship; in the art of "making of a small town a great city"; in the adjustment of authority to liberty; in the concurrence of reason and strength in peace, of force and obedience in war, we have found nothing to recall us from the course of our fathers, nothing to add to our safety or to aid our progress in it. So far from this, all modifications of European politics accept the popular principles of our system, and tend to our model. The movements toward equality of representation, enlargement of the suffrage, and public education in England; the restoration of unity in Italy; the confederation of Germany under the lead of Prussia; the actual Republic in France; the unsteady throne of Spain; the new liberties of Hungary; the constant gain to the people's share in government throughout Europe, all tend one way, the way pointed out in the Declaration of our Independence.

The care and zeal with which our people cherish and invigorate the primary supports and defenses of their own sovereignty have all the unswerving force and confidence of instincts. The community and publicity of education, at the charge and as an institution of the State, is firmly imbedded in the wants and the desires of the people. Common schools are rapidly extending through the only part of the country which had been shut against them, and follow close upon the footsteps of its new liberty to enlighten the enfranchised race. Freedom of conscience easily stamps out the first sparkles of persecution, and snaps as green withes the first bonds of spiritual domination. The sacred oracles of their religion the people wisely hold in their own keeping as the keys of religious liberty, and refuse to be beguiled by the voice of the wisest charmer into loosing their grasp.

Freedom from military power and the maintenance of that arm of the Government in the people; a trust in their own adequacy as soldiers, when their duty as citizens should need to take on that form of service to the State; these have gained new force by the experience of foreign and civil war, and a standing army is a remoter possibility for this nation, in its present or prospective greatness, than in the days of its small beginnings.

But in the freedom of the press, and the universality of the suffrage, as maintained and exercised to-day throughout the length and breadth of the land, we find the most conspicuous and decisive evidence of the unspent force of the institutions of liberty and the jealous guard of its principal defenses. These indeed are the great agencies and engines of the people's sovereignty. They hold the same relations to the vast democracy of modern society that the persuasions of the orators and the personal voices of the assembly did in the narrow confines of the Grecian States. The laws, the customs, the impulses and sentiments of the people have given wider and wider range and license to the agitations of the press, multiplied and more frequent occasions for the exercise of the suffrage, larger and larger communication of its franchise. The progress of a hundred years finds these prodigious activities in the fullest play,—incessant and all-powerful,—indispensable in the habits of the people, and impregnable in their affections. Their public service, and their subordination to the public safety, stand in their play upon one another and in their freedom thus maintained. Neither could long exist in true vigor in our system without the other. Without the watchful, omnipresent, and indomitable energy of the press, the suffrage would languish, would be subjugated by the corporate power of the legions of placemen which the administration of the affairs of a great nation imposes upon it, and fall a prey to that "vast patronage which," we are told, "distracted, corrupted, and finally subverted the Roman Republic." On the other hand, if the impressions of the press upon the opinions and passions of the people found no settled and ready mode of their working out, through the frequent and peaceful suffrage, the people would be driven, to satisfy their displeasure at government or their love of change, to the coarse methods of barricades and batteries.

We cannot then hesitate to declare that the original principles of equal society and popular government still inspire the laws, live in the habits of the people, and animate their purposes and their hopes. These principles have not lost their spring or elasticity. They have sufficed for all the methods of government in the past; we feel no fear for their adequacy in the future. Released now from the tasks and burdens of the formative period, these principles and methods can be directed with undivided force to the every-day conduct of government, to the staple and steady virtues of administration. The feebleness of crowding the statute-books with unexecuted laws; the danger of power outgrowing or evading responsibility; the rashness and fickleness of temporary expedients; the constant tendency by which parties decline into factions and end in conspiracies, all these mischiefs beset all governments, and are part of the life of each generation. To deal with these evils—the tasks and burdens of the immediate future—the nation needs no other resources than the principles and the examples which our past history supplies. These principles, these examples of our fathers, are the strength and the safety of our State to-day: *"Moribus antiquis, stat res Romana, virisque."*†

Unity, liberty, power, prosperity,—these are our possessions to-day. Our territory is safe against foreign dangers; its completeness dissuades from further ambitions to extend it, and its rounded symmetry discourages all attempts to dismember it. No division into greatly unequal parts would be tolerable to either. No imaginable union of interests or passions, large enough to include one-half the country, but must embrace much more. The madness of

† A line from the *Annales* of Ennius. It may be translated: "The Roman state stands on its ancient customs and its men."

partition into numerous and feeble fragments could proceed only from the hopeless degradation of the people, and would form but an incident in general ruin.

The spirit of the nation is at the highest,—its triumph over the inborn, inbred perils of the Constitution has chased away all fears, justified all hopes, and with universal joy we greet this day. We have not proved unworthy of a great ancestry; we have had the virtue to uphold what they so wisely, so firmly, established. With these proud possessions of the past, with powers matured, with principles settled, with habits formed, the nation passes as it were from preparatory growth to responsible development of character and the steady performance of duty. What labors await it, what trials shall attend it, what triumphs for human nature, what glory for itself, are prepared for this people in the coming century, we may not assume to foretell. "One generation passeth away, and another generation cometh; but the earth abideth forever," and we reverently hope that these our constituted liberties shall be maintained to the unending line of our posterity, and so long as the earth itself shall endure.

In the great procession of nations, in the great march of humanity, we hold our place. Peace is our duty, peace is our policy. In its arts, its labors, and its victories, then, we find scope for all our energies, rewards for all our ambitions, renown enough for all our love of fame. In the august presence of so many nations, which, by their representatives, have done us the honor to be witnesses of our commemorative joy and gratulation, and in sight of the collective evidences of the greatness of their own civilization with which they grace our celebration, we may well confess how much we fall short, how much we have to make up, in the emulative competitions of the times. Yet, even in this presence, and with a just deference to the age, the power, the greatness of the other nations of the earth, we do not fear to appeal to the opinion of mankind whether, as we point to our land, our people, and our laws, the contemplation should not inspire us with a lover's enthusiasm for our country.

Time makes no pauses in his march. Even while I speak the last hour of the receding is replaced by the first hour of the coming century, and reverence for the past gives way to the joys and hopes, the activities and the responsibilities of the future. A hundred years hence the piety of that generation will recall the ancestral glory which we celebrate to-day, and crown it with the plaudits of a vast population which no man can number. By the mere circumstance of this periodicity our generation will be in the minds, in the hearts, on the lips of our countrymen at the next Centennial commemoration, in comparison with their own character and condition and with the great founders of the nation. What shall they say of us? How shall they estimate the part we bear in the unbroken line of the nation's progress? And so on, in the long reach of time, forever and forever, our place in the secular roll of the ages must always bring us into observation and criticism. Under this double trust, then, from the past and for the future, let us take heed to our ways, and, while it is called to-day, resolve that the great heritage we have received shall be handed down through the long line of the advancing generations, the home of liberty, the abode of justice, the stronghold of faith among men, "which holds the moral elements of the world together," and of faith in God, which binds that world to His throne. . . .

DOCUMENT 2

(PLATE 1)

The American Soldier

SOURCE: Carl H. Conrads, "The American Soldier" (sculpture in granite), from an engraving in *The Masterpieces of the Centennial International Exhibition*, Vol. I, *Fine Art*, by Edward Strahan (Philadelphia, 1878), opposite p. 62.

The naïve nationalism of the Centennial year is equally explicit in this statue and in the commentary on it by Edward Strahan. "Like the nation he defends," wrote Strahan of the Antietam soldier,

> this colossus is in the bloom of youth and like it he is hard and firm though alert. What art has succeeded in making this monster out of granite? He is twenty-one feet six inches in height. What sempster, working with needles of thrice-hardened steel, has draped him in those folds of adamant, that hang ten feet or farther from his inflexible loins? The sculptors of ancient Egypt, who had their colossi in granite also, worked for years with their bronze points and their corundum-dust to achieve their enormous figures, while the makers of this titanic image, availing themselves of the appliances of American skill, have needed but a few months to change the shapeless mass of stone into an idea. Something rocky, rude and large-grained is obvious still in this stalwart American; his head, with its masculine chin and moustache of barbaric proportions, is rather like the Vatican "Dacian" than like the Vatican "Genius." But, whatever may be thought of the artistic delicacy of the model, Mr. Conrads' "soldier" presents the image of a sentinel not to be trifled with, as he leans with both hands clasped around his gun-barrel, the cape of his overcoat thrown back to free his arm, and

the sharp bayonet thrust into its sheath at his belt. Rabelais' hero, Pantagruel, whose opponents were giants in armor of granite, would have recoiled before our colossus of Antietam, because his heart is of granite too. . . . Compared with the American soldier's face, as defined from the testimony of all our artists and the very photographs of our officers, the faces of soldiers over the rest of the world are those of undeveloped intelligences; the Greek contestants of the Parthenon frieze are but large babies; the English soldiers of Hogarth's "March to Finchley" are good-natured, immature, beef-eating lads; the French soldiers of Vernet are dried out of all individuality—a tinder-box and a spark—a lean cheek and a glowing eye—food for powder, and then nothingness. But our ordinary American phiz has a look of capability, of knowingness, and when handsome of intellectual majesty, that it would take a vast deal of actual achievement to justify us in wearing. It is walking about under false colors to adopt such faces unless we are really the philosophers, tacticians and diplomats of the age!*

* *The Masterpieces of the Centennial International Exhibition*, Vol. I, *Fine Art*, by Edward Strahan (Philadelphia, 1878), pp. 63–66.

DOCUMENT 3

(PLATE 2)

The Century Vase

SOURCE: George Wilkinson and Thomas J. Fairpoint, "The Century Vase" (in silver), from an engraving in *The Masterpieces of the Centennial International Exhibition*, Vol. II, *Industrial Art*, by Walter Smith (Philadelphia, 1878), p. 52.

In its combination of highly conventional themes and motives, ultimately baroque, with an essentially primitive plan of composition, this example of the silversmith's art exhibited at the Philadelphia Centennial by Gorham Manufacturing Company is a near-perfect expression of the culture of the 1870s. Professor Walter Smith's commentary explains the elaborate allegory of the piece:

If the design is carefully studied it will tell its own story—the story of the rise and progress of our republic upon a soil rich in natural resources, triumphing over barbarism and civilized enemies from without, strong in its own integrity and uprightness, until on its hundredth birthday, commanding the respect and admiration of the world, it bids all nations come and see for themselves its progress, offering a hearty welcome to all alike. That the reader may the more thoroughly understand the *motif* of this fine work, we shall give a detailed description of its parts.

The piece is five feet four inches long, and four feet two inches high. With the exception of the slab of polished granite on which the plinth rests, every part is sterling silver. The designs are by George Wilkinson and Thomas J. Fairpoint. Beginning with the base from which the whole fabric of the republic was reared, we have the native red man and the pioneer of civilization representing the first phase of our existence. Native fruit, flowers and cereals, happily combined in groups, typifying the fruitfulness of the soil, ornament the ends. . . . A foliated scroll-work of graceful design connects the several groups. Above and encircling the solid granite slab are the thirty-eight stars of the republic, bound together and resting upon as sure a foundation as the rock itself. On either side of the plinth are groups—one, the Genius of War, holding her dogs in the leash, her whole attitude expressive of her fierce purpose and her surroundings—the shattered tree and the broken cannon-wheel—indicative of the desolation of her course. On the other side we have the contrast—the lion led by little children, and emblems suggestive of peace and security scattered around. Between these two extremes our republic steadily rises upwards, directed and led in those stormy days of trial by the strong hand and inflexible will of Washington. It is fitting, then, that the Angel of Fame, while holding in one hand the palm branch and laurel, should with the other hand place a wreath of immortelles upon the brow of him who was indeed the Father of his Country. On the opposite side is another medallion, the genius of Philosophy and Diplomacy, with one hand resting on the printing-press, and the other holding the portrait of Franklin—the one man of this country who was truly a philosopher and a diplomatist of the highest order. And as from the plinth the perfect vase rises, so from those colonial times sprung at a bound the young republic. On the front panel of the vase we see the Genius of the Arts, ready to inscribe on his tablet the names of those famous in Literature, Science, Music, Painting, Sculpture, and Architecture. In the reverse panel the Genius stands ready to record our advancement in Commerce, Mining and Manufactures. Crowning the vase we have the last and grandest scene in our hundred years of existence. Here is America holding aloft the olive branch of peace and the wreath of honor, summoning Europe, Asia and Africa to join with her in the friendly rivalry with which she enters on the second century of her existence.*

* *The Masterpieces of the Centennial International Exhibition,* Vol. II, *Industrial Art,* by Walter Smith (Philadelphia, 1878), pp. 54–56.

DOCUMENT 4

Inaugural Address

SOURCE: Robert H. Thurston, "Inaugural Address," in *Transactions of the American Society of Mechanical Engineers*, I (1880), 2d ed., 1892, pp. 16–23.

In contrast to Evarts, who represents a kind of nationalism still colored by the intense political emphasis of the American Revolution, Thurston speaks for a cult of technology. The main ideas of his speech had been current since the 1830s, and by the 1850s had become commonplaces. But Thurston's account of the first century of national life is almost totally different from Evarts'. The Founding Father to whom he looks back is not a statesman but Samuel Slater, builder of the first successful power-driven cotton-spinning mill in this country. Independence of Great Britain has nothing to do with the Declaration signed in Independence Hall, but is defined by ten millions of spindles and a quarter of a million looms. Not merely the prosperity and happiness of America, but even the stability of republican institutions is due to pre-eminence in the mechanic arts. It is the engineers who have created the "only real civilization," whose achievements can be precisely measured in dollars. Thurston's list of great names from the past includes two mentioned by Evarts—Aristotle and Bacon —but they are cited for their contribution to the inductive method rather than for their ethical or political wisdom. The "half-knowledge" of Greeks and Romans hardly deserves notice in comparison with the real—and profitable—knowledge bequeathed to mankind by inventors in modern times. In passages not reproduced here, Herbert Spencer, an engineer by training, is called the greatest philosopher of any age. Thurston maintains that inductive science is the true basis of ethics, and even implies a new esthetics when he calls the Bessemer proc-

ess "this beautiful and wonderful illustration of the
marvels of chemical science." Yet he thinks of himself
as an innovator in defending the engineers' claim to
public esteem, and later in his address notes that a committee of Congress had refused to recommend an ap-
propriation of $20,000 for research in the strength of
materials.

As a footnote on the history of American prose style,
one might observe that Thurston has no inkling of a
rhetorical mode appropriate to his new perspective: he
writes in a clumsy imitation of the grand oratorical
manner exemplified by Evarts in Document 1.

Importance of This Body and Its Work

Glancing back for a moment upon the past, and observing the progress in all branches of industry which has been
the result of the efforts of our predecessors and of our
professional colleagues, we cannot fail to be impressed
with the magnitude of the interests which are entrusted
to our charge, and with the importance of doing the work
which we are in these stirring times called upon to do, in
an honest, earnest spirit and with our utmost skill, and we
shall be encouraged to press on hopefully and with unflag-
ging courage.

Ninety years ago Samuel Slater settled at Pawtucket,
Rhode Island, and started the little mill, which was the
first to successfully spin cotton in this country—the first
after many failures.

To-day we raise fifteen hundred million pounds of cotton to supply mills in every New England State, and in
nearly every other State in the Union, as well as to keep
employed thousands of working people in other countries;
and we work up our share into five hundred millions of
dollars worth of manufactured goods, which we put in the
market at a price so low that the very beggars in our metropolitan cities, and the "tramps" sleeping in our fields or
under the roof that shelters our cattle, wear a finer fabric
than kings could boast a century ago.

From the day, in 1794, when the first rude woolen mill was established at Newbury, Mass., our woolen manufactures have grown in extent and in excellence of product with hardly a reverse, until to-day our twelve or fifteen thousand sets of machinery, handled by nearly a hundred thousand of the most skillful operatives to be found in the world, produce two hundred and fifty millions of dollars worth of goods, which, in combined cheapness and excellence, compete with the best work of Europe.

We have seen the silk manufacture, after struggling with difficulties of every imaginable sort for a half century, finally secure a foothold, and enter upon a period of prosperity which is as marvelous as it is encouraging. The enterprise of the Cheneys during the past generation, and the steady persistence and courage of our neighbors at Paterson, N. J., have borne fruit in the erection of two hundred and fifty mills, with a production of thirty millions of dollars worth of silk goods, which, in strength and durability excel, and in beauty fully equal, the finest products of our French competitors at Lyons, the great center of European silk manufacture.

In the iron and steel manufacture the story is the same. We have furnaces which are supplied with every desired variety of the best ores, plentifully and cheaply, and, making two millions of tons of pig iron per annum, to-day are practically free from that threatening foreign competition, which was only prevented from throttling our manufactures in their infancy by a wise policy of legislative protection, which was prompted by just such action as bodies of men, like that here in session, can most intelligently devise, direct, and sustain.

We consume our whole product, and that means nearly fifteen per cent. of all the iron used in this world. Of our enormous coal production—about fifty millions of tons per annum—a large fraction is consumed in making and working this iron, a million or more tons of which goes to market as wrought iron in a thousand different shapes.

The growth of our pneumatic, or Bessemer, steel production is even more marvelous than that of the industries to which I have already made reference; and beside it, the progress of other steel-making processes which to-day, nevertheless, supply seventy-five thousand tons of steel, much of it equal to the best that Sheffield can furnish, seems hardly to claim our casual attention. Twenty years ago, this beautiful and wonderful illustration of the marvels of chemical science was looked upon as merely an interesting and curious process, of no immediate value, and of most uncertain promise. To-day a single establishment is making a hundred thousand tons a year, and one dozen sets of converters are driven to their utmost capacity to supply a demand which, consuming one hundred and seventy-five thousand tons a half dozen years ago, has unceasingly grown, and they have now probably more than quadrupled the output. The increase in production of the standard plant is a most interesting and encouraging feature of this branch of industry. A plant which a few years ago was constructed with a guaranteed production of thirty thousand tons per annum, and such as is still, in all countries in Europe, rated at about the same capacity, has been brought to such efficiency that it has, at times, been known to work up to three or four times its guaranteed rate of production . . . . we are far, very far, in advance of all other nations in the manufacture of this material which is destined, before many years, to supersede absolutely that comparatively crude, weak, brittle, and expensive material which we call wrought iron.

And so we might, did time permit, trace the advances of other departments of manufacturing industry, and see the work of our fellow workmen in every direction, aiding —indeed, more than that, effecting—in all these many ways, the advancement of civilization.

Position and Prospects

The position of our country to-day, among nations, is, then, eminently satisfactory.

With credit restored, with agriculture and all the mechanic arts flourishing as they never flourished before, with every mill wheel in operation, every steam-engine doing its maximum work, with nearly all our blast furnaces and all our rolling mills working to their full capacity, with all the steel works in the land driven beyond their ability to supply orders, with markets for our manufactured, as well as our crude, products opening in all the countries of the globe, we seem to-day entering upon an era that is at once a golden age and an age of steel.

Looking back upon our past history, we have seen the growth of our cotton manufactures, from the small beginnings of Samuel Slater, and his humble rivals in a New England village, grow, until to-day many mills of forty thousand spindles each have been built, and the hum of their machinery and the clatter of their shuttles make music in the ears of two hundred thousand thrifty and happy working people. From absolute dependence upon Great Britain, we have grown to independence, and now, more than ten millions of spindles, and nearly a quarter of a million looms in our thousand mills supply Canada, South America, and even China annually with millions of dollars worth of goods.

Our associates have made this country the most prosperous and happy in the world.

We call from all lands their most enterprising and industrious workers, and we send to all lands the best devices for creating the most essential comforts and the greatest luxuries. The United States is looked upon as the home of all ingenious and effective "labor-saving" devices; this is the natural home of the finest wood-working machinery, and all foreign nations imitate our designs; the American steam engine has revolutionized the steam engine manufacture of the world; the introduction of navigation by steam here, led to the construction of steam vessels on all waters, and one of our steamers—the "Savannah"—was the pioneer in trans-oceanic navigation; our mowers and reapers gather the harvests of every field from Oregon to Maine, and from Great Britain to the most distant countries of Europe, and are even seen among the semi-barbarians of farthest Asia; the American rotary printing press sends out its stories of daily life and its records of the history and of the knowledge of all peoples in every quarter of the civilized world. And thus in myriads of ways the modern civilization, which is reaching its highest development in this new world, is reaching out to touch and to revivify every other nation. It is of this civilization —a civilization which seeks directly useful and practically valuable results—that you, and such as you, are the vitally essential supporters and promoters.

It is by such men that this only real civilization—which had its origin among the ruins of the old worlds of Greece and Rome, and which, checked by the destruction of the wealth and the science schools, the arts and the industries of the Saracens—has been revived within a few centuries, and given its wonderful growth—a growth which is still going on with ever accelerating speed. It is by such men that the value, the absolutely essential necessity, of intelligent labor has been forced upon the world, that the dignity of labor has been made known, and its acknowledgment compelled from those who, moulding general sentiment, had hitherto associated intellectual labor with manual indolence, and had despised the hard-working mechanic and every mental effort which led to other than non-utilitarian ends; that the Rip Van Winkle of the Middle Ages was awakened from that slumber of a thousand years, and taught to work the printing press, to labor at the forge and the loom, and to educate his children in such a manner as, by profitable exercise, to develop together mind and body, and was given the power of making life worth living, while becoming daily better fitted to live the truest life.

Such men have taught the world that the true and only way to secure the greatest good of the greatest number, to obtain the blessings of stable and wise government, to secure a fair and equitable distribution of all those forms of wealth which are most essential to a life of happiness and content, to obtain for all an equal opportunity of gaining with certainty and holding safely, the best fruits of intelligently directed industry, and to bring every nation most promptly, and with most stability, to a state of maximum prosperity, is to educate a people in all the useful arts and in all true philosophy, training mind and hand together, and fitting soul and body to cöoperate in doing the work of a citizen in the community. We have begun to learn to despise mere speculation, whether in finance or philosophy, and to adopt the modern system of philosophy, which bases knowledge on ascertained facts and upon logical deduction from such facts; we are learning to abandon those old habits of thought which come from over-respect for ancient methods and philosophies, to turn from the study of the teachings of less civilized times and peoples, and, leaving the Greek and the Roman to his own half-knowledge and profitless speculations, to devote ourselves to the acquirement of real knowledge, by directly profitable methods. Abstract philosophy, and the deductive method have, at last, been thrown down from the pedestal from which they so long received the homage of the greatest of mankind, and the inductive method of Aristotle, of Galileo, and of many truer men among their disciples than Bacon, has become fruitful of all that tends to make "*Liberté, Egalité, Fraternité*" words having true meaning.

And this is the situation but one hundred and four years after the foundation of our government and the birth of the nation.

The class of men from whose ranks the membership of this Society is principally drawn direct the labors of nearly three millions of prosperous working people in a third of a million mills and other manufactories, are responsible for the preservation and profitable utilization of twenty-five hundred millions of dollars' worth of capital, direct the payment of more than one thousand millions of dollars in annual wages, the consumption of three thousand millions of dollars' worth of raw materials, and the output of five thousand millions of dollars' worth of manufactured products. Fifty thousand steam engines, and more than an equal number of water-wheels, at their command, turn the machinery of these hundreds of thousands of workshops that everywhere dot our land, giving quietly and docilely the strength of three millions of horses, night or day, or all night and all day, whenever the demand comes for their wonderful power.

This Society, when it shall become properly representative of such a class, may well claim position and consideration.

It has been by the work of men whom we are proud to claim as brothers in our own and kindred professions, but whom the world has not always honored as they are honored to-day, that true progress has always been most efficiently promoted. It has been these men who have been made gods and demi-gods in pre-historic times. Vulcan and Thor, the Assyrian Master of Works, the builders of the Pyramids, Archimedes, Hero of Alexandria, Cæsar's engineers and the author of "Theatrum Machinarum," and Leonardo da Vinci, artist and engineer, and a hundred later and equally great men, are entitled to our homage as masters and teachers in a profession for which we may claim an age of certainly not less than five thousand years.

Wyatt and Arkwright, who taught us to spin by machinery more than a hundred years ago, and Hargreaves and Crompton, who followed those inventors; Jacquard, who perfected the pattern-loom, which to-day weaves with equal facility the portrait of him who was "first in war, first in peace, and first in the hearts of his countrymen," and the most beautiful and ingenious combinations of form and color of which decorative art is so wonderfully prolific; and Cartwright, who first harnessed the steam engine to the loom; Hammond and Heathcote, who made the stocking-loom; Watt and Fulton, and Stevens, Fourdrinier, Howe, and McCormick, Whitworth and Siemens, and Bessemer, Hoe and Bullock, Smith and Ericsson, and such great names glitter all along the list upon which we are glad to be permitted to inscribe our own obscure names, while the name, here and there, is seen of a great mathematical genius like Rankine, and of a great philosopher like Spencer, shining with a radiance that never comes but from a towering intellect, enlightened by wisdom and sparkling with that purest brilliancy which is acquired only by study, and thoughtful labor in the loftiest atmosphere of human thought.

The Future

It is by the past we are to judge the future, and the rapid advances of the past century, in all branches of mechanical science and the mechanic arts, are simply indicative of greater advances and more rapid acceleration in the future.

We have seen greater advances made in all the great industries during the past century than during a dozen centuries preceding it. The progress, which to-day apparently culminates in the light and effective reaping machine, cutting in one hour more grain than our sturdy grandfathers could reap in a day, making the clustering stalks into bundles with tireless and deft metallic fingers, which bind them and tie them as could no human hands, in short, almost a miracle of human ingenuity; in the sewing machine, which has done so much to relieve the sad, toilsome monotony of the life of those poor creatures whose hard fate inspired Hood's "Song of the Shirt," and which accompanies American mowers and reapers to every foreign land, there to do one of the truest of all kinds of missionary work; in the spinning and weaving machinery which has been taught to produce the fabrics that comfortably clothe the poorest, as well as the richest and most artistic patterns that wealth demands or art desires; in the printing press, that has made civilization and educated intelligence possible, and which is the great safeguard which preserves our nation from retrogression, from internal decay, and from external aggression more effectively than could the armies of an Alexander, of a Cæsar, or of a Napoleon, which supplies us with newspapers printed by the mile, and with books freighted with all human knowledge so cheaply that the poorest in the land may, at the sacrifice of the least of his few indulgences, read the thoughts of the wisest men of all ages, and learn of the latest and greatest discoveries and inventions of this age of wonders by the light of the street lamp, or of the dim candle that faintly burns in attic or cellar; in the steam engine that drives all these other triumphs of invention, and which impels the great trans-oceanic steamers, carrying thousands of tons of valuable freight and hundreds of precious lives, twenty miles an hour, accomplishing the three thousand miles of heaving ocean which separates us from the mother country, in a single week; which transports us from one great metropolis to another at the rate of a mile a minute—that progress which thus has seemingly culminated in a perfection of invention and a fruitfulness of production that appear to us impossible to greatly surpass, has really, so far, exhibited, we may be confident, but the earliest stages of an onward movement that is like the motion of a meteorite, attracted toward the center of the nearest star with a velocity which increases as it flies, and which continues to increase without lessening and without fluctuating to the very end.

We are now called upon to do our part in the work so well begun by our predecessors, and so splendidly carried on by our older colleagues during the past generation. We have for our work the cheapening and improvement of all textile fabrics, the perfecting of metallurgical processes, the introduction of the electric light, the increase of facilities for rapid and cheap transportation, the invention of new and more efficient forms of steam and gas engines, of means for relieving woman from drudgery, and for shortening the hours of labor for hard-working men, the increase in the productive power of all mechanical devices, aiding in the great task of recording and disseminating useful knowledge; and ours is the duty to discover facts and to deduce laws bearing upon every application of mechanical science and art in field, workshop, school, or household.

Every member of the engineering profession has his share of this work, not only in his private capacity, but as a member of a great body of men of kindred pursuits, each of whom may be rightfully called upon to give to his neighbor of his own light, and to assist in promoting the general welfare.

DOCUMENT 5

Invention and Advancement

SOURCE: Orville H. Platt, "Invention and Advancement," in [Patent Centennial Celebration], *Proceedings and Addresses. Celebration of the Beginning of the Second Century of the American Patent System at Washington City, D.C., April 8, 9, 10, 1891* (Washington, 1892), pp. 57–76.

This oration, delivered ten years after R. H. Thurston's inaugural address before the American Association of Mechanical Engineers and fifteen years after Evarts' speech at the Philadelphia Centennial, synthesizes the contrasting viewpoints of statesman and engineer—although, significantly, with rather more emphasis on technology than on political theory. By proclaiming a "machine age" to succeed the stone age, the bronze age, and the iron age in the typology of human progress, Senator Platt of Connecticut places the industrial present in a long historical perspective and even suggests that an era beyond and above civilization, an "age of spirituality," is opening its roseate portals. Although he confesses that the mind can not grasp "our material advancement," he admits no shadows into his picture of the future. He takes account of the charge that the advance of technology has enriched a few at the expense of the many, but brushes it aside as the wail of the pessimist; industrial progress offers easier, more interesting, more morally beneficial work to thousands and millions. And the future holds even more brilliant promise for mankind. One is tempted to see here the ultimate possible development of Philistinism; but this judgment would fail to do justice to Platt's innocence and basic humanitarianism. His position, in fact, is not far from that with which Mark Twain began writing *A Connecticut Yankee*. On the other hand, he evidently lacks the power of ironic perception that caused Mark Twain to imagine the ultimate defeat of his Promethean inventor-industrialist.

Neither the genius of Irving nor the exquisite acting of Jefferson was required to give the legend of Sleepy Hollow a lasting hold upon the popular heart. It was not wholly the miraculous flavor in the story of the Seven Sleepers of Ephesus that preserved that early Christian myth. In all such tales the mutual astonishment of the awakened sleeper and the wondering beholders is largely due to the fact that the changes which have occurred during the lethargic sleep are suddenly and sharply forced upon the attention. But in all of them it is the domestic, the political, or the social revolution that is thus outlined.

The legend in which the awaking dazed sleeper and the bewildered witnesses shall realize and feel the material, intellectual, and humanitarian development of the last century has yet to be given shape and skillful touch. The marvel is transcendent, but the story will never be wrought. Genius cannot describe nor the public mind appreciate what of human progress has occurred, what of human development has taken place in the United States during the last hundred years. I know of no place where it may be more fitly illustrated or more sharply forced on the attention than in this city of Washington. Imagine, if you can, an individual who witnessed the laying of the cornerstone of the Capitol, now nearly one hundred years ago, to have been suddenly withdrawn from the associations of men, and with the scenes of that day vivid in his mind permitted to stand again upon the spot graced by the completed building, but which to him had been a rural waste. We would appear to him like the inhabitants of a new world, while he would seem as strange a being to us as a visitor from some other planet. The Potomac flowing as before, the outline of the hills, the dip of the valley, the sun and the sky above would be the only features of what to him was the scene of yesterday. The city, with its noble avenues, its architectural structures, and the residences of its people, would have grown as if by magic in a night. These things he might with wonder dimly comprehend. But the steamboat on the river would startle him as the ships of Columbus startled the natives whom they approached. The wavy lines of black smoke and white vapor escaping from chimneys and steam-pipes would be as incomprehensible and awesome as the aurora borealis. The incoming and outgoing locomotives with their trains; street railroads and vehicles moving thereon apparently without propulsive force; the tick of the telegraph, transmitting thought from the ends of the earth; the voice of man sounding through half the continent in his ears, would be as truly miraculous to him as the raising of Lazarus from the dead. The light that illumines our nightly darkness to him would be as truly a miracle as was to Moses that bush which burned with fire and was not consumed. He would find the people engaged in occupations and pursuits of which he had no knowledge. Machinery would have no meaning to him; the thought of his fellowmen and their language in large part would be incomprehensible. . . .

As the miraculous change began to dawn upon his mind, and he began by degrees to understand that it was real—that he had returned after an absence of a hundred years, and that during the century a thousand years of growth and development and increase of human knowledge and comfort and happiness had occurred—his first question of the bystanders would be: "What has done all this? Is this enchantment? What magician has transformed nature and changed mankind? What force, what power has been at work?" And the answer, if truly given, would be, "The spirit of invention has accomplished this; the creative faculty in man hath wrought these wonders."

How little we have realized the progress of the century; how silent its footsteps have been, and how little we have stopped to analyze or appreciate its cause. How barren of suggestion are the standard works on political economy and sociology as to the real underlying cause of the great transformation. Change, improvement, advancement have

come to be so large a part of our history that we should
the rather wonder if they ceased to go forward with accelerated motion. We are satisfied with nothing else. The
world would be slow and dull and intolerable to us if in
every decade we did not outstrip the performance of a
century. We seem to care as little about the cause of it all
as we do about sunlight and air, and health and strength.
We enjoy it as our right. We write and speak of the incidents of progress, the new phases of our existence, of
visible results, and magnify them in our minds above the
invisible force which has produced the results. Away out in
the busy world, if my thought shall ever reach it, men
will receive my statement, that invention is to be ac-
credited with this great progress, with a sceptical sneer.
But you who are workers in the field, who are planning
and devising methods by which still greater progress is to
be achieved, will understand me.

Books without number have been written, showing how
man emerged from savagery to barbarism, from barbarism
to civilization. The whole world has been explored for relics
by which to measure the progress of man on the long and
toilsome way from his prehistoric condition to the period
of civilization. Audiences gather to hear it explained, and
go away satisfied that the weapon, the tool, or the imple-
ment dug up from its buried resting place unerringly
proves how much progress mankind had made at the time
it was used. Science divides the periods of human progress
into ages, and calls them the stone age, the iron age, the
bronze age, but has failed to comprehend that there is another age, the age in which we are living—the machine age.
The first tool that man invented that he might more easily
satisfy his wants does not more truly mark his advancement
than does the invention of the marvelous devices and contrivances by which his comfort and happiness are a thou-
sandfold multiplied in the present time. Savagery, barbarism, civilization—have we reached the end of human
growth and development? Shall we not the rather understand that a new name must be given to the condition of
human society upon which we are about to enter, if we

have not already entered it; that we are reaching or have reached in our progress the age of spirituality. I do not use the word in its religious sense, but as meaning that, in the future of human achievement, mind is to triumph over matter, brain over muscle; that man is entering that period in which he is to subjugate all forces of nature and make them his servants.

Time will not permit me to paint the picture of our progress in detail; a few striking outlines must suffice. I must leave realistic touches to others. Nor can I closely analyze causes; I can merely suggest and generalize.

The establishment of constitutional liberty, the granting of patents for inventions, and the introduction and use of Webster's Spelling Book were practically coincident with the opening of the century, the closing of which we celebrate. Freedom, invention, popular intelligence were thus inaugurated. Who can fail to appreciate their intimate relation? During the century and a-half that preceded the year 1791 we had only succeeded in obtaining a permanent lodgment on the continent. We occupied only what has been called the selvedge of a great country. Our growth and progress had been slow. When the patent system was established we were less than four millions of people, differing little in character, ability, and pursuits from the men who settled at Jamestown and Plymouth. To-day we are more than sixty-three millions, so different in character and civilization that the traces of the Cavalier and Puritan are scarcely discernible. Then our western-most States were Pennsylvania, Virginia, Kentucky, and Georgia; now the line of Commonwealths is unbroken from the Atlantic to the Pacific. Then the Mississippi River marked the western boundary of our possessions, and we had just passed an ordinance for the government of the unoccupied territory northwest of the Ohio River; now we are asking the nations of the world to join us in the Columbian Exposition on the shores of Lake Michigan. Our coal mines, with a present out-put of more than one hundred and thirty million tons per annum, were then practically unknown; our iron mines, with a present annual

production of fourteen million tons of ore, were mainly
unworked. The railroad was undreamed of; now our railroad trackage would encompass the earth six and one-
half times. The steamboat was but an expectation; now
we are using six thousand with an aggregate carrying capacity of two million tons. The telegraph then lay in the
realm of the miraculous; to-day our telegraphic wires
would reach from the earth to the moon, return to earth
and again to the moon, with enough spare wire to girdle
the earth three times. We had in those days about nineteen hundred miles of post-routes, over which the mail
was carried at intervals and deposited in about seventy-
five offices; now our post-routes cover more than four hundred and twenty-five thousand miles, and our post-offices
number more than sixty thousand. The mail matter carried
during the past year weighed more than one hundred and
eighty-two thousand tons, and the persons engaged in
carrying it (not including "free-delivery" carriers) traveled three hundred and twenty-seven million miles. Then
we had a depreciated and really worthless currency, little
of private wealth, and no public credit. Our sound currency now exceeds two billions of dollars; our national
credit stands highest among the nations of the earth; and
the aggregate wealth of our people is estimated to be
more than sixty billions of dollars. Then a few weekly,
semi-weekly or tri-weekly newspapers, scarcely larger than
a sheet of foolscap, supplied and satisfied the popular demand for news. There were no reporters or editors then.
These words are new, as are the professions they signify.
It was the "printer" whom the public knew in connection
with the newspapers of those days. The entire newspaper
publication of 1791 is now surpassed in the weakest of
our Territories; and a single newspaper of our day, The
New York World, has circulated nearly six hundred thousand copies in a single day, requiring for their printing
ninety-four tons of paper.

Manufactures, except in the household, were practically
unknown. There were no "mechanics" in the meaning of
the word as now used. Men knew how to sow and plow,

hoe and chop, reap and mow and cradle, break flax and hackle it, thrash with the flail, winnow with the blanket or fan, and to shell corn by hand; the women knew how to spin, card, weave, and knit. Mechanical knowledge was monopolized by the blacksmith, the carpenter, the millwright, and the village tinker. Production was a toilsome, weary matter, limited by the capacity for muscular endurance. In the absence of reliable statistics we only know that in 1790 the value of our manufactures was but a few millions of dollars, the larger part of which consisted of linen and woolen cloth made in households. The value of our manufactured products in 1880 was between five and six billions. Statistics for 1890 are not at hand, but the sum total of our manufactured products within the census year can hardly be less than eight billions. But I must forbear; our material advancement surpasses the wildest dream of the most vivid imagination. Neither philosopher nor mad man could have predicted it. It is incomprehensible; the mind does not and cannot grasp it. We know that it is great; we try to realize it as in our feeble way we try to comprehend the infinite.

If you would in a measure form a conception of how large a factor invention has been in this progress, try to imagine what our social, financial, educational, and commercial condition would be with an absolute ignorance of how steam and electricity can be used in the daily production of things for our sustenance and comfort; with an absolute ignorance of the steamboat, the railroad, the telegraph, the telephone, the modern printing press, and the machinery in common daily use. Men who acknowledge that the development of invention and national progress have kept even pace in all that makes the people great and happy are yet slow to comprehend that invention has contributed in any large degree to such progress.

To satisfy the doubts of such, a little careful thought is needed. We may well inquire what it is that marks the superiority of our people. And to answer this we need to read the lesson which history teaches—that the people which has known most of the laws of nature, and has had with that knowledge the greatest capacity to apply natural forces in economic production, has always attained the highest point in human development. Human superiority consists in superior capacity to know and superior ability to do. If I understand how it is that invention has promoted the progress of our people, it is because it has enabled them to know more, and has given them the power to do more than any other people. . . .

We must understand that to invent is to create, and that the thing created must be beneficial to mankind. We are wont to say that we live in an environment of invention—that everything we touch, taste, handle, or see, is the result of an invention. We might more properly say that we live in a new creation. Literally, the old things have passed away and all things have become new. Human society is full of creators. Formerly we ascribed creative faculty or force to the Divine Being alone; our commonest thought of God was that He was the Infinite Creator. We said as we gazed on the forms, animate and inanimate, which surrounded us and which we believed contributed to our happiness, "Behold the expressed thought of the Creator— God!" and we were lost in wonder, love, and praise. Now, when we look upon the wondrous contrivances and inventions everywhere contributing to our life wants and adding to our life enjoyments, we are forced to exclaim: "Behold the expressed thought of the creator—man!" Inventions have given us a new and higher idea of the capacity of man. We begin to see how nearly he is related to Divinity; we have found a new meaning in the phrase, "So God created man in His own image." Shakespeare's words—the highest and noblest uninspired estimate of man seem real to us at last—"How infinite in faculty . . . In apprehension, how like a god."

Let me illustrate. Men have often wondered and adored the Infinite Creator as they have dwelt upon the words— "And God said, 'Let there be light,' and there was light." But the hours are not all light; there is the night and darkness as well as the day and light. Now, if you will think as you come to this place this evening how the thought of man has transformed black coal and viewless electricity into the agents which light your pathway, you will feel it scarcely irreverent to exclaim: "And man said, 'Let there be light,' and there was light."

If you will let your mind dwell steadily on the development during the century of the creative faculty in man, you will discover one prominent reason for the advancement of mankind. You will see that the creative faculty is no longer limited to a few great souls, but that it is possessed by the many. You will see that the gap between the scientific discoverer and the practical workman is slowly but surely being closed. When we survey the field of invention our eyes rest inevitably on the figure of Watt. He stands out before us as the great leader in the inventive world. We give him highest place among those who have wrought for mankind. We put him above Alexander and Napoleon. They were destroyers; he was a creator; they devoured; he developed the world's capacity to produce. But do we realize that many greater than Watt are here? There are thousands of men in our midst whose praises are never sung, who pursue their intense work quietly and unnoticed, for whom the world erects no pedestal of fame, but each of whom knows more of the nature and power and adaptation of steam than Watt ever dreamed of. We sing the praises of Morse; we write him down among our greatest; we give him a conspicuous niche in our temple of fame; the world pays tribute to his greatness, to his creative skill; he will go down in history as the first man who by his invention made it possible to crowd into a day's time transactions which would otherwise require a month's time for their accomplishment; who enabled every man who can buy a penny paper to behold as in a moving panorama the events transpiring throughout the whole world. But many greater than Morse are with us. There are thousands of girls in our country who know more of the laws of electricity, and better how to apply their knowledge of these laws in the transmission of human thought, than ever Morse imagined. Such men, such inventors, famous by right in the world's history, were after all but prospectors, locating the rich mine of human invention. They thought out, or by accident discovered, a limited possibility in the application of new forces to the supply of human wants. Then the world's thought became focused like a great burning lens on that possibility, and other men wrought the possible into the actual. . . .

So we see that each invention, great or small, by its own inherent force and power wonderfully stimulates and increases the inventive or creative faculty of man. Reduction to practice requires knowledge and skill equal to that of the man who conceives the idea, and the use of the invention necessitates knowledge akin to that of the inventor. The woman who uses the sewing machine must have knowledge in kind, at least, if not in degree, equal to that of Howe. The field laborer who uses the harvester must know as much of the operation, if not of the principle, of the machine as McCormick. What an advancement in average human knowledge this signifies in the country where we live and move and have our being among inventions! And if, as Bacon said, knowledge is power, how greatly have we advanced in power!

Another thought in this line. Our library shelves are filled with books, written to prove the ennobling influence of the fine arts upon mankind. Painting, sculpture, and music are lauded because they educate and refine society, because they improve and elevate men and women, and advance them in the scale of being. But, is the contemplation of a painting more inspiring than the intelligent study of an engine? Is a statue more beautiful than a machine? The one copies nature, the other compels nature; in the one there is repose and inaction, the other is instinct with life and energy. Are the waves of song more rhythmic than the undulations which fall on the ear from the movement of myriad inventions? The one touches sentiment, the other sings to us of human peace and plenty.

Again. There are books without number which tell us how man grows by the contemplation of nature, of the subtle influence exercised upon the character of man by the scenes in which he dwells, by mountain and forest, by brook and river and ocean, by clear sky and fleecy clouds, by the rare tints of sunset and dawn, by breaking billow and roaring blasts. All this has been portrayed since books were first written—by poet, philosopher, and moralist alike. But who has written, who shall write, of that greater and subtler molding influence exercised upon the character of man by his subjection of the forces of nature to become his ministering spirits? Compare the man who muses on nature, who drinks in the influence of the mountain from afar, with the man who pierces that mountain to make a highway for the distribution of the world's products, or digs out from their dungeon the imprisoned metals, to be wrought into implements for his use, and tell me which man grows most or best. Which is the more a man, he who gazes with awe on the dark storm-cloud and sees in the lightning only the manifestation of the wrath of an angry God, or he who subdues the lightning and makes it his servant, and sends it to and fro on missions of mercy and sympathy to his fellow-man?

Thus far I have spoken of the indirect influence of invention on the progress of mankind, on human advancement. Let me for a moment be more specific and direct. Man is ever wanting something. He may be said to be the creature who wants; and the greater his attainment the more numerous his wants. The man who wants least in the world is of the least use to the world. Sometimes we call this craving, unceasing want of man, aspiration. Our fathers called it the pursuit of happiness, and declared it an "inalienable right." Whatever we may call it, this is true: The more numerous and complex the wants of man (provided they are not born of vicious desire) and the more easily they are satisfied, the better, abler, happier, and nobler mankind becomes. Every human want involves production; something must be produced to satisfy it, and production is useless and objectless except to satisfy human wants. Man's first want is to appease hunger and quench thirst; his next, to be protected from the extremes of cold and heat. If these are all, we call him a savage, and production stands at its minimum. With every step of advancement toward civilization and spirituality his wants multiply, and production must increase. His comfort and happiness, his present and future, depend upon the ease with which he can obtain wherewith to satisfy and gratify these wants.

Now, the true problem of invention—its only purpose and object, indeed—is, first, to enable man to satisfy his present wants with less of effort and cost than before; and, second, to create in him the new wants incident to his higher plane of existence, and the means of supplying those wants, so that as the years go on man can have more of comfort with less of personal effort than ever before. If this does not constitute human advancement, I do not know what does. . . .

The America of to-day is radically different from the America of 1791. We call our improvement the development of Christian civilization; and I would not for a moment forget nor disparage the great influence of Christianity in molding our institutions and directing our pursuits. But what kind of a Christian civilization would it be with the spirit of invention still dormant? Improved printing presses, telegraphs, and the means of rapid communication have given us a different Christianity, and taught us the lessons of the Master more correctly. The religious polemics of a former century interest men no longer. Reasoning

> Of providence, fore-knowledge, will and fate,
> Fixed fate, free-will, fore-knowledge absolute,

is as obsolete now as the argument to prove witchcraft a reality and of satanic origin. Men no longer wander in the mazes of abstract speculation; they seek for practical truths and practical results. The clergyman who should preach the sermon of a hundred years ago would speak to empty pews. The present religion is one that seeks to better man's physical and social condition. We care less for doctrine, and more for human improvement; and we have come at last to dwell with intense satisfaction upon the thought that our Saviour went about "doing good."

Thus we see how the inventive spirit of the age has been

working this change; how the very essence of an invention is to do good to man, to minister to the comfort, the happiness, and the higher intelligence of the people; how it works hand in hand with the spirit of a true religion. For the first time in the history of the world we seem to be making real headway against superstition and bigotry. We no longer count the mysterious as miraculous. What seemed miraculous has in our day too often come to be commonplace to let us sit down in wonder before it. For the first time we have come to learn that true rivalry in manly achievement is the struggle to accomplish most for the benefit of mankind, and that the only real happiness consists in enabling others to become happy.

Nor is the change in the method and system of our education less radical than that in religious thought and effort. The college president of a hundred years ago would bring financial ruin to any college in a twelve-month. We more and more demand that our children shall study the present, and that their expansive powers shall not be imprisoned in the dungeons of a dead past. Roman and Grecian manners, customs, literature and art are no longer the only models upon which we seek to develop the character of our sons. They must be fitted to explore the storehouse of nature and to bring out therefrom unseen treasures for a true enrichment of their fellows. Nothing more strikingly illustrates this change than the public demand for scientific, industrial, and manual training schools. Consider for a moment how impossible such schools would have been when our Constitution was framed, and how their felt necessity is now changing all our educational methods. No education is complete to-day that does not fit the student to deal with the great problems of applied science, the solution of which is still more to enrich and bless mankind. Education is not finished now in the college or professional school; it goes on in the workshop, in the laboratory, by the lathe, in the field, in the mine, in the forest, wherever and so long as man is called upon to wrestle with these great problems. And how intense life has become in consequence! Slow and toilsome processes of thought are now no longer possible by the side of the swiftly-moving machine; thought has been wedded to intuition. Evidence is not wanting that invention and discovery have resulted in lengthening the average of human life. But whether this be so or not, if we count life by its action and experience and what we gain in it and by it, our term of life has been wonderfully lengthened.

The change in human enterprise may be illustrated by contrasting what were once the Seven Wonders of the world with the seven wonders of American invention. The old wonders of the world were: The Pyramids, the Hanging Gardens of Babylon, the Phidian Statue of Jupiter, the Mausoleum, the Temple of Diana at Ephesus, the Colossus of Rhodes, and the Pharos of Alexandria. Two were tombs of kings, one was the playground of a petted queen; one was the habitat of the world's darkest superstition; one the shrine of a heathen god; another was a crude attempt to produce a work of art solely to excite wonder, and one only, the light-house at Alexandria, was of the slightest benefit to mankind. They were erected mainly by tyrants; most of them by the unrequited toil of degraded and enslaved laborers. In them was neither improvement nor advancement for the people.

Let me enumerate the seven wonders of American invention: The cotton-gin; the adaptation of steam to methods of transportation; the application of electricity in business pursuits; the harvester; the modern printing press; the ocean cable, and the sewing machine. How wonderful in conception, in construction, in purpose, these great inventions; how they dwarf the Pyramids and all the wonders of antiquity; what a train of blessings each brought with its entrance into social life; how wide, direct, and far-reaching their benefits! Each was the herald of a social revolution; each was a human benefactor; each was a new Goddess of Liberty; each was a great emancipator of man from the bondage of labor; each was a new teacher come upon earth; each was a moral force. . . .

I must not fail to notice at this point a more or less prevalent idea that the result of invention is to enrich the few at the expense of the many—that capital is assisted while labor is injured. I have little patience with this belief. It is the wail of the pessimist rather than the opinion of the intelligent. Men who give utterance to it forget that in social economy man always builds on the ruins of the past. The first effect of every useful invention is to destroy capital. In the inventive realm the fittest only survives. No invention answers its purpose that does not either supersede the old methods of production or bring forth a new product. If some new motive power should be discovered which would enable us to produce those things which men must have for their sustenance and happiness better and more cheaply than water power, air power, steam power, and electrical power, the capital thus invested would be gradually but surely destroyed; whereas all experience teaches us that there would be no injury to labor—there would simply be a readjustment of labor and an increased demand for it. There would be a demand for more intelligent labor, more skillful labor, more brain labor, as well as a greater demand in new fields for what we term muscular labor.

An illustration or two conclusively proves this. In the beginning of the century there were no railroads; all transportation was by wagons, carts, horses, and oxen. The railroads of the country last year, in railroad parlance, moved sixty-eight billion tons of freight one mile. To have accomplished the same work would have required more horses than there are in the United States, and two-thirds of the able-bodied men of the country to drive them. But all the horses in the country were needed for other work—work which, except for the railroads, would not have been done. With the introduction of the railroad the men who had driven horses found that their services were in demand at prices which teamsters never expected to receive. There would be no such carrying trade as we now have if it had not been developed by the railroads. People who think that invention lessens the demand for labor should remember that millions of people find profitable employment in localities where Indians would now be hunting the buffalo were it not for the inventions which go to make up that vast system of railroads, which is itself one great conglomerate machine acting with the precision of mechanical law. They should remember, too, that to operate the railroads of this country nearly a million persons are employed to fill places that have been created by the railroad, in which intelligence and skill of a high order are required. They should take account, too, of the men who have worked in mines and forests, who have built furnaces and mills, who have produced the rails for one hundred and sixty thousand miles of railroad track, and the necessary equipment of locomotives and cars; of the men who have leveled and graded the roads—who have pierced the mountains and filled up the valleys; of the men who have found employment in supplying all these laborers and artisans with food and comforts and luxuries. That man is sadly deficient in the intelligence of the age who cannot see that every true invention greatly increases the demand for labor, improves the quality of labor, and thereby enhances its price.

About thirty-five years ago men discovered a natural product unknown before; they called it petroleum. Invention seized upon it and began to work it into useful forms for the production of useful results and to supply unquestioned needs. It was a timely discovery. Without it, we can hardly conceive how it would be possible to light the homes of our people. In every stage of its treatment invention has been called into use. By the aid of those inventions the crude article has been resolved into more than one hundred and fifty separate products, each one of which has its commercial designation, its beneficial use—many of them supplying wants unfelt and unknown before. All this has created an army of workmen engaged in employments unheard and unthought of but for the discovery, and for the inventions which have so multifariously utilized the product. What labor has been displaced or injured thereby? So with every invention since the creation of man. Not one of them but has made life more to be desired by the toiler; not one but has made his station more honorable, his environment more agreeable. I count it one of the chief benefits of our unrivaled inventions that labor in the United States has become more intelligent, more skillful, and therefore commands the highest price. I count the advancement of our laborers as the chief wealth of our people. A people may have gold and not be rich, may have lands and be indigent; but a people with intelligence and skill and energy is truly rich and truly great. It is brain power that constitutes real wealth. The old poet of the sixteenth century who sang, "My mind to me a kingdom is," had a better conception of the true nature of wealth than the man who counts only the millionaire as the wealthy man.

One other thought I commend to the pessimist. If, as he believes, invention has augmented and concentrated capital and clothed it with power which is used to the public detriment, it has also made possible the organization and association of labor. Without the railroad, the telegraph, and the press, associated labor could not exist; without these children of invention, no labor combination or organization would extend beyond the city or town in which it was organized. By adding to the intelligence of the masses, by the opportunity which it gives for association, invention has wonderfully increased the power of the masses. The laborer is no longer an isolated toiler. Invention has clothed him with strength as a garment. God grant that he may use it wisely.

We stand in the doorway of a new century. What of the future? Has invention reached its zenith; has man attained his highest development; has he already reached the goal of human progress; can he advance no farther? I ask these questions because I firmly believe that the limit of human invention is also the limit of human advancement; that he who writes the history of invention will write the history of mankind; that if invention has already done its perfect work, man is all he can ever hope to be in this life.

For one, I cannot entertain the gloomy thought that we have come to that century in the world's life in which new and grander achievements are impossible. For one, I am persuaded that we have but just entered the era of improvement; that at no period in his existence has man been so well equipped, so well fitted by his ability, knowledge, and high resolve, to grapple with the problems of life and to make new conquests in the field of invention. Invention is a prolific mother; every inventive triumph stimulates new effort. Man never is and never will be content with success, and the great secrets of nature are as yet largely undiscovered. Though we seem to have accomplished much, we really know but little. Who knows what electricity is? Who understands the properties of any material substance? Who has solved the mysteries of the atom and the germ? Who knows what forces men have passed by in their search for motive power? Who has even catalogued the forces of nature? What wondrous possibilities are yet locked in her storehouse? But, after all, the real wonder of the earth is man; never so wonderful as when he boldly challenges nature to unlock her doors and reveal her mysteries that he may use them for the improvement and advancement of his kind.

DOCUMENT 6

Testimony before the Senate Committee on Education and Labor

SOURCE: Carroll D. Wright, Testimony before the Senate Committee on Education and Labor, Boston, 18 October 1883 (U.S. Congress. Senate. Committee on Education and Labor. *Report of the Committee of the Senate upon Relations between Labor and Capital, and Testimony Taken by the Committee*, "in five volumes" [only four published], Vol. III, Washington, D.C., 1885, pp. 422–25).

Wright, head of the Massachusetts Bureau of Labor Statistics, and soon to be appointed first U.S. Commissioner of Labor, was a celebrated pioneer in the compilation and interpretation of statistics bearing on industrial conditions. The report to General Walker to which he refers, published in the Tenth Census of the United States, 1880, is a landmark in the empirical study of economic and sociological phenomena. Most of the questioning was by the Chairman of the Committee, Senator Henry W. Blair of New Hampshire. "Mr. Pugh" was Senator James L. Pugh of Alabama. Wright's unqualified optimism about the effects of the mechanization of industry represented orthodox conservative opinion.

[BOSTON, *October* 18, 1883]
[CARROLL D. WRIGHT sworn and examined.]

The Factory System an Element of Advancement in Civilization

Q. What is your judgment as to the general influence upon the character, the prosperity, and the happiness of the wage-working population and laboring people, generally, of the introduction of the factory system instead of our former method of performing like labor?—A. I am thoroughly satisfied that the factory has been a wonderful element in our civilization towards its advancement, for this reason: Under the old domestic system of labor, which existed prior to the factory system, there was no centering of thought; everything was diffused; the moral condition of workers under the domestic system was much worse than under the factory system. It was under it that the great pauper class of England grew up, and it was only with the advent of the factory that that pauper class began to be limited in size.

Its Results in America

In this country, while the factory has, on the face of it and in the minds of many, tended to degrade labor, the actual fact is that it has elevated it, for this reason: While processes have been simplified, people who have been obliged to earn their living by the coarsest muscular labor have been able to step up in the grade of employment and become partially skilled in their employment; so that instead of degrading skilled labor the factory has been constantly elevating unskilled labor to the ranks of skilled labor. I believe a very close examination of the subject would bring any one to that conclusion.

I have had the honor to make a report to General Walker on the factory system of the United States, and that is my conclusion after two or three years' special study on that subject.

General Misconception of the Results of the Factory System

Q. You think it has improved the health and the general conditions of life with our own working population?—A. Certainly.

Q. As well here as in the foreign country you refer to?—

A. Certainly. I was speaking more particularly in regard to America. I know the feeling is that the factory system has more and more tended to degrade labor, because under that system thirty or forty years ago, as established in New England, we employed only American girls from our farm houses, &c., while now we see an entirely different class in our factories; but I fail to find that the class who used to be in factories have gone down; they have stepped up into school teaching, telegraphy, and the higher branches of labor, while their places have been filled by a class that have come up from a lower occupation.

Q. Would it or not have been inevitable that those who had possession, if incapable of rising, would have remained?—A. That certainly would have been true; while now the result is that by the factory we are constantly opening wider the field of advancement for that class of people who unfortunately stand on the lower round of the industrial ladder—we are bringing them up closer.

The Elevation of One Class Elevates All

Q. Is not that universally true in the history of human affairs, that where one class of human beings rise, that rising does, of necessity, elevate all that are above?—A. That is the conclusion of my observation and reflection on the subject.

By Mr. Pugh:

Q. Have you ever thought about the influences in factory employment that would have this elevating effect that you describe—the influence on the life of a factory operative that would elevate him more than he would be elevated under other conditions?

The Old Industrial System Compared with the New

A. Yes; if you take things comparatively—and we are obliged always to do that. Under the old system which preceded the factory, the hand-loom weavers and spinners did their work in the same rooms in which they lived. They were left to themselves, and to all the demoralizing influences which came from constant association, and living and working in one room. The machinery for production always disputed with the family for the room for living, and the result was very bad in regard to the morals of the people.

When the factory came, association and co-operation in many respects took place; minds were sharpened by contact, and, as factory centers increased, the mental friction of the factory brought about efforts to introduce the lyceum, and many other of the results which you usually find in factory towns, and rarely, if ever, find in agricultural villages. There is that isolation in the old domestic system and in agricultural labor which prevents much progress. This progress has been greatest in the centers of industry as developed by machinery.

The Factory System in its Bearings on Prostitution and Intemperance

Your question leads me to another thought entertained by some in regard to the old methods, that the factory feeds prostitution and intemperance. It has been a privilege of mine to examine many of the records of different municipalities in Europe, and to gather from them statistics which have never appeared in print with reference to the crimes committed in different boroughs and towns, and I have made the same investigation in this country, and, with very rare exceptions, I have found that the factory population of a place furnished a less proportion of the arrests for crime than the proportion of the factory population to the whole population of that place. Nor have I been able to find that prostitution grows out of the associations of the factory. I am well satisfied from the investigation of original statistics which I have been able to make, that the factory populations not only of this country, but of Great Britain, are making as virtuous and noble a fight for their existence and progress as any other class in the community. I have come to that conclusion, and was glad to arrive at it, because I had a different impression. The facts teach me that that is true.

The Factory System in Large Cities

Q. Have you been able to draw any distinction between operatives in villages outside of the cities, and those in large cities?—A. Certainly. All large cities have a population which is in its nature floating, but which has nothing particular to do with the industries of the place; and the misfortune is that all the misdemeanors of that population are, in a large industrial town, attributed to the presence of the industry. You may take Manchester, England, if you choose. I used to hear very bad statements in regard to the factory population of Manchester; still the facts were that the misdemeanors which were attributed to the factory operatives of Manchester belonged entirely to what we would call the "hoodlum" population of any great city. The factory did not bring it there. It *was* there.

The Factory System in Villages

But of course, the truer idea is to find the town that is built around the village. That is the factory village you refer to. In this factory village, not only in this country but in other countries, I think you will find as good a state of progress as in villages where the industries are entirely formative. I see no reason why, certainly in the future, with the growth of a better sentiment on both sides of the great industrial question, the factory should not be the most powerful agent in bringing the people to a higher moral condition.

The Temperance Question

For instance, the temperance question is more largely under the control of the employers of labor than any other class of men. The experience of the last twenty years clearly proves that in all factory centers where the manufacturers themselves have taken an interest in the question, and have insisted upon employing only men of sobriety, there has been a vast improvement. Take the English factory towns, where twenty years ago Monday was largely lost, and Tuesday worth but little; you can now find but few places where there is any difference in the days of the week about the conduct of the establishment in respect to the drunkenness of the operatives. That old state of things is passing by. Men can be employed for the same wages who do not get drunk. And there is an *esprit du corps* growing up in factories everywhere, which frowns upon any general dissipation among the people in the factories. That is certainly so among the women, and I find, so far as I have been able to observe, that it is growing to be largely so among the men. Improvident habits, of course, among people everywhere is largely the cause of pauperism; but how to check these improvident habits is a great question. In my own mind the most powerful influence that will check them is a sentiment which shall say to a man that without sobriety there is no employment.

DOCUMENT 7

Causes of American Nervousness

SOURCE: George M. Beard, "Causes of American Nervousness," from *American Nervousness, Its Causes and Consequences* (New York, 1881), pp. 96–129.

Beard, a graduate of Phillips Andover, Yale (1862), and the College of Physicians and Surgeons of New York (1866), displayed early in his medical career a remarkable energy and inventiveness in research. His treatise on *The Medical and Surgical Uses of Electricity* (1871) brought him an international reputation. In investigating "neurasthenia" he ranged widely over the field of what would now be called psychosomatic medicine. While both his methods of research and his therapeutic proposals have inevitably been superseded, his treatise on American nervousness provides valuable data concerning the effects of the new industrial environment on human beings.

The causes of American nervousness are complicated, but are not beyond analysis: First of all modern civilization. The phrase modern civilization is used with emphasis, for civilization alone does not cause nervousness. The Greeks were certainly civilized, but they were not nervous, and in the Greek language there is no word for that term. The ancient Romans were civilized, as judged by any standard. Civilization is therefore a relative term, and as such is employed throughout this treatise. The modern differ from the ancient civilizations mainly in these five elements—steam power, the periodical press, the telegraph, the sciences, and the mental activity of women. When civilization, plus these five factors, invades any nation, it must carry nervousness and nervous diseases along with it.

Civilization Very Limited in Extent

All that is said here of American nervousness refers only to a fraction of American society; for in America, as in all lands, the majority of the people are muscle-workers rather than brain-workers; have little education, and are not striving for honor, or expecting eminence or wealth. All our civilization hangs by a thread; the activity and force of the very few make us what we are as a nation; and if, through degeneracy, the descendants of these few revert to the condition of their not very remote ancestors, all our haughty civilization would be wiped away. With all our numerous colleges, such as they are, it is a rarity and surprise to meet in business relations with a college-educated man.

A late writer, Dr. Arthur Mitchell, has shown that if, of the population of Scotland, a few thousands were destroyed or degenerated and their places unsupplied, the nation would fall downward to barbarism. To a somewhat less degree this is true of all lands, including our own land. Of our fifty millions of population, but a few millions have reached that elevation where they are likely to be nervous. In the lower orders, the classes that support our dispensaries and hospitals, in the tenements of our crowded cities, and even on farms in the country, by the mountain side—among the healthiest regions, we find, now and then, here and there cases of special varieties of nervous disease, such as hay-fever, neurasthenia, etc.; but the proportion of diseases of this kind among these people is much smaller than among the in-door-living and brain-working classes, although insanity of the incurable kind is more common among the lower or the middle than in the very highest classes.

Edison's electric light is now sufficiently advanced in an experimental direction to give us the best possible illustration of the effects of modern civilization on the nervous system. An electric machine of definite horse-power, situated at some central point, is to supply the electricity needed to run a certain number of lamps—say one thousand, more or less. If an extra number of lamps should be interposed in the circuit, then the power of the engine must be increased; else the light of the lamps would be decreased, or give out. This has been mathematically calculated, so that it is known, or believed to be known, by those in charge, just how much increase of horse-power is needed for each increase in the number of lamps. In all the calculations, however widely they may differ, it is assumed that the force supplied by any central machine is limited, and cannot be pushed beyond a certain point; and if the number of lamps interposed in the circuit be increased, there must be a corresponding increase in the force of the machine. The nervous system of man is the centre of the nerve-force supplying all the organs of the body. Like the steam engine, its force is limited, although it cannot be mathematically measured—and, unlike the steam engine, varies in amount of force with the food, the state of health and external conditions, varies with age, nutrition, occupation, and numberless factors. The force in this nervous system can, therefore, be increased or diminished by good or evil influences, medical or hygienic, or by the natural evolutions—growth, disease and decline; but none the less it is limited; and when new functions are interposed in the circuit, as modern civilization is constantly requiring us to do, there comes a period, sooner or later, varying in different individuals, and at different times of life, when the amount of force is insufficient to keep all the lamps actively burning; those that are weakest go out entirely, or, as more frequently happens, burn faint and feebly—they do not expire, but give an insufficient and unstable light—this is the philosophy of modern nervousness.

The invention of printing, the extension of steam power into manufacturing interests and into means of conveyance, the telegraph, the periodical press, the political machinery of free countries, the religious excitements that are the sequels of Protestantism—the activities of philanthropy, made necessary by the increase of civilization, and of poverty, and certain forms of disease—and, more than all, perhaps, the heightening and extending complexity of modern education in and out of schools and universities, the inevitable effect of the rise of modern science and the expansion of history in all its branches—all these are so many additional lamps interposed in the circuit, and are supplied at the expense of the nervous system, the dynamic power of which has not correspondingly increased.

Necessary Evils of Specialization

One evil, and hardly looked for effect of the introduction of steam, together with the improved methods of manufacturing of recent times, has been the training in special departments or duties—so that artisans, instead of doing or preparing to do, all the varieties of the manipulations needed in the making of any article, are restricted to a few simple exiguous movements, to which they give their whole lives—in the making of a rifle, or a watch, each part is constructed by experts on that part. The effect of this exclusive concentration of mind and muscle to one mode of action, through months and years, is both negatively and positively pernicious, and notably so, when reenforced, as it almost universally is, by the bad air of overheated and ill-ventilated establishments. Herein is one unanticipated cause of the increase of insanity and other diseases of the nervous system among the laboring and poorer classes. The steam engine, which would relieve work, as it was hoped, and allow us to be idle, has increased the amount of work done a thousand fold; and with that increase in quantity there has been a differentiation of quality and specialization of function which, so far forth, is depressing both to mind and body. In the professions —the constringing power of specialization is neutralized very successfully by general culture and observation, out of which specialties spring, and by which they are supported; but for the artisan there is no time, or chance, or hope, for such redeeming and antidotal influences.

Clocks and Watches—Necessity of Punctuality

The perfection of clocks and the invention of watches have something to do with modern nervousness, since they compel us to be on time, and excite the habit of looking to see the exact moment, so as not to be late for trains or appointments. Before the general use of these instruments of precision in time, there was a wider margin for all appointments; a longer period was required and prepared for, especially in travelling—coaches of the olden period were not expected to start like steamers or trains, on the instant—men judged of the time by probabilities, by looking at the sun, and needed not, as a rule, to be nervous about the loss of a moment, and had incomparably fewer experiences wherein a delay of a few moments might destroy the hopes of a lifetime. A nervous man cannot take out his watch and look at it when the time for an appointment or train is near, without affecting his pulse, and the effect on that pulse, if we could but measure and weigh it, would be found to be correlated to a loss to the nervous system. Punctuality is a greater thief of nervous force than is procrastination of time. We are under constant strain, mostly unconscious, oftentimes in sleeping as well as in waking hours, to get somewhere or do something at some definite moment. Those who would relieve their nervousness may well study the manners of the Turks, who require two weeks to execute a promise that the Anglo-Saxon would fulfil in a moment. In Constantinople indolence is the ideal, as work is the ideal in London and New York; the follower of the Prophet is ashamed to be in haste, and would apologize for keeping a promise. There are those who prefer, or fancy they prefer, the sensations of movement and activity to the sensations of repose; but from the standpoint only of economy of nerve-force all our civilization is a mistake; every mile of advance into the domain of ideas, brings a conflict that knows no rest, and all conquests are to be paid for, before delivery often, in blood and nerve and life. We cannot have civilization and have anything else, the price at which nature disposes of this luxury being all the rest of her domain.

The Telegraph

The telegraph is a cause of nervousness the potency of which is little understood. Before the days of Morse and his rivals, merchants were far less worried than now, and less business was transacted in a given time; prices fluctuated far less rapidly, and the fluctuations which now are transmitted instantaneously over the world were only known then by the slow communication of sailing vessels or steamships; hence we might wait for weeks or months for a cargo of tea from China, trusting for profit to prices that should follow their arrival; whereas, now, prices at each port are known at once all over the globe. This continual fluctuation of values, and the constant knowledge of those fluctuations in every part of the world, are the scourges of business men, the tyrants of trade—every cut in prices in wholesale lines in the smallest of any of the Western cities, becomes known in less than an hour all over the Union; thus competition is both diffused and intensified. Within but thirty years the telegraphs of the world have grown to half a million miles of line, and over a million miles of wire—or more than forty times the circuit of the globe. In the United States there were, in 1880, 170,103 miles of line, and in that year 33,155,991 messages were sent over them.

Effect of Noise on the Nerves

The relation of noise to nervousness and nervous diseases is a subject of not a little interest; but one which seems to have been but incidentally studied.

The noises that nature is constantly producing—the

moans and roar of the wind, the rustling and trembling of the leaves and swaying of the branches, the roar of the sea and of waterfalls, the singing of birds, and even the cries of some wild animals—are mostly rhythmical to a greater or less degree, and always varying if not intermittent; to a savage or to a refined ear, on cultured or uncultured brains, they are rarely distressing, often pleasing, sometimes delightful and inspiring. Even the loudest sounds in nature, the roll of thunder, the howling of storms, and the roar of a cataract like Niagara—save in the exceptional cases of idiosyncrasy—are the occasions not of pain but of pleasure, and to observe them at their best men will compass the globe.

Many of the appliances and accompaniments of civilization, on the other hand, are the causes of noises that are unrhythmical, unmelodious and therefore annoying, if not injurious; manufactures, locomotion, travel, housekeeping even, are noise-producing factors, and when all these elements are concentred, as in great cities, they maintain through all the waking and some of the sleeping hours, an unintermittent vibration in the air that is more or less disagreeable to all, and in the case of an idiosyncrasy or severe illness may be unbearable and harmful. Rhythmical, melodious, musical sounds are not only agreeable, but when not too long maintained are beneficial, and may be ranked among our therapeutical agencies.

Unrhythmical, harsh, jarring sounds, to which we apply the term noise, are, on the contrary, to a greater or less degree, harmful or liable to be harmful; they cause severe molecular disturbance. . . . A professional gentleman whom I know, says that the noise of the elevated railway trains in New York city are so harassing to him that he never goes on the avenue where these trains run unless compelled to do so; the effect he declares is rasping, exasperating, amounting to positive pain; and yet this man is not only well, but is remarkably tough and wiry, capable of bearing confinement and long and severe application. . . .

Railway Travelling and Nervousness

Whether railway travelling is directly the cause of nervous disease is a question of not a little interest. Reasoning deductively, without any special facts, it would seem that the molecular disturbance caused by travelling long distances, or living on trains as an employé, would have an unfavorable influence on the nervous system.

In practice this seems to be found; that in some cases —probably a minority of those who live on the road— functional nervous symptoms are excited, and there are some who are compelled to give up this mode of life.

A German physician has given the name "Fear of Railway Travelling," to a symptom that is observed in some who have become nervously exhausted by long residence on trains; they become fearful of taking a journey on the cars, mainly from the unpleasant sensations caused by the vibrating motions of the train.

That railway travel, though beneficial to some, is sometimes injurious to the nerve system of the nervous, is demonstrable all the time in my patients; many while travelling by rail suffer from the symptoms of sea-sickness and with increase of nervousness.

Rapid Development and Acceptance of New Ideas

The rapidity with which new truths are discovered, accepted and popularized in modern times is a proof and result of the extravagance of our civilization.

Philosophies and discoveries as well as inventions which in the Middle Ages would have been passed by or dismissed with the murder of the author, are in our time— and notably in our country—taken up and adopted, in innumerable ways made practical—modified, developed, actively opposed, possibly overthrown and displaced within a few years, and all of necessity at a great expenditure of force.

The experiments, inventions, and discoveries of Edison alone have made and are now making constant and exhausting draughts on the nervous forces of America and Europe, and have multiplied in very many ways, and made more complex and extensive, the tasks and agonies not only of practical men, but of professors and teachers and students everywhere; the simple attempt to master the multitudinous directions and details of the labors of this one young man with all his thousands and thousands of experiments and hundreds of patents and with all the soluble and insoluble physical problems suggested by his discoveries would itself be a sufficient task for even a genius in science; and any high school or college in which his labors were not recognized and the results of his labors were not taught would be patronized only for those who prefer the eighteenth century to the twentieth.

On the mercantile or practical side the promised discoveries and inventions of this one man have kept millions of capital and thousands of capitalists in suspense and distress on both sides of the sea. In contrast with the gradualness of thought movement in the Middle Ages, consider the dazzling swiftness with which the theory of evolution and the agnostic philosophy have extended and solidified their conquests until the whole world of thought seems hopelessly subjected to their autocracy. I once met in society a young man just entering the silver decade, but whose hair was white enough for one of sixty, and he said that the color changed in a single day, as a sign and result of a mental conflict in giving up his religion for science. Many are they who have passed, or are yet to pass through such conflict, and at far greater damage to the nerve centres.

Increase in Amount of Business in Modern Times

The increase in the amount of business of nearly all kinds in modern times, especially in the last half century, is a fact that comes right before us when we ask the question, Why nervousness is so much on the increase?

Of business, as we moderns understand the term, the ancient world knew almost nothing; the commerce of the Greeks, of which classical histories talk so much, was more like play—like our summer yachting trips—than like the work or commerce of to-day.

Manufacturers, under the impulses of steam-power and invention, have multiplied the burdens of mankind; and railways, telegraphs, canals, steamships, and the utilization of steam-power in agriculture, and in handling and preparing materials for transportation, have made it possible to transact a hundred-fold more business in a limited time than even in the eighteenth century; but with an increase rather than a decrease in business transactions. Increased facilities for agriculture, manufactures, and trades have developed sources of anxiety and of loss as well as profit, and have enhanced the risks of business; machinery has been increased in quantity and complexity, some parts, it is true, being lubricated by late inventions, others having the friction still more increased. . . .

Buying on a Margin vs. Gambling

The custom of buying on a margin that has lately grown so much in popularity is more exciting to the nervous system than ordinary gambling, which it in a measure displaces, in these two respects—

First, the gambler risks usually all that he has; while the stock buyer risks very much more than he has.

Secondly. The stock buyer usually has a certain commercial, social, and religious position, which is thrown into the risk, in all his ventures; whereas, the ordinary gambler has nothing to lose but his money.

For these reasons it is quite clear that gambling—formerly far more prevalent than now—is less pernicious in its action on the nervous system, than buying stocks on a margin.

Increased Capacity for Sorrow—Love and Philanthropy

Capacity for disappointment and sorrow has increased with the advance of civilization. Fineness of organization, which is essential to the development of the civilization of modern times, is accompanied by intensified mental susceptibility. . . .

Organized philanthropy is wholly modern, and is the offspring of a higher evolved sympathy wedded to a form of poverty that could only arise out of the inequalities of civilization. Philanthropy that is sincere suffers more than those it hopes to save; for while "charity creates much of the misery that it relieves, it does not relieve all the misery that it creates."

Repression of Emotion

One cause of the increase of nervous diseases is that the conventionalities of society require the emotions to be repressed, while the activity of our civilization gives an unprecedented freedom and opportunity for the expression of the intellect; the more we feel the more we must restrain our feelings. This repression of emotion and expression of reason, when carried to a high degree, as in the most active nations, tend to exhaustion, the one by excessive toil and friction, the other by restraining and shutting up within the mind those feelings which are best relieved by expression. Laughter and tears are safety-valves; the savage and the child laugh or cry when they feel like it—and it takes but little to make them feel like it; in a high civilization like the present, it is not polite either to laugh or to cry in public; the emotions which would lead us to do either the one or the other, thus turn in on the brain and expend themselves on its substance; the relief which should come from the movements of muscles in laughter and from the escape of tears in crying is denied us; nature will not, however, be robbed; her loss must be paid and the force which might be expended in muscular actions of the face in laughter and on the whole body in various movements reverberates on the brain and dies away in the cerebral cells.

Constant inhibition, restraining normal feelings, keeping back, covering, holding in check atomic forces of the mind and body, is an exhausting process, and to this process all civilization is constantly subjected.

A modern philosopher of the most liberal school, states that he hates to hear one laugh aloud, regarding the habit, as he declares, a survival of barbarism.

Domestic and Financial Trouble

Family and financial sorrows, and secret griefs of various kinds, are very commonly indeed the exciting cause of neurasthenia. In very many cases where overwork is the assigned cause—and where it is brought prominently into notice, the true cause, philosophically, is to be found in family broils or disappointments, business failures or mishaps, or some grief that comes very near to one, and, rightly or wrongly, is felt to be very serious.

The savage has no property and cannot fail; he has so little to win of wealth or possessions, that he has no need to be anxious. If his wife does not suit he divorces or murders her; and if all things seem to go wrong he kills himself.

Politics and Religion

There are two institutions that are almost distinctively American—political elections and religious revivals; for although in other countries both these institutions exist, yet they are far less numerous and far less exacting, and have far less influence than in America. Politics and religion appeal mostly to the emotional nature of men, and have little to do with the intellect, save among the leaders; and in consequence, the whole land is at times agitated by both these influences, to a degree which, however needful it may be, is most exciting to the nervous temperament.

Liberty as a Cause of Nervousness

A factor in producing American nervousness is, beyond dispute, the liberty allowed, and the stimulus given, to

Americans to rise out of the position in which they were born, whatever that may be, and to aspire to the highest possibilities of fortune and glory. In the older countries, the existence of classes and of nobility, and the general contexture and mechanism of society, make necessary so much strenuous effort to rise from poverty and paltriness and obscurity, that the majority do not attempt or even think of doing anything that their fathers did not do: thus trades, employments, and professions become the inheritance of families, save where great ambition is combined with great powers. There is a spirit of routine and spontaneous contentment and repose, which in America is only found among the extremely unambitious. In travelling in Europe one is often amazed to find individuals serving in menial, or at least most undignified positions, whose appearance and conversation show that they are capable of nobler things than they will ever accomplish. In this land, men of that order, their ambition once aroused, are far more likely to ascend in the social scale. Thus it is that in all classes there is a constant friction and unrest—a painful striving to see who shall be highest; and, as those who are at the bottom may soon be at the very top, there is almost as much stress and agony and excitement among some of the lowest orders as among the very highest. . . .

The experiment attempted on this continent of making every man, every child, and every woman an expert in politics and theology is one of the costliest of experiments with living human beings, and has been drawing on our surplus energies with cruel extravagance for one hundred years.

Protestantism, with the subdivision into sects which has sprung from it, is an element in the causation of the nervous diseases of our time.

No Catholic country is very nervous, and partly for this —that in a Catholic nation the burden of religion is carried by the church. In Protestant countries this burden is borne by each individual for himself; hence the doubts, bickerings, and antagonisms between individuals of the same sect and between churches, most noticeable in this land, where millions of excellent people are in constant disagreement about the way to heaven. . . .

Habit of Forethought

Much of the exhaustion connected with civilization is the direct product of the forethought and foreworry that makes civilization possible. In coming out of barbarism and advancing in the direction of enlightenment the first need is care for the future. . . . This forecasting, this forethinking, discounting the future, bearing constantly with us not only the real but imagined or possible sorrows and distresses, and not only of our own lives but those of our families and of our descendants, which is the very essence of civilization as distinguished from barbarism, involves a constant and exhausting expenditure of force. Without this forecasting, this sacrifice of the present to the future, this living for our posterity, there can be no high civilization and no great achievement; but it is, perhaps, the chief element of expense in all the ambitious classes, in all except the more degraded orders of modern society. We are exhorted, and on hygienic grounds very wisely, not to borrow trouble—but were there no discounting of disappointment, there would be no progress. . . .

DOCUMENT 8

(PLATE 3)

Our Centennial—President Grant and Dom Pedro Starting the Corliss Engine

SOURCE: Theodore R. Davis, "Our Centennial—President Grant and Dom Pedro Starting the Corliss Engine" (wood engraving), *Harper's Weekly*, XX (27 May 1876), 421.

Dom Pedro of Brazil figured in the opening ceremonies of the Centennial more or less by accident: he happened to be on hand as a state guest. Much more important was the impression made on visitors to the exposition by the giant Corliss steam engine which provided power for all the exhibits in Machinery Hall. The twenty-five hundred horsepower which the two-cylinder engine could develop seems trivial by twentieth-century standards, but was a source of awe for engineers as well as for the general public. The very monumentality of the machine, with its thirty-foot flywheel, its twenty-seven-foot walking beams, and its towering height of thirty-nine feet above the main floor of the building, lent itself to the kind of statistical boasting that was often noted in this period as an American trait. The artist has chosen to emphasize the height of the engine by making it dwarf the human figures clustered about its base. The effect of the drawing resembles the impression William Dean Howells reported in the *Atlantic Monthly*. In calling the engine a "giant" and an "Afreet" (in Arabic mythology, an evil demon) and the attendant engineer an "enchanter," Howells follows a tendency, common in that day, to regard steam power as a supernatural force kept only precariously under human control. Mark Twain illustrates the same tendency when he has his Connecticut Yankee mechanic impress the people of Arthurian Britain as a magician. Howells' comment follows:

The Corliss engine does not lend itself to description; its personal acquaintance must be sought by those who would understand its vast and almost silent grandeur. It rises loftily in the centre of the huge structure, an athlete of steel and iron with not a superfluous ounce of metal on it; the mighty walking-beams plunge their pistons downward, the enormous fly-wheel revolves with a hoarded power that makes all tremble, the hundred life-like details do their office with unerring intelligence. In the midst of this ineffably strong mechanism is a chair where the engineer sits reading his newspaper, as in a peaceful bower. Now and then he lays down his paper and clambers up one of the stairways that cover the framework, and touches some irritated spot on the giant's body with a drop of oil, and goes down again and takes up his newspaper; he is like some potent enchanter there, and this prodigious Afreet is his slave who could crush him past all semblance of humanity with his lightest touch. It is, alas! what the Afreet has done to humanity too often, where his strength has superseded men's industry; but of such things the Machinery Hall is no place to speak, and to be honest, one never thinks of such things there. One thinks only of the glorious triumphs of skill and invention; and wherever else the national bird is mute in one's breast, here he cannot fail to utter his pride and content. It would be a barren place without the American machinery. All that Great Britain and Germany have sent is insignificant in amount when compared with our own contributions; the superior elegance, aptness, and ingenuity of our machinery is observable at a glance. Yes, it is still in these things of iron and steel that the national genius most freely speaks; by and by the inspired marbles, the breathing canvases, the great literature; for the present America is voluble in the strong metals and their infinite uses.*

* "A Sennight of the Centennial," *Atlantic*, XXXVIII (July 1876), 96.

DOCUMENT 9

Edison in his Workshop

SOURCE: Anonymous, "Edison in his Workshop," *Harper's Weekly*, XXIII (2 August 1879), 607.

This unsigned editorial note accompanied a full-page drawing of Edison on the cover of the same issue which is too dark to warrant reproduction. It reveals the contradictory strands of folklore that went into the slowly forming image of the technological wizard. Edison in the role of alchemist alone in his tower at midnight conjuring mysterious forces of Nature while the world sleeps is evidently a sinister figure; but these implications are immediately offset by reassuring allusions to the enterprising fourteen-year-old train butcher, the boy playing pranks with a cat, and the foolish crank who sets a railway car afire with his inept experiments. Further reassurance is provided by the information that Edison could not take off messages in Morse code at the normal commercial rate of transmission. His income of $50,000 a year at the age of thirty-one embeds him solidly in understandable reality. It is hardly necessary to add that he is careless of his dress, indifferent to social niceties, and fond of fishing: a vernacular character, not a highbrow.

It is utter, black midnight, and the stillness and awe of that lonely hour have settled upon the pleasant hills and pretty homes of the remote New Jersey village. Only one or two windows gleam faintly, as though through dusty panes, and the traveller directing his stumbling steps by their light, enters a door, passes to a stairway guarded by the shadows of strange objects, and gropes his way upward.

A single flaring gas flame flickers at one end of a long room, disclosing an infinite number of bottles of various sizes, carved and turned pieces of wood, curious shapes of brass, and a wilderness of wires, some straight, others coiled and spiral and kinked, the ends pinched under thumbscrews, or hidden in dirty jars, or hanging free from invisible supports—an indiscriminate, shadowy, uncanny foreground. Picking his way circumspectly around a bluish, half-translucent bulwark of jars filled with azure liquid, and chained together by wires, a new picture meets his bewildered eyes. At an open red brick chimney, fitfully outlined from the darkness by the light of fiercely smoking lamps, stands a roughly clothed gray-haired man, his tall form stooping under the wooden hood which seems to confine noxious gases and compel them to the flue. He is intent upon a complex arrangement of brass and iron and copper wire, assisted by magnets and vitriol jars, vials labelled in chemical formulæ, and retorts in which to form new liquid combinations. His eager countenance is lighted up by the yellow glare of the unsteady lamps, as he glances into a heavy old book lying there, while his broad shoulders keep out the gloom that lurks in all the corners and hides among the masses of machinery. He is a fit occupant for this weird scene; a midnight workman with supernal forces whose mysterious phenomena have taught men their largest idea of elemental power; a modern alchemist, who finds the philosopher's stone to be made of carbon, and with his magnetic wand changes every-day knowledge into the pure gold of new applications and original uses. He is THOMAS A. EDISON, at work in his laboratory, deep in his conjuring of Nature while the world sleeps.

The author of the quadruplex telegraph, the telephone, and the phonograph was born at Milan, Ohio, in February, 1847, of parents whose ancestors came from Holland. Going to the public schools until the age of fourteen, he then began to sell newspapers upon the trains of the Grand Trunk Railway, and perceiving the advantage to be derived, conceived the idea of establishing bulletin-boards at the principal stations on his route, and telegraphing ahead the features of the morning's news, which in those war days were likely to be startling enough. Interest was excited, and his sales correspondingly increased. These bulletin-boards are a common institution on Western railways now, but his was the first. Next he wanted to do his own telegraphing, and so got an operator to teach him how. Then, to perfect his knowledge, he and a companion erected a line between their houses at their own expense, which was small, since young EDISON made every thing himself. To get the wire charged was the great difficulty; and not knowing that the sparks thus evolved were not the kind they needed, the two youthful electricians captured a wretched cat, tied the two poles of their circuit to opposite ends of the animal, and diligently rubbed the fur, right way and wrong. This, of course, was a failure, but the amateur line proved a success after all. Then young EDISON got some type and a press, set it up in the baggage-car, and printed the *Grand Trunk Herald* every day on the express train. When this came to an end, he put up a chemical laboratory in the baggage-car, and experimented until an explosion occurred which set the car afire, when he and his laboratory were ignominiously bundled out. After that he was employed as a railway telegraph operator, and then went to Cincinnati in the employment of the Western Union Company. It was here that his *penchant* for experimenting began to be so strongly manifested. Sleeping almost where night overtook him, and living upon the cheapest possible fare, he spent every penny of his salary in buying apparatus and material for his investigations. The results were that he patented the duplex machine, by which two dispatches could be transmitted on the same wire at the same time, and that he was discharged from his place for continually taking the company's instruments to pieces to try to improve them. From Cincinnati EDISON went to Louisville to receive the press reports at midnight. These come at the rate of forty words a minute, and must be taken off as they go by.

EDISON was not proficient enough to do this, and therefore contrived an arrangement by which the paper on which the message was printed in MORSE's characters should pass through a second machine, where an embossing point travelling over the indented paper should make and break the circuit so as to report in sound what the original machine had printed, but only at half the speed, so that he could easily record it. This went on a few weeks, until the printers complained of the lateness of their copy, and the ingenious operator was again discharged; but his invention was far more important than he suspected, for it was the parent of the phonograph.

In 1872 the quadruplex system of telegraphy was got into shape by him, by which four messages can be sent simultaneously on one wire, two one way and two the other, and which is in daily use now. This was quickly followed by other very important inventions, but the two which carried EDISON's fame the farthest, and aroused such widespread popular interest in his work, are the telephone and the phonograph, both of which have been fully described in the journals of the day.

These with other patents now bring him in a large revenue, and the Western Union Telegraph Company pay him a good yearly bonus for the simple refusal of the first right to buy any and all of his discoveries which relate to telegraphy, so that his present annual income is perhaps $50,000. Though only thirty-one, Mr. EDISON's tall form is somewhat bent with much stooping over his work, and his brown hair is streaked with gray. He wears no beard or mustache, and in rest would hardly be called a handsome man; but when he speaks, the face instantly speaks too, and the keen blue eyes, far apart, light up with quick and happy intelligence. Careless in matters of personal appearance, riding rough-shod over the factitious requirements of society, happy only in his laboratory and his home near by, reckless of money when applied to his scientific needs, regarding time as the one precious thing, EDISON is a man of such strong characteristics as make an indelible impress upon the world wherever he goes. He works, and always has worked, incessantly, and with all sorts of irregularity. Never fond of any athletic games, he had his amusement in experimenting, took his exercise in occasional fishing excursions, and finds recuperation in long deep sleep.

His laboratory is a wonderful place. Down stairs are his office and unpacking room, where are hosts of books, and his steam-engines and machinery, where the best workmen turn for him the delicate parts of iron and brass which are to be put together in his cunning constructions. Up stairs is the work-room. Plenty of windows give light and air and a pleasant view. Gearing from the engine can be attached any where needed. Telegraph wires run to New York and Washington, and a circuit of 3000 miles can be secured if necessary to ascertain whether some designed improvement which works well enough in the laboratory will cope with conditions of long out-door lines. Everywhere are the implements and evidences of his craft: a battery of 250 cells; a wilderness of insulated wires, so that anywhere and everywhere electrical attachments can be made; gas jets innumerable, the gas being made on the premises; telegraphic machines, simple, duplex, triplex, and quadruplex; a coil which will throw a spark nine inches; telescopes, microscopes, spectroscopes. The tables are crowded with parts of new models and fragments of old machines. In one corner is a fine organ; in another a photographic kit; in a third a glass case of delicate material; all around the walls shelves full of chemical mixtures in little bottles, more than 2000 of which have been made and retained, labelled, by EDISON. In the middle of the room are several machines whose names end in *phone*, the biggest of which, naturally, is the megaphone, consisting of a tripod supporting two narrow hollow cones of paper, ending at the apex in rubber tubes. You put the tubes in your ear, go off a mile, some one speaks in an ordinary tone, and you hear it plainly. To conclude, there is an instrument so delicate as to detect the heat derived from the rays of a single star!

DOCUMENT 10

(PLATE 4)

Interior of a Southern Cotton Press by Night

SOURCE: J. O. Davidson, "Interior of a Southern Cotton Press by Night" (wood engraving), *Harper's Weekly*, XXVII (24 March 1883), 181.

Davidson was a member of a task force sent by Harper's through the South in the spring of 1883 in the interest both of the *Monthly* and of the *Weekly* published by that house. The expedition was part of a movement among Northern editors to celebrate the industrial development of the New South. But the drawing conveys more than a merely documentary meaning. The dramatic contrast of light and shade, and the representation of the machine as a kind of monster whose upper parts are lost in darkness, express an emotional response that Davidson elaborates in an explanatory note about the drawing:

Few sights impress the visitor in the Gulf States more vividly than one of the huge modern cotton compresses at work. By daylight it is always interesting, but when surrounded by all the mysterious shadows cast by the sombre veil of a tropical night the scene becomes doubly so, and impresses one forcibly with its excessive picturesqueness and truly Southern flavor.

Upon entering one of the immense buildings where these great machines are housed, a strange sight meets the eye. Rising to the height of fifty feet or more in the darkness above may be discerned a massive frame-work of beams and iron girders, holding in its embrace the press whose iron cylinder head rears its crown amid the beams close under the roof.

Beneath the converging rays of electric lamps and

reflectors a most weird effect is produced, for the machine assumes the aspect of a grand and solemn demon face, strangely human, recalling the famed genii of the *Arabian Nights*. Beside it are the furnaces, whose open doors glow with the fires supplying the vitality of the giant, while about them flit the half-naked forms of the firemen—attendant demons of this monster.

As we gaze in awe at this strange scene, a voice rings out in command, and at the pulling of a lever the obedient monster's jaw drops, opening wide a cavernous mouth serrated with teeth of iron. A bale of cotton already squeezed into as small a compass as the strongest plantation machinery, unaided by steam, can reduce it, is for a moment unloosed from its fetters and rolled into the monster mouth. The dusk figures of the workmen now stand aside for a moment, one in the half shadow beside the scaffold pulls down a short lever, and the hideous iron jaw rises swiftly, and with scarcely a perceptible effort crushes the bale. Under this one Titanic bite the hitherto stubborn cotton shrinks and gives way like a sponge beneath an elephant's tread. Closer and closer come the terrible teeth, till the four-foot mass now measures but eighteen inches; but it has not yet been reduced quite enough; further punishment awaits it. Another pull to the lever sends a muffled rush of steam into the caverns of the monster's chest. With this fresh exertion the great structure trembles visibly, and under the enormous strain of 2000 pounds to the inch the teeth almost meet. It is enough. And now another surprise awaits us.

Half a dozen athletic figures spring like gnomes from out the side gloom into the brilliant light, and passing stout steel bands through the interstices of the monster's teeth, double and fold them back, and fasten them firmly. Like elfish sprites they seem while thus binding the helpless victim. This completed, there comes to the startled ear a strange cry. At first it is one musical voice rising alone, clear, distinct, quavering out on the night wind, then it is joined by a burst of full-throated harmonious voices in chorus, which sink down slowly in musical cadence, intermingled with half and quarter and weird fractional African notes impossible to describe, but, once heard, never forgotten. It is a signal that the bale is completely bound. The lever rises again, then the huge jaw relaxes, and the bitten cotton rolls out.

With the opening of that immense mouth comes a mighty steam sigh as the liberated vapor rushes up and bends above the sombre buildings like a great feathery plume before the cool night breeze. Heard through the quiet tropical nights, this panting of the cotton presses has a strangely human sound, but the sound as of the labored breathing of Titans at work —the sighing of Afrits.*

Davidson's images from the *Arabian Nights* develop a theme that almost invariably accompanies descriptions of machinery in this period—the notion of a supernatural quality, which often, as here, is given a sinister aspect by references to "monsters" and "demons." The cotton press, with its "hideous iron jaw" and "teeth of iron," becomes a Polyphemus with cannibal appetites. At the same time, the night is tropical. The attendant Negro workmen, "gnomes" waiting to bind the helpless victim crushed in the monster's jaws, utter an unintelligible African chorus as if to complete a pagan rite. Davidson cannot control his imagery, but he has the materials for a poem on the order of Vachel Lindsay's "The Congo," suggesting dark subterranean forces beneath the brisk ideology of enlightenment to be brought to the South through industrialization.

* *Harper's Weekly*, XXVII (24 March 1883), 182.

PART II

The Titans

DOCUMENT 11

The Vanderbilts

SOURCE: William A. Croffut, ["Cornelius Vanderbilt"], from *The Vanderbilts and the Story of Their Fortune* (Chicago, 1886), pp. iii–v, 272–76.

For most Americans, the power generated by the developing industrial system was not symbolized by the astonishing statistics about miles of railroad built or tons of steel produced, but by the careers of the men in control of the economy—the new millionaires, the captains of industry, the financiers. In order to find out how the public at large viewed such men, Sigmund Diamond has analyzed obituary notices of six Americans, from the early nineteenth century to the 1940s, who were conspicuous for their great wealth.* The period before the Civil War is represented by two names—Stephen Girard (died 1831) and John Jacob Astor (died 1848). For the twentieth century the names are J. P. Morgan (died 1913), John D. Rockefeller (died 1937), and Henry Ford (died 1947). The representative of the period between, from the 1850s on into the post-Civil War period, is Cornelius Vanderbilt, who died in 1877.

Despite the fact that Vanderbilt's fortune was some ten times the size of Girard's or Astor's, Mr. Diamond's study shows a remarkable persistence of certain traits in the popular conception of all three. We are dealing here, in other words, with a partly imaginary hero-type that changes gradually through time but still maintains its historical continuity. And the hero-type operated powerfully on the popular mind. Carl Sandburg, for

* *The Reputation of the American Businessman*, Cambridge, Mass., 1955.

example, recalled that when he was a boy in Galesburg,
Illinois, in the 1880s, he was deeply impressed by a
biography of Cornelius Vanderbilt in a series given
away as premiums with cigarettes. The life stories of
Vanderbilt and other wealthy men convinced him that
"America [is] the land of self-made men—the one
country in the world where it is possible for a man to
rise by his own effort from obscurity and poverty not
only to the highest place in society, but to the more
courted rank of millionaire as well."† In 1889, to mention a quite different observer, one of William Dean
Howells' fictional spokesmen said that the successful
speculator and financier represented "the ideal and ambition of most Americans"; and a decade later Henry
James declared that the millionaire had become "the
typical American figure."‡

Croffut was a newspaperman, commissioned by a
Chicago publisher to write a book about the Vanderbilt
family shortly after the death of William H. Vanderbilt
in 1885. In the early stages of his work he received
encouragement from Chauncey M. Depew, Vanderbilt's
principal legal adviser, and Cornelius Vanderbilt II, but
when Croffut refused to delete references to the noto-
riously rough and vigorous speech of the Commodore,
the relation was broken off. The selections included here
are taken from the Preface and the last chapter of
Croffut's book. It will be perceived that he admires Cornelius Vanderbilt as an American self-made man who
outshone snobbish British aristocrats, and as an industrial genius who rescued important railroads from
"blunderers and plunderers."

This is a history of the Vanderbilt family, with a record
of their vicissitudes, and a chronicle of the method by
which their wealth has been acquired. It is confidently put
forth as a work which should fall into the hands of boys

† *Ibid.*, p. 191, n. 43.
‡ Howells, *A Hazard of New Fortunes* (New York, 1960),
p. 190; James, "The Question of Opportunities" (1898), reprinted in *Henry James: The American Essays*, ed. Leon Edel
(New York, 1956), p. 202.

and young men—of all who aspire to become Captains of Industry or leaders of their fellows in the sharp and wholesome competitions of life.

In preparing these pages, the author has had an ambition, not merely to give a biographical picture of sire, son, and grandsons and descendants, but to consider their relation to society, to measure the significance and the influence of their fortune, to ascertain where their money came from, to inquire whether others are poorer because they are rich, whether they are hindering or promoting civilization, whether they and such as they are impediments to the welfare of the human race. A correct answer to these questions will solve half of the problems which most eagerly beset this generation.

This story is an analogue of the story of all American successes. When Commodore Vanderbilt visited Europe in 1853 at the head of his family, he seemed to defy classification. He was apparently neither lord nor commoner. He was too democratic for a grandee; too self-poised for a plebeian. He was untitled, but his yacht surpassed in size and splendor the ocean vehicles of monarchs. No expense was too great to be indulged, no luxury too choice to be provided, but he moved modestly and without ostentation, with the serene composure of a prince among his equals. There were wealthy English citizens who could have afforded a similar outlay, but they would have been sneered at and charged with pretentiousness and vanity, with aping customs rightly monopolized by the nobility. They would have been rated as snobs, cads, upstarts, and would have been twitted with their humble origin, as if an improvement of one's condition were a reproach instead of an honor.

But the cruising Commodore came from a land where prevalent conditions and not antecedents are considered; where a coat-of-arms is properly regarded as a foolish affectation; where a family's "descent" is of no importance, and its ascent of all importance; where the wheel of fortune runs rapidly around and every man is not only permitted but required to stand for what he is. . . .

America is the land of the self-made man—the empire of the parvenu. Here it is felt that the accident of birth is of trifling consequence; here there is no "blood" that is to be coveted save the red blood which every masterful man distills in his own arteries; and here the name of parvenu is the only and all-sufficient title of nobility. So here, if nowhere else in the world, should such a dominant man without hesitation or apology assume the place to which he is entitled, in commerce or the industrial arts, in professional life or society. . . .

[Cornelius Vanderbilt] dressed no better than his clerk, and ate less than his coachman. He drank chiefly milk. He could sleep in only one room, like others. He had little taste for books, and not time enough to read the newspapers. Envy and ignorance had raised up an army of enemies about him. The public press stormed at him like a harridan and covered the dead walls with infamous caricatures, representing him as a vampire, a dragon, a Gorgon, a Silenus, a Moloch, a malevolent Hurlothrumbo. He was a victim of insomnia and indigestion. The jockey, Anxiety, rode him with whip and spur. He was in constant peril of apoplexy. He could not take needful exercise by walking in the Park for fear of being accosted by tramps or insulted by socialistic philosophers. Every week his life was threatened by anonymous letters. He kept a magnificent servants' boarding-house on Fifth Avenue, where he made his home, and superbly equipped a stable, whose advantages inured chiefly to the benefit of his employés. He organized the finest picture-gallery in America for the enjoyment of lovers of art, but was compelled to limit his hospitality by the fact that some of the guests rifled the conservatory of its choicest flowers, scratched the Meissoniers with the ends of their parasols, invaded the private apartments of the mansion, and carried away portable things as souvenirs of the visit. An enormous fortune is a heavy burden to bear. To be very rich invites attacks, cares, responsibilities, intrusions and annoyances for which there is no adequate offset.

A man like Commodore Vanderbilt, indeed, has the

large satisfaction of feeling that he has given the human race a magnificent endowment in adding to the wealth of the world. He was not a juggler, who managed by a cunning trick to transfer to himself the wealth of others; he created property that did not before have an existence. When he stepped from the deck upon land, the best railroads in the United States had been paralyzed and driven to bankruptcy by blunderers and plunderers. They were largely in the hands of men who cared nothing for them except as they could be made serviceable in the reckless games of Wall Street. Whether they could meet the demands of traffic was regarded by these desperate gamblers as of no consequence. Thieves had pillaged the Erie road till its stock was sold for three cents on a dollar. Michigan Southern was at 5, and Erie at 6.

The Commodore introduced a new policy. Instead of taking money out of the roads, he put millions into them. Instead of breaking them down he built them up. Instead of robbing them, he renovated them and raised them from the grave. He equipped them anew, trusting that the public would respond and give him his money back. He dragged together worthless fragments and made them one; he consolidated parallel roads that were apart and belonged together; he cut down every possible expense, and subjected them to the economic supervision of one despotic will. He fearlessly staked all upon the venture, and upon the belief that the war for the Union would end in the defeat of Secession.

In both he was right. The South was beaten. The public responded. The stock mounted to par and beyond. His roads had all they could do, and he made millions a year from the investment of his marvelous brain. And he made these millions as legitimately as an artisan fashions a hat from wool, or a chair from wood. He received better pay than the artisan, not only because he risked his money where the mechanic risks nothing, but because he invested his consummate brain.

One of the commonest and most pernicious errors is the assumption that the human hand is the chief factor in the creation of wealth, and from this error springs much of the noisy remonstrance of our time. It is not the hand, but the brain, that is the real creator. It was Michael Angelo that built St. Peter's, not the forgotten workmen who, executing the will of the great master, borne to them through a dozen skilled architects and master-artisans, hewed the stone to lines that had been accurately drawn for them. The unit of service underlying all is the faithful workman; but a brigade of workmen cannot do as much effective good as is done by one strong and intelligent capitalist, whose money employs and whose sagacity directs and renders fruitful the sterile hand. The chief productiveness of the world is due mainly to the skill that plans, the audacity that risks, and the prescience that sees through the heart of the future. So to those captains of industry who succeed in their financial ventures should go that premium called profit which society offers to superior foresight.

It used to be thought by all that as wealth accumulated men decayed; that the love of money was the root of all evil; that avarice was a vice; that the world would be better off if the division of property could be more nearly equal; that great riches were a curse to society; that the millionaire capitalist was a sort of bandit-king who plundered the people by methods which were sometimes legal but always highly immoral, and under whose tyrannical exactions industry was paralyzed and laboring men were impoverished.

But it is now known that the desire to own property is the chief difference between the savage and the enlightened man; that aggregations of money in the hands of individuals are an inestimable blessing to Society, for without them there could be no public improvements or private enterprises, no railroads or steamships, or telegraphs; no cities, no leisure class, no schools, colleges, literature, art—in short, no civilization. The one man to whom the community owes most is the capitalist, not the man who gives, but the man who saves and invests, so that his property reproduces and multiplies itself instead of being consumed.

It is now known that civilization is the result of labor put in motion by wealth; that wealth springs from self-denial; that self-denial springs from avarice; and that avarice is the child of an aspiring discontent.

It used to be thought that consolidation was a menace to the people, and that great "Monopolies," as they were called, ought to be forbidden by law. It is now known that such consolidation is a public benefit; that the man who owns a thousand houses rents them cheaper than he who owns but one or two; that the greatest oil company in the world furnishes oil cheaper than it was ever furnished before, or could be by any other means of distribution; that the Western Union Telegraph Company sends dispatches far cheaper than they were sent by any of the score of companies from which it sprung, and cheaper than they are sent by any of the telegraphs in the world which are owned and operated by governments; that A. T. Stewart greatly reduced the profits and losses of merchandising and the cost of goods to the consumer, and that, therefore, while he crushed out small dealers, his career was a tremendous public benefit; that the New York Central Railroad, the net result of the combination of many roads, carries passengers at lower fares than any other road in the world—lower even than is required by law—and transports freight so cheaply that it has driven from successful competition a canal that was built by the State and is free to all! The government has reduced the price of postage only one-half in a quarter of a century, and delivers letters at a loss of millions of dollars a year; but freight from Chicago to New York costs less than a quarter what it did then, and desperate competition keeps the rate at the lowest possible point.

It is to the obvious advantage of society that reproductive wealth shall be concentrated in few hands; for the larger its aggregations the smaller the toll which it will exact from society for the privilege of its use. And before Socialists can rationally demand an abolition of the competitive system and a reconstruction of the industrial methods of society, they must exhibit one railroad somewhere in the world which is owned by a state and managed as wisely and thriftily as are the roads which are allied to the name of Vanderbilt.

Document 12

(Plate 5)

The Vanderbilt Monument

SOURCE: Albert de Groot and Ernest Plassman, "The Vanderbilt Monument" (sculpture cast in bronze, 1869), from a wood engraving in *Harper's Weekly*, XIII (25 September 1869), 620.

Ernest Plassman, the sculptor who executed the work as a decoration for the exterior of the new Hudson River Railroad Depot, cannot be further identified. De Groot, a steamboat captain, belonged to a family long associated with Vanderbilt. An "old Brunswick river captain" explained the relationship to a reporter for the New York *Herald* in 1877: "People wonder why the Commodore had Albert de Groot to make his statue, for the freight depot in New York. Why, sir, Albert de Groot's father, Freeman de Groot, commanded the Cinderella, on Vanderbilt's line. The Commodore wanted to encourage his old friend's son."* Further details concerning the design of the sculpture are presented in Document 13, which follows.

* Anonymous, "Personal Recollections of Vanderbilt," New York *Herald*, 5 January 1877, p. 3.

DOCUMENT 13

The Vanderbilt Monument

SOURCE: Anonymous, "The Vanderbilt Monument," *Harper's Weekly*, XIII (25 September 1869), 620–21.

This straight-faced account of Vanderbilt's monument to himself reflects the popular cult of business success.

Early in October is to be unveiled the colossal bronze statue of Commodore VANDERBILT with its allegorical accessories, of which we give an illustration on this page. This monument is erected on the summit of the western wall of the new Hudson River Railroad Dépôt, situated on the former site of St. John's Park, at the corner of Laight and Hudson streets. This work was conceived by Captain ALBERT DEGROOT, a gentleman well known as prominently connected with the steamboat history of the Hudson River, and also as the commander of the *Niagara*, *Reindeer*, and other river steamers. As soon as Captain DEGROOT had completed his designs he laid them before a committee of leading citizens of New York, fully explaining his plan and ideas, and meeting with the full and cordial approbation, as well as the prompt financial aid, of those whose indorsement he solicited.

Captain DEGROOT at once secured the services of ERNEST PLASSMAN, one of the most skillful artists in the country; and a large sum of money was expended in building a foundry for the purpose of making the required castings, two experienced metal casters, GEORGE and VALENTINE FISCHER, having been engaged to superintend this part of the work. As first planned the design was only thirty feet in length, but new visions continued to dawn on the mind of Captain DEGROOT, until at last his grand conception had unfolded to more than five times its original size; and finally, after ten months of faithful labor, the models were all completed. As giving an idea of the labor involved, every piece of this immense work was first done in clay, then in plaster, and finally in bronze.

The monument is an epitome of the life of CORNELIUS VANDERBILT, both as Commodore and as the great Railway King. It is a well-deserved tribute to the genius and enterprise of MR. VANDERBILT, who is not less noted for his public spirit than for a well-spent life, abounding in works of unostentatious charity.

The work covers an area of 3125 square feet, measures about 150 feet in a straight line, and 31 feet in extreme height; weighs, we believe, nearly 100,000 pounds; and cost, as nearly as can be ascertained, over $500,000. It consists of an immense bronze statue of Commodore VANDERBILT, placed in the centre of a colossal bass-relief, which is contrived not only to illustrate the career and achievements of the Commodore, but also to represent the marvelous inventions of the nineteenth century, and at the same time to portray allegorically the growth and prosperity of the great American Republic.

The base line upon which the bass-relief is erected is a narrow tier of blue-stone. In the centre, just beneath this, and solidly inserted in the dépôt wall, is a huge carved block of granite weighing eleven tons. On this rests a bronze pedestal 5 feet square, 1½ feet high, and bearing the inscription, "Erected 1868." On the pedestal, within a spacious arched recess, stands the statue. This is 12 feet high, nearly solid, weighs four tons, and is the largest in America, if not in the world. It represents the Commodore with head uncovered and wearing a heavy fur-trimmed over-coat, his left foot slightly advanced, his right hand inserted beneath his vest, and his left extended. The bass-relief is 10 feet high at the ends, and is surrounded by an elegant granite cornice, which slopes gradually upward for about one-third the length from each extremity, turns sud-

denly up, runs along horizontally, and finally forms an
arch in the centre over the statue. The middle portion of
the cornice is decorated with ornamental work in bronze.
The bass-relief is terminated at each end by massive scroll-
work representing leaves and plants.

On the right hand, between the statue and the scroll,
is represented the Commodore's marine life, and on the
left his railroad life. At the right hand, in the fore-ground,
appears, in a reclining position, Neptune, with flowing
beard, a wreath of leaves on his head, his right hand grasp-
ing a rudder, a sea-monster rising from the water at his
feet, and a raccoon peering around the corner of the rocks
on which he rests.

In the back-ground at the right arise the forest-crowned
Palisades of the Hudson, then a lighthouse is seen, and
then appears, rocking on the waves of bronze, the *Dred*,
the little two-masted "periauger," in which, half a century
ago, young Mr. VANDERBILT carried passengers from New
York to Staten Island at 25 cents a head. Next comes,
much greater in size, completely rigged, and under full
headway, the famous steamer *North Star*, in which the
Commodore made his well-remembered voyage round the
world.

Finally the climax is capped by the huge form of the
steamer *Vanderbilt*, also completely rigged, and plowing
along at full speed. In the middle fore-ground a dock appears, on which are coils of rope, bananas, pine-apples,
and other tropical fruits, a huge and savage watch-dog
crouched on a cotton bale, and lastly, next to the statue,
a massive capstan, anchor, and chain. At the extreme left,
to match the figure of Neptune on the right, Liberty,
guardian of the scene, sits erect with flowing tresses and
drapery, her left hand holding a sword, and her right arm
resting on the national shield, from behind which an eagle
is emerging. In the back-ground rises a woody slope, and
in the front a rude fence appears, and then two cows, one
idly whisking her tail and the other lying down. Back of
these an engine drawing a train of cars is entering a tunnel
beneath a forest-covered hill, and still farther in the rear

is a gentle eminence crowned with a villa. In the middle of the fore-ground a switchman, flag in hand, is just stepping from the door of his little house.

Captain DEGROOT is certainly entitled to great praise for the boldness and originality of his designs in this great work, and also for the faithful and assiduous labor he has devoted to it from its inception to its final completion. The FISCHER Brothers, and the sculptor, PLASSMAN, are entitled to the best praise for the admirable manner in which they performed their labors, and may be congratulated upon the success that has attended their efforts.

DOCUMENT 14

The Vanderbilt Memorial

SOURCE: Anonymous, "The Vanderbilt Memorial," *Nation*, IX (18 November 1869), 431–32.

The contrast between this editorial and the editorial in *Harper's Weekly* (Document 13) marks the difference between popular and cultivated taste in the arts and, even more significantly, records the dissent of a sophisticated minority from the prevalent admiration for great fortunes regardless of how they were acquired. The burlesque unveiling to which the editorial refers was a ceremony staged by the brokers of the New York Stock Exchange on the day when the monument was dedicated. An actor posing as a statue of Vanderbilt held a watering pot labeled "207," the price he had established for New York Central shares at the time of the consolidation of the system. The speaker of the occasion said that "the use of water, not as a beverage, but as an element of wealth," had been "the distinguishing characteristic of the achievements" of the Commodore. "We may say of him not only that he commenced life as a waterman, but that water has been the Central idea of his life."*

All of Mr. Vanderbilt's acts have been in a sense private acts; which consideration has not, however, exempted all of them from public criticism—some of it, certainly, not gracious. The fact is that many of "the Commodore's" acts have touched the public, more or less nearly, in a spot

* Wayne Andrews, *The Vanderbilt Legend: The Story of the Vanderbilt Family, 1794–1940* (New York, 1941), p. 157.

which is tender. When a gentleman's hand is discovered to
be pretty regularly in the general pocket, he will inevitably
find himself the subject of public remarks; and this
though it be his own proper good that he seeks, and seeks
with energy and industry and admirable consistency. So,
then, though he may have paid for it himself, and has set
it up on his own railroad station, got by his own hand, we
do not apologize for saying an abusive word or two about
the "Vanderbilt Memorial Bronze," which henceforth
charms the eye at the Hudson River Railroad Depot in
St. John's Park.

There is about it in general and in particulars a curious
appropriateness, a fitness to the exploits and fame it is to
celebrate; this at least the artist may claim as an advantage that his work has over most modern sculpture of the
memorial or any other kind. It crowns with monumental
incongruousness one of the most vulgar-looking of all staring brick buildings. The brute utilitarianism—not without
its own perfection—which is expressed by the big brick-
and-mortar freight-depot, is made the more obvious by the
attempt—abortive though it be—to crown the ignoble sub-
structure with something noble and fine. But it merely
suggests the noble and fine, without being such in any
degree; and the attempt makes ridiculous what before was
at worst only disagreeable. Thus unfortunate in its position
and general effect, our bronze is equally so in its detail;
and if it is not on that account less happy in its appropriateness, it certainly is not therefore more to be admired.
Audaciously or ignorantly, it disregards all laws—of harmony, of grace, of perspective, or of anything else. "The
Commodore" himself, larger than life, stands in a niche
in the centre of the work. The figure, stiff and without
dignity, is dressed in the fur-lined or fur-lapelled over-
coat, which is understood to be the usual wear of the
original. At either side, extending for a rod or two, is a
sheet of bronze, filled up, in what may be called the
higgledy-piggledy manner of grouping, with the simulacra
in bronze of various objects, representing symbolically
facts and events in Mr. Vanderbilt's career. There is the

image of the humble boat in which, in the years when he was poor but honest, he carried passengers from the Battery over to Staten Island. There, near it, under a head of steam that she never knew in life, is one of the vessels of the Pacific Mail line, in which, in later years, he transported many more passengers, with much less comfort and much less safety, from this city to the Isthmus and California. There, also, may be seen the vessel which he magnificently gave the Federal Government when the rebellion broke out, and when it was rather more unprofitable to keep a vessel in her dock than it was to give her away to anybody who would take her. There, too, are the figures of bee-hives, which ingeniously typify the industry and devotion to business of a man who never served the country at large, nor the State, nor the city, in any public office; nor ever spent the time which is money in advancing the cause of any charity; nor in promoting education, which the self-made man may despise; nor in fostering the arts, which can always wait. There are the railroads and the river-boats, which are witnesses to an energy and a business sagacity which before now have bought whole legislatures, debauched courts, crushed out rivals, richer or poorer, as the unmoral, unsentimental forces of nature grind down whatever opposes their blind force, and which have given Mr. Fisk and other gentlemen a lesson, which even they have not yet wholly mastered, in watering stock to the discomfiture of small stockholders of all ages and both sexes. In short, there, in the glory of brass, are portrayed, in a fashion quite good enough, the trophies of a lineal successor of the mediæval baron that we read about, who may have been illiterate indeed; and who was not humanitarian; and not finished in his morals; and not, for his manners, the delight of the refined society of his neighborhood; nor yet beloved by his dependents; but who knew how to take advantage of lines of travel; who had a keen eye for roads, and had the heart and hand to levy contribution on all who passed by his way.

Perhaps some of our readers may have had the fortune to go to California or to Europe in steamships of which

Mr. Vanderbilt had the control. They know, then, with how much respect the travelling public ought to recollect him. The accommodations on board the vessels, the food that was served, the condition as to seaworthiness of the ships themselves, and the efficiency of the officers and crews, the way in which the traveller was cared for whenever, by act of Providence, one of the steamers was wrecked or delayed, will be fresh in the memory of everybody who, by seafaring, has ever contributed of his substance to increase Mr. Vanderbilt's store. Others of our readers have perhaps put their earnings into the stock of the recently consolidated Central and Hudson River Railroad; or have paid passage-money on those well-managed roads; or have tramped a mile or two through the snow at midnight to "make connection," and thus assist the Commodore in "fighting" some other "big railroad man" who wanted a certain part of the public all to himself, and probably may have needed to have it for the sake of saving a road which the Commodore wished to capture. And no doubt others may have been "cornered" by "the old man" in Wall Street; or have gone with him before certain of our judges with whom he has acquaintance; or have ridden on ferry-boats with well-armed friends of his, to the number of fifty or sixty, who were crossing the water to levy war on the Erie cash-boxes and Mr. Daniel Drew; or have called on him with subscription papers at the beginning of hard winters; or in some other way have personally had a taste of the qualities in him which Bishop Janes! and Mr. A. O. Hall, and Mr. Horace Greeley now ask us to honor.

Are any of us honoring them? Courage, tenacity, a capacity "to toil terribly," energy—these are of course sure to secure a certain amount of what may be called respect, whether they are found in the butcher or in the noble dirty-white animal which follows at the butcher's heel. But are not some of us honoring them as we see them employed in the careers of our "kings of the street," and "railroad men," and "giants of the stock exchange," and "king pins of the gold room?" Uncharitable judges have charged the Board of Brokers—who, yesterday was a week, had a burlesque "unveiling"—with only pretending to laugh at Mr. Vanderbilt, whom, say these censors, every one of them envies and admires, and would imitate if he could. But there is something essentially laughable in the spectacle of a man's putting out his own cash to pay for civic honors to himself. Read of such things in the dull annals of the later Roman empire—how his fellow-citizens came to the most noble So-and-so, and gravely informed him that it had been voted that a statue of him should be set up in the Market Place, and how the distinguished man as gravely made answer that the honor alone was enough —was too much, and that he must beg to bear, himself, the money charges of erecting the memorial—thus read in musty history, the thing provokes a smile; and how else should it be when we have before us in the flesh the public-spirited citizen who is willing to pay such homage to virtue? Nevertheless, the censors we have mentioned are not, we imagine, so far in the wrong in their view of the brokers' character and views; and should we go too far if we widened the scope of the charge, and made it cover not the Wall-street men alone, but the whole people? Do we not as a people, if not admire, at least not execrate, nor even practically at all visit with condemnation, the acts of men like Drew and Vanderbilt, and, to go a step lower, the Fisks and Goulds? Perhaps those who live in great commercial centres lay too much stress on the evidence which seems to make in this direction. Yet it was in a country of hay-fields, and small shops, and fishing smacks, and little congregations of a hundred or two hundred souls that Butler was sent to Congress. And he was sent because he was "smart."

There is too much truth in the statement that the tendency to-day in this country is to count up our list of peculiarly American virtues as consisting of audacity, push, unscrupulousness, and brazen disregard of others' rights or others' good opinion; that we make no sufficient objection to a display of unmitigated and immitigable selfishness, if only it be a splendid display—if only it be crowned by success, by the acquisition of wealth or power. Yet we are not going to say that this is all the truth; or at all events, that as yet there is more than a tendency among us to this condition of mind; nor that other tendencies are not developing which will in good part neutralize this one. That, after all, is our best hope—to set in motion as soon as possible as many as possible nobler tendencies of thought, and feeling, and better ways of looking at life. Prevention is better than cure—is in fact, if one may say so, the only perfect cure. Meantime the negative mode of procedure—that of scoffing at the so-called successful men —has its uses too.

Cornelius Vanderbilt

SOURCE: Anonymous, "Cornelius Vanderbilt," New York *Herald*, 5 January 1877, p. 3.

Since Vanderbilt, at the age of eighty-two, had been ill for some months, his death was not unexpected; and the biographical sketch that follows the description of his last hours in the New York *Herald* had obviously been prepared in advance with care. Among the easily recognizable traits which assimilated the tycoon to the American ideal of a practical businessman, and presumably endeared him to the average reader, may be noted the insistence upon his lack of schooling, his dislike of books, his commanding appearance, his prowess as horseman and sailor, his astonishing business enterprise at an early age, his indefatigable industry, and his philanthropies. The attacks of critics are met by the flat assertion that Vanderbilt improved the operating efficiency of his steamship and railway lines. Even his notorious stock-market operations are represented as the achievements of a lone wolf in conflict with the legislative "ring" in Albany.

CORNELIUS VANDERBILT

Death of the Great Railroad King Yesterday Morning

SKETCH OF A BUSY LIFE

How the Poor Boatman's Son Became a Millionnaire

WORKING INTO FORTUNE

The Magnificent Monuments of His Successes

Commodore Vanderbilt died yesterday morning at nine minutes to eleven o'clock, at his residence No. 10 Washington place. Though well advanced in years he enjoyed comparative health and strength, far beyond the allotted time of man, and despite his great age no apprehensions of his death were felt until April last, when the spell of sickness which resulted in his death began. Shortly after his attack in that month he so far recovered that he was not believed to be in danger, but on the 3d of August last he suffered a relapse, and since that time has hovered between life and death. The news of his demise will not cause much surprise, as the daily bulletins of his condition have led to a general expectation of the event.

HIS LAST ILLNESS.

During the long months of his illness the patient varied greatly in his condition after rallying, so that some of his friends were sanguine he would regain strength enough to prolong his life for a few years at least. But to the practised eye of the doctors who attended him his decease was near at hand. His extraordinary vitality was admitted, but the change for the worse, though slowly and barely perceptible from day to day, was going on steadily. He suffered most during the morning, improving as the day wore on and sometimes becoming quite bright and cheerful at night. Music had an enlivening effect upon him, and it was when his relatives were gathered around singing for him in the evening that he felt most at ease. Often when in pain and troubled looking he would ask to have them sing for him, and as they sang in low tones some hymn or melody his countenance would change and a pleased expression light it up. On Wednesday night at ten o'clock he was reported to be somewhat stronger, which only meant that the decline was momentarily checked. This was a short time after he had listened to his usual evening concert, which always had a soothing effect on him. He retired at his usual hour, after receiving a visit from Mr. Turnbull. At about four o'clock yesterday morning Dr. Elliott, who was in attendance, saw that his patient was failing rapidly and sent at once for the Rev. Dr. Deems, Mr. Vanderbilt's spiritual adviser, and also for Dr. Linsly. There was nothing to be done for his temporal welfare. Every thing that wealth and his physicians' skill could devise had been supplied to prolong the life that was ebbing out. Feeble as he was Mr. Vanderbilt was perfectly conscious of his fast approaching death, and held a close and fervent conversation with his religious counsellor. The young and devoted wife, who has so incessantly watched over her dying husband, was present to the last, aiding in every way to ease his path into the other world. At eight o'clock in the morning, when it became evident that Mr. Vanderbilt was *in articulo mortis,* the members of his family were telegraphed for. Among those present at the closing scene of life were his son, Mr. William H. Vanderbilt, and family; his six daughters and their husbands, Mr. and Mrs. Cross, Mrs. D. B. Allen, Mrs. George A. Osgood, Mr. and Mrs. Daniel Torrance and daughter, Mr. and Mrs. William K. Thorne, Mrs. M. B. LaBau, his granddaughter and her husband, Mr. and Mrs. Meredith Howland; his nephews, Mr. C. V. Deforest and Mr. Samuel Barton; Mr. Worcester, Mr. Elliott F. Shepard, Rev. Dr. Deems and Drs. Linsly and Elliott.

THE LAST SCENE OF ALL.

An intimate friend of the family who was present at the Commodore's death gave the following description of the scene:—Late last evening Dr. Deems called on his way from a church meeting, and he was told in response to his inquiries that the invalid was somewhat brighter as compared with his condition in the morning. The Commodore talked a good deal on general subjects with his friends. After the company departed he conversed for some time with Mrs. Vanderbilt on religious subjects very closely. She asked him as to the ground of his faith, and he expressed himself very deliberately and decidedly. Among other things he said:—

"No; I shall never cease to trust Jesus. How could I let that go?"

He spoke also of his consciousness of his ignorance in regard to spiritual things—for instance, the existence and operations of the Holy Ghost, but said that ignorance did not stand in the way of his faith. He understood the Bible as far as he could, and whatever the Bible said that he believed to be true.

The invalid found great difficulty in speaking, and could make but few utterances during the last two hours of his life. He took no little interest in the passages of Scripture recited to him from time to time. Upon a suggestion by one of the ladies that some singing might be had, he misunderstood the speaker, but shortly after turned to his wife and said:—

"I thought you would sing."

A few of his favorite hymns were then sung at brief intervals. He showed great interest in the singing, and even attempted with his hoarse voice to join in a hymn which always pleased him:—

> Come ye sinners, poor and needy,
> Weak and wounded, sick and sore.

Before he was so low, when that hymn was sung he invariably tried to participate in the singing, adding, at the close:—

"I am poor, and I am needy, I am weak and wounded, sick and sore."

Dr. Deems proposed prayer, to which he seemed gladly to agree. At that time it looked as though his strength was failing so rapidly that the friends about him thought the final struggle had come at last. Among other things the pastor prayed that "God would be pleased in His mercy to vouchsafe unto the sufferer an easy departure out of his great pain into everlasting life." The Commodore evidently followed the whole prayer, and when it was closed with the benediction he repeated with the minister, the "blessing of God Almighty, the Father, the Son and the Holy Ghost." Then his voice failed. He afterward attempted to make several remarks, but he could not articulate with sufficient distinctness to be understood. After the lapse of some time he turned to his wife, who was sitting beside him, and, recurring to the prayer, he gave utterance to the last words he ever spoke:—

"That was a good prayer."

"Yes," replied Mrs. Vanderbilt, "because it expressed just your sentiments now."

He nodded assent. The obstruction in his throat did not now seem so painful. He closed his mouth a few minutes, as he had often been seen by his friends to do when thinking deeply on some subject. His eyes brightened, and then his mouth opened, after which he closed his eyes. He breathed a few times quietly, and at nine minutes to eleven o'clock expired.

GREAT IN SUFFERING.

The Rev. Dr. Deems, Commodore Vanderbilt's pastor, said to a *Herald* reporter, yesterday, that he grieved over the death of the good man, not as simply having lost a parishioner, but as a very near and dear friend.

"After all," said the reverend gentleman, "it has come like a surprise. I have looked for it so often, and so often has it been postponed, that I can hardly realize that my dear old friend has gone. I have seen him every day, except eight, since the 26th day of last April, and I have seen more to admire in him during his sickness than ever when he was well. He must have been a very great man, for, like all things that are truly great, he grew and grew upon your regard the longer you knew him. I have never known a grander man. He could take in so much so quickly. He had an immense daring and yet he possessed the best kind of womanly tenderness. In matters of faith he had the simplicity of a little child. I have never been able to find that during all his sickness he complained once. In the beginning he was nervous and irritable sometimes, as he would say 'ugly.' I have gone into his room after a paroxysm of pain, and he has taken my hand and burst into tears, saying at the same time

" 'Dr. Deems, will God forgive me? I've been so bad and ugly toward the people that are nursing me so faithfully.'

"But that passed away. Even then he never prayed that pain might be taken away, but would often say, 'Dear God, do not take it away if it be necessary for me.' I have never met, even in the ranks of the clergy, a man who had a more thorough belief in the divine authenticity of the Bible than Mr. Vanderbilt.

"Of course the public know of the gift of the Church of the Strangers to me, and will naturally believe I am grateful. But they never can know the personal affection I bear for the man, founded on my knowledge of his character. It was his desire that he should be buried from the Church of the Strangers." . . .

THE FEELING IN WALL STREET.

The death of Mr. Vanderbilt was known on Wall street before noon, and although the event has been daily looked for it created a profound sensation in financial circles, in which he was so well known as an operator who took great chances and rarely failed to be on the winning side. It was noticed that the feeling was generally one of regret at the demise of a man whose life and labors have been so intimately connected with the commerce and finance of the country. None spoke of him but in praise. Even those who at some time had suffered, owing to his manipulation of stocks, now that the veteran was no more, extolled his daring and admitted that Commodore Vanderbilt had not lived in vain; that, with all his errors, he had been a public benefactor, as shown in the great steamship and railroad enterprises that he had conceived and fostered. Strange to say, the taking off of this active worker in railroad enterprises did not materially affect the price of railway securities, and consequently "the street" was not subjected to any unusual excitement. For more than a year it had been known in commercial circles that the Commodore's worldly affairs had been carefully arranged, and as a result it was believed that the market would sustain no disarrangement. At the office of the Commodore's brokers, Messrs. Davis & Freeman, there were anxious inquiries made by operators for particulars, and for some hours the place was besieged by them. But the business of the street proceeded as usual, and to all outward appearances no one could have noticed that any unusual event had occurred to disturb the equilibrium of the street. . . .

THE LIFE OF CORNELIUS VANDERBILT.

The Vanderbilts were natives of Holland, and were prosperous, though poor and economical, farmers and tradesmen. Several persons of the name ventured to cross the ocean to New York in the early days of American colonization. They were of pure Knickerbocker stock, and they carried their home training into practice by settling, not on the island of Manhattan, but on the neighboring and less protected Staten Island. At the time when the father of Cornelius (whose name also was Cornelius) came to America, Staten Island was being divided up into large estates, which were worked by persons who furnished supplies for the city. The elder Vanderbilt took one of these farms. He was fond of ease and pleasure, and many a time he engaged in speculations which frequently resulted in loss. He probably gave the speculative impulse to his son. It was among the duties of the old Dutch farmer to carry his produce across the harbor to the city in boats, and in this labor he was greatly assisted by his sons when they came to an age when their work was efficient. The mother was a hard working old Dutch woman, who, like most peasant women of that day, did her household work, weeded and tended the turnip and cabbage patches, and herself many times sailed the ferryboat of her husband, with its loads of vegetables, to New York. This Frau Vanderbilt was a woman of great energy and industry; moreover she was more thrifty and prudent than her husband, who would speculate, like the over-ambitious Dutchman than he was; and it happened once on a time that, when the husband had fallen into debt through indiscreet investments, and the farm was about to be sold, the good old woman went to a secret corner and found that her savings, of which nobody besides herself knew anything, amounted to the sum of $3,000 at least, all in brightest gold; and how much more, for no more was necessary, the world will never discover. If the natural bent of Commodore Vanderbilt's genius came from his speculative father his sturdy, discreet and "bird-in-hand" education, which led to his great success, came from the judicious old lady whom he called his mother.

HIS BIRTH AND EARLY YOUTH.

Cornelius Vanderbilt the younger was born on Staten Island on the 27th day of May, 1794. It is said of him that he was a very noisy baby and made himself heard. He was the oldest of nine children. He was always a wild young fellow, who knew more about hoeing weeds out of his mother's cabbage patches than he knew of the addition table. The times, and the customs of the class from which he sprung, did not make him a lover of books; nor, indeed, had he any natural inclination toward them. When he entered manhood he could read fairly, write badly and cipher inexcusably. But for breaking a horse there was not the young fellow's equal on the whole island.

HE RODE A RACEHORSE

when he was only six years old. His love for a horse was a passion that grew out of his earliest days. This robust boy would have no love for books. His father whipped and his mother expostulated with him, but anxious poring over books was not to his liking, and he would have none of them. He was a very practical and not a very studious boy. He was always full of plans about a horse or a boat, and he was many a time found experimenting with them when he ought to have been at his meals. He excelled all his companions in whatever became the accomplishments of a robust boy. He would swim further into the surf that swept up on the island beach; he could jump further upon the sand; he could row further out to sea.

BOATING.

More than all things else he loved a boat. This was in the early part of the nineteenth century—in Jeffersonian days, when New York was glad to roll its census numbers up to 60,000. Mynheer Vanderbilt was the owner of a superior boat, one much better than any that was owned by his neighbors, and as he had more room in it than he required for the transportation of his own produce to the city he afforded advantages for pay to those of his fellow farmers who needed a ferry. Young Cornelius became a part of this boat, which went over to New York every morning with the tide and returned with the tide every night. So profitable did the old man find the carrying of vegetables and fish that when he had none of his own to take to the city he regularly transported those of his neighbors. The mother, meanwhile, did not give up her share in the business of sailing, and young Cornelius was always found efficient in trimming a sail or in handling an oar.

HIS FIRST VESSEL.

Cornelius had the ambition to possess a boat of his own. On the 1st of May, 1810, he being then in his sixteenth year, he went to his mother and asked her for $100, a large sum in those times, to buy himself a boat. The prudent old lady would not give him the money, but insisted that he should do something to pay for the vessel.

"On the 27th of this month," said the mother, "is your birthday. If by that time you have ploughed, harrowed and planted that field with corn (pointing to a tract of eight acres, rough, stumpy and stony), I'll give you the money."

"It's a bargain," said Cornelius; "I'll do it."

"No boat," said she, "if you don't do it."

"All right," said the boy; "I understand; and I'm going to do it."

Afterward, when the Commodore was speaking of this conversation, he said:—"Mother thought she had the best of me on that eight-acre lot, but I got some boys to help me, and we did the work, and it was well done too: for mother wouldn't allow any half way of doing it. On my birthday I claimed my money, got it, hurried off, bought a boat, hoisted sail and was the happiest boy in the world."

SAILS IT HOME.

But even then his prudent mother tried to dissuade him from his object, and his father vigorously protested. The boy, however, had performed the conditions by a stroke of enterprise in getting his youthful companions to aid him, and the boat he had. He bought it at Port Richmond and sailed home. It was a smaller, swifter boat than any that was running between the island and New York, and he now knew that he was without a rival. As the elder Vanderbilt had been the first regular ferryman to Staten Island, so the younger became the best. The boats ran from and to the same parts whence and when they run to at this day. The place where the Staten Island ferryboats start from New York, near the Battery, was then a beach.

CAPTAIN.

Vanderbilt was the captain of his own boat at the age of sixteen. With great enterprise he succeeded in running his father and mother out of the ferry business in about six months' time. His youthful face did not always attract those who had freight to carry, any more than it attracted those who as passengers wished to risk in a single trip their lives on the rough waters of the harbor. One thing helped him; he was always at his post. Neither wind nor weather prevented his boat from being at her regular landing place at the time when she was expected to be there. Vanderbilt could carry twenty passengers at a time more rapidly than any other man could carry them.

FREIGHTS.

In order that his freight business might not interfere with the regularity of his trips for the accommodation of passengers he frequently worked all the night long. He obtained plenty of business. The government was at that time building fortifications on Staten and Long Islands, and needed both supplies for the men and materials for the work. Young Vanderbilt sought the labor of transportation, and obtaining it, did it well and made much money. He soon repaid his mother the $100 which she had given him to buy his boat.

HIS FIRST EARNINGS.

Besides this he gave all his savings to his parents, as the custom was in those days for boys under age to do. Yet he was permitted to retain half of his earnings at night, so that every summer for three years he saved for himself $1,000. It should be known that with some forty boatmen competing with him in the harbor, and every one of them a grown and sturdy man, the boy must have had to do a deal of energetic work, not only in obtaining but also in performing contracts.

AS A BOATMAN.

But he was no common boatman. He had no vices. He was always seen to be doing his work, in clear weather and in foul, scrupulously and promptly. This boy was never behind time. He always had money in hand, because he did not spend as much as he made, as other boatmen did. His parents, through his industry, were placed in good circumstances. When he was nineteen years old they remitted the term of service to which he was bound by custom, and permitted him to achieve success for himself. His mother was the cause of this doing, and he honored her to the last, saying that he owed everything to her. She lived to be eighty-five years old.

INVESTMENTS.

Cornelius Vanderbilt was always a money making man. From his savings he invested in other sailboats than his own. Moreover, he was a lucky man, succeeding where other men failed. The ice gave way for him; the wind never capsized him. But much of his luck belonged to his in-

domitable spirit of enterprise. At one time during the war
of 1812—though the date was in September, 1813—the
British fleet was endeavoring to penetrate the harbor of
New York during a severe southeast storm, and it was
repulsed at Sandy Hook. After the fight the garrison of
Fort Richmond, which had served in the contest on the
American side, returned to quarters; but it was necessary
that some of the officers should go to New York to report
upon the occurrence and obtain a requisition for reinforcements in expectation of a renewal of the attack when the
storm abated. But the storm was now at its fearful height.
There was but one boatman who would or could brave that
great tempest, "Corneile" was sought and found, and when
he was asked whether he could take the officers up to the
city he promptly replied, "Yes; but I shall have to carry
them under water part of the way." He did take them, and
he landed them soaking wet. But he landed them.

PLENTY OF WORK.

This little adventure, though it was not without its great
consequences in securing reinforcements to the garrison at
Fort Richmond, led to much work for "Corneile, the boatman." During the War of 1812 he transported the sick
and furloughed soldiers from the forts to the city. He
found also much to do with his clean, neat boat in carrying
pleasure seekers to the fortifications. In addition to these
advantages it happened that when the three months militia
was called out for the defence of the city and harbor he
was the one who received the contract for carrying provi-
sions to the fort. But, after all, it was not luck that aided
him. The commanding generals had invited bids from the
boatmen, under the condition that the man who took the
contract should be exempt from military duty and from
liability to the draft. In consequence of this provision all
the boatmen in the harbor bid for the contract on ridicu-
lously low terms. "Corneile" did not bid at all. His father
urged him to make a bid, but the young man replied that
there was no use of bidding upon work that would, at that
rate of competition, be done at half price. To please his

father, he did, at the last hour, put in his bid at a price which would yield him a fair profit. The contract, to the utter surprise of all who knew of it, was given to him. While he was in the office of the Commissary General waiting to sign the papers he asked the commander why the award was granted to him?

"Because," said the General, "we want the work done, and we know you will do it."

He asked, in his own favor, that the stores that he was to carry should be ready at six o'clock in the evening. Young Vanderbilt did all his carrying at night, faithfully supplying Fort Richmond, Bedloe's Island, Governor's Island, Hell Gate, Ward's Island and Harlem. He slept when he could find time for sleep, and when he did not find time he did not sleep. He might always be found in the daytime with his boat at the regular place. He was never obsequious.

INDEPENDENT AS HONEST.

From the very beginning he was independent. His rights were his rights. During the war he was one day sailing his boat, with a load of soldiers on board, from one of the forts at the Narrows toward New York city, when, near Quarantine, he was hailed by the officer of a boat which was approaching from the Staten Island shore. The boat belonged to one of the ferrymen. As the boats came alongside of each other the officer jumped on board Vanderbilt's boat and ordered the soldiers ashore for inspection. Vanderbilt refused to permit the soldiers to leave his boat. The officer, stung to rage, drew his sword upon the young boatman; but in a moment Vanderbilt knocked him down. It is unnecessary to say that without further molestation Vanderbilt landed his soldiers at the Whitehall dock.

MARRIED.

Cornelius Vanderbilt was just out of his time of service to his parents—he was nineteen years old—when he married Miss Sophia Johnson, of Port Richmond, Staten Island.

NEW BOATS.

Very soon after young Vanderbilt became the owner of the finest boat in the harbor. He built a little schooner—the Dred. Then he, in conjunction with a brother-in-law, built the Charlotte. He was always improving upon the vessels of the day. On his twenty-third birthday he found that he was the owner of $10,000 in money. At that time, for this was in 1817, $10,000 was considered to be a nice fortune. He now began, in the winter time, in the Charlotte, to voyage along the Southern coast, taking out and bringing back freights. He was already owner of three boats.

STEAM.

Meanwhile Captain Vanderbilt was observing the progress made by Fulton and others in the operation of boats by means of steam, and, when at last it was evident to him that steamboats were bound to supersede sailboats, he gave all his attention to the former. About this time he became acquainted with Thomas Gibbons, a large capitalist of New Jersey, who was engaged in the transportation of passengers between New York and Philadelphia. Mr. Gibbons took Vanderbilt into his employ, as the captain of a little steamer, at a salary of $1,000 a year. Vanderbilt was not a miscalculating man in giving up the profits of sailboating, which amounted to $2,200 a year, for the salary of a steamboat captain at $1,000. He saw that the day of sailboats had gone by, and he wished to learn the steamboat business; so that in 1819 Cornelius Vanderbilt became a steamboat captain. The boat which he commanded was so little that its owner called it "The Mouse of the Mountain." This vessel was at once employed in carrying passengers between New York and New Brunswick, *en route* for Philadelphia. The Philadelphia passengers, after arriving at New Brunswick from New York, were compelled to remain at New Brunswick over night, so as to be ready for the Philadelphia stage in the morning. Mr. Gibbons was the owner of the stage house at New

Brunswick; but becoming unfortunate in the management of the hotel he offered it to Captain Vanderbilt, free of rent, provided he would take charge of it. Captain Vanderbilt immediately moved his family there, took charge of the hotel and made a considerable profit.

"FULTON'S LICENSE"—A LADY IN THE CASE.

At this time—it was in the early days of steam navigation—an act of the Legislature was in force subjecting any vessel propelled by steam and entering the waters of New York State to forfeiture, unless it sailed under the license of Robert Fulton, so when Captain Vanderbilt touched with his vessel at New York he always had a lady at the helm, and he disappeared in order to avoid arrest.

THE FERRIES.

In 1827 he leased the New York and Elizabethport ferry of Mr. Gibbons for seven years and ran it on his own account. Then he took it for seven years longer. By this means he increased the amount of an already large fortune. The main line owned by Gibbons and managed by Vanderbilt was making $40,000 net profit in a year. Vanderbilt was always increasing the quality of the boats.

FIDELITY.

Captain Vanderbilt remained with Mr. Gibbons for twelve years. Gibbons was engaged in lawsuits over the legislative restriction laws, and Vanderbilt would not leave him. When the suits were settled Captain Vanderbilt refused a salary from Gibbons of $5,000 a year. He was now worth $30,000. This was in 1829. When Gibbons offered to give Vanderbilt the Philadelphia line, allowing him to pay for it when he could, the latter declined, because he was unwilling to put himself under obligation to any one.

AT THIRTY-FIVE.

At this time he was thirty-five years old. He built the Caroline, which afterward went, historically, over Niagara Falls. But his business of building steamboats had its difficulties. His competitors were wealthy and formidable. But he had a plan of building a better boat than his rivals would build, and in this endeavor he was successful. He risked everything. The Stevenses, of Hoboken, tried to ruin him, and a few days of good luck saved him. He was always successful. He built boats and became a steamboat king. This was accomplished in the twenty years succeeding the time when he began the steamboat business for himself.

THE CALIFORNIA EXCITEMENT.

Now came the gold excitement in California. The Pacific Mail Steamship line having been established in connection with Panama, Mr. Vanderbilt determined to find another route than that across the Isthmus, and for this purpose he, in 1849, obtained from the government of Nicaragua a charter for a ship canal and a transit company. He had the exclusive right to transport between the Atlantic Ocean and the Pacific, over the land and waters of Nicaragua, by railroad, steamboat or otherwise, all freights and passengers. The line was soon put in operation. The ships began to sail semi-monthly from New York in July, 1851. The price of the trip was made $300, instead of $600, as it was on the Pacific Mail route. The ships on the Atlantic side landed at Greytown, small boats ascended the San Juan River, and after landing at Virgin Bay, on the western side of Lake Nicaragua, the route was continued overland with horses for sixteen miles to San Juan del Sur on the Pacific coast, where ocean steamers were again taken for California. This was a great enterprise for those days.

THE PACIFIC MAIL ROUTE

had fewer inconveniences, but it was longer and dearer. In January, 1853, Vanderbilt sold his steamers and his franchise to the Transit Company, and became its president. But it was during the time of his presidency of the company that William Walker, the filibuster, took possession of Nicaragua. Vanderbilt refused to transport his men and stores, and Walker retaliated by annulling, or pretending to annul, Vanderbilt's contracts with the Nicaraguan government. Vanderbilt showed as great resolution as Walker showed; but the difficulty was ended by the closing of the route, the San Juan River having poured down mud and sand until a bar had formed at its mouth. It is remarkable, however, that the route chosen by Commodore Vanderbilt in 1849 is . . . one of the three which are now considered the only practicable routes for a ship canal from the Atlantic to the Pacific, and, indeed, there are many considerations which make it the best of the three.

UNIVERSAL.

His ships now fretted every harbor and every sea; and, besides being known as the leading steamboat owner of America, he was a very wealthy man. In the early part of [1853] he had finished a new steamship, which he called the North Star. It was the first steamer fitted with a beam engine that ever attempted to cross the Atlantic. Up to that time many prominent steamship manufacturers were of the opinion that beam engines were impracticable for ocean steamers. The North Star was a perfect vessel of its kind. Commodore Vanderbilt, on the 19th of May, 1853, sailed in this vessel with his family for a foreign tour. The idea of a republican citizen travelling abroad with a steamship for his own private family use created a considerable sensation. At Southampton the North Star attracted great attention. She was more than a yacht; she had 200 feet length of keel and 270 feet overall, with 38 feet breadth of beam. There were twenty-three persons of the Commodore's family on board of her. The Mayor and other civil officers of Southampton gave the Vanderbilts a *fête*, and in return for the reception the Commodore treated his entertainers to a sail around the Isle of Wight.

FROM SOUTHAMPTON

the North Star went to the Hague, to Copenhagen, to the Gulf of Finland, to St. Petersburg, where the Grand Duke Constantine and the Chief Admiral of the Russian Navy visited the ship and obtained permission for a corps of engineers to take drafts of her. Thence the North Star went through the Mediterranean, visiting all the principal Italian cities and Gibraltar, finally reaching Constantinople, where the Vanderbilts were fêted.

SALUTES THE OLD HOME.

After a four months' sail the North Star returned home, and after passing the Narrows the Commodore fired a salute opposite his mother's old cottage.

OCEAN STEAMSHIP LINE.

Soon after his return Commodore Vanderbilt made a proposal to the Postmaster General to run a semi-monthly line to England, alternating with the ships of the Collins line, and carrying the mails back and forth for $15,000. At that time the Cunard line was withdrawn from the mail service on account of the Crimean war. The proposal being refused, Commodore Vanderbilt, in the summer of 1855, established a steamship line between New York and Havre, and for that purpose he built several new steamers, among them the Ariel and the Vanderbilt. There was now an exciting contest, in which the Commodore had great sympathy in America. It was a matter of much public curiosity which line would do the fastest sailing. Of the Cunard line there were the vessels Arabia and Persia, of the Collins line the Baltic and Atlantic, and of the Vanderbilt line the Vanderbilt and the Ariel. The Vanderbilt was victorious in making the fastest time ever then made by an American or a European steamer.

PATRIOTISM.

When the civil war broke out and the Merrimac had disabled some of our naval vessels, Commodore Vanderbilt presented the steamship bearing his name to the government.

Congress thereupon voted him a gold medal.

When he was a steamboat king he refused to have his boats insured, and, in order that our readers may understand how vast his business was, we give the names of

SOME OF THE PRINCIPAL VESSELS

built by him. Those names will be familiar. Steamships—
Prometheus, Daniel Webster, Star of the West, Northern
Light, North Star, Granada, Ariel, Vanderbilt, Ocean
Queen, Galveston, Opelousas, Magnolia, Matagorda,
Champion, Costa Rica, Port Jackson, New York.

Steamboats—Citizen, Cinderella, Westchester, Union,
Nimrod, Champion, Lexington, Cleopatra, Augusta, Clif-
ton, C. Vanderbilt, New Champion, Commodore, Gladia-
tor, Staten Island, Huguenot, Sylph, Hunchback, Red
Jacket, Kill Von Kull, Westfield, Clifton No. 2, Westfield
No. 2, Clifton No. 3, Cornelius Vanderbilt, Wilmington,
North Carolina, George Dudley, Traveller, Director, Cen-
tral America, Clayton, Bulwer.

HIS RAILROAD ENTERPRISES.

Already in 1862, when Vanderbilt virtually abandoned
the water, he was supposed to be worth about $40,000,000.
He now turned his attention to railroad enterprises, in
which he was destined to achieve his greatest successes.
He first acquired a controlling interest in the Harlem
road, buying the stock at a low rate when it sold as low
as six in Wall street. He improved the road wonderfully,
and soon astonished the stockholders by paying them eight
per cent annual dividend. The Harlem was ultimately
leased to the New York Central on a guarantee of eight
per cent, in addition to which the stockholders receive
two per cent from the profits of the Fourth avenue horse
line. But the acquisition of the New York Central was his
greatest ambition, and as a preliminary step he bought a
controlling interest in the Hudson River. Having once control of these two roads it was comparatively easy for a man
of his gigantic resources to achieve his object. Mr. Cor-
ning, the President of the Central, in 1864 secured the co-
operation of Vanderbilt to frustrate an attempt to supersede him, and by Vanderbilt loaning him half a million of
his stock this was accomplished. It was in 1866 that he
obtained full control of this great road, and at the annual

election in 1867, Cornelius Vanderbilt deposited the entire vote, representing thirteen millions of stock. Of course part of this stock was held by him as proxy for other shareholders, but the result was the same, and made him president of the road. His subsequent purchases of the stock of this road were at the rate of about two millions a year, the money being for the greater part the vast accumulation of dividends. He soon was the personal owner of the greater portion of the Central railroad, and, consolidating it with the Hudson River, he gave the public one line from New York to Buffalo. The great improvements which he carried out, the laying of steel rails and four tracks, the erection of the Grand Central depot, of the St. John's Park freight depot and of the grain elevators and cattle yards on the North River, are widely known. To compete with other lines from Buffalo to Chicago he made heavy purchases of Lake Shore at a high price and made Horace F. Clark president of the road. After his death Vanderbilt assumed the presidency of the road himself, and subsequently he was said to have bought a large interest in the Canada Southern Road. Since 1873 the Lake Shore and Michigan Southern have been operated in conjunction with the New York Central and Hudson River roads as one continuous route, 978 miles in extent, and with the Harlem and side lines and branches, presenting an aggregate capital of about $150,000,000, of which about one-half is said to belong to the Vanderbilt family, making, in railroad stock alone, a fortune of about $75,000,000.

ON WALL STREET.

As a prominent banker said yesterday—"Vanderbilt was the heaviest operator in stocks which not only Wall street, but which the world has ever seen. He would frequently risk $10,000,000 or $15,000,000 in a day, but he was nearly always successful, and was not only the heaviest, but also the most successful operator the world ever saw." His first great *coup* was the famous "Harlem" corner, in 1864, when a legislative "ring" sold the stock short, and by refusing to confirm the grant of the railway in Broadway expected to knock down the price of the shares, but Commodore Vanderbilt had bought all the stocks and made a close corner upon the "ring," compelling them to settle at an enormous loss. One of the heaviest sufferers was Daniel Drew. After having sold as low as 86 in January of that year Harlem sold at 285 in June, and the Commodore was said to have netted about $10,000,000 in this "corner." Daniel Drew alone was reputed to have lost $1,000,000. In 1868 followed his heavy and complicated transactions in Erie in which Vanderbilt carried on a gigantic contest with Fisk, Gould and Drew, with what result will be still remembered. In July, 1868, a compromise was finally effected which protected the Commodore against loss. Then came the declaration of the 80 per cent scrip dividend on New York Central, which brought up the price of the scrip to 218 before it was converted into stock. His success in paying 8 per cent dividend upon all this stock established for him a great reputation as a railroad financier. Among his latest financial transactions were his heavy purchases of Western Union and the assistance rendered to the Lake Shore in 1873, which helped to re-establish the Union Trust Company after its failure during the panic. The Commodore came comparatively seldom down to Wall street, preferring to give his orders to his brokers every morning at his home. The last time he was seen in Wall street was during the panic.

VANDERBILT'S PUBLIC GIFTS.

The institution which will be principally associated with the memory of the deceased is the Vanderbilt University, situated in the western suburbs of Nashville, Tenn. It was chartered in 1872 as the Central University of the Methodist Episcopal Church, South, but the efforts to raise funds for its organization were unsuccessful. Its condition was in a critical juncture when, in 1873, Cornelius Vanderbilt gave to the enterprise $500,000, and the institution was named in his honor. Subsequently he increased this amount to nearly $700,000, $300,000 of which is to remain as a permanent invested endowment. On October

4, 1875, the institution was opened for students. It has a theological department with four professors, a law department with three, a medical department with eleven, and a department of philosophy, science and literature with eleven. The total number of students in 1875–76 was 300. It has a library of 6,000 volumes, scientific apparatus that cost more than $50,000, and extensive geological and mineralogical cabinets. Tuition is free to all in the theological department, and in the literary and scientific departments to all preparing for the ministry.

HIS WEALTH.

While Vanderbilt's railroad wealth is estimated at $75,000,000 his accumulations of real estate were comparatively small. His house in East Washington place is worth $48,000; his office, stable, &c., on Fourth street, $51,000; his property in Bowling Green, $27,000; in Cortlandt street, $31,000, and in Twenty-second street, $15,000. He was also said to have owned Gilmore's Garden, worth about $1,000,000. His personal estate for 1876 was assessed at $3,000,000. On Staten Island he owned a park and hotel, worth $200,000, and several thousand acres of wild land. Dr. Deems' church, which will also revert to the Vanderbilt estate (Dr. Deems has a life lease of it) is worth $50,000. Vanderbilt was the richest man in the world who ever made his own fortune, unless, possibly, Krupp, the German gunmaker should have outstripped him.

HIS PERSONAL APPEARANCE.

Commodore Vanderbilt was generally described as a most kingly looking man of about six feet one, with a fine, large, bold head, fair complexion and ruddy cheeks, aquiline, powerful nose and lively, dark eyes of keen expression. His hair was beautifully white, and even now the bankers in Wall street say, "He is the finest looking man I ever saw." He was straight as an arrow and carried himself in an imposing manner. He generally wore black, with a white silk necktie, and in winter a peculiar heavy, fur trimmed

overcoat, by which he was generally known about Wall
street. . . .

"DO YOUR BUSINESS WELL."

Commodore Vanderbilt had few maxims of life. When
he was asked for one he would reply, "Do your business
well." And he was sometimes fond of adding, "Don't tell
anybody what you are going to do until you have done it."

AMUSEMENTS.

He was very fond of games with cards, and he spent a
great sum of money for fast horses. He himself was an
excellent driver. . . .

DOCUMENT 16

A Railroad Eulogy

SOURCE: Anonymous, "A Railroad Eulogy," New York *Herald*, 6 January 1877, p. 3.

This memorial resolution, of course, makes no claim to impartiality; but the anonymous writer employed by the railroad executives to draft it was skillful in assigning to Vanderbilt the major traits of the American hero-image of the rich man: power so great that it sets in motion processes and institutions surviving the man himself; the ability to dominate circumstances instead of submitting to them; a rise to the pinnacle of success without any outside help; and "frank simplicity of character and habits." On the other hand, few even moderately well-informed readers could have accepted at face value the flat assertion that Vanderbilt's invariable policy was to develop and improve the properties he controlled "instead of seeking a selfish and dishonorable profit through their detriment and sacrifice," or that he always had in mind "the rights and the welfare of the smallest stockholder."

At a joint meeting of the Board of Directors of the New York Central and Hudson River Railroad Company, the New York and Harlem Railroad Company, and the Lake Shore and Michigan Southern Railway Company, held at Grand Central depot, on Friday, the 5th day of January, 1877, Augustus Schell was called to the chair and Edwin D. Worcester was appointed secretary.

The object of the meeting was stated to be an expression of regard for the memory of Cornelius Vanderbilt, the late President of the respective companies, whereupon Samuel F. Barger, Chauncey M. Depew, William C. Wetmore, William H. Leonard and William L. Scott were appointed a committee to prepare and present a suitable expression to be entered upon the minutes of the companies.

Mr. Barger, from such committee, presented and read the following, which was adopted:—

The Directors of the New York Central and Hudson River Railroad Company, the New York and Harlem Railroad Company and the Lake Shore and Michigan Southern Railway Company, assembled together by the sorrowful announcement of the death of their honored President, Cornelius Vanderbilt, direct that the following expression of their deep and lasting regard for his cherished memory be entered in full upon the minutes of their respective companies.

Though the lamented dead passes away at an age beyond the allotted period of man and at the close of a complete and rounded career, with his great work in the full course of successful and enduring operation, yet the sense of personal and public loss on the part of all his associates is none the less keen and poignant. The entire public will unite in paying the tribute of sincere respect for one who stood as the foremost representative of public enterprise and material progress; but to those who were identified with him in these Boards his death comes with a closer and deeper touch. In their personal relations they lose a kindly and beloved friend; in their business relations one whose intrepid, penetrating and sagacious leadership was the inspiration of unfailing success.

While deploring the great loss thus sustained it is a source of satisfaction to these Boards to know, as it was a just solace to our departed friend to reflect, that the gigantic work he inaugurated and the sound policy he established find, in two generations of trained and worthy successors, the complete assurance that they will be faithfully and ably carried out by those who follow him in control. It is the mark of power to leave its impress beyond its own immediate sway; and the truest monument to Cornelius Vanderbilt is the fact that he so organized his creation that the work will go on, though the master workman is gone.

His career was a dazzling success. In an age and a country distinguished for their marvellous personal triumphs his achievements rank among the most extraordinary and distinctive of all. Thoroughly practical and faithfully wrought out, their splendor yet gives them the tinge of romance. Nor was this glittering success due to any early adventitious advantages. He was essentially the creator, not the creature, of the circumstances which he moulded to his purposes. He was the architect of his own fortune. Beginning in an humble position, with apparently little scope of action and small promise of opportunity, he rose, by his genius, his indomitable energy and his clear forecast, to the control of vast enterprises involving millions of property and connected with the interests of millions of people.

The diverse and complicated character of his business was as remarkable as its magnitude. He created a large merchant marine, and then turned with equal aptitude and skill to the organization and management of great railroad combinations. And it is to his lasting honor that his uniform policy was to protect, develop and improve the interests with which he was connected, instead of seeking a selfish and dishonorable profit through their detriment and sacrifice. The rights and the welfare of the smallest stockholder were as well guarded as his own. In a period of crafty devices for sinister ends he taught the way of success through legitimate means.

It was a further evidence of his essential and rugged manhood that, with all his brilliant success, his frank simplicity of character and habits remained unchanged. In the height of his rare fortune he was the same direct, provident, unostentatious man as before he had mounted to his large opportunities. The sterling qualities of his strong and commanding individuality were deeply appreciated by all who were associated with him. He was firm and true in his friendships, and the unerring sagacity with which he selected the best agents to administer his great trusts was only equalled by the sincerity of his attachment for those who proved worthy of his confidence. In his relations with the members of these boards he was uniformly courteous and genial, and the association will ever be a fragrant memory.

As a citizen, he was true to the honor and welfare of his country. His public spirit was attested by his liberal donation to the government, in the hour of its need, of the steamer bearing his own name—a contribution which, in a critical emergency, when there was urgent demand for the promptest naval equipment, was even more important than its intrinsic value, great as that was. If his patriotism was thus substantial, his philanthropy was equally generous and effective. Without ostentatious profession he wrought practical good. His own training had been in the severe experience of affairs rather than in the fine culture of the schools; but his nature was great enough to appreciate advantages of the finished education he had not himself been permitted to enjoy, and his munificent gift for the endowment of the University at Nashville will be gratefully remembered by the large number who will share its benefits.

While exacting needed and effective discipline among those intrusted with the care of the property and lives of the people, he always manifested a strong attachment for them and a kindly interest in their welfare. It was among his cherished purposes that adequate provision should be made, upon some comprehensive plan, for injured and needy railroad employés; and even while suffering under fatal disease his thoughts and utterances often recurred to those associated in every variety of capacity with his great enterprises, and evinced his earnest regard for their prosperity.

He was peculiarly happy in his domestic relations. Passing beyond the golden anniversary with the cherished companion of his early manhood, whose memory was deeply revered by her survivor and by her children, he was fortunate in the choice of his later life; and his declining years were sustained and brightened by the tender devotion of one whose rare endowments of heart and mind shone throughout their union, who ministered with unaffected grace to his comfort and happiness, and to whom, with the other members of his family, we extend our sincere sympathy in their bereavement.

He endured a protracted and painful illness at a remarkable age with heroic fortitude and Christian spirit; and when the sun of his life, unclouded through its long day, peacefully sank below the horizon a true man, a sincere friend, a devoted husband and father, a liberal employer, an extraordinary genius of affairs and a citizen of high public spirit went to his final rest.

AUGUSTUS SCHELL, Chairman,
E. D. Worcester, Secretary

Testimony before the Senate Committee
on Education and Labor

SOURCE: Jay Gould, Testimony before the Senate Committee on Education and Labor, New York, 5 September 1883 (*Report of the Committee*, Vol. I, 1062–68).

The autobiographical reminiscences elicited from Gould by the Committee have a convincing air of literal fact, yet correspond closely to the current stereotype of the successful business man. Although Gould's early business career followed a much more circuitous path than Vanderbilt's, the general features are much the same; the only significant difference is Gould's eagerness to educate himself. In later life he was a much more cultivated man than the Commodore; indeed, his interests might even be called scholarly, for he published a history of his native Delaware County, New York, based on conventional research. But the precocious spirit of enterprise and self-reliance, the intuitive power to recognize a bargain in securities of near-bankrupt concerns, the air of simplicity and innocence in describing financial operations, and the claim to have been always building up railroads or developing natural resources—these are the dominant features of the self-made man's career in the popular press.

[NEW YORK, *September* 5, 1883]
[JAY GOULD sworn and examined.]

By the CHAIRMAN: I would like, in the first place, if you please, that you would give us some account of your earlier, your continued, and your present connection with the business enterprises of the country, and, if you do not deem it impertinent at all, I wish you to begin with your early life and give us a statement as minute as you please of your commencement in life, your earlier business experiences, and the road by which you have reached your present position, together with a statement of your knowledge and your views of the business affairs of the country generally, growing out of your long and extensive connection with them. . . . You were born in this State, I believe?—Answer. Yes; I was born at Roxbury, Delaware County, New York.

Q. About how far is that from this city?—A. It is about 150 miles from New York City. I was born there on the 27th day of May, 1836. My father was a small farmer, and kept a dairy of twenty cows. As I was the boy of the family, I generally brought the cows in the morning, and assisted my sisters to milk them, and drove them back, and went for them again at night. I went barefooted and I used to get thistles in my feet, and I did not like farming in that way; so I said one day to my father that I would like to go to a select school that was some twelve or fifteen miles from there. He said all right, but that I was too young. I said to him that if he would give me my time I would try my fortune. He said all right; that I was not worth much at home and I might go ahead. So next day I started off. I showed myself up at this school, and finally I found a blacksmith who consented to board me, as I wrote a pretty good hand, if I would write up his books at night. In that way I worked myself through the school. Then I got a clerkship in a country store.

Q. What was your age at that time?—A. I think I was about fourteen when I left home, as I spent about a year at the school. Then I got into a country store, where I made myself useful, sweeping it out every morning and learning what I could about the business during the day. My duties in the store occupied me from 6 o'clock in the morning until 10 o'clock at night. In the mean time I had got quite a taste for mathematics, especially surveying and engineering. I took that up after I left school, and as I was pretty busy during the day, I used to get up at 3 o'clock in the morning and study from that time until 6 o'clock, and

I very soon found that I got a pretty good idea of that branch, so I concluded I would start out as a surveyor. I don't know but this is rather silly stuff, but it is in response to your question.

The CHAIRMAN. It is just what we want. Go right ahead and tell your story as minutely as you are willing to give it to us.

The WITNESS. Well, I heard of a man in Ulster County who was looking for an assistant in making a map of the county—a surveyor. I wrote to him, and he wrote back engaging me; so one spring morning I started off home. This man's bargain with me was "$20 a month and found." When I came to start I questioned whether I should take any money with me or not. I could have had it; but I thought it was better to break down the bridge behind me; so I took only enough to pay my fare. I met this gentleman and he started me out to make these surveys. The map he was making was one such as you have probably seen, one on which all the roads and the residences are located—a map showing the general topography of the country. They are useful for reference. When this man came to start me out he gave me a small passbook and said, "As you go along you will get trusted for your little bills, what you will eat, and so on, and I will come round afterwards and pay the bills." I thought that was all right. I think it was on my second or third day out that I met a man who took a different view. I had staid at his house overnight. They charged in that part of the country at that time a shilling for supper, sixpence for lodging, and a shilling for breakfast, making two shillings and sixpence in all. I took out my little book and said, "I will enter that." The man turned on me with an oath, and said (referring to my employer), "Why, you don't know this man! He has failed three times. He owes everybody in the county, and you have got money and I know it, and I want the bill paid." There I was. I hadn't a cent in my pocket; so I just pulled my pockets out and said to him: "You can see that I tell the truth. There are my pockets." So finally, he said he would trust me. "I'll

PLATES 1 THROUGH 19

PLATE 1. Carl H. Conrads, "The American Soldier" (sculpture in granite), from an engraving in *The Masterpieces of the Centennial International Exhibition*, Vol. I, *Fine Art*, by Edward Strahan (Philadelphia, 1878), opposite p. 62.

PLATE 2. George Wilkinson and Thomas J. Fairpoint, "The Century Vase" (in silver), from an engraving in *The Masterpieces of the Centennial International Exhibition*, Vol. II, *Industrial Art*, by Walter Smith (Philadelphia, 1878), 52.

PLATE 3. Theodore R. Davis, "Our Centennial—President Grant and Dom Pedro Starting the Corliss Engine" (wood engraving), *Harper's Weekly*, XX (27 May 1876), 421.

PLATE 4. J. O. Davidson, "Interior of a Southern Cotton Press by Night" (wood engraving), *Harper's Weekly*, XXVII (24 March 1883), 181.

PLATE 5. Albert de Groot and Ernest Plassman, "The Vanderbilt Monument" (sculpture cast in bronze, 1869), from a wood engraving in Harper's Weekly, XIII (25 September 1869), 620.

PLATE 6. Arthur J. Goodman, "B. P. Hutchinson ('Old Hutch'), the Great Chicago Grain Operator" (pen-and-ink drawing), *Harper's Weekly*, XXXIV (10 May 1890), 357.

PLATE 7. Taylor and Meeker [first names unknown], "A Blockade on Broadway" (pen-and-ink drawing), *Harper's Weekly*, XXVII (29 December 1883), 845.

PLATE 8. Gray Parker, "The Drive—Central Park—Four O'Clock" (pen-and-ink drawing), *Harper's Weekly*, XXVII (19 May 1883), 317

PLATE 9. Sol Eytinge, Jun., "Rich and Poor" (wood engraving),
Harper's Weekly, XVII (11 January 1873), 33.

PLATE 10. Anonymous, "Under-Ground Life" (wood engraving), Harper's Weekly, XVII (12 July 1873), 604.

PLATE 11. Winslow Homer, "Station-House Lodgers" (wood engraving), *Harper's Weekly*, XVIII (7 February 1874) 132.

PLATE 12. Sol Eytinge, Jun., "Among the Tenement-Houses During the Heated Term—Just before Daybreak" (wood engraving), *Harper's Weekly*, XXIII (9 August 1879), 629.

PLATE 13. R. N. Brooke, "Way Down upon the Swanee Ribber" (wood engraving), *Harper's Weekly*, XVII (28 June 1873), 552.

PLATE 14. Thomas Nast, "Colored Rule in a Reconstructed (?) State" (wood engraving), *Harper's Weekly*, XVIII (14 March 1874), 229.

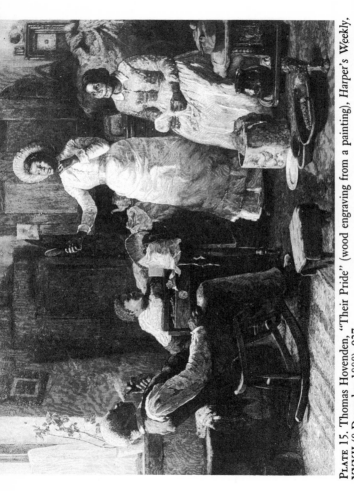

PLATE 15. Thomas Hovenden, "Their Pride" (wood engraving from a painting), *Harper's Weekly*, XXXII (8 December 1888), 937.

PLATE 16. Thomas Nast, "The Greek Slave" (wood engraving),
Harper's Weekly, XIV (16 April 1870), 248.

PLATE 17. Thomas Nast, "The Unconditional Surrender—July 11th" (wood engraving), *Harper's Weekly*, XV (29 July 1871), 697.

PLATE 18. Thomas Nast, "The Usual Irish Way of Doing Things" (wood engraving), *Harper's Weekly*, XV (2 September 1871), 824.

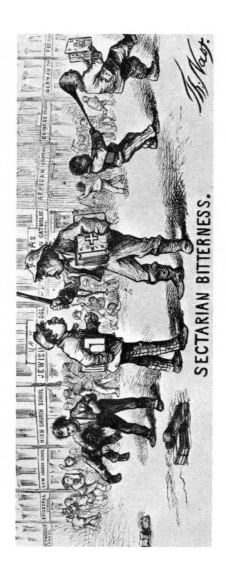

PLATE 19. Thomas Nast, "Sectarian Bitterness" (wood engraving), *Harper's Weekly*, XIV (26 February 1870), 140.

trust *you*," said he, "but I won't trust that man." This incident had such an effect on me that it seemed to me as though the world had come to an end. This was in the morning, and I could not have the heart that day to ask anybody to give me a dinner, so along about 3 o'clock in the afternoon I got faint and I sat down for a few minutes.

The CHAIRMAN. Your voice is so low, Mr. Gould, that I fear the reporters do not get all you say.

The WITNESS. It is a lot of silly stuff, but you have got me into it.

The CHAIRMAN. No, it is not so; and I wish you would give it to us as minutely as you can.

The WITNESS. Well, after this rebuff I was naturally timid. It had a great effect upon me, and I debated with myself whether I should give up and go home, or whether I should go ahead. I came to a piece of woods where nobody could see me, and I had a good cry. Finally I thought I would try my sister's remedy—a prayer. So I got down and prayed, and felt better after it, and I then made up my mind to go ahead. I set my lips close together and made up my mind that I would go ahead and "die in the last ditch." So I went on and the first house I came to I determined right then and there to go in and get something to eat. I went in and the woman treated me kindly, gave me some bread and milk and cold meat, and one thing and another, and when I got ready to leave I said to her, "I will enter it down." She said all right. In the mean time her husband came in and they both said it was all right. I started and had got, I guess, about forty rods away from the house when I heard him hallooing to me. Well, after the morning scene I thought *he* was going to finish me; but he came right on and when he got up to me he said, "I want you to take your compass back and make me a noon-mark." That, as you perhaps know, is a north and south line right through the window, marked in so that the farmers can regulate their clocks by it. When the sun strikes the line it is 12 o'clock. I took my compass back and made the noon-mark for him. When I had made it, and was about to go away he said: "How much is that?"

"Oh," said I, "nothing." "Oh, yes," said he, "I want to pay you for it." I thought a moment, and he went on to say, "Our surveyor always charges a dollar for these jobs." Said I, "Very well. Take out a shilling for my dinner." So he paid me the seven shillings. Everything went by "shillings" in those days—eight shillings to the dollar, and he kept one and paid me the other seven. That was the first money I made in that business, and it opened up a new field to me, so that I went on from that time and completed the surveys and paid my expenses all that summer by making noon-marks at different places. When I got through with the summer's work my employer had failed, and was unable to pay me. There were two other young men, wealthy men's sons, who had been engaged on the same work, and we three together had the control of it. I proposed to them that we should go on and finish the map ourselves, and finally we decided to do so. Then, as they lived in the county and were pretty conspicuous, they wanted to put their names to the map, so I said to them, "Very well; I will sell you out my interest;" and I sold out my interest to them for $500.

That was the result of my first summer's work. I went on and finished the work and got it ready for the engraver, so that what I sold was the perfected map. That was a map of Ulster County. With this little capital (which was a great deal to me then) I went forward and made similar surveys of Albany and Delaware Counties. I had made up my mind that I would go alone, and I made those surveys alone and completed them, and they were very successful in sale, so that I made about $5,000 out of those maps. About that time, while I was carrying on these surveys, I met a gentleman who seemed to take a fancy to me, Mr. Zadoc Pratt, of Prattsville. He was at that time one of the largest tanners in the country. I had done some surveying for him. He had a very beautiful place at Prattsville, and I fixed that up for him, and finally he proposed to me to go into the tanning business with him. He knew my whole history. I accepted this proposal, and next day I started for Pennsylvania. The Delaware and Lackawanna Railroad had just been completed. I went over that road, and found some very large lots of hemlock timber land, and I came back and reported to Mr. Pratt what I had found, and we decided to go on. He sent me back, and I made the purchase of the land—made all the contracts myself, and then came back, and took about fifty or sixty men down there with me to start the work. It was right in the woods, fifteen miles from any place. I went in there and chopped down the first tree. We had a portable saw-mill, and we sawed the tree up, and that day we built a blacksmith's shop out of the timber. I slept in it that night, on a bed made of hemlock boughs. We went on and built the tannery. It was a very large one, the largest in the country at that time. We carried on the business for a while, and then I bought Mr. Pratt out, and sold the interest to a firm in New York, at the head of which was a Mr. Loup. About that time the panic of 1857 came, and of course everything was very much disturbed—confidence was gone in almost every kind of business, and money was almost impossible to get. I thought once or twice that we would fail, but we went through. Mr. Loup afterwards committed suicide. That left the property in such a condition that litigation grew out of it. In the mean time I still retained my early love of engineering, and I was watching the railroads, and after the panic everything went down very low, and I found a road whose first-mortgage bonds were selling at about 10 cents—The Rutland and Washington Railroad, running from Troy, N. Y., to Rutland, Vt. I went in and bought on credit a majority of the bonds at 10 cents on the dollar, and I left everything else and went into railroading. That was in 1860. I took entire charge of that road. I learned the business, and I was president and treasurer and general superintendent, and I owned the controlling interest in the road.

Q. What points does that road connect?—A. It is now a part of the Rensselaer and Saratoga consolidation.

Q. How long was it?—A. Sixty-two miles. I gradually brought the road up, and I kept at work, and finally we made the Rensselaer and Saratoga consolidation, which still exists. In the mean time my bonds had become good, and the stock also; so that I sold my stock for about 120, I think, and then I went West into Western roads.

The next road I took hold of I think was the Cleveland and Pittsburgh. The stock was selling pretty low. A friend of mine had bought more of it than he could take care of, and he came to me one night and said that the next day he had got to fail; that he had bought more of the capital stock of the Cleveland and Pittsburgh road than he could pay for. He had bought it for about 70, and it was then down to about 65. I did not have very much confidence in this man, but I had in the property, so I told him I would do only one thing. Said I, "I will take your hand; you may give me it to-morrow on those purchases." He did so and was glad to do it, and in that way I became the owner of that interest in the Cleveland and Pittsburgh road. I think his purchase was made on an average at about 70, and as soon as people saw that there was some one there that could take care of it the stock went up and reached about 120 before it stopped. I took the road and brought it up, made a success of it, and paid dividends right from the start. I finally sold that out or leased it to the Pennsylvania road.

From that I went into the Union Pacific. My attention was attracted to that road at that time I think. I met the late Mr. Horace F. Clark in Chicago. He and Mr. Schell had been out over the road, and they gave me a good account of it; spoke about the coal deposits and one thing and another, and I concluded to buy a lot of it. I telegraphed to New York an order to buy in the neighborhood of 30, from 30 down. I did not expect to get much. Mr. Clark came home and was taken sick, and as soon as his brokers found that his illness was to be a fatal one they sold his stock. That broke the market down and filled up orders which I never expected to get filled, so that when I got home I found myself a very large owner in that property, and I began to inquire into its condition. I found that there was a large floating debt to begin with, which I did not know about before. Then I found that there was

$10,000,000 of bonds that came due in about a month or two, income bonds. It was rather a blue condition of things. In the mean time some of the directors were consulting as to who should be the receiver of the road. I made up my mind that I would carry it through, so I told the directors that if they would furnish half the money I would furnish the other half, and we would carry it through, and finally I pressed them into it. The stock went down to 15. I bought it and kept buying it, and finally I had a very large loss staring me in the face if I had made it; but instead of that I kept on buying, so that when the turn came there didn't seem to be any top to it; it went right along up to 75. I immediately went to work to bring the road up. I didn't care anything about the price in the market; I wanted to give it a substantial foundation. I went out over the road and started coal mines to develop that interest, and very soon we began to pay dividends to the surprise of everybody, and the road came up. It never passed a dividend.

The CHAIRMAN. Would it be difficult for you to speak somewhat louder, Mr. Gould?

The WITNESS. I can talk louder.

The CHAIRMAN. I see directions in which this testimony of yours may be of great interest and value, and I think if you will talk somewhat louder the reporters for the press will be able to hear you better.

The WITNESS. I do not like to parade myself before the public, but inasmuch as you have got me into it I had better give it frankly, I suppose.

The CHAIRMAN. It is distinctly understood that I ask these questions for a public purpose, and it is quite apparent that you answer with some reluctance. I have asked Mr. Gould to give us as much of his personal history and connection with the great business interests of the country as he will, and I do not think it will do any harm to the American people to hear it.

The WITNESS. [Continuing.] When this road began to be a financial success there arose at once a great clamor that it was "Jay Gould's road." After it became a dividend-paying property and a demonstrated success, there seemed to arise all at once on the part of the public a great outcry that it was "Jay Gould's road," as though it were a dangerous thing to have one man control a road. However, I thought it was better to bow to public opinion, so I took an opportunity whenever I could to place the stock in investors' hands, and in the course of a very few months, instead of my owning the control of the road I was entirely out, and the stock was 20 per cent. higher than the price at which I had sold it, and was all in the hands of investors, men who had bought it for income. Instead of there being thirty or forty stockholders, there were between six and seven thousand, the investments representing the savings of many widows and orphans, for there were a great many lady stockholders.

Q. That was about what year?—A. That was about three or four years ago after Congress had enacted some very harsh legislation, which really amounted to an abrogation of the contracts which they had made in order to get the road through in its early stages.

Q. Do you refer to the Thurman act?—A. I refer to the Thurman act. That closed my connection with the Union Pacific road.

The next great enterprise that I became connected with (I don't know that I should call it a great enterprise, though) was the Missouri Pacific road. I one day bought of Mr. Commodore Garrison the control of that road. It was a road running from Saint Louis to Kansas City, 287 miles long. After a short negotiation with Mr. Garrison he gave me his price just as we are talking here, and I said, "All right, I will take it," and I gave him a check for it that day and closed the matter up and took the road. Railroads had then got to be a sort of hobby with me—I didn't care about the money I made, I took the road more as a plaything to see what I could do with it; I had passed the time when I cared about mere money-making. My object in taking the road (if you can appreciate that) was more to show that I could make a combination and make it a success. So I took this road and commenced developing it, bringing in other lines which would be tributary to it, extending branches into new country where I could develop coal mines, and so on. I continued to develop that road until, I think, we have now in the system controlled by it about 10,000 miles of railroad.

Q. What are the other roads that make up that system, and what are the points connected by them?—A. The roads extend now from Saint Louis through to Kansas City and to Omaha. That is on the west side. There is another line extending on the east side. They both run to Omaha. Then there are two lines extending from Saint Louis through to Mexico, one connecting at El Paso with the Texas Pacific and the other at Laredo, which is on the direct line to the City of Mexico. Another line runs from Saint Louis to Galveston on the coast.

Q. What is the point where all those roads concentrate? —A. They concentrate at Saint Louis, Chicago, Detroit, and Toledo. Those are the eastern termini. I think the property when I took it was earning about $70,000 a week gross. I have just received a statement of the gross earnings for last month, which amount to $5,100,000 for the month.

Q. That would be over $61,000,000 per annum?—A. Yes, sir.

By Mr. CALL:

Q. Is that the earnings of that road alone or the earnings of the system?—A. The earnings of the system controlled by that road. While we have been doing this we have made the country through which the lines pass rich; we have developed coal mines; we have developed cattle raising, and we have largely developed the production of cotton; so that we have in fact created this earning power by the development of that railroad system.

DOCUMENT 18

The Genesis of a Money-Maker

SOURCE: Henry F. Keenan, "The Genesis of a Money-Maker," from *The Money-Makers: A Social Parable* (New York, 1885), pp. 132–40.

By the side of the actual careers of Vanderbilt and Gould may be placed this social parable of how financial tycoons are made. Keenan—obviously no novelist, but an intelligent journalist who knew what he was talking about—is presenting a thinly disguised biography of Amasa Stone, father-in-law of John Hay. *The Money-Makers* is in fact a *roman à clef* written as a rebuttal to Hay's novel *The Bread-Winners* (1884), which took the side of Cleveland employers against labor unions. "Valedo" is Cleveland, "General Ajax" is Ulysses S. Grant, and so on. Keenan makes the parallel between the fictional career of Aaron Grimstone and the actual career of Amasa Stone almost literal by having Grimstone commit suicide after many persons are killed in the collapse of an auditorium he has built of flimsy materials. Stone committed suicide after the collapse of a railroad bridge for which he had been the contractor. But at the same time Keenan is following a fictional convention in his hostile treatment of Grimstone: the financier-protagonist of H. H. Boyesen's *A Daughter of the Philistines* (1883) also kills himself; Erastus Brainard, the domineering banker in Henry B. Fuller's *The Cliff-Dwellers* (1893), is murdered by his dissolute son; and both Charles Dudley Warner (in *A Little Journey in the World*, 1889) and William Dean Howells (in *A Hazard of New Fortunes*, 1889) present highly unfavorable portraits of millionaires. In calling Grimstone a "consummate product of the survival of the social fittest" Keenan is of course alluding to a pseudo-

Darwinian doctrine popularized in the United States by Herbert Spencer, and expounded for example by Andrew Carnegie in *Triumphant Democracy* (1886).

Aaron Grimstone, as a type of that consummate product of the survival of the social fittest, the self-made man, requires a retrospective glimpse, not only for the better understanding of a very curious personality, but to enable us, by beginning at the outset, to comprehend the complex traits that lead to the catastrophe. Not only this, but, at a time when the world is emulous of winning wealth by the arts that make the Grimstones the arbiters of our destinies, no detail can be too trivial, no incident too *banal*. When, in 1847, Aaron, then a stalwart lad of twenty-one, set up his anvil in Valedo, that slatternly hamlet gave no promise of the urban wonder it is to-day. Fixed upon as an Indian trading-post in 1812, the oldest inhabitant, thirty years later, looked forward to no better fortune for the place than a red-brick custom-house, and a post-office, that should outshine the rival Canadian edifices on the opposite shore. Contrasted with the shifty New England quarry he had been starved out in, Aaron looked upon the careless abundance of his new home as the promise of a subsistence at least. When later he found work for his brawny arms twelve hours a day, and excellent pay for his toil, he was sure that he had done well, and that the future need have no terrors for him.

Early rising was not general in Valedo in those days. Beyond the publican who gave his sleepy countenance to the trim breakfast-room, as he speeded the parting guest, and the lad who sat in the lighthouse, waiting the sun as a signal to go to bed, there were few stirring in Valedo's windy street. But these few were sure to see the red glow in Aaron's smithy, and hear the cheery clangor of his hammer as he wrought the shoon that soon became the wonder of the country-side. The latest loiterer at night, too, was sure to see the smithy's glowing flame, and it soon became as natural to look for Grimstone's fire as the village-clock.

For years his was the only anvil in Valedo, and, though the grimy corner behind the bellows became presently the village rostrum, it was remarked that Aaron never remitted a blow to give an opinion, nor stifled a blaze to hear the momentous whisper in which some vicinage scandal was breathed. The fame of his handiwork brought him custom from all the neighboring towns, where the rich farmers set store by their horses. He had become as much a part of the vital energies of the town as the doctor, the preacher, or the town-clock, when an event came to pass that gave him the hearts of his fellow-citizens, and opened the way to that wonderful career which finally made him a power in the councils of the nation. A company, chartered to connect two great lakes by water, had reached Valedo in its operations; but, as the town was small, and its political ambition dormant, the contractors carelessly ignored its existence, both in buying stores and employing the idle. Worse than that, however, to bear, as I gather from the archives, was the insolence with which the company landed in the very streets of Valedo stores and munitions shipped to the neighboring and rival port of Carleo, whose harbor and docks were absurdly inferior to the capacious curves upon which Valedo clustered its scattered tenements. For weeks the town bore the indignity of seeing the contractors' stores dragged from Carleo and dumped along the outlined channel of the canal, and then actually carted through the town and stacked beyond the surveyed line.

Nor was this all, as the vivacious records of the time tell it; while the autumn was at hand, and hundreds of farmers were idle, the contractors' gangs "swarmed with foreigners, imported into the country by these canal monopolies to crush the natives to beggary, by reducing wages. These impoverished aliens, used to starvation at home, were content to take a mere pittance, to live on corn and pork, sleep under a mud hut, and work sixteen hours a day." The whole country about was in deep anger. The Valedoans took prompt action. A public meeting was called in the blacksmith's shop. Aaron was chosen "moderator," and the wrongs of the township were recited in a very imposing list of whereases, which were in due time presented by a committee, of which Aaron was one, to the contractors and the manager of the Valedo section of the canal. The company paid no heed to the remonstrances. Valedo had held out longer than any of the other towns when the charter was before the Legislature, and had exacted high rates when the survey was made; as a consequence, the company, foreseeing that the canal was to greatly benefit the town, were quite indifferent to the outcry.

The season advanced, the winter came late and light, and work was pushed on vigorously, as, under their stipulations, the contractors were obliged to have the cut a mile or more through and beyond Valedo by the first of May. Now, it had not been supposed that the work could be kept on in all its branches so late. Hence the horses, having worn their shoes out, were useless, and the company was forced to call in such smiths as could be found about the neighboring villages. Aaron, so soon as he learned this condition of things, made a swift journey to Carleo. The company's stores of ready-made shoes, and the iron and nails for others, were in luggers lying at the wharf. Aaron bought up every ounce of iron and nails in the town, and at dark mounted his horse to return to Valedo. There was a fierce November wind during the night, and the next morning, when the canal contractors reached the wharf, the boats with their precious stores of iron had disappeared. Search was made for miles about in the lake, but they could not be found. It was not until the next spring that boys, diving in the water, came upon them a few yards from the wharf, in the deepest channel of the harbor. There was no suspicion at the time that the heavy scows had not drifted away from the shore, their fastenings being found worn away near the capstans. There was great disgust among the canal people. Work would be brought to a stand unless five hundred horses could be instantly shod. Not a shoe or nail was to be obtained in Carleo.

Grimstone had paid in advance for every vestige of shoeing in the town. It would take six weeks to send to Pittsburg or Troy, where, in those days, such work was supplied. Before noon the chief contractor was in Grimstone's shop. Aaron listened to the tale of disaster, and remarked that it was fortunate that he had just received a cargo from Canada, and besides had a good supply on hand. He was given a contract for shoeing five hundred horses, which he accepted only on condition that the company's stores should be landed at Valedo, for that section of the canal, and that, wherever the foreign help gave out, preference should be given the able-bodied men of Valedo County. The contractor listened with surprise. He went out and saw the scow laden with Aaron's Canadian cargo, he listened once more to the blacksmith's review of the situation, and then he burst into a loud laugh. That was the only comment he made, but he scrutinized the phraseology of the paper drawn up for his signature, and went away pensive.

Whether he suspected the extent of Aaron's handiwork in the *ruse*, he never said; but, thereafter, he never took action without consulting the blacksmith. Nor did the company find cause to repent their bargain. His work was so honest, rapid, and enduring, that it was found an economy to intrust him with that branch of it; then he was given the whole line, and no objection put in the way when he established the main depot of the company in Valedo. This brought people, the people brought money, and the need for new buildings. Valedo soon began to show signs of its future possibilities. His new enterprise had taken Aaron from Valedo a good deal; but when he came back Marcellus returning to delivered Rome with the spoils of the Veiintians was not more rapturously welcomed than Aaron, as he surveyed the busy wharves, the extemporized cranes and warehouses, where waste had been but a few months before. This was the wonder the unobtrusive Yankee had wrought. But, in all this effusive adulation, the blacksmith showed another side of his character that presaged the qualities of the self-maker—he kept his own counsels; he never was surprised or flattered into an admission of his handiwork in the affair that had brought such luck to Valedo.

I don't know what the Church said of the matter, but it is on record that, so far as the popular sentiment could be ascertained, the end justified the means. There were a few, it seems, who held the sinking of the scows immoral, but these croakers were silenced by the derisive taunts of the town. It was envy, the majority said, that found wrong in a stroke of genius which had despoiled the Philistines of Carleo, and crowned the saints of Valedo with their own. It was the place of the Valedoans to be grateful, and trust to Providence: when was Providence ever known to repulse the efforts of a long head?

Aaron's time became too precious to bestow upon the forge. He had gathered a good deal of money in the canal contracts, and had learned casually that the Eastern railway system was to be extended to Valedo and thence westward to Bigbrag, then a town not any larger than Valedo, though now the second or third largest city in the Union. When the surveys for the road-bed were finished, it was found that the blacksmith had bought all the village lands adjacent, as well as miles of farms through which the route lay. This all brought money, and plenty of it. He was set down as a demi-millionaire. In 1848 he married the daughter of one of his associate railway directors in Louisville, and her fortune was considered large for those days. Anecdotes illustrating his fecundity in devising means to frustrate rivals were the staple of Valedo gossip for years. But, as he amassed money, Grimstone's reticence grew upon him. He was never known to open a conversation first, unless on business requiring his initiative. In 1863 he became a banker, accepting from the Government a larger deposit than any institution out of New York city. When the war broke out, Valedo had grown to be a city of quite one hundred thousand inhabitants. The sudden crash threw everybody into disorder, and it was soon whispered that Grimstone held a third of the realty of the town in mortgages and foreclosures. Mrs. Grimstone was fond of company. The family occupied an imposing mansion in a

pleasant, grassy avenue of Valedo, where the wealth of
the town had set its bourns. The edifice was characteristic
of the man. He had before his marriage built a white
sandstone house, two stories high, and painfully plain.
With the growth of their children, and the increasing social demands brought about by the city's rank, more room
was found necessary. A house in New York had once impressed him, and sketching the outlines he gave the paper
to a builder in Valedo, ordering him to make that cover as
much of the old structure as he could. When the work was
done the effect was a never-exhausted source of mirth to
the Valedoans. The combination was as incongruous as a
Cairene dome upon a Gothic temple. Nor was the interior
less *bizarre*.

The new edifice was broken up into spacious *salons*
and recesses; while just across the hallway the bewildered
stranger stumbled down two awkward steps, and was lost
in a labyrinth of low-ceiled rooms and old-fashioned cran-
nies, that made the neighboring grandeur grotesque. No
one ever remembered seeing Grimstone in the new part
of his house. His own room was in the old wing, far from
the street, and far from the intrusion of the household.
Not a member of the family had ever seen much of the
interior of his sanctum. The keeping it in order was intrusted to a gigantic negro, who had been a slave in his
youth on the plantation of Mrs. Grimstone's mother. The
doors of this *cachot* were of sheet-iron, the windows were
lined with sliding panels of the same; the floor was of
brick, and the walls of granite. As the dwelling was far
from the settled part of the city, these precautions were
not regarded as excessive, when the treasures to be guarded
were considered.

His marriage made no difference in the passion of Aaron
Grimstone's life. The devotion he had shown the forge he
lavished upon each enterprise upon which he embarked
in turn. He took a notion that he wanted a better hotel
in Valedo. He offered a fair price for the existing one. The
owner, knowing Grimstone's wealth, refused to sell.

Grimstone promptly bought ground facing the hotel,

called in an architect, named the figures he was willing to expend, and set him to work. But, when the plan was submitted, Grimstone declined to pay within one hundred thousand dollars of the sum estimated. The architect explained that it was absolutely essential for the security of the building that this sum should be put in, that is, if Grimstone's idea was to be carried out. It could be done for one hundred thousand dollars less, but it would be unsafe, neither fire-proof nor shock-proof. Cheaper materials would have to be used, and as a man proud of his profession the architect declined to accept the responsibility of putting up such a building. Grimstone dismissed him coldly, called in another architect, gave him the plan, and told him to build it, and that he, the architect, was to be responsible for every penny over the specified sum. When the edifice was completed, it was given to a Swiss manager rent-free for a year, with the sole condition that the prices should be so low that the other hotel must close its doors. That came to pass within the stipulated year, and the old building came into Grimstone's hands through foreclosure.

The minister of one of the Valedo churches had, in the course of one of those personal sermons which began to enliven the pulpit at the close of the war, alluded to Grimstone's heartlessness in money-getting. The church was situated in the center of a square but sparsely built upon. Within a year Grimstone had bought the ground surrounding the church, had reared masses of brick on three sides, and set the hammers of a bolt factory in operation. The body of the church was dark by day, and when the windows were open the fumes from the forges made the place intolerable. The society offered the ground for sale, but no one would buy it. They began negotiations for a dozen sites, but at the last moment found them taken from their hands. In despair, the offending preacher called his flock together, and, refusing to be the cause of their persecution, he quit the place. The society thereafter found not the least difficulty in transferring their ruined site to

Grimstone for a far more desirable one under fine trees in the outskirts of the town.

A reckless little journal, published by a group of flighty college graduates, made sarcastic reference to Grimstone's *amours fragiles*, known and winked at by all the town. The paper was run to the ground in a month, and Grimstone held the mortgage when the scant property was knocked down. In 1870 Aaron Grimstone could do with the State of Appalachia what a baron under Barbarossa could do with *Rittergut*. He could, by a word, decide the choice of the men who were to be Governor, Senator, Congressmen, legislators, as in 1872 he was omnipotent in making General Ajax President. His own ambition no one knew; even his politics were in doubt. Sometimes he favored the Optimate, and sometimes the Ultrocrats. He had made Killgore Senator, causing his election by a Legislature in which the Ultrocrats held a majority on joint ballot. In those days Killgore was a poor man; but he was counted worth not less than a million in 1872, six years after his election.

Though one of the earlier settlers of Valedo, Grimstone was, if not a mystery, the least understood personality in the city. His interests were known to exist in every large town of the State of Appalachia. He owned mines in one place, coal-fields in another, blast-furnaces here, machine-shops there. He was director in forty railway lines in 1870, and president of two. He held controlling interests in lake and ocean lines, and had invested half a million in exploiting a newly invented watering-place on the sea-shore. He was, in short, one of that extraordinary group of men which has grown up in this country since the war, who, reversing the saying of Thiers, "govern, but do not reign." He was indulgent and undemonstratively affectionate with his son and daughter. Herbert's faults were all known to his father, who made no sign. He gave him an ample allowance, which he increased under no circumstances. When Herbert's money ran short, which it did every term, it was his mother and sister who slyly made up the deficit. In the evening, while the children were at home, Grimstone would sit with them in the dull, stuffy little sewing-room, and, though he said but little, he seemed to enjoy their prattle. If a stranger were announced, he would get up instantly and slip up-stairs by the rear, and be seen no more that night.

At the table he rarely spoke unless pointedly addressed. He was never known to talk to Mrs. Grimstone. When he went to Washington or New York, he never took his wife; and, when she went off for the summer, her husband never formed one of the party. They were not divided, quarrelsome, or unhappy in any way. Mrs. Grimstone was one of the rare women who look on a husband as a poet looks on a publisher—as a necessity; that is, tolerable, in proportion as he keeps himself at a distance, and holds to his prescriptive functions, claiming no rights! She was tranquilly happy in the possession of an abundant allowance—the most expensive diamonds in Valedo, the handsomest equipage, the best horses, the most spacious house, the handsomest son, if not the handsomest daughter, in the city. She always said "Mr. Grimstone," in speaking to or of her husband, and would hear details of his enterprises, unknown to her, from callers with perfect composure. Gossip busied itself industriously with the affairs of the family; but while it was undisputed that Grimstone had neither heart nor scruples, nor his wife any self-assertion, it was admitted that the hearth-stone was a peaceful one; that if it were true that Grimstone ruled by fear, he managed to give his sway the air of love. The boy and girl were left to grow up under such influences as chance threw them into.

DOCUMENT 19

The Rich

SOURCE: James W. Buel, "The Rich," from *Mysteries and Miseries of America's Great Cities* (San Francisco, 1883), pp. 93–106.

Buel, a reporter and editorial writer for Kansas City and St. Louis newspapers, wrote some twenty non-fiction books, all originally published by the Historical Publishing Co. of St. Louis. By the end of the nineteenth century his works are said to have sold more than six million copies. His point of view, even in this short passage, can be recognized as Middle Western. The air of presenting an exposé of exotic and probably wicked urban glamor continues the tradition of George Lippard and other American fictional disciples of Eugène Sue (author of *Les Mystères de Paris*, 1842–43), but Buel's sensationalism is comparatively mild. It really amounts to little more than the time-honored cliché—ultimately pastoral—that proclaims the honest laborer to be happier than the millionaire.

The detailed description of the Vanderbilt mansion foreshadows Dreiser's fascinated attention to the palaces constructed by Chicago and New York millionaires in his Cowperwood trilogy.

The wealth of New York is enormous, so great in fact that she is recognized as the financial center of America, to which nearly all business pays tribute. And yet, as a manufacturing city, Gotham is hardly half so important as Pittsburg or St. Louis, and the tax yielding wealth of Boston is much greater. But several advantages have combined to make her the chief commercial entrepot, and money gravitates to her financial institutions, and is held there by a magnetic force. Wall street controls the stock market and New York's rich magnates hold our railroads and shipping by a firm grip. It is a trite but well proved adage that "money is the root of all evil," and while we may all be striving for some of the root, yet its evils are too apparent in the great Metropolis for us to neglect the lesson which its acquisition teaches.

Gould, Vanderbilt, Astor, Goelet, Seligman, Jerome, Bennett, Belmont, Sage, Field, Tilden, and scores of other New York capitalists estimate their wealth by millions, but if they are happy we cannot discover the fact by any of the evidences of their living and surroundings. Jay Gould, although perhaps the richest man in the Metropolis, possibly excepting Vanderbilt, manifests some of the general symptoms of contentment, because he is a philosopher, and has made life a pleasant study. His family are rarely mentioned in the newspapers, because he forbids it; none of the members belong to the recognized gilt-edged aristocracy, because he knows the shams and dissipations of that supercilious class; his son, George, now of age, is never seen at club meetings, horse-races, fashionable weddings, or other places of that loose indulgence which induces crapulence, because the father's teachings are heeded, and wholesome advice is as a lamp unto his feet. He, too, is a student like his father, and in consequence now gives promise of a career more brilliant than that of any other young man in New York. Jay Gould has tried to cultivate home pleasures, making his hearth-stone so Eden-like that his family find all their happiness in domestic associations and acts of private charity. But for the care of such vast interests I could believe Gould a happy man, and I cannot say he is not, for his family certainly are, and to such an extent, too, that their happiness cannot but reflect joy on him.

Those who are most familiar with the other millionaires of New York have no hesitancy in declaring that these monied princes are infinitely less happy than are the honest laborers, whose daily duties are a constant striving for only limited comforts. There is much reason to confirm this truth. [William H.] Vanderbilt betrays a lack of confidence in his own abilities, and it is said he is the victim of a singular delusion—that he may some day become a pauper. To guard against such an impossible event, he has purchased government bonds to the amount of $65,000,000, which he has deposited in the United States treasury.

As an example of the sumptuous surroundings which are characteristic of nabob life in New York, a description is here introduced of Mr. Vanderbilt's private residence, which was completed and occupied about the first of January, 1882. This house, said to be the finest in America, is located on Fifth avenue and Fifty-first street. There is nothing attractive about its outer appearance, but on the other hand there are several architectural eccentricities observable which are decidedly forbidding. The building is tripartite in arrangement, being designed as a home for himself and also the families of his two married daughters.

One of the most striking points in connection with the work has been the rapidity of its execution; what would, it is said, in any European country have taken from five to ten years to accomplish has been done here in a little more than two years.

The house is entered by the large vestibule which gives admission both to Mr. Vanderbilt's own dwelling and to those of his two daughters. The ceiling of this vestibule is of bronze and stained glass, filled in with mosaic made by Facchina, of Venice, after designs drawn in New York. The walls are of light African marble, surmounted by a frieze containing figures in mosaic. There are fixed marble seats, and the floor is of marble and mosaic. The doors leading to Mr. Vanderbilt's house are reduced copies of Ghiberti's famous gates in Florence, and were exhibited in the Paris exposition of 1878 by Barbedienne. Passing through these one finds himself in the private vestibule, furnished with a high wainscoting of marble and with three bronze doors, the one on the right leading to a small dressing-room; that on the left to Mr. Vanderbilt's private reception room, and the third to the main hall. This hall extends to the full height of the house, and is surrounded on the upper stories by galleries leading to the different private living rooms. A high wainscoting of English oak surrounds it. Square columns of African marble of a dark red color, with bronze capitals, support the gallery, and facing the entrance is a large and beautiful open fireplace, with a full-sized bronze female figure in relief on each side, and a massive sculptured marble chimney piece.

Carved oaken seats flank the door on the eastern side, which leads to the drawing-room. The paintings for the ceiling of the drawing-room, by Gallaud, of Paris, are now on their way to this country, the present ceiling of blue and gold being merely temporary. The woodwork is a mass of sculpture, gilded and glazed with warm tints. The walls are hung with pale red velvet, embroidered with designs of foliage, the flowers and butterflies scattered through it being enriched with cut crystals suggesting dewdrops and precious stones. The carpet of a similar tone, which was manufactured in Europe from special designs made in New York, unites with the walls in giving a wealth of color and richness of effect. The lights are arranged in eight vases of stained and jewelled glass, disposed at the corners and at the angles of the large east window and flanking the entrance doors. Some of these vases stand on columns of onyx with bronze trimmings, while the lights in the corners are backed by mirrors and stand on black velvet bases—an arrangement which is designed to heighten the general effect of brilliancy, and at the same [time] to divest the room of any possible appearance of angularity or bareness. The door to the north connects the drawing-room with the library.

In the library the most striking feature is the inlaid work, on the woodwork, of mother-of-pearl and brass on mahogany and rosewood in a beautiful design of an antique Greek pattern. This work is handsome and striking. A table of similar work stands in this room, and the general furniture is all designed to correspond in style. The ceiling is fretted and has rich gilt work and small square mirrors. Over the door-way to the west of the library hang heavy,

rich curtains, which separate it from Mr. Vanderbilt's
private reception-room, which is fitted with a high mahogany wainscoting, with seats and book-cases of the same
material, and a massive mahogany ceiling. The walls and
ceiling spaces are covered with stamped leather.

To the south of the drawing-room is a parlor. It is
modeled and furnished entirely in a free Japanese fashion.
The ceiling is of bamboo, with rafters left exposed. A
rich, low-toned tapestry is covered in places with velvet
panels. Around the room runs a low cabinet of Japanese
pattern (to all appearance of Japanese lacquer, although it
was made here) which contains innumerable shelves, cup-
boards and closets. The whole is the work of men in New
York under the direction of Herter Bros. A large open
fireplace and a seat covered with uncut velvet, manufactured in Japan, add to the attractions of this apartment.

By the door leading west of this room, which is also
successful as a finish resembling the Miaco or Soochon
lacquers, one enters the dining-room. This is in the style
of the Italian Renaissance, and entirely distinct, in character of treatment, from the other rooms. It consists of an
arrangement of glass-faced cases supported by rich consoles
that rest upon a beautiful wainscot. The wood is English
oak, of a rich, light brown or golden hue of great beauty;
and, after a general impression of the room is received, a
closer examination reveals delicate carving, in different degrees of relief, on almost all surfaces of the component
parts. The elliptical arch ceiling is subdivided into small
oblong panels, carved in reliefs of fruit and foliage, modeled and decorated in various tints of gold. The spaces
between the top of the wainscot and the ceiling, at either
end of the room, and the large centre panel on the ceiling,
are filled with paintings by Lummais of Paris, representing
hunting scenes. The furniture is from special designs, and
the coverings of the chairs are unusually rich and handsome.

At the west end of the hall is the entrance to the picture
gallery, which is also provided with a separate entrance
from Fifty-first street.

The aquarelle room opens on this from above by means of a foyer on the north wall. A balcony for music connects on the east with this gallery of the main hall, and on the south a similar one connects with the conservatory.

The main staircase leads from the north of the main hall, and is lighted by nine glass windows, by John La-Farge, noticeable for the arrangement of color, and especially for the arrangement of greens and blues. Most of the marble, particularly that from Africa, has been especially imported, but the working and finishing have been done in this country.

There are several private residences projected by New York millionaires which are promised to exceed in cost and grandeur that of Commodore Vanderbilt's, and in a few years we may expect to see a dozen palaces with domes and spires kissing the heavens above Fifth avenue. We cannot have royalty, but American moneybags have a penchant for nuncupative titles which the worshipers of aristocracy are quite willing to bestow.

Of the rich men named nearly all have acquired their wealth by inheritance, and are therefore incapable of appreciating their fortunes; they can only live like other men, by eating, and but little money suffices for nature's wants; large investments create anxiety, for with so much wealth in active employment some of their enterprises are languishing while others are profitable; the consolation which the latter may bring is therefore destroyed by the former, and no point is reached where contentment is in full fruition.

But the absence of happiness is more noticeable in the homes of these favored sons of Mammon. Wealth is like blasted fruit if it is not made the means for display, and society only rears its superstructure on a gilded foundation. The rich of New York, speaking always in general terms, are slaves to society, which places them in a straight-jacket of punctilious mannerisms. The parlors and drawing-rooms, though filled with antique bric-a-brac, elegant paintings and the rarest productions of sculptor genius, are animated by senseless conversation, betraying a want of intellectual training. There is scarcely such a thing as domestic privacy—those moments when man and wife may survey the fields of love together and watch the full, round honeymoon as it blazes out upon a sky bejeweled with laughing stars of affection. Under social separation all the sentiment of conjugal devotion and that holy relation becomes pulseless, leaving only bonds of convenience and a mummified love holding them together. Is it strange, under such circumstances, that the rich man's home becomes little less than a sepulchre for young hearts' ambitions, with dead leaves of myrtle entwining Love's sarcophagus?

Life, to the wives and daughters of millionaires, is a problem only in the opportunities they may find for destroying its *ennui;* surfeited with idle vaporings from fawning associates, stupefied by excesses and enervated by a variety of dissipations, existence not infrequently becomes a burden grievous in its oppressiveness.

The abstinence observed during Lent is a blessing only too brief for many women, and the saturnalia which follows wastes the nerve force and vitality that has accumulated. There is no cessation, for if a lady holds membership in an exclusive circle of wealth she must be a part of the social gatherings, *soirees, bal-masques,* weddings, funerals, receptions, dinner parties, private theatricals, fencing practice among sturdy belles, and the endless category of society pastimes. If exhausted nature becomes painfully felt, there is wine to warm the sluggish blood, cosmetics for blanching cheeks and *pastilles* for ageing furrows.

To-night there is a *bal-masque* at Music Hall, at which all first-class society ladies and men of various positions are expected to be present. The hall is magnificently decorated, and an excellent band discourses such music as sets every foot in nervous motion. The ladies are masked beyond recognition, so that little *contretemps* defy remark, and with wine on the brain and music in their feet, there succeeds an uproarious scene of flying limbs, babbling tongues, whispering forms in amorous arms, and all the welkin of an over-excited crowd. As the hours speed by abandon grows more noticeable, and when the gray of dawn bespeaks approaching day, carriages are hastily filled with pot-valiant cavaliers and temulent feminines, crowded together in a wealthy profusion of crinoline, puffs, topees and variegated silk stockings. What a delicious time at the fancy dress ball!

The permissibilities of New York society not only promote discord and alienation, but are equally efficacious in making drunkards, male and female. The rich of to-day may become the poor of to-morrow; speculation runs through the city like an infectious fever, and all classes become victims. A poor man may invest a few spare dollars in stocks and if fortune should place him on the breast of an incoming tide he may gather a harvest of wealth at high-water mark absolutely bewildering. Suddenly accumulated riches become a passport for his family to enter the gay circle of fashion, though ignorance and boorishness be his only inherent characteristics. It is quite sufficient to be rich, regardless of personal qualities or the means employed. A metamorphosis so radical often disconcerts the ephemerally rich and causes them to plunge into excesses which they would have considered abhorrent before their acquisition. Circumstances are the very reverse, when the rich take a tumble under a pressure of bad investments. Fifth avenue princes very often doff their ermine out of deference to adverse fortune, and become street-car drivers, with philosophical if not stoical cheerfulness. Society is therefore a melange of shocking composition, full of idiosyncrasies, if not monstrosities.

Around the festal board of assembled fashionables the cup that cheers makes graceful circuit, nor stops short of the borders of inebriety. Many young men, old ere of age, besotted and degraded in their adolescence, with the slavery of intemperance full upon them, can see through the mists of their reeling brains a vision of some bright-eyed girl with a cup of wine in her jewelled fingers pleading for a social bumper,—forging the first chains which bind the soul to appetite and make them votaries of vice.

Young ladies of aristocratic antecedents are nearly always subjects of superstition, and with intellects fed on puerile sentimentality they become peculiarly susceptible to what are called supernatural influences. But in this respect they are not materially different from men under similar circumstances.

In New York more than in any other American city are the services of spirit mediums and fortune-tellers sought for. Some of the richest men in the Metropolis are in daily communication with these occult philosophers, and are controlled by their advice. It is well known that Singer, the rich sewing machine manufacturer, was a firm believer in Spiritualism; and, moreover, that all his business transactions were conducted upon advice received through mediums at private seances. These facts would never have been known to the general public, perhaps, had they not been disclosed in the courts during a contest of his will, when upon these facts the contestants sought to prove his mental weakness. But there are hundreds of leading men in New York who are controlled by influences identical with those which affected Mr. Singer, though they generally succeed in keeping the truth secret.

Among wealthy women there is an almost general belief in the revelations of fortune-tellers, and particularly in palmistry. There are many *Fata Morganas* in Gotham whose profession yields them a flattering competence, enabling them to maintain sumptuous quarters in fashionable neighborhoods. The all-important question with young ladies is, "Does he love me? is he true?" and for its ascertainment they usually repair to some popular seer, who divines an answer by tracing prominent lines of the palm. If the question should be replied to affirmatively, what lady would refuse the payment of five dollars or more out of her abundance? So it is always "Yes" to fair questions and "No" to the foul, for in pandering to that phase of human nature fortune-tellers see their reward.

"All is vanity," sayeth the preacher, and this clerical aphorism has many illustrations in the ways of the wealthy that prove its truthfulness.

DOCUMENT 20

(PLATE 6)

B. P. Hutchinson ("Old Hutch"), the Great Chicago Grain Operator

SOURCE: Arthur J. Goodman, "B. P. Hutchinson ('Old Hutch'), the Great Chicago Grain Operator" (pen-and-ink drawing), *Harper's Weekly*, XXXIV (10 May 1890), 357.

The lean, angular body and the lounging posture depicted in this full-page portrait on the cover of *Harper's Weekly* were considered characteristically American. The physical type, as the editorial comment points out, was that of Abraham Lincoln. It was represented in folklore by the stereotype of the shrewd Yankee trader (who was apotheosized as Uncle Sam), and it appeared in fiction both in Henry James's Christopher Newman (protagonist of *The American*, 1877) and in Mark Twain's Hank Morgan (of *A Connecticut Yankee in King Arthur's Court*, 1889). The editorial writer attributes to Hutchinson the traits of character regularly associated with the self-made tycoon: "judgment, the instinct of industry, audacity, and grit." It is significant that although speculating in commodities is explicitly distinguished from "more legitimate business," the activities of this full-time speculator are described with no hint of moral censure:

"Hutch" was trained in New England, and in his youth went West, and succeeded there by reason of his pluck and energy. He "grew up with the country," and made for himself all that could be made from the early development of a Western city—of Chicago. To succeed thus is to succeed as a matter of course; it is to make the most of the opportunities. Anticipating the requirements of a growing community, "Hutch" early allied himself with the enterprises to provide them. He was a pioneer in the pork-packing industry of the West, and active in establishing a business that profited by his foresight and ability. He is not to be regarded as phenomenal because he has made so much money; he is rather to be regarded as an expression of a force. He had judgment, the instinct of industry, audacity, and grit, and now, at sixty-three, these qualities remain unimpaired.

"Hutch" is striking in appearance. Tall, erect, with a deep sunken eye that takes in everything, with a memory that forgets nothing, he moves about the Chicago Board of Trade seemingly isolated from every member, but the most progressive factor in it. He dresses in black, is seldom seen without his felt hat, and when in repose reminds one of President Lincoln as he appeared in 1861.

A speculator, such a one as "Hutch" is—for he long since neglected his more legitimate business—must possess superior discernment, nerve, and be able to command the best information. Operations in products are conducted on what seem to be the most reasonable grounds, with a fine calculation for chances. While the factors of demand and supply establish the tendency of values for a long-run, the constant interruption in the movement toward higher or lower prices results in fluctuations, of which it is the province of the speculator to take advantage. "Old Hutch" is skilled in counter operations against the well-laid plans of other speculators, and he delights in leading in an action contrary to the apparent logic of the situation.*

The tone of this article would have been inconceivable in the 1870s, when speculation was regularly condemned as mere gambling, and admirers of a Vanderbilt or a Gould maintained that these men were not speculating but creating new wealth by their organizing and administrative genius. Even twenty years later, the morality of speculation was still open to debate. During the previous year, *Harper's Weekly* had serialized William Dean Howells' *A Hazard of New Fortunes*, in which Jacob Dryfoos is denounced because his great wealth has been gained through speculation in stocks

* *Harper's Weekly*, XXXIV (10 May 1890), 367.

without his making any real contribution to the welfare of society. On the other hand, by 1903 Frank Norris would make a speculator in wheat, Curtis Jadwin, protagonist of *The Pit*, allowing him a certain grandeur even in defeat; and after another decade Theodore Dreiser would depict his amoral financier and master speculator Frank Cowperwood as a superman whom the author explicitly admired.

PART III

The City
DIVES AND LAZARUS

DOCUMENT 21

New York

SOURCE: Mary L. Booth, ["New York"], from *History of the City of New York*, 2 vols. (New York, 1851, rev. 1867), II, 879–81.

For the general public, the most conspicuous results of industrial development in the post-Civil War decades were the creation of a new group of multimillionaires and the dramatic growth of cities as the centers of manufacturing and finance. The increase in the population of Chicago from only a little more than one hundred thousand in 1860 to more than a million and a half in 1900 was the most spectacular example of urbanization in this period, but New York was the undoubted center of the new economic system. In the same period, it grew from about one million inhabitants to almost three millions and a half; and its financial power far outstripped that of its competitors. The melodramatic contrast between the garish opulence of Fifth Avenue and the squalor of slums in the lower reaches of Manhattan was a constant theme of discussion. As Josiah Strong remarks in Document 23, "It is the city where wealth is massed; . . . Dives and Lazarus are brought fact to face."

The varied materials collected here do not exhaust the range of attitudes expressed by contemporary observers. For example, Walt Whitman's delight in the sheer spectacle of the streets of Manhattan in the 1850s was echoed many times in later decades. On the other hand, William Dean Howells suggests that his character Basil March (in *A Hazard of New Fortunes*) is guilty of callousness when he enjoys the streets of the city as mere theater and finds the "low life" of the slums "immensely picturesque."

The conventional view of New York inherited from an earlier period is illustrated in the concluding paragraphs of Mary L. Booth's history, first published in 1851, with a revised edition in 1867. A native of Long Island, Miss Booth became a celebrated figure during the Civil War, when she translated French works useful to the anti-slavery cause. In 1867 she became editor of *Harper's Bazar,* and continued in this position until a short time before her death more than twenty years later.

. . . in palatial splendor, in gorgeous magnificence, and in lavish display of inexhaustible wealth, New York may well be regarded as bearing off the palm from all other cities in the Union. Yet were this all, did her claims to her proud title of the Empire City rest merely upon the power of riches, were she but the Golden City, the Venice of the Western Continent, then indeed we might tremble for her future, sure that the seeds of decay were lurking in her heart. But that she has played a far different part in the history of her country, her annals give sufficient proof. The first to practice that religious freedom which the Eastern colonists emigrated from the Old World to secure for themselves only to deny to others, and to throw open her doors to the poor and oppressed of her sister settlements; the first to vindicate the freedom of the press; the first to enter a practical protest against the arbitrary Stamp Act by dooming herself to commercial ruin; the first to shed her blood on the battle-fields of the Revolution, and the chief in furnishing the sinews of war without which the late gigantic conflict could never have been conducted to a successful termination, New York has not falsified in maturer years the promises of her youth. Not only has she given an impetus to gigantic schemes of internal improvement that challenge the admiration of the whole world—the Ocean Telegraph, the Steamboat, the Erie Canal, the Croton Aqueduct and the magnificent Central Park; not only does she, by her open-handed liberality, attract to herself men of science, enterprise, and broad and earnest thought, ingenious mechanics, far-seeing merchants, talented artists, and brilliant literary men, but she has fostered within her own bosom statesmen, philosophers, inventors, and authors, who may compete advantageously with any in the world. . . .

The future destiny of New York rests with the present generation; their verdict must decide whether she will patiently bear the name of the Golden City, by some so tauntingly bestowed upon her, or vindicate herself not only by past proof but by present action. That it is in her power, through her immense resources, her boundless wealth, her buoyant elasticity, her composite population, the vast array of talent which lies at her disposal, and most of all, by the breadth, cosmopolitanism and geniality of the character of her people, to mould herself into what she will—to become the Athens of America, the centre of culture and of art—must be evident to all. Her fate is in her own hands; whether her future fame is to rest on marble palaces or erudite universities—on well-filled warehouses or wealth of brain, she alone can decide. Let her but choose the latter position—let her but expend her wealth, regardless of outside display, in fostering talent, in encouraging art, in attracting to herself by liberal patronage the intellectual power of the whole country, in endowing universities, and in developing the mental resources of her own citizens, not by a lavish expenditure of money alone, but by an earnest appreciation of talent, and the time is not far distant when she will be cordially acknowledged, both by friends and foes, as the EMPIRE CITY, not only of the UNION but also of the WORLD!

DOCUMENT 22

Testimony before the Senate Committee on Education and Labor

SOURCE: Edward H. Ludlow, Testimony before the Senate Committee on Education and Labor, New York, 29 August 1883 (*Report of the Committee*, Vol. I, 830–31).

At the beginning of his appearance before the Committee, Ludlow (then in his seventies) described himself as "an auctioneer and real-estate broker," a native and lifelong resident of New York. He recalled that when he was a boy, "there was not many houses above Canal Street," and in illustrating the rise in prices paid for real estate in the city he said that he had recently been offered $300,000 for six lots adjoining Central Park which had sold for $40,000 twenty years before. Ludlow's remark that "anybody who is industrious and anxious to do right will get along here" illustrates the comfortable outlook of an earlier day, before the "influx of people of large wealth" and the appearance of a "fashionable society."

[NEW YORK, *August 29, 1883*]

[EDWARD H. LUDLOW sworn and examined.]

By the CHAIRMAN:

Q. I take it, from what I learn of you, that you have known as intimately as anybody the business growth of the city of New York for a lifetime. You have resided here always yourself?—A. Yes, sir; except for three or four years.

Q. Your business has been dealing in real estate in a large way?—A. Yes, sir.

Q. You have witnessed the growth of the city ever since you came to years of discretion?—A. Yes, sir.

NEW YORK, PAST AND PRESENT

Q. Such a man must know a great deal outside of real-estate. I wish, therefore, that you would tell us how things have been in New York for as long as you can remember.

The WITNESS. Do you mean socially?

The CHAIRMAN. Socially, financially, industrially—I do not care about politically at all, but I want you to tell us how the old times and the more recent times compare in these other respects, in your judgment.

The WITNESS. We old fellows, you know, always think that the old times were a great deal the best.

The CHAIRMAN. All right. We will concede that. It is just the kind of information which an old man who has a great deal of knowledge on the subject can give us young people that we want.

A. Well, in answer to your question, I will say, that I think the people who lived here a good many years ago, back about 1825 and 1830, were a great deal happier than people are now. They did not have so much money, but they had plenty of social good feeling; everybody knew everybody; there were but very few great establishments in New York then, and the man who was worth $100,000 was looked upon as a pretty rich man. At that time we had a population composed very largely of Dutch and English elements; they were very conservative people; they did not like to venture much on the ice. At that time this city was a pleasant place of residence. It was more like a large village, more like some of our western villages in this State now. A man was known then and he could not shirk anything. He was known by his acts, and pretty much everybody who had any standing or character was well known and appreciated in this community. Now, sometimes the most brillant characters are appreciated more than the more modest ones. I think New York is a very nice place still, but I think they are carrying the love of show a great deal beyond common sense.

Q. It costs some money, too, does it not?—A. Yes, and I am sorry to see it. It is due in a great degree to the influx of people of large wealth who come here and want to show how much they are worth, and they not only make a display of their wealth but also of artificial foreign manners and things of that kind, all seeking to seem to be as rich as Mr. Vanderbilt or any other of those big capitalists.

Q. Your idea is that their example begets emulation among those who are not able to spend so much?—A. That is what I am driving at. That is the fact, and I am sorry to see it.

Q. Do you say that that is becoming very prevalent?—A. It seems to be among our richer men, and also among men who are not quite so rich. The general desire seems to be to make a great display. Some of our old Knickerbockers hold back and are modest and plain as they ever were, but there is a fascination about fashionable society that leads most people into making these displays.

Q. Do you think that that spirit which is communicated from the wealthy to the classes nearer them, is transmitted all the way down until it affects society clear down to the humblest?—A. I think so. I know that girls that used to be satisfied with calicoes and muslins want silk gowns now. You see them yourselves in the streets and you see how they are dressed. They all must have ostrich feathers in their hats now, no matter how hard they have to work for a living.

Q. There are a great many poor people in this city. The evidence that we have taken here shows that, and anybody can see it?—A. Yes; there are a great many poor people. The very poor people probably have themselves to blame generally, except in some cases. There is always a chance of making a living in this city for anybody who wants to do right. There is plenty of employment. There may be some exceptions to the rule, as there are to every rule, but I think that anybody who is industrious and anxious to do right will get along here.

Perils.—The City

SOURCE: Josiah Strong, "Perils.—The City," from *Our Country: Its Possible Future and Its Present Crisis* (New York, 1885), pp. 128–44.

Our Country was intended to gain support for the Protestant home missionary endeavor, especially in the West, somewhat in the manner of Lyman Beecher's celebrated pamphlet *A Plea for the West* (1835). It expressed so accurately the growing social concern of the leading denominations that 130,000 copies were sold within five years, and chapters were widely reprinted in newspapers throughout the country. The author was a clergyman who had served as Secretary for the Congregational Home Missionary Society in Ohio, Kentucky, West Virginia, and western Pennsylvania, and was General Secretary of the Evangelical Alliance for the United States. His special gift as a writer was the power to create by rhetorical means, including the skillful use of statistics and rudimentary charts, a sense of crisis facing the country and the world. Another source of his appeal was the jingoism which was blended with his genuine concern for the survival of Protestant Christianity. Eight years before the young Frederick Jackson Turner published his paper "The Influence of the Frontier in American History" in 1893, Strong proclaimed that the United States would face a climactic test of its power to survive when free land in the West should be exhausted—an event he considered imminent. His portrayal of the city as unnatural and threatening bespeaks a deep-rooted conviction that the authentic America is rural and pre-industrial. It is this half-imaginary agrarian society that faces the "perils" enumerated in Strong's chapter headings. His extensive quotation from Henry George's *Social Problems* (1886) attests George's status as spokesman for widely divergent forms of alarm over the problems created by industrialization.

The city is the nerve center of our civilization. It is also the storm center. The fact, therefore, that it is growing much more rapidly than the whole population is full of significance. In 1790 one-thirtieth of the population of the United States lived in cities of 8,000 inhabitants and over; in 1800, one twenty-fifth; in 1810, and also in 1820, one-twentieth; in 1830, one sixteenth; in 1840, one-twelfth; in 1850, one-eighth; in 1860, one-sixth; in 1870, a little over one-fifth; and in 1880, 22.5 per cent., or nearly one-fourth.* From 1790 to 1880 the whole population increased twelve fold, the urban population eighty-six fold. From 1830 to 1880 the whole population increased a little less than four fold, the urban population thirteen fold. From 1870 to 1880 the whole population increased thirty per cent., the urban population forty per cent. During the half century preceding 1880, population in the city increased more than four times as rapidly as that of the village and country. In 1800 there were only six cities in the United States which had a population of 8,000 or more. In 1880 there were 286.

The city has become a serious menace to our civilization, because in it, excepting Mormonism, each of the dangers we have discussed is enhanced, and all are focalized. It has a peculiar attraction for the immigrant. Our fifty principal cities contain 39.3 per cent. of our entire German population, and 45.8 per cent. of the Irish. Our ten larger cities contain only nine per cent. of the entire population, but 23 per cent. of the foreign. While a little less than one-third of the population of the United States is foreign by birth or parentage, sixty-two per cent. of the population of Cincinnati are foreign, eighty-three per cent.

* "Compendium of the Tenth Census," Part I., pp. xxx and 8. [The footnotes in this document are those of the author, not the editor.]

of Cleveland, sixty-three per cent. of Boston, eighty per cent. of New York, and ninety-one per cent. of Chicago.†

Because our cities are so largely foreign, Romanism finds in them its chief strength.

For the same reason the saloon, together with the intemperance and the liquor power which it represents, is multiplied in the city. East of the Mississippi there was, in 1880, one saloon to every 438 of the population; in Boston, one to every 329; in Cleveland, one to every 192; in Chicago, one to every 179; in New York, one to every 171; in Cincinnati, one to every 124. Of course the demoralizing and pauperizing power of the saloons and their debauching influence in politics increase with their numerical strength.

It is the city where wealth is massed; and here are the tangible evidences of it piled many stories high. Here the sway of Mammon is widest, and his worship the most constant and eager. Here are luxuries gathered—everything that dazzles the eye, or tempts the appetite; here is the most extravagant expenditure. Here, also, is the *congestion* of wealth the severest. Dives and Lazarus are brought face to face; here, in sharp contrast, are the *ennui* of surfeit and the desperation of starvation. The rich are richer, and the poor are poorer, in the city than elsewhere; and, as a rule, the greater the city, the greater are the riches of the rich and the poverty of the poor. Not only does the proportion of the poor increase with the growth of the city, but their condition becomes more wretched. . . . Is it strange that such conditions arouse a blind and bitter hatred of our social system?

Socialism not only centers in the city, but is almost confined to it; and the materials of its growth are multiplied with the growth of the city. Here is heaped the social

† The Compendium of the Tenth Census gives the number of persons, foreign-born, in each of the fifty principal cities, but does not give the native-born population of foreign parentage. We are enabled to compute it, however, by knowing that the total number of foreigners and their children of the first generation is, according to the Census, 2.24 times larger than the total number of foreign-born.

dynamite; here roughs, gamblers, thieves, robbers, lawless and desperate men of all sorts, congregate; men who are ready on any pretext to raise riots for the purpose of destruction and plunder; here gather foreigners and wage-workers; here skepticism and irreligion abound; here inequality is the greatest and most obvious, and the contrast between opulence and penury the most striking; here is suffering the sorest. As the greatest wickedness in the world is to be found not among the cannibals of some far off coast, but in Christian lands where the light of truth is diffused and rejected, so the utmost depth of wretchedness exists not among savages, who have few wants, but in great cities, where, in the presence of plenty and of every luxury men starve. Let a man become the owner of a home, and he is much less susceptible to socialistic propagandism. But real estate is so high in the city that it is almost impossible for a wage-worker to become a householder. The law in New York requires a juror to be owner of real or personal property valued at not less than two hundred and fifty dollars; and this, the Commissioner says, relieves seventy thousand of the registered voters of New York City from jury duty. Let us remember that those seventy thousand voters represent a population of two hundred and eighty thousand, or fifty-six thousand families, not one of which has property to the value of two hundred and fifty dollars. "During the past three years, 220,976 persons in New York have asked for outside aid in one form or another."‡ Said a New York Supreme Judge, not long since: "There is a large class —I was about to say a majority—of the population of New York and Brooklyn, who just live, and to whom the rearing of two or more children means inevitably a boy for the penitentiary, and a girl for the brothel."§ Under such conditions smolder the volcanic fires of a deep discontent.

We have seen how the dangerous elements of our civilization are each multiplied and all concentered in the city. Do we find there the conservative forces of society equally numerous and strong? Here are the tainted spots

‡ Mrs. J. S. Lowell, in *The Christian Union*, March 26th, 1885.
§ Henry George's "Social Problems," p. 98.

in the body-politic; where is the salt? In 1880 there was in the United States one Evangelical church organization to every 516 of the population. In Boston there is one church to every 1,600 of the population; in Chicago, one to 2,081; in New York, one to 2,468; in St. Louis, one to 2,800. The city, where the forces of evil are massed, and where the need of Christian influence is peculiarly great, is from one-third to one-fifth as well supplied with churches as the nation at large. And church accommodations in the city are growing more inadequate every year. . . .

If moral and religious influences are peculiarly weak at the point where our social explosives are gathered, what of city government? Are its strength and purity so exceptional as to insure the effective control of these dangerous elements? In the light of notorious facts, the question sounds satirical. It is commonly said in Europe, and sometimes acknowledged here, that the government of large cities in the United States is a failure. "In all the great American cities there is to-day as clearly defined a ruling class as in the most aristocratic countries in the world. Its members carry wards in their pockets, make up the slates for nominating conventions, distribute offices as they bargain together, and—though they toil not, neither do they spin—wear the best of raiment and spend money lavishly. They are men of power, whose favor the ambitious must court, and whose vengeance he must avoid. Who are these men? The wise, the good, the learned—men who have earned the confidence of their fellow-citizens by the purity of their lives, the splendor of their talents, their probity in public trusts, their deep study of the problems of government? No; they are gamblers, saloon-keepers, pugilists, or worse, who have made a trade of controlling votes and of buying and selling offices and official acts."❡ It has come to this, that holding a municipal office in a large city almost impeaches a man's character. Known integrity and competency hopelessly incapacitate a man for any office in the gift of a city rabble. In a certain western city, the administration of the

❡ "Progress and Poverty," p. 382.

mayor had convinced good citizens that he gave constant aid and comfort to gamblers, thieves, saloon-keepers, and all the worst elements of society. He became a candidate for a second term. The prominent men and press of both parties and the ministry of all denominations united in a Citizens' League to defeat him; but he was triumphantly returned to office by the "lewd fellows of the baser sort." And now, after a desperate struggle on the part of the better elements to defeat him, he has been re-elected to a third term of office.

Popular government in the city is degenerating into government by a "boss." During his visit to this country Herbert Spencer said: "You retain the forms of freedom; but, so far as I can gather, there has been a considerable loss of the substance. It is true that those who rule you do not do it by means of retainers armed with swords; but they do it through regiments of men armed with voting papers, who obey the word of command as loyally as did the dependents of the old feudal nobles, and who thus enable their leaders to override the general will, and make the community submit to their exactions as effectually as their prototypes of old. Manifestly those who framed your Constitution never dreamed that twenty thousand citizens would go to the polls led by a 'boss.'"

As a rule, our largest cities are the worst governed. It is natural, therefore, to infer that, as our cities grow larger and more dangerous, the government will become more corrupt, and control will pass more completely into the hands of those who themselves most need to be controlled. If we would appreciate the significance of these facts and tendencies, we must bear in mind that the disproportionate growth of the city is undoubtedly to continue, and the number of great cities to be largely increased. The extraordinary growth of urban population during this century has not been at all peculiar to the United States. It is a characteristic of nineteenth century civilization. In England and Wales two-thirds of the entire population are found in cities of 3,000 inhabitants and over, and the urban population is growing nearly twice as rapidly as that of the country. And this growth of the city is taking place not only in England and Germany, where the increase of population is rapid, but also in France, where population is practically stationary, and even in Ireland, where it is declining. This strong tendency toward the city is the result chiefly of manufacturers and railway communication, and their influence will, of course, continue. If the growth of the city in the United States has been so rapid during this century, while many millions of acres were being settled, what may be expected when the settlement of the West has been completed? The rapid rise in the value of lands will stimulate yet more the growth of the city; for the man of small means will be unable to command a farm, and the town will become his only alternative. When the public lands are all taken, immigration, though it will be considerably restricted thereby, will continue, and will crowd the cities more and more. This country will undoubtedly have a population of several hundred millions, for the simple reason that it is capable of sustaining that number. And it looks as if the larger proportion of it would be urban. There can be no indefinite increase of our agricultural population. Its growth must needs be slow after the farms are all taken, and it is necessarily limited; but the cities may go on doubling and doubling again. Unless the growth of population is very greatly and unexpectedly retarded, many who are adults to-day will live to see 200,000,000 inhabitants in the United States, and a number greater than our present population—over 50,000,000—living in cities of 8,000 and upwards. And the city of the future will be more crowded than that of to-day, because the elevator makes it possible to build, as it were, one city above another. Thus is our civilization multiplying and focalizing the elements of anarchy and destruction. Nearly forty years ago De Tocqueville wrote: "I look upon the size of certain American cities, and especially upon the nature of their population, as a real danger which threatens the security of the democratic republics of the New World." That danger grows more real and imminent every year. . . .

These dangerous elements are now working, and will continue to work, incalculable harm and loss—moral, intellectual, social, pecuniary. But the supreme peril, which will certainly come, eventually, and must probably be faced by multitudes now living, will arise, when, the conditions having been fully prepared, some great industrial or other crisis precipitates an open struggle between the destructive and the conservative elements of society. As civilization advances, and society becomes more highly organized, commercial transactions will be more complex and immense. As a result, all business relations and industries will be more sensitive. Commercial distress in any great business center will the more surely create widespread disaster. Under such conditions, industrial paralysis is likely to occur from time to time, more general and more prostrating than any heretofore known. When such a commercial crisis has closed factories by the ten thousand, and wage-workers have been thrown out of employment by the million; when the public lands, which hitherto at such times have afforded relief, are all exhausted; when our urban population has been multiplied several fold, and our Cincinnatis have become Chicagos, our Chicagos New Yorks, and our New Yorks Londons; when class antipathies are deepened; when socialistic organizations, armed and drilled, are in every city, and the ignorant and vicious power of crowded populations has fully found itself; when the corruption of city governments is grown apace; when crops fail, or some gigantic "corner" doubles the price of bread; with starvation in the home; with idle workmen gathered, sullen and desperate, in the saloons; with unprotected wealth at hand; with the tremendous forces of chemistry within easy reach; then, with *the opportunity, the means, the fit agents, the motive, the temptation to destroy, all brought into evil conjunction,* THEN will come the real test of our institutions, then will appear whether we are capable of self-government.

DOCUMENT 24

(PLATE 7)

A Blockade on Broadway

SOURCE: Taylor and Meeker [first names unknown], "A Blockade on Broadway" (pen-and-ink drawing), *Harper's Weekly*, XXVII (29 December 1883), 845.

The picture represents a view northward along Broadway from a point just south of its intersection with Park Row, which comes in from the northeast. In the immediate foreground is Fulton Street. At the left is the rear portico of St. Paul's Church (1766), with a section of its graveyard—the rather forlorn tree providing a note of contrast with the hurlyburly of traffic just outside. The imposing structure at the visual center is the New York Post Office, completed in 1878 (demolished 1939). It was designed by Alfred B. Mullett (1834–90), Supervising Architect of the Treasury Department, and various New York architects. Benson J. Lossing, in his *History of New York City* (New York and Chicago, 1884, p. 532), says that "The architecture is a mixture of the Doric and the Renaissance, and the material of the walls is a light-colored granite from Dix Island, Maine." Behind the Post Office to the north is City Hall Park.

The highly anecdotal drawing strikes a true New York note. The congestion of traffic is obviously intolerable, and the pedestrians risk life and limb merely by being in the street. Yet the artist finds a grotesque comedy in the scene, sustained perhaps by a sense of participating in the incredible outpouring of energy. The city is so vast and vital that it can function even at the cost of appalling waste and discomfort institutionalized in the daily routine. Although the tone of the drawing is comic, a pertinent commentary on it is provided by James W.

Buel in his *Mysteries and Miseries of America's Great Cities:*

The first visit to New York is always productive of a singular sensation—a realization of your utter inconsequence in the world; a feeling that every one who swells the crowd and rush of Broadway is of infinitely more importance than yourself, and that you are as much out of your sphere as though some mighty occult force had suddenly transported you to a strange planet, the inhabitants of which were rushing wildly about in their efforts to destroy themselves and every world in the infinite firmament. In such a mass of princes and beggars, natives and strangers, the visitor is kept dodging, halting and shuffling to avoid the pressing throng, which, though utterly unobserving, he believes are tickling themselves at his unsophisticated and ludicrous actions. The confusing rattle of 'busses and wagons over the granite pavement in Broadway almost drowns his own thoughts, and if he should desire to cross the street a thousand misgivings will assail him, for although he sees scores of men and women constantly passing through the moving lines of vehicles, it gives him little courage to attempt it himself, because his confidence has deserted him the moment he leaves the car that has brought him to the city. It happens, therefore, not infrequently that a stranger will suffer the pressure of a hurrying and jostling crowd on the sidewalk for an hour before plucking up sufficient resolution to attempt a crossing, and even when the effort is made he feels like shutting his eyes to hide from sight the result.*

* *Mysteries and Miseries of America's Great Cities* (San Francisco, 1883), pp. 26–28.

DOCUMENT 25

The Great Fancy Dress Ball

source: William A. Croffut, ["The Great Fancy Dress Ball"],
from *The Vanderbilts and the Story of Their Fortune* (Chicago,
1886), pp. 192–97.

Croffut presents a newspaperman's factual account of
the dazzling amusements of the new millionaire class
that supplies concrete meaning for Miss Booth's reference to "marble palaces" and Edward Ludlow's statement
that the rich "are carrying the love of show a great
deal beyond common sense." The old Commodore had
seemed "a most kingly looking man" to a newspaper
reporter (Document 15), but this was a matter of
physical presence rather than costume. In the "royal
entertainment" described here, the next generation is
embarked on a conscious emulation of past grandeurs.
The William K. Vanderbilt mansion is a reproduction
of a renaissance French chateau; it is adorned with
antique Italian tapestries; the hostess personates a Venetian princess; her husband is dressed as the Duke de
Guise; various guests wear the costumes of glamorous
European aristocrats, including "the old German court
costume"; and Cornelius Vanderbilt II appears as Louis
XVI. One is charmed to learn, however, that his wife
represents "the Electric Light," in a costume emphasiz-
ing diamonds.

The Vanderbilts obtained their first secure foothold in
New York's leading society by the great fancy-dress ball
given by Mrs. William K. Vanderbilt in her beautiful
house at Fifth Avenue and Fifty-third Street on the evening
of March 26, 1883, which was an event never before

equaled in the social annals of the metropolis, and one that interested the whole country. It is impossible to give here more than a brief outline of this truly marvelous entertainment, which surpassed in splendor, in beauty, in brilliancy, and in luxurious and lavish expense any scene before witnessed in the new world.

For weeks beforehand the costumers, milliners, and dressmakers, not only of New York, but of all the larger eastern cities, were engaged in preparing the richest and most varied of garments for this wonderful entertainment. Histories, novels, and illustrated books of all periods were ransacked by the expectant guests to obtain either suggestions or models upon which their own costumes could be patterned. All else was forgotten in society during the forty days of Lenten penitence which preceded the event, and the most improbable and fantastic tales and rumors of the forthcoming splendor were constantly circulated in the community. Even the daily press became affected by the prevailing excitement which the ball occasioned in the atmosphere, and assigned their ablest and most skilled reporters for two weeks beforehand to the preparation of lists of the costumes of the guests and more or less accurate foreshadowings of the event. In fact they devoted more attention to it, than they have ever done before or since to any purely social affair.

Although Mrs. W. H. Vanderbilt had already given a ball in her own palace which was largely and fashionably attended, and although the names of two or three of her daughters and daughters-in-law had already figured as patronesses of the distinctive society balls of the metropolis, two or three of the leaders of New York society, notably Mrs. William Astor, had never called upon any of the ladies of the Vanderbilt family. It was Lady Mandeville, who with her family had been making Mrs. W. K. Vanderbilt a visit of a year, who first suggested the entertainment to her hostess, and it is largely due to her society experience, cleverness, and tact that the ball was in every way the grandest ever given on this continent, and one which fully established the Vanderbilt family as

THE CITY   183

social leaders. According to the generally accepted story
in society, soon after the first announcement of the ball
Miss Carrie Astor, the only unmarried daughter of Mrs.
William Astor, organized a fancy-dress quadrille to be
danced at the ball by several young ladies and gentlemen.
Mrs. Vanderbilt heard of this, and stated in the hearing of
some friends that she regretted that she could not invite
Miss Astor to her ball, as her mother had never called
upon her. This reached Mrs. Astor's ears, and soon afterward she called upon Mrs. Vanderbilt and they were
invited. Thus did the ball break the last barriers down.

The brilliant scene was well framed in one of the most
beautiful of New York houses—the reproduction of one
of those fascinating chateaux of the French renaissance
which are the pride of Touraine. Seen, as it was on the
night of this entertainment, under a blaze of light, and
kindled into splendor everywhere by masses of flowers
and a moving throng of varied and magnificent costumes,
it was the most fitting frame-work an artist could have
asked for a succession of pictures so heterogeneous, so incongruous in detail, yet in their general effect so dazzling
and so attractive. The guests, on arriving, found themselves in a grand hall about 65 feet long, 16 feet in height,
and 20 feet in width. Under their feet was a floor of
polished and luminous marble, and above them a ceiling
richly paneled in oak, while over a high wainscoting of
richly-carved Caen stone hung antique Italian tapestries.
Over this hall, to the right, rose a grand stairway of the
finest Caen stone, carved with superb delicacy and vigor,
to the height of fifty feet.

By eleven o'clock the members of the six organized
quadrilles assembled in the gymnasium, on the third floor,
a beautiful apartment, 50 feet in length by 35 feet in
width. These quadrilles, six in number, comprised in all
nearly a hundred ladies and gentlemen, and, having
formed in the gymnasium in order, they moved in a glittering processional pageant down the grand stairway and
through the hall into a room in the front of the house
fitted and furnished in the style of Francis I., 25 feet in

width by 40 in length, whose whole wainscoting of carved
French walnut was brought from a chateau in France, and
whose ceiling was painted by Paul Baudry. Thence the
procession swept on into the spacious dining-hall, which
was converted for a night into a ball-room, and the dancing
began.

The first quadrille was the "hobby horse," led by Mr.
J. V. Parker and Mrs. S. S. Howland, a daughter of Mr.
August Belmont. The horses took two months in construction. They were of life-size, covered with genuine hides,
and were light enough to be easily and comfortably attached to the waists of the wearers. The costumes for the
men were red hunting-coats, white satin vests, yellow satin
knee-breeches, and white satin stockings. The ladies wore
red hunting-coats and white satin skirts, elegantly embroidered. The other quadrilles danced were the "Mother
Goose," led by Mr. Oliver Northcote and Mrs. Lawrence
Perkins, in which the famous characters of Mother Goose
were personated; the "Opera Bouffe," the "Star," the
"Dresden China," and the "Go-as-you-please." In the
"Star" quadrille, which was organized by Mrs. William
Astor, the ladies were arrayed as twin stars, in yellow,
blue, and white. The "Dresden China" quadrille, in which
the dancers personated those dainty porcelain figures of
the famous pottery, was perhaps the most notable of the
evening, and even the photographs in costume of those
who appeared in it are cherished as household treasures
to-day. The dancers all wore ivory-white satin costumes,
every appurtenance of which was pure white; their hair
was powdered and dressed high. The gentlemen wore the
old German court costume of white satin knee-breeches
and powdered wigs, while the two crossed swords, the mark
of the Dresden factory, were embroidered on all the costumes.

Among the hundreds of striking and unique costumes
only a very few can possibly be noted. Mrs. W. K. Vanderbilt herself personated a Venetian princess, as painted
by Cabanel. The underskirt of her dress was of white and
yellow brocade, shading from the deepest orange to the

lightest canary, while the figures of flowers and leaves were outlined in gold and white and iridescent beads; her white satin train was embroidered magnificently in gold, and lined with Roman red. The waist was of blue satin covered with gold embroidery, and on her head was a Venetian cap covered with magnificent jewels, among them a peacock in many-colored gems.

Lady Mandeville, who received the guests with Mrs. Vanderbilt, wore a costume copied from a picture by Vandyke of the Princess Marie-Claire Decroy.

Mr. W. K. Vanderbilt appeared as the Duke de Guise; Mr. Cornelius Vanderbilt as Louis XVI. Mrs. Cornelius Vanderbilt went as the Electric Light, in white satin trimmed with diamonds, and with a superb diamond head-dress. Miss Amide Smith, Mrs. Vanderbilt's sister, came as a peacock, in a dazzling costume of peacock-blue satin, and Mrs. Seward Webb, Mr. Vanderbilt's sister, as a hornet, with a brilliant waist of yellow satin with a brown velvet skirt and brown gauze wings. Other notable costumes were those worn by Miss Work, as Joan of Arc; by Miss Edith Fish, as Marie Antoinette; by Miss Turnure, as an Egyptian Princess, and by Mrs. Bradley Martin, as Marie Stuart. The Duc du Morny wore a court dress; Madam Christine Nilsson a mourning costume of the time of Henry III.; Mrs. Pierre Lorillard appeared as a Phoenix, and Mr. Hurlburt as a Spanish knight.

It was a royal entertainment, which had never before been equaled in the social annals of America, and which it is probable will not be surpassed for many years to come. It was the wonder not only of the year but of the decade, and the Vanderbilt ball will be remembered when other events much greater in their significance and in their bearing on the time have been quite forgotten.

The World of Fashion

SOURCE: Ward McAllister, ["The World of Fashion"], from *Society as I Have Found It* (New York, 1890), pp. 160–62, 210–17, 233–36.

McAllister, son of a Northern mother and a Southern father, grew up in Savannah, Georgia, but entered the practice of law with his father and brother in San Francisco in 1850. In two years he made a comfortable fortune which, with the inherited wealth of his wife, enabled him to devote all his great energies to perfecting the practice of Society as an art. He spent a few years in Europe learning food and wine, and making distinguished social connections (especially in England); then revolutionized entertaining in the summer colony of the rich at Newport, Rhode Island; and by the late 1860s had established himself as the social arbiter of New York. The capsule rationalization of the social utility of fashionable life reprinted here is no more than half-hearted; McAllister's true commitment was to elegant entertaining as an end in itself, needing no justification. His establishment of the Patriarchs in 1872 was, from his standpoint, a necessary revolution in the social habits of upper-class life in the city to accommodate the more presentable among the new-rich families of the Gilded Age. After he had stabilized New York Society and supervised it for two decades, he attained his greatest notoriety in 1892, only a few years before his death, when he assisted Mrs. William Astor in pruning the guest list for a ball to four hundred— the figure at which he set the limits of those who really belonged to the fashionable world of New York. His unquestioning faith in the self-evident importance of elegance in food, wine, costume, and the ritual of social intercourse impresses the reader with a kind of inno-

cence, but at the same time McAllister's almost fero-
cious concern with technique resembles the industrial
ethos of the era.

The mistake made by the world at large is that fashionable people are selfish, frivolous, and indifferent to the
welfare of their fellow-creatures; all of which is a popular
error, arising simply from a want of knowledge of the true
state of things. The elegancies of fashionable life nourish
and benefit art and artists; they cause the expenditure of
money and its distribution; and they really prevent our
people and country from settling down into a humdrum
rut and becoming merely a money-making and money-
saving people, with nothing to brighten up and enliven
life; they foster all the fine arts; but for fashion what
would become of them? They bring to the front merit of
every kind; seek it in the remotest corners, where it modestly shrinks from observation, and force it into notice;
adorn their houses with works of art, and themselves with
all the taste and novelty they can find in any quarter of
the globe, calling forth talent and ingenuity. Fashionable
people cultivate and refine themselves, for fashion demands this of them. Progress is fashion's watchword; it
never stands still; it always advances, it values and ap-
preciates beauty in woman and talent and genius in man.
It is certainly always most charitable; it surrounds itself
with the elegancies of life; it soars, it never crawls. I know
the general belief is that all fashionable people are hollow
and heartless. My experience is quite the contrary. I have
found as warm, sympathetic, loving hearts in the garb of
fashion as out of it. A thorough acquaintance with the
world enables them to distinguish the wheat from the
chaff, so that all the good work they do is done with knowledge and effect. The world could not dispense with it.
Fashion selects its own votaries. You will see certain members of a family born to it, as it were, others of the same
family with none of its attributes. You can give no explanation of this; "One is taken, the other left." Such and such a
man or woman are cited as having been always fashiona-

ble. The talent of and for society develops itself just as does the talent for art.

. . . I resolved in 1872 to establish in New York an American Almack's, taking men instead of women, being careful to select only the leading representative men of the city, who had the right to create and lead society. I knew all would depend upon our making a proper selection. . . . I went in this city to those who could make the best analysis of men; who knew their past as well as their present, and could foresee their future. In this way, I made up an Executive Committee of three gentlemen, who daily met at my house, and we went to work in earnest to make a list of those we should ask to join in the undertaking. One of this Committee, a very bright, clever man, hit upon the name of Patriarchs for the Association, which was at once adopted, and then, after some discussion, we limited the number of Patriarchs to twenty-five, and that each Patriarch, for his subscription, should have the right of inviting to each ball four ladies and five gentlemen, including himself and family; that all distinguished strangers, up to fifty, should be asked; and then established the rules governing the giving of these balls—all of which, with some slight modifications, have been carried out to the letter to this day. The following gentlemen were then asked to become "Patriarchs," and at once joined the little band:

JOHN JACOB ASTOR,	ROYAL PHELPS,
WILLIAM ASTOR,	EDWIN A. POST,
DE LANCEY KANE,	A. GRACIE KING,
WARD MCALLISTER,	LEWIS M. RUTHERFURD,
GEORGE HENRY WARREN,	ROBERT G. REMSEN,
EUGENE A. LIVINGSTON,	WM. C. SCHERMERHORN,
WILLIAM BUTLER DUNCAN,	FRANCIS R. RIVES,
E. TEMPLETON SNELLING,	MATURIN LIVINGSTON,
LEWIS COLFORD JONES,	ALEX. VAN RENSSELAER,
JOHN W. HAMERSLEY,	WALTER LANGDON,
BENJAMIN S. WELLES,	F. G. D'HAUTEVILLE,
FREDERICK SHELDON,	C. C. GOODHUE,

WILLIAM R. TRAVERS.

The object we had in view was to make these balls thoroughly representative; to embrace the old Colonial New Yorkers, our adopted citizens, and men whose ability and integrity had won the esteem of the community, and who formed an important element in society. We wanted the money power, but not in any way to be controlled by it. Patriarchs were chosen solely for their fitness; on each of them promising to invite to each ball only such people as would do credit to the ball. We then resolved that the responsibility of inviting each batch of nine guests should rest upon the shoulders of the Patriarch who invited them, and that if any objectionable element was introduced, it was the Management's duty to at once let it be known by whom such objectionable party was invited, and to notify the Patriarch so offending, that he had done us an injury, and pray him to be more circumspect. He then stood before the community as a sponsor of his guest, and all society, knowing the offense he had committed, would so upbraid him, that he would go and sin no more. We knew then, and we know now, that the whole secret of the success of these Patriarch Balls lay in making them select; in making them the most brilliant balls of each winter; in making it extremely difficult to obtain an invitation to them, and to make such invitations of great value; to make them the stepping-stone to the best New York society, that one might be sure that any one repeatedly invited to them had a secure social position, and to make them the best managed, the best looked-after balls given in this city. I soon became as much interested in them as if I were giving them in my own house; their success I felt was my success, and their failure, my failure; and be assured, this identifying oneself with any undertaking is the secret of its success. One should never say, "Oh, it is a subscription ball; I'm not responsible for it." It must always be said, "I must be more careful in doing this for others, than in doing it for myself." Nothing must be kept in view but the great result to be reached, i.e. the success of the entertainment, the pleasure of the whole. When petitioned to curtail the expense, lower the subscription, our reply has always been, "We cannot do it if it endangers the success of the balls. While we give them, let us make them the great social events in New York society; make our suppers the best that can be given in this city; decorate our rooms as lavishly as good taste permits, spare no expense to make them a credit to ourselves and to the great city in which they are given."

The social life of a great part of our community, in my opinion, hinges on this and similar organizations, for it and they are organized social power, capable of giving a passport to society to all worthy of it. We thought it would not be wise to allow a handful of men having royal fortunes to have a sovereign's prerogative, i.e. to say whom society shall receive, and whom society shall shut out. We thought it better to try and place such power in the hands of representative men, the choice falling on them solely because of their worth, respectability, and responsibility. . . .

Just at this time [1884] a man of wealth, who had accumulated a fortune here, resolved to give New Yorkers a sensation; to give them a banquet which should exceed in luxury and expense anything before seen in this country. As he expressed it, "I knew it would be a folly, a piece of unheard-of extravagance, but as the United States Government had just refunded me $10,000, exacted from me for duties upon importations (which, being excessive, I had petitioned to be returned me, and had quite unexpectedly received this sum back), I resolved to appropriate it to giving a banquet that would always be remembered." Accordingly, he went to Charles Delmonico, who in turn went to his *cuisine classique* to see how they could possibly spend this sum on this feast. Success crowned their efforts. The sum in such skillful hands soon melted away, and a banquet was given of such beauty and magnificence, that even New Yorkers, accustomed as they were to every species of novel expenditure, were astonished at its lavishness, its luxury. The banquet was given at Delmonico's, in Fourteenth Street. There were seventy-two guests in the large ball-room, looking on Fifth Avenue. The table covered the whole length and breadth of the room, only leaving a passageway for the waiters to pass around it. It was a long extended oval table, and every inch of it was covered with flowers, excepting a space in the centre, left for a lake, and a border around the table for the plates. This lake was indeed a work of art; it was an oval pond, thirty feet in length, by nearly the width of the table, inclosed by a delicate golden wire network, reaching from table to ceiling, making the whole one grand cage; four superb swans, brought from Prospect Park, swam in it, surrounded by high banks of flowers of every species and variety, which prevented them from splashing the water on the table. There were hills and dales; the modest little violet carpeting the valleys, and other bolder sorts climbing up and covering the tops of those miniature mountains. Then, all around the inclosure, and in fact above the entire table, hung little golden cages, with fine songsters, who filled the room with their melody, occasionally interrupted by the splashing of the waters of the lake by the swans, and the cooing of these noble birds, and at one time by a fierce combat between these stately, graceful, gliding white creatures. The surface of the whole table, by clever art, was one unbroken series of undulations, rising and falling like the billows of the sea, but all clothed and carpeted with every form of blossom. It seemed like the abode of fairies; and when surrounding this fairyland with lovely young American womanhood, you had indeed an unequaled scene of enchantment. But this was not to be alone a feast for the eye; all that art could do, all that the cleverest men could devise to spread before the guests, such a feast as the gods should enjoy, was done, and so well done that all present felt, in the way of feasting, that man could do no more! The wines were perfect. Blue seal Johannisberg flowed like water. Incomparable '48 claret, superb Burgundies, and amber-colored Madeira, all were there to add to the intoxicating delight of the scene. Then, soft music stole over one's senses;

lovely women's eyes sparkled with delight at the beauty of their surroundings, and I felt that the fair being who sat next to me would have graced Alexander's feast

> "Sitting by my side,
> Like a lovely Eastern bride,
> In flower of youth and beauty's pride."

DOCUMENT 27

(PLATE 8)

The Drive—Central Park—Four O'Clock

SOURCE: Gray Parker, "The Drive—Central Park—Four O'Clock" (pen-and-ink drawing), *Harper's Weekly*, XXVII (19 May 1883), 317.

This drawing depicts a daily ritual of New York society at a level just below the peak of status protected by Ward McAllister. The spirited horses, the footmen in livery, and the costumes of the women all bespeak wealth, but perhaps too insistently: the artist's tone is mildly satiric, and he has given prominence in the foreground to a threatened contretemps in the traffic.

DOCUMENT 28

(PLATE 9)

Rich and Poor

SOURCE: Sol Eytinge, Jun., "Rich and Poor" (wood engraving), *Harper's Weekly*, XVII (11 January 1873), 33.

This is the basic allegory of urban contrasts. The artist renders the pathos of poverty without doctrinaire intent. He does not express hostility toward the over-dressed wealthy mother and children inside the brownstone house. At the same time, the poor woman outside has dignity despite her rags and hunger. She conveys none of the menace that Charles L. Brace perceived in the "dangerous classes" of the city (Document 29).

DOCUMENT 29

The Prolétaires of New York

SOURCE: Charles L. Brace, "The Prolétaires of New York," from *The Dangerous Classes of New York, and Twenty Years' Work among Them* (New York, 1872), pp. 25–31.

Brace's *The Dangerous Classes of New York* (based on a series of articles in *Appleton's Journal* which had an obvious relation to the Paris Commune of 1871) was the first and one of the most widely read among the many books by clergymen and devout laymen recording the shock with which middle-class Protestant America became aware of the mass of poverty, disease, vice, and crime in the slums of the new industrial cities. Brace was still to some extent under the influence of the post-Calvinist attitude tersely summarized by an anonymous reviewer in the *Presbyterian Quarterly*: ". . . as a general rule, poverty comes from vice, rather than vice from poverty."* But his long experience in social work had taught him that the abominable living conditions of the urban poor made it difficult for them to maintain middle-class virtues. His pioneering philanthropies, especially the establishment of the Children's Aid Society in New York—which over a period of years found homes and employment in the country for more than one hundred thousand city waifs—brought him an international reputation and the friendship of distinguished men on both sides of the Atlantic, including Emerson, Theodore Parker, Asa Gray, and in England, Darwin and John Stuart Mill. Developing a historical context for his humanitarian crusade, Brace published

* *Presbyterian Quarterly and Princeton Review*, series 3, II (January 1873), 189. Quoted by Henry F. May in *Protestant Churches and Industrial America* (New York, 1949), p. 62.

in 1882 *Gesta Christi; or, A History of Humane Progress under Christianity.* (William Dean Howells found this book impressive, and urged Mark Twain to read it in order to modify the anti-clericalism expressed in *A Connecticut Yankee in King Arthur's Court.*†)

Brace's career represents the more attractive side of American evangelical Protestantism after the Civil War. The general tendency was anti-intellectual in the sense that it involved an increasing disregard for doctrinal niceties. In the preaching of Henry Ward Beecher it appeared as an outpouring of warm, cheerful, empty sentiment; in Dwight L. Moody's revivalism it became an excruciating but socially sterile preoccupation with personal guilt. Brace's humanitarianism seems more relevant to the actual situation, but his program was vitiated by a naïvely invidious class-consciousness: he maintained that the best way to redeem the poor was "to draw them under the influence of the moral and fortunate classes. . . ."‡ On the other hand, his sincerity and responsibility contrast favorably with the unabashed sensationalism of the superficially similar "exposure" of conditions in the slums contained in the sermons of the Reverend T. DeWitt Talmage, published in the *Christian World* and collected in such widely read volumes as *The Night Sides of City Life* (1878). (On Talmage, see Document 74.)

New York is a much younger city than its European rivals; and with perhaps one-third the population of London, yet it presents varieties of life among the "masses" quite as picturesque, and elements of population even more dangerous. The throng of different nationalities in the American city gives a peculiarly variegated air to the life beneath the surface, and the enormous over-crowding in portions of the poor quarters intensifies the evils, pe-

† Howells to Clemens, Cambridge, Mass., 17 October 1889, in *Mark Twain-Howells Letters*, eds. William M. Gibson and Henry Nash Smith, 2 vols. (Cambridge, Mass., 1960), II, 614.
‡ *The Dangerous Classes of New York*, p. ii.

culiar to large towns, to a degree seen only in a few districts in such cities as London and Liverpool.

The *mass* of poverty and wretchedness is, of course, far greater in the English capital. There are classes with inherited pauperism and crime more deeply stamped in them, in London or Glasgow, than we ever behold in New York; but certain small districts can be found in our metropolis with the unhappy fame of containing more human beings packed to the square yard, and stained with more acts of blood and riot, within a given period, than is true of any other equal space of earth in the civilized world.

There are houses, well known to sanitary boards and the police, where Fever has taken a perennial lease, and will obey no legal summons to quit; where Cholera—if a single germ-seed of it float anywhere in American atmosphere— at once ripens a black harvest; where Murder has stained every floor of its gloomy stories, and Vice skulks or riots from one year's end to the other. Such houses are never reformed. The only hope for them is in the march of street improvements, which will utterly sweep them away.

It is often urged that the breaking-up of these "dens" and "fever-nests" only scatters the pestilence and moral disease, but does not put an end to them.

The objection is more apparent than real. The abolishing of one of these centres of crime and poverty is somewhat like withdrawing the virus from one diseased limb and diffusing it through an otherwise healthy body. It seems to lose its intensity. The diffusion weakens. Above all, it is less likely to become hereditary.

One of the remarkable and hopeful things about New York, to a close observer of its "dangerous classes," is, as I shall show in a future chapter, that they do not tend to become fixed and inherited, as in European cities.

But, though the crime and pauperism of New York are not so deeply stamped in the blood of the population, they are even more dangerous. The intensity of the American temperament is felt in every fibre of these children of poverty and vice. Their crimes have the unrestrained and sanguinary character of a race accustomed to overcome all

obstacles. They rifle a bank, where English thieves pick a
pocket; they murder, where European *prolétaires* cudgel
or fight with fists; in a riot, they begin what seems about
to be the sacking of a city, where English rioters would
merely batter policemen, or smash lamps. The "dangerous
classes" of New York are mainly American-born, but the
children of Irish and German immigrants. They are as
ignorant as London flash-men or costermongers. They are
far more brutal than the peasantry from whom they de-
scend, and they are much banded together, in associations,
such as "Dead Rabbit," "Plug-ugly," and various target
companies. They are our *enfants perdus*, grown up to
young manhood. The murder of an unoffending old man,
like Mr. Rogers, is nothing to them.§ They are ready for
any offense or crime, however degraded or bloody. New
York has never experienced the full effect of the nurture
of these youthful ruffians as she will one day. They showed
their hand only slightly in the riots during the war. At
present, they are like the athletes and gladiators of the
Roman demagogues. They are the "roughs" who sustain
the ward politicians, and frighten honest voters. They can
"repeat" to an unlimited extent, and serve their employers. They live on *"panem et circenses,"* or City-Hall places
and pot-houses, where they have full credit.

We shall speak more particularly of the causes of crime
in future chapters, but we may say in brief, that the young
ruffians of New York are the products of accident, ignorance, and vice. Among a million people, such as compose
the population of this city and its suburbs, there will always be a great number of misfortunes; fathers die, and
leave their children unprovided for; parents drink, and

§ "Mr. Chas. M. Rogers, aged 60, and proprietor of a
boarding-house at No. 42 East 12th St." was assaulted by two
men "without provocation and for the purpose of robbery" on
31 December 1868 (*New York Times*, 1 January 1869, p. 8,
col. 2). The case became celebrated because, despite numerous
arrests, the murderer was not discovered. A confession to the
murder by an inmate of Sing Sing was reported in 1871 (*ibid.*,
15 January 1871, p. 1, col. 7).

abuse their little ones, and they float away on the currents of the street; step-mothers or step-fathers drive out, by neglect and ill-treatment, their sons from home. Thousands are the children of poor foreigners, who have permitted them to grow up without school, education, or religion. All the neglect and bad education and evil example of a poor class tend to form others, who, as they mature, swell the ranks of ruffians and criminals. So, at length, a great multitude of ignorant, untrained, passionate, irreligious boys and young men are formed, who become the "dangerous class" of our city. They form the "Nineteenth-street Gangs," the young burglars and murderers, the garroters and rioters, the thieves and flash-men, the "repeaters" and ruffians, so well known to all who know this metropolis.

THE DANGERS

It has been common, since the recent terrible Communistic outbreak in Paris, to assume that France alone is exposed to such horrors; but, in the judgment of one who has been familiar with our "dangerous classes" for twenty years, there are just the same explosive social elements beneath the surface of New York as of Paris.

There are thousands on thousands in New York who have no assignable home, and "flit" from attic to attic, and cellar to cellar; there are other thousands more or less connected with criminal enterprises; and still other tens of thousands, poor, hard-pressed, and depending for daily bread on the day's earnings, swarming in tenement-houses, who behold the gilded rewards of toil all about them, but are never permitted to touch them.

All these great masses of destitute, miserable, and criminal persons believe that for ages the rich have had all the good things of life, while to them have been left the evil things. Capital to them is the tyrant.

Let but Law lift its hand from them for a season, or let the civilizing influences of American life fail to reach them, and, if the opportunity offered, we should see an explosion from this class which might leave this city in ashes and blood.

To those incredulous of this, we would recall the scenes in our streets during the riots in 1863, when, for a short period, the guardians of good order—the local militia—had been withdrawn for national purposes, and when the ignorant masses were excited by dread of the draft.

Who will ever forget the marvelous rapidity with which the better streets were filled with a ruffianly and desperate multitude, such as in ordinary times we seldom see—creatures who seemed to have crept from their burrows and dens to join in the plunder of the city—how quickly certain houses were marked out for sacking and ruin, and what wild and brutal crimes were committed on the unoffending negroes? It will be recalled, too, how much *women* figured in these horrible scenes, as they did in the Communistic outbreak in Paris. It was evident to all careful observers then, that had another day of license been given the crowd, the attack would have been directed at the apparent wealth of the city—the banks, jewelers' shops, and rich private houses.

No one doubted then, or during the Orange riot of 1871, the existence of "dangerous classes" in New York. And yet the separate members of these riotous and ruffianly masses are simply neglected and street-wandering children who have come to early manhood.

The true preventive of social catastrophes like these, are just such Christian reformatory and educational movements as we are about to describe.

Of the number of the distinctively homeless and vagrant youth in New York, it is difficult to speak with precision. We should be inclined to estimate it, after long observation, as fluctuating each year between 20,000 and 30,000. But to these, as they mature, must be added, in the composition of the dangerous classes, all those who are professionally criminal, and who have homes and lodging-places. And again to these, portions of that vast and ignorant multitude, who, in prosperous times, just keep their heads above water, who are pressed down by poverty or misfortune, and who look with envy and greed at the signs of wealth and luxury all around them, while they themselves have nothing but hardship, penury, and unceasing drudgery.

DOCUMENT 30

(PLATE 10)

Under-Ground Life

SOURCE: Anonymous, "Under-Ground Life" (wood engraving), *Harper's Weekly*, XVII (12 July 1873), 604.

The editorial comment on this drawing employs a vivid metonymic imagery to associate poverty with moral depravity, and to convey a violent revulsion against both. The quotation marks around "landlady" and the leering references to a "boarding-house for young ladies" and to the "interesting lodgers" brand the dive as a brothel; and the mention of holy pictures along with the bottles of perfume makes it clear that the prostitutes are Catholic—probably Irish:

> The Sanitary Inspectors of the Health Department of this city have commenced a good work in clearing out the vile under-ground dens—"dives," in the slang of the street—in which hundreds and thousands of the lower classes of our population herd together in filth and squalor too dreadful to be described. Mr. C. S. REINHART, one of the artists of *Harper's Weekly*, accompanied the officers on several of their "raids," and to his pencil our readers are indebted for the graphic and faithful illustrations. . . .
>
> Among the places, and one of the worst of all, cleared out by the inspectors was a basement in Mott Street. The cellar was pitch-dark, and the only chance for ventilation was through the passage-way. As soon as the inspector entered, the woman who kept the place began to beg piteously for mercy and delay; but the officers were inexorable, and in a few minutes the wretched furniture was flung out into the street, and nothing but the bare walls remained. It was a most disagreeable task for the officers, who staggered

out from the gloomy, reeking cellar, bending under
the weight of heaps of foul rags, piles of dirty straw,
and broken bedsteads that were covered with hideous
vermin. The scene was horrible. Brooms, stove-pipes,
bedsteads, lamps, shovels, chests, quilts, blankets,
spreads, mattresses, stoves, straw hats, radishes,
looking-glasses, holy pictures, soup signs, torn books,
and bottles of perfume were all heaped together, and
formed a disgusting barricade on the sidewalk.

In the basement of a house in Madison Street,
where nightly lodgers were taken in, there were a
number of bunks of very curious construction. They
were turned up on one side against the wall, and were
lowered by means of a swivel. The bunks were
smashed to pieces and thrown out into the street,
while the women were swearing, cursing, and crying.
One of them had a terrible black eye. "Well, what of
that?" she said; "my husband gave it to me, and there's
no one has a better right than him."

A basement in Mulberry Street, labeled "Lodgings," was entirely below the level of the sidewalk,
without any means of ventilation except the low, narrow passage-way, and was pervaded by a damp,
cavern-like smell. This cellar was cut up in small
box-like rooms, closed, with the exception of a section
half the width of an ordinary door, through which
the lodger might enter. These boxes were filled with
berths, and were five feet in length by three and a
half in breadth. When the straw ticks were pulled
up, the damp, matted muck stuck to the boards, and
the rotten bedclothing fell apart of its own weight.
Every possible corner had a bed in it, and there was
sleeping room for thirty persons.

The "landlady" of one of the basements was very
indignant at the invasion of her premises by the officers, whom she informed, with an air of dignity, that
she kept a "boarding-house for young ladies." She
and her interesting lodgers were unceremoniously
ejected, and her furniture thrown out into the street.

Horrible and disgusting as these under-ground
tenements were, the occupants were loath to quit
them, and in many cases had to be removed by main
force. Women wept, moaned, and raved, and men

blustered and threatened; but the officers were inflexible, and the wretched people were compelled to
seek lodgings elsewhere. Better the open street than
the noisome dens from which they were ejected.*

* "Under-Ground Life," anonymous editorial note in *Harper's
Weekly*, XVII (12 July 1873), 606.

Document 31
(Plate 11)

Station-House Lodgers

source: Winslow Homer, "Station-House Lodgers" (wood engraving), *Harper's Weekly*, XVIII (7 February 1874), 132.

Although this is not one of Winslow Homer's best compositions, the drawing distinguishes itself at once from other illustrations in *Harper's Weekly* by the bold pattern of lights and darks and by the interesting contrasts between tension and repose in the figures.

In his autobiography Jacob Riis tells how, as a young immigrant from Denmark, penniless and unable to find work, he spent a night in the autumn of 1870 in a police lodginghouse, where he was brutally treated by the custodians. "The outrage of that night," he wrote, "became, in the providence of God, the means of putting an end to one of the foulest abuses that ever disgraced a Christian city, and a mainspring in the battle with the slum as far as my share in it is concerned." His "battle" began in 1883, when he was a reporter for the *Tribune,* and lasted until 1895, when with the help of Police Commissioner Theodore Roosevelt he succeeded at last in bringing about the abolition of the station-house lodgings. They were replaced by municipal lodginghouses not operated by the police department, which provided for the homeless "a clean shirt and a decent bed and a bath . . . and something to eat in the morning, so they did not have to go out and beg the first thing."*

The difference in tone between the editorial comment on this drawing and the comment on "Under-Ground Life" (headnote to Document 30) illustrates a conflict in attitudes toward poverty and vice in the

* *The Making of an American* (New York, 1901), pp. 74, 252.

slums that appears often during the 1870s and 1880s.
Here the editorialist provides a perspective on the scene
of misery by citing statistics of poverty and death, and
by implication places the blame for the ghastly total of
suffering and crime on forces beyond the control of the
victims. The reference to "misrule and riotous influences" implies that urban poverty is caused by corrupt
politicians and the careless rich. And the stark contrast
between the pleasures of the well-to-do and the prayers
and curses arising from cellars and garrets states the
theme of "two nations" in a way that anticipates the
strong humanitarian sympathy of Jacob Riis's *How the
Other Half Lives* almost two decades later. The mention
of Brace's Children's Aid Society (see Document 29)
also implies that poverty is the cause rather than the
result of immorality:

It is a little past midnight when the sergeant on
duty throws open the door of the large hall in the
basement of the Seventeenth Precinct Station-house,
and we step on the stone flagging where some fifty
men are lying. Behind us is a grated doorway opening
upon a corridor, and there half a dozen women sit
crouching about an immense stove, red from the
seething heat. Around us, as shown in the sketch
in almost inextricable confusion, are stretched the
sleepers, and here and there a wakeful or restless
one turns and looks toward us for a moment. They
lie mostly with their heads resting upon low rude
benches, and from their garments and their persons
comes an offensive odor. There is a Babel-like confusion of snoring, and now and then a young man at
the edge of the throng starts nervously and sighs,
and an old man near the centre moves his hands
tremulously about his face and groans in his sleep.
Between this man so near us, and, as it were, just
entering upon a career with which prison life and
prison scenes will have more and more to do as he
advances, and the poor wreck going to pieces over
there, we see the shadow of New York—the shadow
of a city where misrule and riotous influences have
done their work; where one hundred thousand human beings, men, women, and children, are sent to

the penitentiary, the asylums, the almshouse, the hospitals, and the prisons in a single year! One hundred and thirty thousand persons who have been convicted criminals living at large in our midst!

These men at our feet are "only lodgers." There are fifty-one of them, whose names will on the morrow swell the list of 935 who that night sought the shelter of the station-houses. Looking at these poor crouching forms, columns of well-remembered figures assume a strange vitality, and go dancing around before our eyes, and seem to beckon us farther into the shadow. One column sums up in red numerals 1321 deaths from violence in the city of New York in a single year. The skeleton of the old year stands behind these men, and points with a ghastly leer at 101 suicides and fifty homicides, including two men killed on the scaffold in the year of our Lord 1873. These are the facts and figures that are constantly arising, like a ghostly exhalation, from what we are pleased to call "the lower strata of the city." Is it to be wondered at that the metropolis can swallow up so many lives pouring in each year from the country?

The island of Manhattan contains sixteen and three-fourths square miles of land, 10,722 acres, with a population, according to the census of 1870, of 952,000. This gives an average of fifty-five square yards of space to each person. Yet 468,492 human beings are crowded into 14,872 tenements, or more than an average of thirty-one persons to each house. The rooms are necessarily small, often without windows, and the great majority of the sleeping apartments have, as their only means of ventilation, a narrow transverse opening into the close common room where the cooking is done. Yet the inmates of these poor abodes are comparatively happy and comfortable, for there are still people wandering in the streets, with no roof, however humble, to shelter them from the drenching rain, the biting frost, or the falling snow.

While eleven thousand six hundred and sixty homeless boys have been provided with lodgings and meals by the Children's Aid Society alone in a single year, there have been thousands of boys and adult

men left to sleep in hallways, in empty carts and
wagons, in the corners of areas, in the hay barges at
the docks, and in the open boats and upon sunken
cribs under the wharves and piers.

All America has heard of the little boy, a street
musician, who, like "petit Gervais," came from Savoy,
and was found lying dead beside his harp on the
steps of a Fifth Avenue mansion. It was said he died
from "nostalgia"—longing for home. This may have
been true; but there are scores of his kind drooping
away and dying weekly from an unsatisfied longing
for food and shelter. Death from hunger, the wasting
away of the flesh, "made light and thin by heavy-
handed fate," is more common in this city of New
York than one would think—only the reader of the
daily paper is not so shocked by its mention in the
columns of reports from the Bureau of Vital Statistics
under the form of "deaths from marasmus." The
deaths from "marasmus" during the year 1873 were
over 900 in number. If we add to this the fact that
3000 infants are annually abandoned, sent to the
public hospitals, left in the public streets, or placed
in the hands of those who "keep them till *death*" for
a small sum, while 113 more were found during the
past year dead and lying in ash-barrels, in vacant
lots, in areas, in the streets and rivers, we may get
some idea of the terrors of life among the very poor
in New York city. We may understand better why,
when bright eyes are glancing merrily at the falling
snow, and bright little feet are gliding over the ice
in the Park, muttered prayers and bitter curses go
up from cellars and garrets, while wan hands, bony
hands, and little hands quiver about the embers of a
dying fire. On such nights the "lodgers" throng the
entrance to the station-houses from dusk till midnight,
and when unable to gain admission to one, wander
away to another, often faltering, often falling, often
freezing. Sometimes they feel the snow-blight falling
upon them, and they wander till they fall in the dark
waters of the river, from whence in good time they
are conveyed to a slab at the Morgue, and thence
in a rough box to the Potter's Field. The snow that
brings joy with its pure soft flakes in the country

carries death on its wings to the dark quarters of the city. We were thinking then it might be the harbinger of an opening spring-time for these poor souls in some far-off land where poverty would lose its sting, when we were interrupted by the door-man.

"Get out of this!" he cried, roughly, to the sleepers; "stir lively now!" Then he turned apologetically, saying, "It is half past five." As they passed, still half asleep, through the corridor, they were roughly pushed and shoved about, and those at the head of the column were made to carry out and empty the ash tanks. That finished, they disappeared in the fog and gloom of the early morning, and the Croton was turned on in their late sleeping-place, while the women lodgers entered it with scrubbing-brushes and brooms.†

† Anonymous, *Harper's Weekly*, XVIII (7 February 1874), 133–34.

Prostitution

SOURCE: Edward Crapsey, "Prostitution," from *The Nether Side of New York; or, The Vice, Crime and Poverty of the Great Metropolis* (New York, 1872), pp. 138–39, 142–45.

Crapsey's circumstantial account of prostitution in New York (based on a series of articles in *Galaxy* in 1871–72) contrasts with the timid handling of the topic in *Harper's Weekly* (see the headnote to Document 30). It is true that he takes a conventional moral stance and uses the standard clichés ("poor painted wrecks of womanhood," "the leprosy of their vice"). Yet, just as Charles L. Brace maintains that the wickedness of slum dwellers is at least partly caused by their environment, so Crapsey argues that along with the "insane desire for display," economic and social forces play a major part in causing prostitution: not only "faulty education," but the threat of starvation forces girls who find "the doors of productive industry" closed to become prostitutes in order to survive. His use of interviews to collect data on the origins and motivation of prostitutes, although hardly up to modern standards of sociological research, nevertheless represents an effort to understand pathological social conditions instead of merely denouncing them in the moralistic manner of an Anthony Comstock or a DeWitt Talmage. Perhaps the journalistic tendency toward neutral reporting of fact forshadows the revolutionary change in attitudes toward the "fallen woman" that would enter fiction with Stephen Crane's *Maggie: A Girl of the Streets* (1893) and Theodore Dreiser's *Sister Carrie* (1900).

Take the lowest type first, and find it in the middle of any night by merely sauntering through Broadway from

Grand to Fourteenth street, or again from Twenty-third
to Thirtieth street, or in some of the side streets. The
type is the night-walker, and gradations of the class are
almost as numerous as its representatives. To meet the
worst, Greene, Wooster, Houston, Bleecker, or Amity
streets must be traversed. There was a time, and it is not
long past, when only the Fourth Ward could show the
prowling prostitute in her most abject degradation, but it
is not necessary now to get lost in the tortuous mazes of the
old town, to find the most repulsive phases of female
frailty. The Eighth Ward has taken the place of the
Fourth, and the stranger need only turn three hundred
feet out of Broadway anywhere between Grand and Amity
streets, to encounter the most startling evidence of the
possibility of total depravity.

To see the worst, stand for the hour before midnight on
the corner of Houston and Greene streets. In that time a
hundred women apparently will pass, but the close observer will notice that each woman passes the spot on an
average of about twice, so that in fact there are not more
than fifty of them. This frequency of appearance leads to
the supposition that they do not go far, which is the fact.
Each set of prostitutes has its metes and bounds laid down
by an unwritten code of its own enactment, which is rarely
violated. The set now under consideration travels Houston,
Bleecker, Wooster, and Greene streets, with occasional
forays upon Broadway, which is the common property of
all. But these poor fallen creatures rarely go there to put
themselves in fruitless competition with more attractive
sin. They are poorly dressed, have nothing of beauty in
form or face, and are always uncouth or brazenly vulgar in
manner. They are miserably poor, herding in garrets or
cellars, and are driven by their necessities to accost every
stranger they meet with what the silly law of New York
calls "Soliciting for the purpose of prostitution." When a
woman offers to sell her body to a man she never saw before, for fifty cents, she has fallen low indeed, and this
offer will be made at least a dozen times within the hour
to any observer at the spot mentioned, whose appearance
does not absolutely forbid advances.

Next stand for the same period at Amity and Greene streets. As many women will pass, and in about the same ratio as to reappearances. They are a shade better in appearance as to dress, and some of them have the faint remnants of former personal beauty. They are vulgar yet, but are a vast improvement on the set first seen. All of them will so look at you as to invite advances, but only about one in five will speak first. When they do, it is merely to say "Good evening" or "How are you, my dear," instead of a direct invitation to go home with them, which is the first greeting of the other set. These Amity street women are, as a rule, better housed and fed than the first set, as they live in the houses bordering their tramping-ground, which are all well built and finished. Some of the women have attained to, or more correctly speaking, have not fallen below the prosperity of occupying a room in one of these houses alone, and none of them have more than one female room-mate. Instead of the rough pine furniture of Houston street, the rooms here are given an almost decent appearance by imitation oak, or else are filled up with those strainings for respectable adornments known as "cottage furniture." Another decided proof of better condition is the absence of the cooking stove, for these girls either board with the "Madam" or obtain their food at restaurants. This class, which is thus better housed, better dressed, better behaved, has the middle rank, and contains the majority of all women plying their vocation in the public streets. Although I have mentioned only Amity and Greene streets as a post of observation, it can be seen at many other points, and notably so at Twelfth street and University Place, which latter stately thoroughfare has lately become a chief tramping-ground for abandoned females. . . .

In all the great cities of the United States, so far as my personal observation extends—and I have been in all of them—the walking of the streets after nightfall by prostitutes has become an alarming evil; but New York is entitled, I am afraid, to preëminence in this respect. Not only is the city first in the number of its street-walkers, but

nowhere else has the class become so degraded. I have
hinted something of the profanity and obscenity of the
women who can be found after midnight in any of the
side streets, but it is not possible to describe in detail the
scenes which will be forced upon the observer any night in
Houston, Bleecker, Amity, and Fourth streets, as well as
in the lower Bowery, Chatham street, and some other east-
side thoroughfares. Singly, in couples, or groups, these
girls, many of whom are mere children and very few of
whom have scarcely passed maturity, plunge along the
sidewalks, accosting every man they meet, or, stopping at
the street corners, annoy all passers until they are driven
away by the police. Many of them are under the influence
of liquor, and not a night passes but some of these degraded creatures are carried into the station-houses helplessly or furiously drunk. Until within the past two years
I never saw any of these women drinking in public bar-
rooms, but now it has become so common that it has
ceased to be remarked; it is true there are few of the
saloons which will serve them, but there is always one on
each route of the tramps which will sell to any one, and
here these poor painted wrecks of womanhood can be seen
standing at the bar, drinking vile liquors until they have
won the beatitude of stupefaction, or until they reel out
into the streets indecently drunk. If the unconsciousness
of inebriety is ever a blessing, it is such in the case of these
lost women, as it permits them for the time to forget
what they are and must be always. Often suffering for the
necessaries of life, burdened almost without exception with
"lovers" who despoil them of the pittance they receive for
moral and physical death, harassed by the police, shunned
by their more prosperous sisters in sin, corroded morally
and physically with the leprosy of their vice, no class needs
so much of pity, none has less of it, and none is so little
aware that it needs commiseration. Calloused by crime
which is unnatural and bestializing, the street-walkers have
forgotten that they were ever undefiled and lost all desire
to be other than they are. Numbering about two thousand,
constantly infesting the public thoroughfares, inoculated

and inoculating with loathsome diseases, they are the great
danger and shame of civilization found in all cities, but
here more numerous more dangerous and more shameful
than anywhere else on the continent.

It has not been from any wish to pander to a morbid
desire for the repulsive that I have set this type of prostitution in the foreground. Palpable facts cannot be ignored,
and a vice that is thus obtruded upon every passer through
the public streets cannot be too soon or too fully described;
but having presented the facts in such plain terms that
they cannot be misunderstood, I gladly take leave of this
lowest type of metropolitan prostitution. It is hardly more
agreeable to speak of the next grade, which is found in the
lowest of what are known as "parlor houses." The chief
difference between the inmates and the street-walkers is
that the former do not cruise the streets to entice strangers
to their dens. If this is a comparative virtue it is the only
one these women can boast, as they are fully as bestial in
every other respect as their sisters of the pave. The houses
in which they live and ply their infamous vocation are
always unmistakable even to the novice. In Greene and
Wooster streets several blocks are almost wholly taken up
by such houses, but others but little less open and degraded can be found in many other quarters of the city. In
many of these houses there is a public bar; in all of them
the orgies are indecent to such a degree that they cannot
be described. Next above these dens are houses a shade
more sufferable, which attempt to hide their infamy behind cigar stores or some other kind of shop, and are filled
with women who do not shock at the first glance. Above
these again are houses which really have parlors, and in
which the women make a pretence to decency in their
demeanor while in public. After these come the grand
saloons where the evil is painted in the most alluring
colors. The houses are of the largest and stateliest, the
furniture the most elegant, the inmates beautiful, accomplished, captivating in dress and manner, who, with woman's only priceless jewel, would adorn any circle. It is
difficult to persuade one who has no personal knowledge of

the matter, that, taken into the parlors of one of these houses and meeting the inmates without a previous intimation of the character of the place, he would believe himself in a pure, refined home. Yet such is the fact. Such houses as these can be found in every desirable neighborhood, and no man can be sure that he has not one of the sepulchres next door.

But the vice has taken in New York a more insidious if less alluring form than this. For some years past a most deplorable change has been going on which has had the effect of greatly decreasing the number of parlor houses, while houses of assignation have multiplied in the same ratio. The effect has been to intrude prostitution into circles and places where its presence is never suspected. Hundreds of houses are thus defiled, and the corroding vice creeps into families of every social grade. Women of high position and culture, no less than the unlettered shop girls, resort to the houses of assignation, which are of every grade, from the palaces in the most aristocratic quarters of the city to the frowsy rooms in the slums. Many of the frequenters of these houses are married women, who are driven by an insane desire for display to thus add to a scanty income; others are young girls led astray by faulty education, and yet others are driven by starvation to sell their virtue to any casual buyer. Many of these cases have come to the knowledge of the police, and there is nothing which pleads so strongly against the flagrant injustice which has closed the doors of productive industry against women, as the fact that when forced to fall back upon their own resources, so many of them have been compelled to choose between prostitution and destitution. But for this fact the chief evil of the age could not have become so prevalent as it is. Woman is naturally chaste, and if those who have fallen can be induced to tell the cause, it will be found that at least six in every ten are forced by sheer necessity to become confirmed prostitutes. I do not mean to say that they will plead this as the cause of the first lapse from virtue, as nine cases out of ten of them will charge that to their betrayal by men whom they loved.

But after that first lapse, and after their desertion by these men, they claim they had no choice between their way of life and death from starvation. The story is told by types of every class of prostitutes, from the adroit adventuress who lays her snares in the great hotels, to the poor drunken creature who tramps the streets. . . .

It may be that here the evil in its covert form is more general in its ramifications through all circles of society, and is thus corroding where its presence is not suspected. I believe such to be the case, and if it is, the moral stamina of the community is being undermined, and it is impossible to imagine what will be the debasement it will entail upon the next generation. It is a terrible state of affairs when the chastity of men is hooted at as an absurdity, and the virtue of women seeming to be virtuous is suspected; yet such is the condition of New York. That such things can be asserted and believed is in itself a proof of a profligacy that has become ominous; that houses of assignation into which women can steal from reputable homes have gradually replaced the houses of prostitution, is a startling evidence that there is too much foundation for these assertions and this belief. As I look upon it in the light of many facts which are of such character that they cannot be hinted at, much less mentioned, the chief danger that threatens the city from the social evil does not come from the street-walkers, nor the inmates of public houses of prostitution. These are women known to be unchaste, who are without home ties and without influence except to a very limited extent. On the contrary, those women who are unsuspected prostitutes occupy and defile the holiest positions of domestic life, and there is no limit to the evil which their crime produces. And this form of the plague is more deplorable because it is one which no law can cure, although it might be mitigated to some extent by statutory remedies. . . .

The Common Herd

SOURCE: Jacob A. Riis, "The Common Herd," from *How the Other Half Lives. Studies among the Tenements of New York* (New York, 1890), pp. 162–75.

The motivation of Riis's vigorous "battle with the slums" was an intuitive sense of outrage rather than the piety which impelled Charles L. Brace to establish the Children's Aid Society. Riis had the crusading journalist's belief that the best way to bring about reforms is "to make the facts of the wrong plain." His aggressive exposure of conditions in New York tenements and the political corruption that was partly responsible for them brought him to the notice of prominent humanitarians such as Felix Adler and Theodore Roosevelt. With their help he managed to mobilize public opinion in support of tenement house commissions and other official investigating bodies. His greatest influence came in the 1890s, following the publication of *How the Other Half Lives*—a book which grew out of an article published in *Scribner's Magazine* in 1889. Over a period of ten years (according to Riis's figures) the death rate in the New York slums was brought down from 26.32 to 19.53 per thousand through a combination of measures he advocated, including protection of the city water supply from contamination, slum clearance, more rigorous enforcement of sanitary codes, and legislation controlling the architecture of tenement houses. While Riis was far from radical in his politics, he had a more realistic view of urban poverty than Brace's dependence on the safety valve of emigration to the West as a solution for the problem of urban poverty. His unshaken belief that the environment was a major cause of crime as well as of disease was in accord with the increasingly

secular attitude toward social problems in the 1880s and
1890s, but his freely expressed sympathy for the urban
poor contrasts with the hard-boiled, "objective" pose
of that other newspaperman, Stephen Crane, who gave
an equally memorable description of the slums in *Maggie: A Girl of the Streets,* published only three years
after *How the Other Half Lives.*

In the dull content of life bred on the tenement-house
dead level there is little to redeem it, or to calm apprehension for a society that has nothing better to offer its
toilers; while the patient efforts of the lives finally attuned
to it to render the situation tolerable, and the very success of these efforts, serve only to bring out in stronger
contrast the general gloom of the picture by showing how
much farther they might have gone with half a chance.
Go into any of the "respectable" tenement neighborhoods
—the fact that there are not more than two saloons on the
corner, nor over three or four in the block will serve as a
fair guide—where live the great body of hard-working Irish
and German immigrants and their descendants, who accept naturally the conditions of tenement life, because
for them there is nothing else in New York; be with and
among its people until you understand their ways, their
aims, and the quality of their ambitions, and unless you
can content yourself with the scriptural promise that the
poor we shall have always with us, or with the menagerie
view that, if fed, they have no cause of complaint, you
shall come away agreeing with me that, humanly speaking,
life there does not seem worth the living. Take at random
one of these uptown tenement blocks, not of the worst nor
yet of the most prosperous kind, within hail of what the
newspapers would call a "fine residential section." These
houses were built since the last cholera scare made people
willing to listen to reason. The block is not like the one
over on the East Side in which I actually lost my way
once. There were thirty or forty rear houses in the heart
of it, three or four on every lot, set at all sorts of angles,

with odd, winding passages, or no passage at all, only "runways" for the thieves and toughs of the neighborhood. These yards are clear. There is air there, and it is about all there is. The view between brick walls outside is that of a stony street; inside, of rows of unpainted board fences, a bewildering maze of clothes-posts and lines; underfoot, a desert of brown, hard-baked soil from which every blade of grass, every stray weed, every speck of green, has been trodden out, as must inevitably be every gentle thought and aspiration above the mere wants of the body in those whose moral natures such home surroundings are to nourish. In self-defence, you know, all life eventually accommodates itself to its environment, and human life is no exception. Within the house there is nothing to supply the want thus left unsatisfied. Tenement-houses have no æsthetic resources. If any are to be brought to bear on them, they must come from the outside. There is the common hall with doors opening softly on every landing as the strange step is heard on the stairs, the air-shaft that seems always so busy letting out foul stenches from below that it has no time to earn its name by bringing down fresh air, the squeaking pumps that hold no water, and the rent that is never less than one week's wages out of the four, quite as often half of the family earnings.

Why complete the sketch? It is drearily familiar already. Such as it is, it is the frame in which are set days, weeks, months, and years of unceasing toil, just able to fill the mouth and clothe the back. Such as it is, it is the world, and all of it, to which these weary workers return nightly to feed heart and brain after wearing out the body at the bench, or in the shop. To it come the young with their restless yearnings, perhaps to pass on the threshold one of the daughters of sin, driven to the tenement by the police when they raided her den, sallying forth in silks and fine attire after her day of idleness. These in their coarse garments—girls with the love of youth for beautiful things, with this hard life before them—who shall save them from the tempter? Down in the street the saloon, always bright and gay, gathering to itself all the cheer of the block, beckons the boys. In many such blocks the census-taker found two thousand men, women, and children, and over, who called them home.

The picture is faithful enough to stand for its class wherever along both rivers the Irish brogue is heard. As already said, the Celt falls most readily victim to tenement influences since shanty-town and its original free-soilers have become things of the past. If he be thrifty and shrewd his progress thenceforward is along the plane of the tenement, on which he soon assumes to manage without improving things. The German has an advantage over his Celtic neighbor in his strong love for flowers, which not all the tenements on the East Side have power to smother. His garden goes with him wherever he goes. Not that it represents any high moral principle in the man; rather perhaps the capacity for it. He turns his saloon into a shrubbery as soon as his back-yard. But wherever he puts it in a tenement block it does the work of a dozen police clubs. In proportion as it spreads the neighborhood takes on a more orderly character. As the green dies out of the landscape and increases in political importance, the police find more to do. Where it disappears altogether from sight, lapsing into a mere sentiment, police-beats are shortened and the force patrols double at night. Neither the man nor the sentiment is wholly responsible for this. It is the tenement unadorned that is. The changing of Tompkins Square from a sand lot into a beautiful park put an end for good and all to the Bread or Blood riots of which it used to be the scene, and transformed a nest of dangerous agitators into a harmless, beer-craving band of Anarchists. They have scarcely been heard of since. Opponents of the small parks system as a means of relieving the congested population of tenement districts, please take note.

With the first hot nights in June police despatches, that record the killing of men and women by rolling off roofs and window-sills while asleep, announce that the time of greatest suffering among the poor is at hand. It is in hot weather, when life indoors is well-nigh unbearable with cooking, sleeping, and working, all crowded into the small rooms together, that the tenement expands, reckless of all restraint. Then a strange and picturesque life moves upon the flat roofs. In the day and early evening mothers air their babies there, the boys fly their kits from the house-tops, undismayed by police regulations, and the young men and girls court and pass the growler. In the stifling July nights, when the big barracks are like fiery furnaces, their very walls giving out absorbed heat, men and women lie in restless, sweltering rows, panting for air and sleep. Then every truck in the street, every crowded fire-escape, becomes a bedroom, infinitely preferable to any the house affords. A cooling shower on such a night is hailed as a heaven-sent blessing in a hundred thousand homes.

Life in the tenements in July and August spells death to an army of little ones whom the doctor's skill is power-less to save. When the white badge of mourning flutters from every second door, sleepless mothers walk the streets in the gray of the early dawn, trying to stir a cooling breeze to fan the brow of the sick baby. There is no sadder sight than this patient devotion striving against fearfully hope-less odds. Fifty "summer doctors," especially trained to this work, are then sent into the tenements by the Board of Health, with free advice and medicine for the poor. De-voted women follow in their track with care and nursing for the sick. Fresh-air excursions run daily out of New York on land and water; but despite all efforts the grave-diggers in Calvary work over-time, and little coffins are stacked mountain high on the deck of the Charity Commissioners' boat when it makes its semi-weekly trips to the city cemetery.

Under the most favorable circumstances, an epidemic, which the well-to-do can afford to make light of as a thing to be got over or avoided by reasonable care, is excessively fatal among the children of the poor, by reason of the practical impossibility of isolating the patient in a tene-ment. The measles, ordinarily a harmless disease, furnishes a familiar example. Tread it ever so lightly on the avenues, in the tenements it kills right and left. Such an epidemic ravaged three crowded blocks in Elizabeth Street on the heels of the grippe last winter, and, when it had spent its fury, the death-maps in the Bureau of Vital Statistics looked as if a black hand had been laid across those blocks, over-shadowing in part the contiguous tenements in Mott Street, and with the thumb covering a particularly packed settlement of half a dozen houses in Mulberry Street. The track of the epidemic through these teeming barracks was as clearly defined as the track of a tornado through a forest district. There were houses in which as many as eight little children had died in five months. The records showed that respiratory diseases, the common heritage of the grippe and the measles, had caused death in most cases, discovering the trouble to be, next to the inability to check the contagion in those crowds, in the poverty of the parents and the wretched home conditions that made proper care of the sick impossible. The fact was emphasized by the occurrence here and there of a few isolated deaths from diphtheria and scarlet fever. In the case of these diseases, considered more dangerous to the public health, the health officers exercised summary powers of removal to the hospital where proper treatment could be had, and the result was a low death-rate.

These were tenements of the tall, modern type. A little more than a year ago, when a census was made of the tenements and compared with the mortality tables, no little surprise and congratulation was caused by the discovery that as the buildings grew taller the death-rate fell. The reason is plain, though the reverse had been expected by most people. The biggest tenements have been built in the last ten years of sanitary reform rule, and have been brought, in all but the crowding, under its laws. The old houses that from private dwellings were made into tenements, or were run up to house the biggest crowds in defiance of every moral and physical law, can be improved by no device short of demolition. They will ever remain the worst. . . .

Every once in a while a case of downright starvation gets into the newspapers and makes a sensation. But this is the exception. Were the whole truth known, it would come home to the community with a shock that would rouse it to a more serious effort than the spasmodic undoing of its purse-strings. I am satisfied from my own observation that hundreds of men, women, and children are every day slowly starving to death in the tenements with my medical friend's complaint of "improper nourishment." Within a single week I have had this year three cases of insanity, provoked directly by poverty and want. One was that of a mother who in the middle of the night got up to murder her child, who was crying for food; another was the case of an Elizabeth Street truck-driver whom the newspapers never heard of. With a family to provide for, he had been unable to work for many months. There was neither food, nor a scrap of anything upon which money could be raised, left in the house; his mind gave way under the combined physical and mental suffering. In the third case I was just in time with the police to prevent the madman from murdering his whole family. He had the sharpened hatchet in his pocket when we seized him. He was an Irish laborer, and had been working in the sewers until the poisonous gases destroyed his health. Then he was laid off, and scarcely anything had been coming in all winter but the oldest child's earnings as cash-girl in a store, $2.50 a week. There were seven children to provide for, and the rent of the Mulberry Street attic in which the family lived was $10 a month. They had borrowed as long as anybody had a cent to lend. When at last the man got an odd job that would just buy the children bread, the week's wages only served to measure the depth of their misery. "It came in so on the tail-end of everything," said his wife in telling the story, with unconscious eloquence. The outlook worried him through sleepless nights until it destroyed his reason. In his madness he had only one conscious thought: that the town should not take the children. "Better that I take care of them myself," he repeated to himself as he ground the axe to an edge. Help came in abundance from many almost as poor as they when the desperate straits of the family became known through his arrest. The readiness of the poor to share what little they

have with those who have even less is one of the few
moral virtues of the tenements. Their enormous crowds
touch elbow in a closeness of sympathy that is scarcely to
be understood out of them, and has no parallel except
among the unfortunate women whom the world scorns as
outcasts. There is very little professed sentiment about it
to draw a sentimental tear from the eye of romantic philanthropy. The hard fact is that the instinct of self-
preservation impels them to make common cause against
the common misery.

No doubt intemperance bears a large share of the blame
for it; judging from the stand-point of the policeman perhaps the greater share. Two such entries as I read in the
police returns on successive days last March, of mothers in
West Side tenements, who, in their drunken sleep, lay
upon and killed their infants, go far to support such a position. And they are far from uncommon. But my experience
has shown me another view of it, a view which the last report of the Society for Improving the Condition of the
Poor seems more than half inclined to adopt in allotting to
"intemperance the cause of distress, or distress the cause
of intemperance," forty per cent. of the cases it is called
upon to deal with. Even if it were all true, I should still
load over upon the tenement the heaviest responsibility.
A single factor, the scandalous scarcity of water in the hot
summer when the thirst of the million tenants must be
quenched, if not in that in something else, has in the past
years more than all other causes encouraged drunkenness
among the poor. But to my mind there is a closer connection between the wages of the tenements and the vices
and improvidence of those who dwell in them than, with
the guilt of the tenement upon our heads, we are willing
to admit even to ourselves. Weak tea with a dry crust is not
a diet to nurse moral strength. Yet how much better might
the fare be expected to be in the family of this "widow
with seven children, very energetic and prudent"—I quote
again from the report of the Society for the Improvement
of the Condition of the Poor—whose "eldest girl was employed as a learner in a tailor's shop at small wages, and one

boy had a place as 'cash' in a store. There were two other
little boys who sold papers and sometimes earned one
dollar. The mother finishes pantaloons and can do three
pairs in a day, thus earning thirty-nine cents. Here is a
family of eight persons with rent to pay and an income of
less than six dollars a week."

And yet she was better off in point of pay than this
Sixth Street mother, who "had just brought home four
pairs of pants to finish, at seven cents a pair. She was
required to put the canvas in the bottom, basting and sewing three times around; to put the linings in the waist-
bands; to tack three pockets, three corners to each; to put
on two stays and eight buttons, and make six buttonholes;
to put the buckle on the back strap and sew on the ticket,
all for seven cents." Better off than the "churchgoing
mother of six children," and with a husband sick to death,
who to support the family made shirts, averaging an income of one dollar and twenty cents a week, while her
oldest girl, aged thirteen, was "employed down-town cutting out Hamburg edgings at one dollar and a half a week
—two and half cents per hour for ten hours of steady labor
—making the total income of the family two dollars and
seventy cents per week." Than the Harlem woman, who
was "making a brave effort to support a sick husband and
two children by taking in washing at thirty-five cents for
the lot of fourteen large pieces, finding coal, soap, starch,
and bluing herself, rather than depend on charity in any
form." Specimen wages of the tenements these, seemingly
inconsistent with the charge of improvidence.

But the connection on second thought is not obscure.
There is nothing in the prospect of a sharp, unceasing battle for the bare necessaries of life to encourage looking
ahead, everything to discourage the effort. Improvidence
and wastefulness are natural results. The instalment plan
secures to the tenant who lives from hand to mouth his
few comforts; the evil day of reckoning is put off till a
to-morrow that may never come. When it does come, with
failure to pay and the loss of hard-earned dollars, it simply
adds another hardship to a life measured from the cradle

by such incidents. The children soon catch the spirit of this sort of thing. I remember once calling at the home of a poor washer-woman living in an East Side tenement, and finding the door locked. Some children in the hallway stopped their play and eyed me attentively while I knocked. The biggest girl volunteered the information that Mrs. Smith was out; but while I was thinking of how I was to get a message to her, the child put a question of her own: "Are you the spring man or the clock man?" When I assured her that I was neither one nor the other, but had brought work for her mother, Mrs. Smith, who had been hiding from the instalment collector, speedily appeared.

Perhaps of all the disheartening experiences of those who have devoted lives of unselfish thought and effort, and their number is not so small as often supposed, to the lifting of this great load, the indifference of those they would help is the most puzzling. They will not be helped. Dragged by main force out of their misery, they slip back again on the first opportunity, seemingly content only in the old rut. The explanation was supplied by two women of my acquaintance in an Elizabeth Street tenement, whom the city missionaries had taken from their wretched hovel and provided with work and a decent home somewhere in New Jersey. In three weeks they were back, saying that they preferred their dark rear room to the stumps out in the country. But to me the oldest, the mother, who had struggled along with her daughter making cloaks at half a dollar apiece, twelve long years since the daughter's husband was killed in a street accident and the city took the children, made the bitter confession: "We do get so kind o' downhearted living this way, that we have to be where something is going on, or we just can't stand it." And there was sadder pathos to me in her words than in the whole long story of their struggle with poverty; for unconsciously she voiced the sufferings of thousands, misjudged by a happier world, deemed vicious because they are human and unfortunate. . . .

DOCUMENT 34

(PLATE 12)

Among the Tenement-Houses During the Heated Term—Just before Daybreak

SOURCE: Sol Eytinge, Jun., "Among the Tenement-Houses During the Heated Term—Just before Daybreak" (wood engraving), *Harper's Weekly*, XXIII (9 August 1879), 629.

Winter was grim in the slums, but as Riis points out, sweltering summer could be even more oppressive. The factory chimneys in the background, sending out smoke as the boilers are fired up for another day, are a reminder that after a sleepless night the slum-dwellers face a day of labor in shop and factory.

PART IV

Racial Stereotypes

Although it is difficult to avoid using such terms as "liberal" and "conservative" or "left" and "right" in discussing political and social issues in the 1870s and 1880s, one must be careful not to assume that the polarization of opinions and attitudes in that period was similar to the patterns of our own day. One of the most conspicuous changes that has occurred in popular culture during the past hundred years is marked by the fact that in public discourse outside the South, racial prejudice is no longer reputable. It is not an exaggeration to say that in the mid-twentieth century, a belief in the biological inferiority and superiority of races is characteristic only of a reactionary minority. In the nineteenth century, however, many influential men who were considered to represent enlightened and humane attitudes were firm believers in the innate inequality of the races of mankind. Such doctrines were regarded as "scientific" in the sense that they were based on versions of the theory of organic evolution.

Belief in the biologically determined inferiority of the Negro was of course the most conspicuous form of American racial prejudice. It was implanted in popular culture by the long and tragic heritage of slavery, but the belief was by no means confined to the South. Many of the most determined crusaders for the abolition of slavery had been convinced that Negroes were inferior beings who needed to be protected and guided by the dominant whites. Rayford W. Logan points out that in the post-Civil War period the New York monthly literary magazines—*Harper's, Scribner's, Century*—regularly published drawings and cartoons as well as fiction holding Negroes up to scorn, raucous amusement, or at best sentimental patronizing. In fact, he maintains that the "nadir" of American attitudes toward the Negro was the 1880s and the 1890s.

The loyalty of Irish immigrants and their descendants to the Democratic machines in Northern cities exacerbated latent ethnic prejudice in zealous Republicans such as Thomas Nast. Furthermore, the increasing tide of immigration from central and southern Europe after the Civil War, because it introduced an unfamiliar element into American society, aroused apprehensions that could readily be converted into hostility.

The subject of racial prejudice is vast and complex, and it has been dealt with extensively by historians—not only by Logan (*The Negro in American Life and Thought: The Nadir, 1877–1901*, New York, 1954), but also by Edward N. Saveth (*American Historians and European Immigrants, 1875–1925*, New York, 1948) and, most comprehensively with regard to explicit theory, by Thomas F. Gossett (*Race: The History of an Idea in America*, Dallas, 1963). It is impossible to represent adequately in this anthology the complex of popular racial and ethnic prejudices. The illustrations grouped in the following section are the merest gesture, a shorthand reminder of attitudes that were taken for granted. They are all chosen from *Harper's Weekly*, and they are limited almost entirely to two topics, the Negro and the Irishman.

DOCUMENT 35

(PLATE 13)

Way Down upon the Swanee Ribber

SOURCE: R. N. Brooke, "Way Down upon the Swanee Ribber" (wood engraving), *Harper's Weekly*, XVII (28 June 1873), 552.

One of the most familiar racial stereotypes was that of the old Negro male who, having served his master long and faithfully before Emancipation, remains loyal through Reconstruction, and functions as a celebrant of the nostalgic myth of the pre-War Southern plantation. Some of Thomas Nelson Page's most affecting stories make use of this character—for example, "Ole 'Stracted," which appeared in *Harper's Monthly* in 1886 (LXXIII, October). Joel Chandler Harris's Uncle Remus is a version of the same stock figure, and Stephen Foster's song (composed in 1851 but widely popular through the remainder of the century) also uses it. The importation of the Foster song from its original context of the black-face minstrel show to the more genteel pages of *Harper's Weekly*, emphasized by the reprinting of the words of the song in the same issue with Brooke's drawing, indicates the increasing currency of the plantation myth: it would flower luxuriantly in the next decade in national magazines. The aged Negro is apparently a fiddler selling sheet music in the streets of a Northern city (his feet rest on paving stones, the placard reads "Songs 5¢," and the stove suggests cold weather; it may also provide roasted chestnuts for sale). The vision of past happiness ascribed to him in a dream has the standard characteristics of plantation romance: an exotic landscape, idle and carefree Negroes dancing to the music of a banjo, and in the background the mansion of the white "quality" in evident but benign contrast with the Negro hut on the banks of the stream. The insistence of popular culture on the venerable age of the faithful former slave is of course in accord with chronology as the pre-War era receded further into the past; but it also serves to play down the threatening sexuality of the young Negro male which contemporary lynchings show to have been an equally strong component of the prevalent conception of the Negro.

DOCUMENT 36

(PLATE 14)

Colored Rule in a Reconstructed (?) State

SOURCE: Thomas Nast, "Colored Rule in a Reconstructed (?) State" (wood engraving), *Harper's Weekly*, XVIII (14 March 1874), 229.

Nast, who used his cartoonist's pen for some of the most powerful editorializing in the history of American journalism, was normally a strict follower of the orthodox Republican party line. The violently hostile representation of Negro politicians in this drawing (which clothes them in the garish costumes of the Negro dude of minstrel tradition) foreshadows Hayes's withdrawal of Federal troops from the South as a result of the Republican bargain with Southern white leaders in the electoral crisis of 1876–77.

Nast gives his cartoon the subtitle, "The Members call each other Thieves, Liars, Rascals, and Cowards," and represents Columbia as saying: "You are Aping the lowest Whites. If you disgrace your Race in this way you had better take Back Seats."

DOCUMENT 37

(PLATE 15)

Their Pride

SOURCE: Thomas Hovenden, "Their Pride" (wood engraving from a painting), *Harper's Weekly*, XXXII (8 December 1888), 937.

Hovenden was of Irish birth but made his career in the United States; he succeeded Thomas Eakins as professor of painting in the Philadelphia Academy of Fine Arts. His capacity for warmth and pathos in the depiction of genre subjects, exemplified for example in his famous "Breaking Home Ties" (1890), made him one of the most popular painters of the later nineteenth century. He was noted for his sympathetic interest in the Negro; one of his best known paintings ("Last Moments of John Brown," *circa* 1881) shows Brown pausing as he leaves his prison for the scaffold, under heavy guard, to kiss a Negro infant in its mother's arms. "Their Pride" indicates that by the end of the 1880s popular culture could accept an affirmative treatment of the Negro relatively free of the patronizing attitude long familiar in local-color fiction. The family in Hovenden's painting are capable of arousing interest and sympathy in their own right. The artist has rejected the usual stereotype of the Negro (compare the face of the father with that of the old musician in Document 35). It is significant, further, that a beautiful Negro girl can be made the visual center of interest without any suggestion of uneasiness on the score of her sexual attractiveness.

Document 38

(Plate 16)

The Greek Slave

SOURCE: Thomas Nast, "The Greek Slave" (wood engraving), *Harper's Weekly*, XIV (16 April 1870), 248.

The justifiable bitterness that Nast felt toward the Tweed Ring for its corrupt dominance of New York City and state politics took an unfortunate form in his many variations on the theme represented in this cartoon. He sets forth the thesis that the Tammany machine lured Irish peasants to emigrate, then enslaved them upon their arrival in the United States and kept them chained to the Democratic Party. The bottles of liquor and the papal emblem on top of the post to which the caricature Irishman is chained suggest the means by which the ignorant voters are held in bondage. The slave driver with his lash is Peter B. Sweeny, one of Tweed's most prominent lieutenants, and a constant target for Nast's invective.

In *The Damnation of Theron Ware* (1896) Harold Frederic describes the "tacit race and religious aversion" against the Irish implanted in the young Methodist minister by his provincial upbringing in small towns of upstate New York. Theron Ware's prejudice resembles "some huge, shadowy, and symbolical monument . . . an abhorrent spectacle, truly!"

The foundations upon which its dark bulk reared itself were ignorance, squalor, brutality, and vice. Pigs wallowed in the mire before its base, and burrowing into this base were a myriad of narrow doors, each bearing the hateful sign of a saloon, and giving forth from its recesses of night the sounds of screams and curses. Above were sculptured rows of lowering, ape-like faces from Nast's and Keppler's cartoons, and out of these sprang into the vague upper gloom, on the one side, lamp-posts from which negroes hung by the neck, and on the other gibbets for dynamiters and Molly Maguires; and between the two glowed a spectral picture of some black-robed, tonsured men, with leering satanic masks, making a bonfire of the Bible in the public schools.*

* *The Damnation of Theron Ware*, John Harvard Library ed. (Cambridge, Mass., 1960), p. 51. Joseph Keppler was Nast's principal rival as a political caricaturist, first for *Frank Leslie's Illustrated Weekly*, and later in *Punch*, an illustrated humorous weekly founded by Keppler in 1877.

DOCUMENT 39

(PLATE 17)

The Unconditional Surrender—July 11th

SOURCE: Thomas Nast, "The Unconditional Surrender—July 11th" (wood engraving), *Harper's Weekly*, XV (29 July 1871), 697.

Protestant Orangemen in New York had announced a parade for 12 July 1871 to commemorate the Battle of the Boyne (1690), in which the forces of William III had defeated the Irish Catholic supporters of James II. An organization of Irishmen called the Hibernians had threatened to break up the parade by force. Mayor Oakley Hall, a member of the Tweed Ring, had then prohibited the parade, and Superintendent of Police James J. Kelso had issued General Order No. 57 to that effect. This is the surrender that Nast, following as usual the Republican party line, condemns in his cartoon. The figures represented kneeling in obeisance before the caricature Irishman with drawn sword include the Mayor (wearing a pince-nez), Peter B. Sweeny (with black mustache but no beard), and Boss Tweed himself (the last figure on the right). The United States flag is lowered in token of surrender before the ranks of the National Guard, as is the flag in the facing rank of policemen, while high above flies a flag bearing the Hibernian emblem of the harp.

The subsequent history of the incident throws light on contemporary attitudes toward Irish slum-dwellers. Governor John T. Hoffman, also a Democrat, responded to the uproar of criticism that greeted the General Order by countermanding it and coming to the city to take personal charge of the situation. On the afternoon of 12 July approximately one hundred Orangemen set out on their march through the streets of lower Manhattan under the protection of five hundred policemen and four regiments of New York militia. Some bystanders—described by one reporter as an aged crone and an adolescent boy—threw paving stones toward the paraders, and there were apparently other threatening gestures, although no actual injuries were reported at this stage. One of the militia regiments, at the command of its officers, halted and fired into the crowd, killing at least twenty persons and wounding perhaps twice that number. (The newspapers published varying statistics of casualties.) The fire was returned by snipers concealed behind chimneys and in the upper stories of buildings along the street; several policemen and militiamen were killed and others wounded. The parade then continued without further disturbance.

Nast's denunciation of the order forbidding the parade implies general support for the use of armed force to intimidate the Hibernians. The simian distortion of the faces of the two Irishmen reveals not only his astonishing command of his medium but also the fanatical virulence of a man who believed himself to be waging political warfare in a just cause.

The Usual Irish Way of Doing Things

SOURCE: Thomas Nast, "The Usual Irish Way of Doing Things" (wood engraving), *Harper's Weekly*, XV (2 September 1871), 824.

Nast is still hammering away at the riot of 12 July. Here he relies too heavily on printed and lettered texts for maximum effect in a cartoon, but the brutalized face of the rioter is hauntingly vivid.

DOCUMENT 41

(PLATE 19)

Sectarian Bitterness

SOURCE: Thomas Nast, "Sectarian Bitterness" (wood engraving), *Harper's Weekly*, XIV (26 February 1870), 140.

Attacking a proposal for state aid to church schools, Nast presents a gallery of racial stereotypes that includes along with the familiar Irishman and Negro the less common caricature figures of Chinese and Jew.

PART V

Immigrants

DOCUMENT 42

Perils.—Immigration

SOURCE: Josiah Strong, "Perils.—Immigration," from *Our Country: Its Possible Future and Its Present Crisis* (New York, 1885), pp. 30–45.

Josiah Strong's treatment of the problem of immigration illustrates how racist ideas could be integrated with a "liberal" theological position and a strong if misguided humanitarianism. Strong believed that a divine purpose was constantly furthering the progress of mankind by causing the evolutionary triumph of "higher" over "lower" races. The dominant position in his scheme was occupied by the Anglo-Saxon race, which he identified with the European peoples who had settled in this country during the first two centuries of its history. With a deliberately invidious reference to Roman Catholicism, Strong asserted that the Anglo-Saxons had a religious life "more vigorous, more spiritual, more Christian" than that of any other race. He insisted that one of the most urgent tasks of the Protestant Home Missionary movement was to "Americanize" and to "Christianize the mixed multitude of the down-town city." Although he deplored the racial prejudice expressed in such terms as "sheeny," "dago," or "coon," he maintained that the immigration of the post-Civil War period, mainly from central and southern Europe, was a "peril" for the United States because it threatened the long-established supremacy of the older Anglo-Saxon stock.*

Political optimism is one of the vices of the American people. There is a popular faith that "God takes care of

* Thomas F. Gossett, *Race: The History of an Idea in America* (Dallas, 1963), pp. 185–90.

children, fools, and the United States." We deem ourselves a chosen people, and incline to the belief that the Almighty stands pledged to our prosperity. Probably not one in a hundred of our population has ever questioned the security of our future. Such optimism is as senseless as pessimism is faithless. The one is as foolish as the other is wicked. . . .

America, as the land of promise to all the world, is the destination of the most remarkable migration of which we have any record. During the last four years we have suffered a peaceful invasion by an army more than twice as vast as the estimated number of Goths and Vandals that swept over Southern Europe and overwhelmed Rome. During the ninety years preceding 1880, ten million foreigners made their homes in the United States, and three-quarters of them came during the last third of that period. Not only are they coming in great numbers, but in numbers rapidly increasing. A study of the causes of this great world movement indicates that as yet we have seen only beginnings. . . .

In view of the fact that Europe is able to send us nearly nine times as many immigrants during the next thirty years as during the thirty years past, without any diminution of her population, and in view of all the powerful influences co-operating to stimulate the movement, is it not reasonable to conclude that we have seen only the advance guard of the mighty army which is moving upon us?

The Tenth Census gives our total foreign-born population as 6,679,943; but we must not forget their children of the first generation, who, as we shall see, present a more serious problem than their parents, the immigrants. This class numbers 8,316,053, making a total foreign population of nearly 15,000,000. . . . So immense a foreign element must have a profound influence on our national life and character. Immigration brings unquestioned benefits, but these do not concern our argument. It complicates almost every home missionary problem and furnishes the soil which feeds the life of several of the most noxious growths of our civilization. I have, therefore, dwelt at some length upon its future that we may the more accurately measure the dangers which threaten us.

Consider briefly the moral and political influence of immigration. 1. Influence on morals. Let me hasten to recognize the high worth of many of our citizens of foreign birth, not a few of whom are eminent in the pulpit and in all the learned professions. Many come to us in full sympathy with our free institutions, and desiring to aid us in promoting a Christian civilization. But no one knows better than these same intelligent and Christian foreigners that they do not represent the mass of immigrants. The typical immigrant is a European peasant, whose horizon has been narrow, whose moral and religious training has been meager or false, and whose ideas of life are low. Not a few belong to the pauper and criminal classes. "From a late report of the Howard Society of London, it appears that 'seventy-four per cent. of the Irish discharged convicts have found their way to the United States.'"† Moreover, immigration is demoralizing. No man is held upright simply by the strength of his own roots; his branches interlock with those of other men, and thus society is formed, with all its laws and customs and force of public opinion. Few men appreciate the extent to which they are indebted to their surroundings for the strength with which they resist, or do, or suffer. All this strength the emigrant leaves behind him. He is isolated in a strange land, perhaps doubly so by reason of a strange speech. He is transplanted from a forest to an open prairie, where, before he is rooted, he is smitten with the blasts of temptation.

We have a good deal of piety in our churches that will not bear transportation. It cannot endure even the slight change of climate involved in spending a few summer weeks at a watering place, and is commonly left at home. American travelers in Europe often grant themselves license, on which, if at home, they would frown. Very

† Dorchester's Problem of Religious Progress, p. 423. [The footnotes in this document are those of the author, not the editor.]

many church-members, when they go west, seem to think they have left their Christian obligations with their church-membership in the East. And a considerable element of our American-born population are apparently under the impression that the Ten Commandments are not binding west of the Missouri. Is it strange, then, that those who come from other lands, whose old associations are all broken and whose reputations are left behind, should sink to a lower moral level? Across the sea they suffered many restraints which are here removed. Better wages afford larger means of self-indulgence; often the back is not strong enough to bear prosperity, and liberty too often lapses into license. Our population of foreign extraction is sadly conspicuous in our criminal records. This element constituted in 1870 twenty per cent. of the population of New England, and furnished seventy-five per cent. of the crime. That is, it was twelve times as much disposed to crime as the native stock. The hoodlums and roughs of our cities are, most of them, American-born of foreign parentage. Of the 680 discharged convicts who applied to the Prison Association of New York for aid, during the year ending June 30th, 1882, 442 were born in the United States, against 238 foreign-born; while only 144 reported native parentage against 536 who reported foreign parentage. . . .

Moreover, immigration not only furnishes the greater portion of our criminals, it is also seriously affecting the morals of the native population. It is disease and not health which is contagious. Most foreigners bring with them continental ideas of the Sabbath, and the result is sadly manifest in all our cities, where it is being transformed from a holy day into a holiday. But by far the most effective instrumentality for debauching popular morals is the liquor traffic, and this is chiefly carried on by foreigners. In 1880, of the "Traders and dealers in liquors and wines,"‡ (I suppose this means wholesale dealers) sixty-three per cent. were foreign-born, and of the brewers

‡ The Tenth Census.

and maltsters seventy-five per cent., while a large proportion of the remainder were of foreign parentage. Of saloon-keepers about sixty per cent. were foreign-born, while many of the remaining forty per cent. of these corrupters of youth, these western Arabs, whose hand is against every man, were of foreign extraction.

2. We can only glance at the political aspects of immigration. As we have already seen, it is immigration which has fed fat the liquor power; and there is a liquor vote. Immigration furnishes most of the victims of Mormonism; and there is a Mormon vote. Immigration is the strength of the Catholic church; and there is a Catholic vote. Immigration is the mother and nurse of American socialism; and there is to be a socialist vote. Immigration tends strongly to the cities, and gives to them their political complexion. And there is no more serious menace to our civilization than our rabble-ruled cities. These several perils, all of which are enhanced by immigration, will be considered in succeeding chapters.

Many American citizens are not Americanized. It is as unfortunate as it is natural, that foreigners in this country should cherish their own language and peculiar customs, and carry their nationality, as a distinct factor, into our politics. Immigration has created the "German vote" and the "Irish vote," for which politicians bid, and which have already been decisive of state elections, and might easily determine national. A mass of men but little acquainted with our institutions, who will act in concert and who are controlled largely by their appetites and prejudices, constitute a very paradise for demagogues.

We have seen that immigration is detrimental to popular morals. It has a like influence upon popular intelligence, for the percentage of illiteracy among the foreign-born population is thirty-eight per cent. greater than among the native-born whites. Thus immigration complicates our moral and political problems by swelling our dangerous classes. And as immigration is to increase much more rapidly than the population, we may infer that the dangerous classes are to increase more rapidly than hitherto.§ It goes without saying, that there is a dead-line of ignorance and vice in every republic, and when it is touched by the average citizen, free institutions perish; for intelligence and virtue are as essential to the life of a republic as are brain and heart to the life of a man.

A severe strain upon a bridge may be borne with safety if evenly distributed, which, if concentrated, would ruin the whole structure. There is among our population of alien birth an unhappy tendency toward aggregation, which concentrates the strain upon portions of our social and political fabric. Certain quarters of many of the cities are, in language, customs and costumes, essentially foreign. Many colonies have bought up lands and so set themselves apart from Americanizing influences. . . . Our safety demands the assimilation of these strange populations, and the process of assimilation will become slower and more difficult as the proportion of foreigners increases.

§ From 1870 to 1880 the population increased 30.06 per cent. During the same period the number of criminals increased 82.33 per cent.

Document 43

(Plate 20)

Land, Ho!—Scene on Board an Emigrant Ship

source: Anonymous, "Land, Ho!—Scene on Board an Emigrant Ship" (wood engraving), *Harper's Weekly*, XV (3 June 1871), 509.

The most interesting feature of this drawing is the artist's favorable attitude toward his subjects. The passengers, representing a variety of European types, are presented as intelligent, clean, orderly, and healthy. Several handsome young men and women are depicted. The guitar and the violin are reminders of the musical cultivation of many Europeans, and the family group in the left foreground suggests quiet domestic habits. The male figure pointing toward the land is probably meant to be Jewish, but it is not a hostile portrait.

Document 44

(Plate 21)

The Modern Ship of the Plains

source: R. F. Zogbaum, "The Modern Ship of the Plains" (wood engraving), *Harper's Weekly*, XXX (13 November 1886), 728.

The scene is the interior of one of the cars specially constructed to transport immigrants cheaply on Western railroads. The mood is quite similar to that of Document 43. The surroundings are austere but tidy. The cap and boots worn by the young man in the aisle—probably German—suggests a university background. The sleeping child, the boy watching a man prepare food, and the kitten all convey a reassuring sense of domesticity.

Document 45

(Plate 22)

Immigrants Waiting to be Distributed in the Coal Regions of Pennsylvania

SOURCE: W. A. Rogers, "Immigrants Waiting to be Distributed in the Coal Regions of Pennsylvania" (pen-and-ink drawing), *Harper's Weekly*, XXXII (28 July 1888), 557.

Whereas the scenes on board ship (Document 43) and in the railroad car (Document 44) suggest Western European origins of the immigrants, here the conspicuous figures in the foreground seem to be Central European, perhaps Slavic. The landscape is desolate. These tired, submissive, and apparently aged men and women are not looking forward to a new life in a new country, but at best to a slight improvement in a way of life that has always been hard. The artist's relatively unsympathetic attitude toward his subjects may be due to the presumption that they will compete with American industrial workers instead of making homes for themselves on Western farmlands.

DOCUMENT 46

(PLATE 23)

A Question of Labor

SOURCE: W. A. Rogers, "A Question of Labor" (pen-and-ink drawing), *Harper's Weekly*, XXXII (29 September 1888), 721.

Here, as in Thomas Nast's drawings of the Irish (Documents 38–41), political emotions have entered into the visual representation of the immigrant. The man walking down the gangplank is a sullen brute with only a handful of possessions, bearing a numbered tag as if he were a parcel of merchandise. The shovel suggests that he is equipped for nothing beyond unskilled manual labor. The slogans attacking trusts and monopolies in behalf of "American labor" are not consonant with the animal stupidity ascribed to the peasant on the gangplank, for a skilled and intelligent competitor would presumably be a more alarming threat to American labor than this lout with his shovel.

PART VI

Protest

The belief that technological advance would solve all economic and social problems, as set forth for example by Robert H. Thurston (Document 4) and Senator Orville H. Platt (Document 5), was placed under an increasing strain during the 1870s by revelations of misery in the slums of large cities and by conflicts between workers and employers that developed into open warfare. The great railway strike of 1877 was especially disturbing, not only because it involved the whole country, from coast to coast, but also because it broke out in a highly mechanized industry. The question had to be asked: Was the early promise of the machine being made good?

In *Progress and Poverty* (1879) Henry George hammered home his answer with a rhetoric as powerful as Tom Paine's. "The present century," declared George in his opening paragraph, "has been marked by a prodigious increase in wealth-producing power. The utilization of steam and electricity, the introduction of improved processes and labor-saving machinery, the greater subdivision and grander scale of production, the wonderful facilitation of exchanges, have multiplied enormously the effectiveness of labor." If a man of the eighteenth century—a Franklin or a Priestley—could have foreseen the development of technology in the advanced societies of the world, "in the sight of the imagination he would have beheld these new forces . . . lifting the very poorest above the possibility of want . . . ; he would have seen these slaves of the lamp of knowledge taking on themselves the traditional curse, these muscles of iron and sinews of steel making the poorest laborer's life a holiday, in which every high quality and noble impulse could have scope to grow."

The vision that George develops with such eloquence is almost identical with the generalized descriptions of the actual state of society advanced by Thurston and Platt. But George maintains that the idea of prosperity and happiness created by mechanization is everywhere belied by the facts. The reality is the reverse of the golden dream:

The "tramp" [he asserted] comes with the locomotive, and almshouses and prisons are as surely the marks of "material progress" as are costly dwellings, rich warehouses, and magnificent churches. Upon streets lighted with gas and patrolled by uniformed policemen, beggars wait for the passer-by, and in the shadow of college, and library, and museum, are gathering the more hideous Huns and fiercer Vandals of whom Macaulay prophesied. . . . The march of invention has clothed mankind with powers of which a century ago the boldest imagination could not have dreamed. But in factories where labor-saving machinery has reached its most wonderful development, little children are at work; wherever the new forces are anything like fully utilized, large classes are maintained by charity or live on the verge of recourse to it; amid the greatest accumulations of wealth, men die of starvation, and puny infants suckle dry breasts; while everywhere the greed of gain, the worship of wealth, shows the force of the fear of want.*

George's perception became the common property of many dissident groups and movements in the 1880s. The influence of his celebrated "remedy"—a single tax

* Henry George, *Progress and Poverty. An Inquiry into the Cause of Industrial Depression and of Increase of Want with Increase of Wealth. The Remedy* (1879), Fiftieth Anniversary Edition (New York, 1929), pp. 3, 4, 7–8.

amounting to one hundred per cent of the unearned increment in the value of land—can be recognized for example in the attacks on monopoly that run through the documents included in this section of the anthology. The Anti-Monopoly League was an active propaganda organization. But in the light of subsequent history, George's proposal for reform seems much less impressive than his description of the ills of industrialism. His preoccupation—it might almost be called an obsession— with monopoly of land was anachronistic; it represented the survival of an essentially agrarian viewpoint into a period when agriculture had ceased to be the dominant force in the American economy. George's contention that the basic conflict was between labor and monopoly, not labor and capital, led him to underestimate the significance of labor unions and made much of his vigorous reformist effort irrelevant.

The inhibiting force of agrarian tradition on George's social theory is especially clear in his continued reliance on the idea of the West as a safety valve for social and economic discontent. This notion, already current in the eighteenth century, and restated by Franklin, by Washington, by Jefferson, by virtually all American statesmen for more than a century, was one of the most deeply rooted articles of agrarian faith. Much of its hold on the popular mind lay in its simplicity. The doctrine asserted, in brief, that the inexhaustible store of free land awaiting settlement on the Western frontier made American society immune to the economic and social ills of the Old World. Poverty, unemployment, low wages, the existence of a working class without hope of bettering its condition, were bound to be transitory phenomena in this country because the unsuccessful or merely discontented man could always go West and earn a good living for himself and his family by farming.† With the passage of the Homestead Act in 1862, it was almost universally believed that the federal government had enacted the only legislation necessary to ensure the automatic operation of this panacea for social ills. Both the theory of the safety valve and the single

† "The Garden as Safety Valve," Chap. xx in Henry N. Smith, *Virgin Land: The American West as Symbol and Myth*, Cambridge, Mass., 1950.

tax that George proclaimed as an infallible remedy are
deeply American; they are the quintessence of vernacular thought, the economic equivalent of homemade
theologies and cracker-barrel metaphysics. They could
have been conceived and cherished only by men of an
Adamic innocence whose deepest belief was in the be-
neficence of Nature and the primordial sanctity of the
husbandman's labor in the good earth.

Ironically enough, George's uncritical reliance on
agrarian tradition aligned him with the most conservative businessmen, who used it repeatedly to prove that
no intervention by the government was needed to solve
American problems. Shrewder spokesmen for the left
emphatically repudiated the safety-valve doctrine, dem-
onstrating with an abundance of detail that urban industrial workers could not hope to make a living by
going West and becoming farmers. Furthermore, the
rural West was suffering economic distress during the
1880s that would burst out at the end of the decade in
the Populist revolt.

The ideologies and counterideologies generated by
conflicts between industrial workers and employers in
this period are a large and important topic, to which has
been devoted a copious monographic literature.‡ In one
direction, the many-voiced debate moved upward toward
a searching analysis of the major social and economic
issues of the modern world. At the level of popular culture, it proliferated into an amusing or pathetic array
of gimmicks and slogans and nostrums advocated as cures
for social and economic ills—grave or trivial, general or
local, real or imaginary—that can hardly be displayed
adequately in the brief compass of an anthology. What
is presented here is a selection from the testimony offered by witnesses before the Senate Committee on
Education and Labor at hearings conducted in New
York during a few weeks in the late summer and early
autumn of 1883. The witnesses differed as much in
their degrees of sophistication as they did in their

‡ A convenient list of relevant materials is contained in the
bibliographical notes at the end of Edward C. Kirkland, *Industry
Comes of Age: Business, Labor, and Public Policy, 1860–1897*,
New York, 1961. Also worth consulting is Chester M. Destler,
American Radicalism, 1865–1901, New London, Conn., 1946.

opinions. Whereas many of them represented important segments of current opinion, some were parroting the dogmas of this or that miniscule group of true believers, and still others were obviously cranks representing no one except themselves. The Committee was remarkably permissive; it tried to give everyone who wished it an opportunity to be heard.

In drawing upon the transcript of the hearings I have tried to convey an impression of the ideas about public policy that were circulating in popular culture—ideas one might have expected to encounter in larger or smaller public meetings, or hear from the pulpit or in casual conversation, or read in newspaper editorials. The sample has the defect of being limited to a single year, but it has the compensating advantage of being a reasonably full cross section and of showing what diverse opinions could exist side by side. A similar sample taken ten years earlier would probably reveal less variety but greater confusion; in 1893 the ideas would be more nearly crystallized because the Populist Party had entered the national elections of the previous year and had hammered out a number of platforms defining temporary coalitions among diverse left-wing groups, and the conservative defense had come into focus around key doctrines and dogmas under attack. But the differences observable over the twenty-year period would lie in emphasis rather than in substance.

The main themes which emerge in the following bits of testimony are a marked disillusionment with the outcome of the mechanization of industry; the laborers' specific complaints about wages, the cost of living, and the conditions of work; and a growing awareness of a class conflict between employers and employees. The list of solutions advocated, such as the organization of workers into unions, federal laws against monopoly, the single tax, a socialist revolution on Marxian lines, profit-sharing plans, and the Utopian ideal of a co-operative commonwealth, is by no means exhaustive, but it shows that the great debate over the consequences of the technological revolution had begun in earnest.

DOCUMENT 47

Testimony before the Senate Committee on Education and Labor

SOURCE: Henry George, Testimony before the Senate Committee on Education and Labor, New York, 22 August 1883 (from *Report of the Committee*, Vol. I, pp. 466–511).

The Committee evidently took George's views seriously. His testimony runs to almost fifty pages in the published transcript, and members of the Committee entered into prolonged debates with him on various points of fact or interpretation. His attitude toward the labor movement is curiously ambiguous: on occasion he seems to believe that unions can improve the lot of the workers by direct action, yet again he maintains that their function is mainly educational. As has already been noticed, however, some quite devoted and aggressive union spokesmen considered themselves George's disciples.

NEW YORK, *August 22*, 1883.

HENRY GEORGE sworn and examined.

By Mr. CALL:

Question. Please state your place of residence.—Answer. I reside at 70 Hancock street, Brooklyn.

Q. You have been engaged for some years, I believe, in looking into the labor question, the condition of the laboring population, and the relations of labor and capital, have you not?

THE LABOR QUESTION

A. For some time, with a great deal of attention.

Q. We should be glad to have a statement from you in

your own way of any facts that may be within your knowledge in regard to the condition of labor in its relations to
capital, and any suggestions of remedies which you think
would bring about an improved condition of things.—A. As
for specific facts I presume you could get them with much
more advantage from other persons, from those who are
familiar with each locality and the particular facts relating
to it. The general fact, however, is that there exists among
the laboring classes of the United States a great and growing feeling of dissatisfaction and discontent. As to whether
the condition of the laboring classes in the United States
is getting any worse, that is a difficult and complex question. I am inclined to think that it is; but whether it is or
not, the feeling of dissatisfaction is evidently increasing. It
is certainly becoming more and more difficult for a man in
any particular occupation to become his own employer.
The tendency of business of all kinds, both in production
and in exchange, is concentration, to the massing of large
capital, and to the massing of men. The inventions and
improvements of all kinds that have done so much to
change all the aspects of production, and which are still
going on, tend to require a greater and greater division of
labor, the employment of more and more capital, and to
make it more and more difficult for a man who has nothing
but his labor to become his own employer, or to rise to a
position of independence in his craft or occupation.

Q. Can you state any economic reasons why that is the
case?

THE CONFLICT BETWEEN LABOR AND MONOPOLY

A. I do not believe that there is any conflict of interest
between labor and capital, using those terms in their large
sense. I believe the conflict is really between labor and
monopoly. Capital is the instrument and tool of labor,
and under conditions of freedom there would be as much
competition for the employment of capital as for the employment of labor. When men speak of the aggressions of
capital and of the conflict between labor and capital I
think they generally have in mind *aggregated* capital, and

aggregated capital which is in of some way or other a monopoly more or less close. The earnings [of] capital, purely as capital, are always measured by the rate of interest. The return to capital for its employment, risk being as nearly as possible eliminated, is interest, and interest has certainly, for some time past, been falling, until now it is lower than it ever has been in this country before. The large businesses which yield great returns have in them always, I think, some element of monopoly.

Do you wish me to go right on and give my views generally, or do you desire me to limit myself to answers to your questions?

Q. I wish you would first give us the economic reasons why there are such aggregations of capital. I would like also to have you explain the sense in which you use the term "monopoly" when you speak of these aggregations of capital.

MONOPOLY DEFINED AND ILLUSTRATED

A. I use the term "monopoly" in the sense of a peculiar privilege or power of doing certain things which other persons have not. There are various kinds of monopolies. As, for instance, the monopolies given by the patent laws which give to the inventor or to his assigns the exclusive right to use a particular invention or process. There are certain businesses that are in their nature monopolies. For instance, in a little village if one puts up a hotel which is sufficient to accommodate all the travel there, he will have a virtual monopoly of that business, for the reason that no one else will put up another to compete with him, knowing that it would result in the loss of money; and for that reason our common law recognizes a peculiar obligation on the part of the innkeeper; he is not allowed to discriminate as between those who come to him for lodging or food. Again, a railroad is in its nature a monopoly. Where one line of road can do the business, no one else is going to build another along side of it, and, as we see in our railroad system, the competition of railroad companies is only between what they call "competing points" where two or

three roads come together, and as to these the tendency
is to do away with competition by contract or pooling. The
telegraph business is in its nature a monopoly; and so with
various others. Then again, there is a certain power of
monopoly that comes with the aggregation of large capital
in a business. A man who controls a very large amount of
capital can succeed by under-selling and by other
methods, in driving out his smaller competitors and very
often in concentrating the business in his own hands.

Q. You use the term in a broader sense then, than that
of a monopoly created by law. You include in it any exclusive right, whether created by facts and circumstances
or by law?—A. Yes. As I have said, there are businesses
which are in their very nature monopolies. The two most
striking examples of that are the railroad and the telegraph.

THE TENDENCY TOWARD THE AGGREGATION
OF CAPITAL AND LABOR

Q. In your opinion, what are the economic reasons why
business tends to become concentrated and why all industries have a tendency to aggregation in the hands of a
few?—A. I think that is the universal tendency of all progress. It is because larger and larger capitals are required
and because labor becomes more and more divided. For
instance, when boots and shoes are made by hand the only
capital required is a lap-stone and a little kit of tools, and
any man who has learned the trade and can get a piece of
leather can sit down and make a pair of shoes. He can do
it in his own house and can finish his product there and
sell it. But when a machine is invented to be used in that
business, the shoemaker requires capital enough to purchase that machine, and, as more and more machines are
invented, more and more capital is needed, while the skill
required becomes less and less. I believe you have it in
testimony here that in the process of shoemaking now there
are sixty-four different branches, thereby requiring that
number of costly machines and differentiating the trade
into that number of subdivisions.

Q. The reason, then, is that production is cheaper when it is done by concentrated capital?—A. Certainly.

Q. You had better proceed now and state your views in your own way.—A. The subject is so wide a one that I might wander further than you would care to follow me, and as you have been investigating these matters perhaps it would be better that you should question me; but if you prefer, I will go on in my own way.

Q. I think you had better do so.—A. Well, we have been speaking of the telegraph business. I should like to say a word or two more in regard to that, and I will do it now or afterwards, just as the committee prefer.

Mr. CALL. We shall be glad to hear your views on that subject at any period of your examination that may suit you, and you can begin with it if you think proper.

THE RELATIONS OF MACHINERY TO LABOR

A. Machinery, in my opinion, ought to be an advantage to labor. Its primary effect is simply to increase the product of labor, to add to the power of labor, and enable it to produce more. One would suppose, and in fact it was supposed at the beginning of the era of modern inventions, that the effect of the introduction of machinery would be to very greatly improve the condition of the laboring classes and largely to raise wages. I think it quite certain that its effect has not been that; that, while very many articles have been greatly cheapened in cost and in price, wherever there has been an increase in the wages of labor it can be traced to something else; generally to the efforts of the laborers themselves, by the formation of trades unions and organizations which have wrested from their employers a higher rate of wages, or to improvements in government, or improvements in intelligence, or improvement in morals. I think that whoever will thoroughly examine the facts will come to the conclusion that John Stuart Mill is right when he says that "all the labor-saving machinery that has hitherto been invented has not lessened the toil of a single human being." While, on the other hand, by permitting and requiring this great subdivision

of labor and dispensing to a great extent with skill on the
part of the laborer, it has reduced him to a far more dependent condition than that which he occupied before.
That is illustrated by the case we were speaking of awhile
ago. The old-fashioned shoemaker, having learned his
trade and purchased his kit of tools, was his own master.
If he did not find work in one place he could find it in
another place. He had the means of earning a livelihood
wherever he could find people who wanted shoes. But now
the shoemaker must find a great factory, and an employer
with a large amount of capital. Without such an employer
he is utterly helpless: he cannot make a shoe; he can only
make one-tenth or one sixty-fourth part of a shoe, or whatever the proportion may be. It is the same way with all
other trades into which machinery has largely entered. The
effect of the introduction of machinery in any trade is to
dispense with skill and to make the laborer more helpless.
I think you all understand that effect of machinery.

Q. Your idea is that the introduction of machinery in
the trades tends to prevent a man from mastering the
whole of his trade—that he learns a part of the trade instead of the whole trade?

THE MONOPOLY OF LAND

A. Yes. That in itself might not be a disadvantage; but it
is a disadvantage under present conditions; those conditions being that the laborers are driven by competition
with each other to seek employment on any terms. They
must find it; they cannot wait. Ultimately, I believe the
whole trouble to come from the fact that the natural field
of employment, the primary source of wealth, the land,
has been monopolized and labor is shut off from it. Wages
in all occupations have a certain relation to each other;
fixed by various circumstances, such as the desirability of
the employment; the continuity of the work; the ease or
difficulty of learning it; the scarcity of the peculiar powers
required, and so on; but in a large sense they must all
depend upon the wages in the widest occupation. That
occupation in this country is agriculture, and everywhere

throughout the world the largest occupations are those which concern themselves directly and primarily with the soil. Where there is free access to the soil wages in any employment cannot sink lower than that which, upon an average, a man can make by applying himself to the soil—to those natural opportunities of labor which it affords. When the soil is monopolized and free access to it ceases, then wages may be driven to the lowest point on which the laborer can live. The fact that in new countries wages, generally speaking, are higher than they are in old countries, is simply because in those new countries, as we call them, the soil has not yet passed fully into private hands. As access to the land is closed, the competition between laborers for employment from a master becomes more intense, and wages are steadily forced down to the lowest amount on which the laborer can live.

In a state of freedom the introduction of machinery could but add to wages. It would increase the productive power of labor, and the competition with each other of those having such machinery and desiring to employ labor would suffice to give the laborer his full share of the improvement. Where natural opportunities are closed up, however, the advantages resulting from the use of machinery, minus that part retained by monopolies arising from its use, must ultimately go to the owners of land, either in higher rents or higher prices. You can see that very readily if you consider a community in which one person or a small number of persons had full possession of the land. In such a case no one could work upon the land or live upon it save upon their terms. Those who had no land, having no means of employment, would have to compete with each other for the privilege of working for those who had the land, and wages would, of course, steadily sink to the point at which a man could barely live. Now, if you imagine a labor-saving invention introduced there, no matter how much it might add to the productiveness of labor, the landlord could necessarily claim the whole advantage, just as he could claim any advantage arising from increased fertility of the soil. If invention were carried to the farthest imaginable point, so that labor could be entirely dispensed with in the production of wealth, the raw material must still be obtained from the land, and therefore the land-owners would have all the wealth that could be produced, and would be absolutely independent of labor. There would be no use for anybody else, save as their servants or as pensioners on their bounty. This point is of course unattainable, but towards it labor-saving inventions tend, and their general effect is to raise the price of land. This is illustrated in the effect of railroads. Railroads very much reduce the cost of transportation, but that does not add anywhere to the wages of labor, nor yet, generally, to the profits of capital. It simply adds to the value of land. Where a railroad comes wages do not increase; interest does not rise; but land goes up in value. All human production in the last analysis is the union of labor with land; the combination, transportation, or modification of materials furnished by nature so as to adapt them for the use of man. Therefore where land is monopolized labor becomes helpless. Where one man owns the land he must necessarily be the master of all the other men that live upon it. Where one class own the land they must necessarily be the ruling class. Those who have not land must work for those who have it. In a ruder state of society, such as that which existed in Poland and in many other countries of the world, the system of serfdom resulted simply from the ownership of the land. The laborer was a serf because he must get his living out of the land which another man owned. In a state of society like ours, where the land is very largely divided up, you do not see this so clearly; but you can see it, on one side, in the large sums which the owners of land are enabled to obtain without doing anything themselves, and on the other, in the conditions which exist among the lowest class of laborers. . . .

BENEFITS OF TRADES UNIONS MAINLY EDUCATIONAL

Senator GEORGE. Have you no confidence in combination and cooperation among the workingmen?

The WITNESS. Yes, I have, to a certain extent. They

can accomplish something, and the larger and more extensive the combination the more it can accomplish; but I still regard the educational feature of those trades organizations as the most useful one. I believe that a great deal can be gained by a reduction of the hours of labor. I believe that that would mean an increase in the intelligence of the workingman, because it would give him time to think. Everything of that kind is good.

Senator GEORGE. Do you think there is nothing in the idea of the workers in a particular craft combining so as to act as one man in negotiating with the employers—do you think there is nothing in that to benefit labor?

The WITNESS. I think that to some extent the workingmen can benefit themselves in that way; but I do not think they can secure any very large benefit in that way; because if any very large benefit were brought about in any particular trade that trade would be brought down again to the general level by the influx from other trades.

Senator GEORGE. But suppose all the trades were to combine?

The WITNESS. Even so; you have outside of the trades the great mass of unorganized workmen, the unskilled laborers, who are incapable of organization, and, therefore, for any large and permanent benefit, there must be something which will take in the whole mass, which will include labor of all kinds.

Senator GEORGE. The number of unskilled laborers will probably exceed that of skilled laborers, will it not?

The WITNESS. I think so. The real foundation of industry in this country is, of course, agricultural labor, as that is the largest class. You cannot raise the wages in any particular trade or avocation much above the general level unless you can adopt some means to prevent people from rushing into that particular avocation; and even if you could do that, the benefit would be only a partial one, confined in its good effects to that one class. I think all these questions are ultimately questions of organization, that the community must act as a whole.

DOCUMENT 48

Testimony

SOURCE: Louis F. Post, Testimony before the Senate Committee on Education and Labor, New York, 29 August 1883 (from *Report of the Committee*, Vol. I, pp. 783–86).

Speaking as the official co-ordinator of testimony to be offered by witnesses representing the Central Labor Union of New York, Post refers approvingly both to Henry George and to the anti-monopoly movement. This strategy indicates something like a coalition among dissident groups with quite varied programs. Post is especially eager to maintain solidarity between the labor unions and the small businessmen whose opposition to "aggregated capital" (or Big Business) was the central animus of the Anti-Monopoly League.

NEW YORK, *August 29, 1883.*

LOUIS F. POST sworn and examined.

By the CHAIRMAN:

Question. Mr. Post, you are familiar with the scope of the investigation which this committee is engaged in, and I will therefore ask you to proceed to make your statement in your own way.—Answer. Very well. I am a lawyer by profession, practicing in the city of New York. I appear before this committee as the representative of the Central Labor Union of New York, and in that capacity I have introduced the witnesses who were examined here yesterday afternoon. I testify now somewhat out of order, to save the time of the committee, and shall therefore be obliged, instead of referring to all our evidence as being in, to make a statement of the substance of some of it which I shall produce to-day.

THE FACTS PROVED BY THE CENTRAL LABOR UNION

In presenting the case in behalf of the Central Labor Union, we have proved so far, with reference to the city of New York, first, that the productive power of labor here has been vastly increased by machinery; and secondly, that, concurrently with this increase of productive power, the wages of labor have at least been at a stand-still, if they have not decreased; while at the same time we have shown that the workingman's style of living and his social condition have deteriorated, and that, in many cases, his wages are actually lower in dollars and cents, while the price of living is considerably higher, than some years ago. We have also shown that a workingman nowadays learns no complete trade, and, therefore, never becomes an independent workman, but must always seek a master. We have shown that it is almost, if not quite an impossibility, for a workman going into the mechanical trades to ever become the employer of himself; that in consequence of that, in many cases, he loses spirit and becomes despondent and thriftless, and in other cases desperate and disorderly. We have shown, to some extent, that children, instead of being at school, are put to work here at a very early age merely to eke out the income of their parents, and we may yet be able to show specifically by employers instances of the employment of child-labor in factories. I know of my own knowledge that in one dry-goods house, that of Erich Brothers, children who I should say are not above ten years of age are kept busily at work during the week, from about 6 or 7 o'clock in the morning until 6 or 7 o'clock at night, every day except Saturday, and on Saturday until 11 o'clock at night. I have seen Erich Brothers' store open and crowded as late as 11 o'clock at night, and those children still on duty. It is my intention, at present, to try to have Mr. Erich on the stand as a witness to testify on this subject. We have proved these facts which I have thus rapidly recited by intelligent witnesses of various trades representing, probably, ten or twelve of the principal mechanical trades carried on in this city, and, if the committee desired, it would be possible for us to offer additional proof in regard to other trades in which the same general state of facts would be found to exist.

EXCEPTIONAL TRADES

There are, however, two or three trades that are exceptional in that respect, and to which the same statement would not apply to an equal extent. The painters' trade and, to a certain extent, the plumbers' trade may be exceptions.

GREAT INCREASE OF WEALTH—WHO GETS IT?

And yet, coexisting with this deteriorated condition of the laboring classes of New York, we find an immense increase of wealth, which is due undoubtedly to the increase of population and the introduction of labor-saving machinery. One object of the Central Labor Union has been and is to ascertain in what directions and to whom this increased wealth goes. We have thus far shown, by the witnesses we have produced here, that it does not go to the workers in these trades, and, if the committee desire, we can show that it does not go to the workers in any trade; that they are no better for the introduction of this labor-saving machinery, but that, on the contrary, in many cases they are far worse off than they were before.

CAPITAL UNAIDED BY MONOPOLY
FARES NO BETTER THAN LABOR

From the workers in the mechanical trades we have to pass to the small capitalists. We have not introduced many witnesses on that branch of the subject, yet our testimony in relation to it has been pretty comprehensive and can be made much more so if the committee desire, or if they entertain any doubt of the truth of the proposition that a man with a small capital unprotected by a monopoly of some sort has no better opportunity of advancing under the present condition of things than the wage-worker him-

self. As Mr. McGuire testified, a man with a capital sufficient in his business to buy an express wagon and horses
had better, instead of buying them, hire himself out for
wages, put his capital in bank, at even 3 per cent. interest,
and work for somebody else. The object of that testimony
is to show that capital as such—capital not supported or
protected by monopoly in some form—is not getting the
advantage of this great increase of wealth that we find
here. Our purpose has been to show that this increased
wealth does not go either to the laborer or to the capitalist;
I mean the small capitalist—the man not protected by any
franchise or other form of monopoly.

By Mr. GEORGE:

Q. You mean simply capital, without anything else—
capital simply?—A. I mean capital simply, because aggregated capital is to some extent a monopoly. A man with
a vast capital is able to, more or less, monopolize the
business in which he engages, but capital not so supported
is not worth more in business than the interest which can
be got on undoubted security, where the element of risk
is eliminated.

INCREASE OF WEALTH ACCOMPANIED BY LOWERING
OF THE RATE OF INTEREST

I do not know that it will be necessary to show formally
that the rate of interest in New York, instead of increasing
with the increase of wealth, has diminished; that whereas
the interest on investments on undoubted security where
there was no risk was formerly 7 or 8 per cent., or there-
about, it is now down to 3 or 4 per cent. That fact will
not be disputed. I am speaking now of cases where the
element of risk is entirely eliminated. Of course, where
there is risk, there the question of insurance comes in. The
object of this evidence is to show that capital as such is not
reaping the benefit of this increase of wealth. It is a matter
of common knowledge that that has been the course of
things—that interest has gone downward just as wages have
gone downward.

WHERE THE INCREASE OF WEALTH GOES

I have not been able yet, but I shall be this afternoon, to go into the other branch of the question, Where has this increase of wealth gone? It must go to somebody, because it is proved to exist, and one of the objects of the Central Labor Union, as I have said, is to ascertain and show where it does go. As this increased wealth does not go to the wage-worker, and does not go to the small capitalist, we believe there is no other place where it can go except to aggregated capital and to the holders of public franchises. There is no other place to look for it, no other place to which it goes, as I think you will find, but to aggregated capital and to the public franchises granted to individuals and corporations. There has been testimony before the committee, which we adopt as a part of our own, showing the profits of large establishments to which workingmen are compelled to resort for employment by reason of their inability to go into business for themselves. As Mr. Henry George has put it, these men are compelled to seek a *master* at this day, just as in a more distant period men were compelled to seek a *lord* for the protection of life and liberty and the opportunity to earn their own living.

Other testimony shows the tendency of railroads and telegraphs in private hands to attract to their owners a large proportion of this increased production which now exists, and we intend this afternoon to show specifically another set of franchises which are great absorbers of the wealth of the community, namely, those franchises which appropriate natural gifts, such as mines, water-courses, the natural productive powers of the soil, and what I believe is termed, and what I shall call for want of a better term, "the unearned increment."

DOCUMENT 49

Testimony

SOURCE: John Morrison, Testimony before the Senate Committee on Education and Labor, New York, 28 August 1883 (from *Report of the Committee*, Vol. I, pp. 755–64).

Morrison's testimony is particularly vivid in its account of the devaluation of the craftsman's skills by mechanization and the consequent decline in the economic and social status of skilled workers. The long exchange between him and Senator Wilkinson Call of Florida probably resembles much street-corner debate in the 1880s. Morrison may have read Marx and Lassalle but he has not really thought through what he means by his ominous references to "forcible revolution"; and the Senator has an even more primitive conception of socialism.

NEW YORK, *August* 28, 1883.

JOHN MORRISON sworn and examined.

By Mr. GEORGE:

Question. State your age, residence, and occupation.—Answer. I am about twenty-three years old; I live in this city; I am a machinist, and have been in that business about nine years.

Q. Do you work in a shop?—A. Yes, sir; I work in different shops.

CHANGED CONDITIONS—SUBDIVISION OF THE TRADE

Q. Is there any difference between the conditions under which machinery is made now and those which existed ten years ago?—A. A great deal of difference.

Q. State the differences as well as you can.—A. Well, the trade has been subdivided and those subdivisions have been again subdivided, so that a man never learns the machinist's trade now. Ten years ago he learned, not the whole of the trade, but a fair portion of it. Also, there is more machinery used in the business, which again makes machinery. In the case of making the sewing-machine, for instance, you find that the trade is so subdivided that a man is not considered a machinist at all. Hence it is merely laborers' work and it is laborers that work at that branch of our trade. The different branches of the trade are divided and subdivided so that one man may make just a particular part of a machine and may not know anything whatever about another part of the same machine. In that way machinery is produced a great deal cheaper than it used to be formerly, and in fact, through this system of work, 100 men are able to do now what it took 300 or 400 men to do fifteen years ago. By the use of machinery and the subdivision of the trade they so simplify the work that it is made a great deal easier and put together a great deal faster. There is no system of apprenticeship, I may say, in the business. You simply go in and learn whatever branch you are put at, and you stay at that unless you are changed to another.

Q. Does a man learn his branch very rapidly?—A. Yes, sir; he can learn his portion of the business very rapidly. Of course he becomes very expert at it, doing that all the time and nothing else, and therefore he is able to do a great deal more work in that particular branch than if he were a general hand and expected to do everything in the business as it came along.

Q. About what fractional part of a machinist is a worker in one of those machine shops now? How many men does it take to make a machine generally?—A. I could not answer that definitely, because there are so many different kinds of machines. Take the sewing-machine: I understand that it takes 300 men to make the different parts of the machine to the finish. That is my understanding. I have never worked at that branch, though.

Q. What branch do you work at?—A. I work as a vise hand; more in repairing work, more as a general hand.

Q. You learned the whole business, I suppose?—A. Not entirely; only the lathe and the vise. But, of course, we are expected to know how to do and to do a good deal more than those other men who get a great deal less wages.

Q. You say that the man who learns his part of making a machine acquires a knowledge of that particular part quite rapidly.—A. Yes.

Q. His function, I suppose, is principally to hold the metal to the machine and adjust it properly so as to have the machine work upon it right, is it not?—A. That is so with the lathe and the subdivisions of that particular branch, but in vise work it is altogether different. In some cases instead of using the file for bringing down anything, they use the emery wheel, and the planer, and so on. Our trade is really different from other trades, from the fact that the invention of machinery produces a little more work; but at the same time there are inventions in our own trade which take it away again. Take it in all branches of our trade, wherever there is one particular kind of machinery built, every man learns his particular part and is kept steadily at that and knows no other part; but in shops where they do all kinds of work the men are expected to be pretty good machinists.

Q. Have you noticed the effect upon the intellect of this plan of keeping a man at one particular branch?—A. Yes. It has a very demoralizing effect upon the mind throughout. The man thinks of nothing else but that particular branch; he knows that he cannot leave that particular branch and go to any other; he has got no chance whatever to learn anything else because he is kept steadily and constantly at that particular thing, and of course his intellect must be narrowed by it.

Q. And does he not finally acquire so much skill in the manipulation of his particular part of the business that he does it without any mental effort?—A. Almost. In fact he becomes almost a part of the machinery.

By the CHAIRMAN:

Q. Then if he gets so skilled that he has not to think about his work, why cannot he compose poetry, or give range to his imagination, or occupy his mind in some other way while he is at work?—A. As a rule a man of that kind has more to think of about his family and his belly than he has about poetry.

The CHAIRMAN. That is right.

By Mr. GEORGE:

Q. Has there been in the last ten or fifteen years any very great revolution in the making of machinery so far as regards the capital that is required to start the business?—A. Well, I understand that at this present day you could not start in the machinist's business to compete successfully with any of these large firms with a capital of less than $20,000 or $30,000. That is my own judgment. There have been cases known where men started ten or fifteen years ago on what they had earned themselves, and they have grown up gradually into a good business. One of those firms is Floyd & Sons, on Twentieth street. That man started out of his own earnings; he saved enough to start a pretty fair-sized shop, and he is occupying it to-day; but since that time it appears the larger ones are squeezing out the smaller, and forcing more of them into the ranks of labor, thus causing more competition among the workers.

DIFFICULTY OF RISING OUT OF THE WAGE-WORKING CLASS

Q. What is the prospect for a man now working in one of these machine shops, a man who is temperate and economical and thrifty, to become a boss or a manufacturer of machinery himself from his own savings? Could a man do it without getting aid from some relative who might die and leave him a fortune, or without drawing a lottery prize, or something of that sort?—A. Well, speaking generally, there is no chance. They have lost all desire to become bosses now.

Q. Why have they lost that desire?—A. Why, because the trade has become demoralized. First, they earn so small wages; and, next, it takes so much capital to become a boss now that they cannot think of it, because it takes all they can earn to live.

Q. Then it is the hopelessness of the effort that produces the loss of the desire on their part; is that it?—A. That is the idea.

Q. What is the pay generally of those workers in these machine shops?—A. It ranges from $1.25 to $3.50 or $4 a day, but these last are, of course, exceptional wages. The average wages I should say is about $2 a day.

Q. In New York, do you mean?—A. Taking New York and vicinity, it might be $2.25 a day. You must remember that good machinists have more responsibility on their shoulders than men have in the average trades, as in fact the safety of society itself rests on their shoulders as far as regards steam engines, locomotives, steamboats, and all kinds of machinery. Still, in spite of all that, in spite of all the knowledge which it is necessary for a man to have who works on this general machine work, he is compelled to go along with less wages than a hod-carrier. And yet we have on iron one of the highest protective tariffs possible.

SOCIAL CONDITION OF MACHINISTS IN NEW YORK

Q. What is the social condition of the machinists in New York and the surrounding towns and cities?—A. It is rather low compared to what their social condition was ten or fifteen years ago.

Q. Do you remember when it was better?—A. When I first went to learn the trade a machinist considered himself more than the average workingman; in fact he did not like to be called a workingman. He liked to be called a mechanic. To-day he recognizes the fact that he is simply a laborer the same as the others. Ten years ago even he considered himself a little above the average workingman; he thought himself a mechanic, and felt he belonged in the middle class; but to-day he recognizes the fact that he is simply the same as any other ordinary laborer, no more and no less.

Q. What sort of houses or lodgings do the machinists

occupy as a general rule?—A. As a general rule they live in tenement houses, often on the top floor.

Q. How is it as to the size of the apartments that they occupy, the conveniences and comforts they afford, their healthfulness, the character of the neighborhood and the general surroundings?—A. That depends a great deal upon the size of the families. In most cases they are compelled to send their families to work, and of course they have to have rooms in proportion to the size of their families, and of course it often robs them of their earnings to pay rent; but as a rule the machinists live in the lowest quarters of the city, between Eighth and Eleventh avenues, on the west side, and on the east side between Third avenue and the river. You will find the machinists stuck in those quarters on both sides of the city.

TOO MANY MACHINISTS IN NEW YORK

One great trouble with our trade is that there is such a surplus of machinists in the market now that every day sees seven or eight at the door of every shop looking for a job. In fact they are denied the right to labor, and that is what we kick about. About two months ago, I believe there was about one-fifth of our trade in this city entirely out of work.

Q. Do you know from reading the papers or from your general knowledge of the business whether there are other places in other cities or other parts of the country that those men could have gone and got work?—A. I know from general reports of the condition of our trade that the same condition existed throughout the country generally.

Q. Then those men could not have bettered themselves by going to any other place, you think?—A. Not in a body.

MACHINISTS HAVE SUNK FROM
THE MIDDLE TO THE LOWER CLASS

Q. I am requested to ask you this question: Dividing the public, as is commonly done, into the upper, middle, and lower classes, to which class would you assign the average workingman of your trade at the time when you entered it, and to which class you would assign him now? —A. I now assign them to the lower class. At the time I entered the trade I should assign them as merely hanging on to the middle class; ready to drop out at any time.

Q. What is the character of the social intercourse of those workingmen? Answer first with reference to their intercourse with other people outside of their own trade— merchants, employers, and others.—A. Are you asking what sort of social intercourse exists between the machinists and the merchants? If you are, there is none whatever, or very little if any.

Q. What sort of social intercourse exists among the machinists themselves and their families, as to visiting, entertaining one another, and having little parties and other forms of sociability, those little things that go to make up the social pleasures of life?—A. In fact with the married folks that has died out—such things as birthday parties, picnics, and so on. The machinists to-day are on such small pay, and the cost of living is so high, that they have very little, if anything, to spend for recreation, and the machinist has to content himself with enjoying himself at home, either fighting with his wife or licking his children.

Q. I hope that is not a common amusement in the trade. Was it so ten years ago?—A. It was not; from the fact that they then sought enjoyment in other places, and had a little more money to spend. But since they have had no organization worth speaking of, of course their pay has gone down. At that time they had a form of organization in some way or other which seemed to keep up the wages, and there was more life left in the machinist then; he had more ambition, he felt more like seeking enjoyment outside, and in reading and such things, but now it is changed to the opposite; the machinist has no such desires.

Q. What is the social air about the ordinary machinist's house? Are there evidences of happiness, and joy, and hilarity, or is the general atmosphere solemn, and somber, and gloomy?—A. To explain that fully, I would state first of all, that machinists have got to work ten hours a day in New York, and that they are compelled to work very hard. In fact the machinists of America are compelled to do about one-third more work than the machinists do in England in a day. Therefore, when they come home they are naturally played out from shoving the file, or using the hammer or the chisel, or whatever it may be, such long hours. They are pretty well played out when they come home, and the first thing they think of is having something to eat and sitting down, and resting, and then of striking a bed. Of course when a man is dragged out in that way he is naturally cranky, and he makes all around him cranky; so, instead of a pleasant house it is every day expecting to lose his job by competition from his fellow-workman, there being so many out of employment, and no places for them, and his wages being pulled down through their competition, looking at all times to be thrown out of work in that way, and staring starvation in the face makes him feel sad, and the head of the house being sad, of course the whole family are the same, so the house looks like a dull prison instead of a home.

Q. Do you mean to say that that is the general condition of the machinists in New York and in this vicinity?— A. That is their general condition, with, of course, a good many exceptions. That is the general condition to the best of my knowledge.

INTIMIDATION AND "BLACKLISTING" BY EMPLOYERS

Q. Where do you work?—A. I would rather not have it in print. Perhaps I would have to go Monday morning if I did. We are so situated in the machinist's trade that we daren't let them know much about us. If they know that we open our mouths on the labor question, and try to form organizations, we are quietly told that "business is slack" and we have got to go.

Q. Do you know of anybody being discharged for making speeches on the labor question?—A. Yes; I do know of several. A little less than a year ago several members of the organization that I belong to were discharged because it was discovered that they were members of the organization.

Q. Do you say those men were members of the same organization that you belonged to?—A. Yes, sir; but not working in the same place where I work. And in fact many of my trade have been on the "black list," and have had to leave town to find work.

REVOLUTIONARY MACHINISTS

Q. Are the machinists here generally contented, or are they in a state of discontent and unrest?—A. There is mostly a general feeling of discontent, and you will find among the machinists the most radical workingmen, with the most revolutionary ideas. You will find that they don't so much give their thoughts simply to trades unions and other efforts of that kind, but they go far beyond that; they only look for reform through the ballot or through a revolution, a forcible revolution.

By Mr. CALL:

Q. You say they look for relief through a forcible revolution. In the alternative of a forcible revolution have they considered what form of government they would establish?—A. Yes; some of them have and some of them have not.

Q. What kind of government would they establish?—A. Yes. They want to form a government such as this was intended to be, a government "of the people, for the people, and by the people"—different entirely from the present form of government.

Q. Well, we say that we have such a government now, although some of us think it has not worked out just right. Now what is the particular form of institutions which you would propose to establish to give us such a government?—A. Do you want that question answered?

Q. Yes; I want to know what particular form of government you propose—I do not mean you individually, but you speaking in a representative character.—A. Well, if you want my own ideas or if you want their ideas, those are two different things. I can give the general feelings of those

I am connected with first, and then I can give my own ideas.

By the CHAIRMAN:

Q. And I suppose there are others who hold the same opinions that you do?—A. Unquestionably; but I do not like to speak as a representative and as an individual at the same time.

Q. But, as an individual, representing some others, those who think like you, you can answer the question, I suppose?—A. Well, I and a great many more believe in a form of government where all the means of production, of public transportation and of exchange, and also the land should become the public property of the people and be under the administration of the Government.

By Mr. CALL:

Q. What do you mean by that?—A. I mean that anything that would tend to become a monopoly should be owned by the Government.

Q. Well, that is a general expression. Let us take an instance. Here is a merchant; he is one of the means of exchange. His business consists in exchanging different kinds of products. Now, what would you do with him under your new government? Is he to get all he makes in that business, or is somebody else?—A. He is to have all he *earns*; no more.

Q. Is he to have all he makes?—A. No.

Q. How much will you let him have?—A. For exchanging things?

Q. Yes.—A. Well, if his services were necessary, I should give him all he *earned*.

Q. Is not that the way now; merchants don't get any more than they earn, do they?—A. Yes. Jay Gould never earned a great deal, but he owns a terrible lot.

Q. But how would you do with the merchant? Under our law and our system of society as it stands, if he does not make anything the public does not pay him anything. Now, what do you propose?—A. I would like to know in the first place what you mean by "make"?

Q. I mean that he gets something now which remains in

his hands over and above what he pays out. That is what I mean when I speak of what he *makes.*—A. Then he is not entitled to that.

Q. But he has to live.—A. He has no right to live in that way. He ought to produce something. As Saint Paul says, "He that will not work shall not eat."

Q. Well, then, we understand that you will not have any merchants in your new government?—A. No; not of that class.

Q. As I understand the matter a merchant now is a man who assumes without any direct authority from the State to buy and sell commodities, that is, to conduct exchange. We have money which is a measure of value. Gold and silver have no intrinsic value, but all nations have recognized them as a measure of value as money, and therefore they are representatives of value. The merchant uses them to buy and sell in order to exchange products of one kind for those of another. Now, how are you going to supply his function under your new form of government? Will you appoint somebody by State authority to do that business?—A. I will answer that question as I understand it. The object of your merchant is, first, to buy cheap in order to sell dear—in other words to get something for nothing. That is the class of merchants that according to my idea have no right to exist, because I consider them taking something without giving an equivalent—therefore stealing something.

Q. Now, how are you going to get your exchanges made under your government?—A. Then, too, the telegraphs and the railroads, we think, should be public property, owned by the Government.

Q. Hold on. Let us not talk now about telegraphs, but about wheat, corn, and other products, and the means of exchanging them. You have not told us how exchange is to be conducted under your form of government.—A. Well, it is necessary to say what I was going to say in order to answer your question.

Q. How are you going to supply, under your new government, the wants of the city of New York, for instance?—

A. In my new government I supply it in this way: The government itself would have to do its own farming to begin with, and, therefore, an employé of the government would be acting in the place of that merchant that you speak of.

Q. But suppose the government was a bad farmer, how would your crops come out then? for sometimes you know the Government does things badly.—A. Then the nation itself, the people in general, would be bad farmers. The whole nation would have to sink. If the nation aint able to support itself, it must of necessity die.

Q. How would you create the head farmer under your system, the one that would direct the farming operations? Would you elect him by a popular vote?—A. No; I would have each branch of the trade separate by itself; each branch of trade to elect its own heads, and they to take that particular branch under their control, subject to the supervision of all the branches of trade acting together as a government.

Q. You would put all the farmers together, then, in a trades' union, and provide that they should regulate all the farming?—A. Yes, sir.

Q. Supposing one piece of land is better than another (as we know is the case), to whom are you going to give that superior land?—A. I aint going to *give* the land to anybody.

Q. Well, who is to determine who shall be permitted to use it? How will the distribution of the good land and the bad land be regulated?—A. The land itself will be owned by the government.

Q. Yes; but you are going to give the use of it to somebody. Now, suppose you had that all arranged, and you had established your industrial government, or whatever you might choose to call it, how are you going to divide out the land? Are you going to select one man to take this piece of land and another man to take that piece? Some of the land, you know, is very good and some very bad, and what I want to know is how you are going to distribute it satisfactorily among your farmers throughout the country.

We all know that we are bound to have something to eat, and that it is a point of the highest importance to assign the land to those who are going to make a good use of it. How are you going to arrive at that result?—A. Oh, that is very simple. They are all producing for one common party; producing for themselves. They in common own all they produce. Therefore, each one produces as a part of a united and common family, and it does not matter which one goes on one piece of land or which gets another.

Q. Then I understand you that all the farm products will belong to them in common; that is, the man who has got one child or the one who has no child will get as much as the man who has ten children. Is that the idea?—A. That will depend on how much he produces.

Q. Then we will assume that a man who has got ten children will produce just as much as the man who has but one child. I understand your theory to be that all the farmers all over the United States are going to have everything connected with farming in common, and you say that for that reason it does not matter who occupies this piece of land or who occupies that. We will overlook for the present the fact that there is a great deal more work to be done on a poor piece of land to produce a given result than there is on a rich piece, and that, therefore, a given amount of labor will produce much less in the one case than in the other. Now, how are you going to regulate the division of the products under such circumstances?—A. When I work ten hours a day I get so much wages; when I work five hours I get only so much. The same rule would apply to farmers; if they worked so many days they would get so much; if they worked so many more days they would get so much more; and so on.

By the CHAIRMAN:

Q. I suppose they would be paid at the same rate per hour that you would be?—A. That is entering into the price that they would get.

By Mr. CALL:

Q. But is not the rule which you suggest the present rule? If a man works ten hours on his own farm does he not get more than the man who works but two hours?—A. That may be so when he works on his farm, providing he aint in debt.

Q. If you hire a man to work ten hours don't you pay him more than you pay a man who works but two?—A. Well, if I owned the farm, I might work only two hours, or I might not work at all, and still get far more money out of it than the man who worked ten hours a day.

Q. But on the basis on which we are talking now, we have done away with all that question of ownership. When you hire a man——A. [Interrupting.] But you don't hire a man on my plan.

Q. You do not?—A. No, sir. How can the State hire a man and you hire him at the same time.

Q. I should be in favor of a better state of things if you can find a definite and practical way of getting at it. I, too, think that every man and woman and child in the world ought to have plenty to eat and wear, and I am in favor of every reasonable measure that looks in that direction; but I would not like to get into a state of things where we would be all starved before we got through. Now, I understand that you propose to divide the product out among different men according to the number of hours that each man works. Suppose another man who has eight or ten children is a much better skilled farmer than you are, and you have not got any children, and you work twelve hours a day, and suppose you come to this man who has this large family, and who has produced twice as much as you have, and propose an even division because you and he have worked the same number of hours, do you think that a division on that basis would be reasonable in such a case? What are you going to do with the element of skill?—A. Well, in fact that has already disappeared. It has already disappeared from farming, because the small farmers of the West are compelled to sell out and go to work for the larger farmers.

Q. Then I understand that we are to have a state of things in which superior skill and aptitude for any given occupation is to be ignored or is to disappear entirely?—A. It is disappearing under the present system.

Q. Do you find that one machinist has just as much skill as another? Is that your practical experience?—A. No.

Q. Then why do you think that that is the case in regard to farmers? That is not my observation. My observation is that one man is a good farmer, while another man can hardly make the seed that he plants?—A. I believe that under the system of large farming and the concentration of all the economic forces for production, the machinery instead of the man is the brains.

Q. That is a good idea. If we can make brains by machinery we will solve all our difficulties. But how is that to be done?—A. I am not saying that we can make brains by machinery.

Q. If we can make a substitute for brains, that will do. —A. Well, that is done now.

The CHAIRMAN. I have received a letter from a workingman at a distance, who puts the protection question in this way: He says, that the tariff was imposed in order to protect American manufactures; and, therefore, he insists upon it that the immigration of foreign cheap labor should be prohibited, because the American workingman is an article of American manufacture, which should be protected like all other articles.

By Mr. CALL:

Q. I think the glory of the American mechanic is that he has developed a wonderfully superior capacity so as to elevate himself to be a superior kind of man; but we will suppose that that is not true; that every man is alike, and that by this substitution of machinery for brains we have arrived at a state of equality as to capacity; still the question arises, how are you going to distribute what you produce? The farmers have got it all (I am talking of farming products now), and the question is how are you going to get it out of their hands—the corn, the wheat, the pork, the cotton, the sugar, and all the other products that we need—how are you going to get that out of the hands of those who produce it, and get it properly distributed to the community generally?—A. By the same system as that on which the post-office works now. We exchange our ideas through the mails, don't we?

Q. Yes.—A. Then, why cannot we have a similar system of exchange of our commodities? If I want a pair of shoes in exchange for my iron work, why cannot the exchange be effected in that way?

Q. Then you *are* going to have somebody do that business of exchange?—A. Undoubtedly.

Q. That is, you will bring all the surplus that the farmers raise, after taking out the supply for their own families, and distribute it. We make now a surplus of six or seven billion bushels of wheat. That is all going to be deposited in some place, I suppose, if you can find a place big enough to hold it. Then, how are you going to regulate the distribution, the exchange? How much machinery, for instance, is a man to get for his wheat and his corn? In short, how will you regulate that whole business of exchange?—A. Of course, it is not for me to define what portion each shall get.

Q. But somebody will have to regulate that?—A. Undoubtedly.

Q. And your idea is that the state shall appoint people to do that. Now, do you think the farmers will be satisfied with what that somebody does about that business? Do you think you could provide any way in which everybody would be satisfied, in which nobody would feel that he was cheated, or would be disposed to say, "I do not get enough of this for my wheat or my corn," or *vice versa?* Suppose some of them were to say, for instance, "You are dividing this in such a manner that I and my family are going to starve; we do not get enough to clothe us comfortably; we do not get enough of the things that are brought from abroad." How would you regulate that?—A. You want me to lay down the whole industrial system in a nut-shell, in about three minutes.

Q. I know it is a puzzling matter, but that is not strange. For two thousand years we have been experimenting and trying to find out the best way of doing these very things?

—A. Yes; one portion of us have, and the other portion have been trying to find out how to make all they can out of the rest.

Q. No doubt there have been thieves and robbers in all ages and countries of the world, but good men have always been trying to find out the best means of making a just and equitable distribution of the world's products.— A. I think all that has been pretty clearly proven by such men as Karl Marx and Lassalle and others of that class, and I think it would be well to study those men. I think it is more than I can do to lay down that whole matter in a few minutes.

Q. But I thought you said that there had been a tendency of opinion among workingmen toward the conclusion that, if necessary, there must be a forcible revolution on the principle that every man should be perfectly free to do what he sees fit to do?—A. I said nothing of the kind.

Q. Well, our present system of government is built upon that theory; and in the Federal Constitution and in every State constitution there is a bill of rights commencing with the Declaration of Independence, asserting that the whole scheme of government shall be constructed so as to enable every man to be free to do exactly what he pleases to do, except——

A. [Interrupting.] Yes; "except"——

Q. I was going to say that it is provided that he shall do it lawfully and peaceably; not by force. Personal security and personal liberty: those are the foundations of this Government. Now, you say that our present system does not work out right, and that we must forcibly revolutionize it and establish a common system by which individuals shall not be free to do as they do now, but the Government shall take charge of all these matters. You see, of course, that your idea and the idea on which the present system of society rests are in direct contravention of each other. If every man is free to farm, of course your plan of having the Government do all the farming cannot be established. Now, what I want to know is: What practical shape is this opinion of the workingmen, of which you speak, taking in regard to the form of Government which they propose to establish when the present Government is revolutionized?—A. In the first place, the workingmen believe that personal liberty should cease where it interferes with the liberty of others. That is why this present form of Government has failed; why it is inconsistent with the Declaration of Independence; inconsistent with even the very first part of the Declaration, which asserts that all men have a right to live.

Q. Then you propose a form of government in which personal liberty is to be denied?—A. When it interferes with the liberty of others.

Q. Who is to decide that? Under our present form of Government no tribunal has a right to decide that a man's personal liberty interferes with that of anybody else unless he commits a crime; his liberty is absolute. Now, to whom will you give the authority to decide when a man's personal liberty to be a mechanic or a farmer or something else that he wishes to be interferes with the welfare of the whole? [The witness did not answer.]

DOCUMENT 50

Testimony

SOURCE: Samuel Gompers, Testimony before the Senate Committee on Education and Labor, New York, 16 and 18 August 1883 (from *Report of the Committee*, Vol. I, pp. 282–84, 376, 377).

In the course of testimony running to more than fifty pages in the published transcript, Gompers shows himself to be well-informed about many occupations besides that of the cigar makers whom he represented. His comments on the working conditions of the drivers of horse-drawn streetcars in New York are reproduced here because of their bearing on William Dean Howells' *A Hazard of New Fortunes* (see headnote to Document 51). It will be noticed that although Gompers declares class conflict between workers and employers to be inevitable, he defines the goal of union organization as improvement in wages and working conditions and does not set forth a political program.

[NEW YORK, *August 16 and 18, 1883*]
[SAMUEL GOMPERS sworn and examined.
MR. GOMPERS:]

GRIEVANCES OF CAR-DRIVERS IN NEW YORK

The car-drivers of the city of New York are working from fourteen to sixteen hours a day in all weathers, and receive $1.75 a day.

Q. Now, why is not that enough?—A. Because it will not purchase the commonest necessaries of life.

Q. You understand, of course, that my question is designed to draw you out fully in regard to that class of workmen, their condition, &c. I understand your assertion to be that it is not enough; it does not seem to me, either, that it is enough; but I want to know from you what chance a man has to live on $1.75 a day?—A. He has this chance: his meals are served to him by his wife or friend or child, as the case may be, in a kettle, while he is driving his team, and at the end of the route he may possibly have two or three minutes to swallow his food. It is nothing more than swallowing it, and when he comes home he is probably too tired or perhaps too hungry to eat.

Q. There is no cessation in his work during the day of any consequence, then?—A. If there is, that which is termed relays or switches he has still the same number of hours to work.

Q. Do you mean that that is deducted from his fourteen or sixteen hours?—A. Yes, sir.

Q. Then, if the relays amounted to an hour, he would be absent from his home seventeen hours?—A. Yes, sir.

Q. And if two hours, eighteen?—A. Yes, sir. And in the matter of these relays, in some instances men who do not and cannot live, on account of the meagerness of their wages, on the route of the railroad, are compelled to live at some distance, and when they have these relays or switches it takes them sometimes twenty or thirty minutes to reach their homes, and to return again takes another half or three-quarters of an hour.

Q. Then, do I understand you that these relays and the time occupied morning and evening going to and returning from their work are to be added to the fourteen or sixteen hours of actual service required?—A. The actual service is from fourteen to fifteen hours. Then there is the looking after their horses and cleaning the car besides.

Q. From the time that a car-driver leaves home in the morning until he returns for the night how much of the twenty-four hours will ordinarily be consumed?—A. I cannot tell you exactly as to how long a time they have at home, for the reason that it depends to some extent upon how far they live from the route of travel.

Q. State it approximately as near as you can.—A. Well, I do not believe that they have more than seven and a half hours out of the twenty-four.

By Mr. CALL:

Q. At what hour in the morning do they commence ordinarily, and what time do they quit?—A. Several of the street railroads of this city run all day and night; and on those, of course, the men commence at various hours. During the day the traffic on some routes is not so much as on others, and then they will be relayed; and, although they may go on to work at 5 o'clock in the morning, they probably would not get off before 11 or 12 o'clock at night, or probably later still. I would not say later still positively, but I think in some instances later.

By Mr. PUGH:

Q. Have they ever been paid higher wages?—A. Yes, sir. About two years ago they were on a strike to obtain, I think, $2 a day, but were starved into submission.

Q. What do they get now?—A. One dollar and seventy-five cents.

By Mr. GEORGE:

Q. Does the conductor get the same wages, or more?—A. I think he gets 25 cents more, by reason of his position of trust.

By the CHAIRMAN:

Q. Have you any knowledge with regard to those who operate the elevated railways?—A. The men who work at ticket collecting or at the boxes where the tickets are deposited receive $1.25 a day, I think. I would rather wait until I can give you information definitely. I think I can do so now, but I prefer to wait.

By Mr. GEORGE:

Q. Are the car-drivers allowed to have seats?—A. They are not. They have to stand all the time.

By Mr. CALL:

Q. How many hours do they stand?—A. Fourteen or fifteen.

Q. Do you mean fourteen hours' standing without intermission?—A. Very little intermission. They sometimes rest back against the door of the car for a while. They also, in some instances, have to act as conductors; that is, give change, count the passengers, and register the number of passengers on an indicator. And then they are sometimes held responsible when somebody is run over on account, perhaps, of their having to perform two men's work. The greed of the horse-railroad companies has been such that they have introduced on several lines what is known as the bobtailed car, and have dispensed with the services of a conductor.

By the CHAIRMAN:

Q. Don't you think that is because they cannot afford to pay any more?—A. I hardly believe that. Judging from the traffic, they are capable of paying it, and judging from what is currently reported as their dividends, they are more than capable of paying it. I must acknowledge, though, that so far as their dividends are concerned, I am personally uninformed. I take merely current rumor and the appearance of the traffic, the number of passengers I see on the cars. . . .

[GOMPERS' testimony continued on *August* 18, 1883:]

I have quoted a statement made by a Massachusetts manufacturer, a member of the legislature, when he said in substance, "I regard my employés the same as I would an old machine, which, when it becomes rusty, I thrust into the street."

Q. That was an expression of the feeling of the employers toward the employed. Now, I ask you about the feelings of the employed towards the employer.—A. Well, I think I said then, in substance, that the employed, the workingmen, believe that that is about the view generally entertained by employers as to their help, and they resent it by about the same feeling—not quite the same, but they resent it and feel it strongly.

Q. Is the present tendency of affairs to increase or intensify that feeling, or to remove it?—A. To intensify it. The views are gaining upon every side that the classes in society are becoming decidedly more distinct, and, as the lines are drawn, so does this feeling become intensified; in fact, I believe I can best describe that by reading from the preamble adopted by the Confederation of the Labor Unions of the United States and Canada at Pittsburg, Pa. (of which I am at present chairman), in November, 1881:

> Whereas a struggle is going on in the nations of the civilized world between the oppressors and the oppressed of all countries, a struggle between capital and labor, which must grow in intensity year by year, and work disastrous results to the toiling millions of all nations, if not combined for mutual protection and benefit, for the history of the wage-workers of all countries is but the history of constant struggle and misery engendered by ignorance and disunion; and, whereas the history of the non-producers of all ages proves that a minority thoroughly organized may work wonders for good or evil, and so on.

That extract, I believe, sets forth in as few words as possible the feeling that prevails among the working classes, that there is an ever-recurring conflict between the two classes, and that the employers are ever on the watch to see whether they cannot take advantage of their employés, the same as the stock speculator looks at the ticking of the indicator to see whether he cannot take advantage of those with whom he is dealing; except that in this instance the fellow stock-broker is generally as alert to take advantage as the first, and is at the other end looking at the wire with the same object, while the workingman is not so vigilant in looking out for himself.

Q. Explain fully, if you can, the nature and extent of the social intercourse between the wage-receivers and the wage-payers.—A. Where the wage-payers are small manufacturers, employing one or two hands, a spirit of cordiality and friendship may exist; but as the employer engages a larger number of hands, just in proportion does he become removed from the social status of his employé. His own status is raised, and the intercourse which may have formerly existed is cut off. The ties of friendship gradually become lessened, and there is no cordiality existing between the two after that. The workingman works as well as he possibly can to retain his employment, and when he looks after the interests of his employer it is because he wishes to retain his employment, and not because he loves him.

By the CHAIRMAN:

Q. I would like to draw out your idea a little more definitely as to the exact thing that is to be accomplished before you undertake to state your remedies. All concede, I suppose, that whatever is to go to the capitalist or to the laborer must be derived from the sale of the article produced. That is so, is it not?—A. Decidedly.

Q. Now, is it or is it not your claim that, before any portion of what is produced goes to the capitalist, a full and fair remuneration to the laborer should be deducted, upon the ground that his reasonable and just claim is primary to all others. That is the main point, is it not?—A. Yes, sir.

Q. That is the first thing to be secured—that the laborer's remuneration shall take precedence, in the order of time, of any compensation to the capitalist?—A. Yes, sir.

Q. And the next thing you wish to secure is that the amount of his compensation shall be just and reasonable?—A. Yes, sir.

Q. Those are two objects that are to be attained?—A. Yes, sir. And further, the treatment of the men in the factories—not as slaves, but as men. The machinery is guarded against rust, and, when passing, if one of the arms or wheels or belts is rather lower than the other, the employer will take off his hat and pass beneath it. We do not ask the employer to take off his hat to his employés, but we do say that "good morning" will not hurt him, more especially when he is spoken to.

DOCUMENT 51

(PLATE 24)

A Riot on Forty-Second Street, Near Broadway

SOURCE: Graham and Durkin [first names unknown], "A Riot on Forty-Second Street, Near Broadway" (wood engraving), *Harper's Weekly*, XXXIII (9 February 1889), 105.

According to Samuel Gompers' testimony before the Senate Committee on Education and Labor in 1883 (Document 50), the drivers of the horse-drawn street-cars had struck unsuccessfully for higher wages in 1881. In 1883 they were paid $1.75 for a fourteen- to sixteen-hour day. A later strike, in 1886, involving fifteen thousand men, resulted in an advance in wages to $2, with a reduction of the working day to twelve hours. In comparison with the railway strikes of the previous decade and other strikes in major industries during the 1880s, the car drivers' strikes were minor affairs, but because they occurred in New York and directly affected the daily lives of ordinary citizens, they were more readily available for use in fiction. Howells introduces just such an incident as is portrayed in this drawing to bring to a climax the plot of *A Hazard of New Fortunes*. The novel began running as a serial in *Harper's Weekly* on 23 March 1889; the chapter dealing with the strike (Book Fifth, Chapter V) appeared in the issue for 12 October 1889 (XXXIII, 811).

Document 52

Testimony

source: Edward King, Testimony before the Senate Committee on Education and Labor, New York, 27 August 1883 (from *Report of the Committee*, Vol. I, pp. 687–90).

King was another member of the delegation from the Central Labor Union. An immigrant from Great Britain who earned his living as a patternmaker, he had educated himself and had been a pioneer in adult education for workers. In addition to a ten-hour day in the shop, he regularly taught evening classes in psychology and sociology in the University Settlement House in New York.

[New York, *August 27*, 1883]
[Edward King sworn and examined.
Mr. King:]

SOCIETY NEEDS A BROADER BASIS
THAN "BUSINESS PRINCIPLES" FURNISH

A. On that score I will state, generally, as to the general spirit which underlies all the propositions from every section of organized labor that has expressed itself in any organized form authoritatively, that you will observe when you look over the testimony presented before this committee that, underlying all those propositions which have been presented here, there are ideas which set entirely at naught the recognized rules of business, or "business principles" as they are called, and that those ideas have reference to questions of health, questions of morals, and other matters of that kind, not generally included or recognized in a business bargain. Now, the conviction I hold myself, and it is a growing conviction among the working-men, is that, as a witness has already testified here to-day, what the organized working classes mean and desire when they say they do not believe in strikes, has reference purely to what ought to be, and not to what they are compelled to do while they profess to found the trades-union move-ment upon the principles of political economy.

Q. They regard strikes as a medicine to be taken when they are sick?—A. Exactly; and when they are sick under a régime of medical science which they desire to supplant by a better medical régime, but under which, while it prevails, it is understood that, as a last resort, a man has a right to suppress all sentiments of sympathy and of hu-manity, and which teaches, according to the prevailing doctrines of political economy, that that is right and best in the long run.

"BUSINESS PRINCIPLES" TO BE SUBORDINATED TO MORALITY

Now, I declare that under all the forms of labor organi-zations, and under all the different methods of expressing themselves there lie views which are totally opposed to any such conception. This idea you will find fault with, perhaps, as being inconsistent with much of the testimony given before this committee, for you will find conservative workingmen professing to desire to act within the recog-nized laws of business; but you will find also that the remedies which they suggest imply something more than "business principles;" they imply the subordination of what are regarded as "business principles" to morality. It is beyond all dispute that the question of child labor, for instance, might be presented by a very clever advocate in opposition to the workingmen's view in a light in which the claims of the working classes on that point would ap-pear not to be justified; but you will observe, also, that every person who presents any advanced views on that sub-ject claims, and it is claimed by all the organizations, both conservative and radical, that their views are based upon and have reference to the future good of the whole community. That is, they claim that the prohibition of child-labor is a *social* measure, justified on *social* grounds, and not necessarily on business grounds; and upon *social* grounds the workingmen advocate the prohibition of such labor even though it be, as in some cases it will be, at the expense of possible inconvenience and sacrifices on their own part. If you examine the manufacturers, as you probably will, you will find that their defense will be that these children are many of them poor orphans, and that they have to live, and that it is the same with women. In England John Bright, and some of the most distinguished men in the country, opposed the Factory law on the ground that there was no means provided in the law called for by the trades unions of supplying bread to those who were to be deprived of it by the enforcement of the proposed law. You will observe, therefore (and I desire to impress it upon the committee), that this question of child labor, as well as the desire of the working classes to live better generally—the battle, as I may call it, not merely for bread but the battle for pie—that is, for the luxuries of life so far as they are attainable, the assumption of the working classes that we have a right to live as well as we possibly can, and not to live as poorly as it suits the convenience of organized capital to keep us living—you will observe that that assumption also is prompted by other views and considerations than those of mere "business."

When I spoke the other day before this committee about morals and religion having a part to play in these questions, and being the ultimate solution of them, of course I referred to the action of such motives upon the labor organizations of the country. Now, the organizations of skilled mechanics of different kinds endeavor to conduct their affairs strictly with regard to their own interests as separate trades, and no doubt if you were looking over the evidence given here you might discover some inconsistencies (as I have frequently observed in the answers given)—some inconsistencies between the demands of the special occupation in question and the general demands of humanity. That may be observed, for instance, in the cross-questioning and the testimony as to the exclusion of foreign labor brought here under contract, as well as in the disposition to deny the right of other people to come in here and share the benefits of our form of government. The general principle underlying the free trade agitation is a general principle which relates to the rights of humanity as opposed to the interests of any number of people gathered within a certain geographical limit. Now, I say the men who are devoting their time to forming the opinions of the workingmen with whom they meet have recognized this distinction, and while they maintain that in the competitive market, under the existing régime, those skilled organizations are compelled to conduct the business of their special occupations as far as possible within the recognized limits; yet, underlying all these agitations and organizations, no matter how conservative they may profess to be, you will find these other principles working their way out and deciding the degree of intensity and faithfulness of the agitation and of the men engaged in it. Now, these principles cannot be described, nor can they be justified on the bald and bare doctrines of political economy as generally understood, and as regulating the current business affairs of great nations. In England there was a striking test of this, and I think it is a very fair example. There was a great famine in India (it is commented on by John Ruskin in one of his works), and in that famine a great number of people, I forget how many, died. However, there was at the same time in the country quite a sufficient amount of food, and an appeal was sent from some of the authorities in England connected with the Government authorities in India asking why this famine was not arrested or allayed by the adoption of some method of procuring food and sending it up to the places where the people needed it. What was the answer? The answer was that to do that would be to interfere with the laws of trade. Shortly after that, however, some more families of poor Hindoos died, and then the proper authorities in India did interfere with the laws of trade and sent the people food. Thus, simply by the absolute pressure of circumstances, humanity asserted itself as above "business," and morality dictated to business and subordinated "business principles" to its laws.

DOCUMENT 53

Testimony

SOURCE: Karl Daniel Adolf Douai, Testimony before the Senate Committee on Education and Labor, New York, 20 September 1883 (from *Report of the Committee*, Vol. II, pp. 702–21).

Douai represents the doctrinaire strain in American radicalism, nourished from Europe, that has always seemed somewhat exotic. (Note, for example, that he was "affirmed" rather than sworn.) He was a native of Germany with a Ph.D. from Leipzig. After being imprisoned for his part in the revolutionary disturbances of 1848, he had emigrated to Texas, where he edited a German-language newspaper and helped to organize the Free-Soil Party. Driven from Texas because of his anti-slavery views, he had served as schoolmaster and editor in various cities of the East. At the time of his testimony he was editor of the New York *Volks Zeitung*.

The contrast between Douai's carefully prepared lecture on Marxism, and Gompers' untheoretical emphasis on wages and hours and working conditions, is highly characteristic. Douai's Marxist interpretation of the Civil War must have seemed novel indeed to virtually all his auditors. It is amusing to observe that Senator Call, who had managed to score sophistical debating points against Morrison, the twenty-three-year-old machinist, finds more than his match in this veteran of decades of ideological fencing-bouts.

NEW YORK, *September* 20, 1883.

Dr. A. DOUAI affirmed and examined.

By the CHAIRMAN:

Question. Please state your residence.—Answer. My

residence is in Williamsburg, or what is called "Brooklyn, E. D."

Q. In what capacity do you appear before the committee?—A. I appear in the capacity of representative of the Socialistic Labor Party of the United States.

Q. You are deputed by them to represent them here?—A. Yes; I am deputed by them to represent their interests and demands here.

The CHAIRMAN. You may proceed in your own way, and say to the committee what you think to be pertinent, as the representative of your body and as instructed, to the committee under this resolution of the Senate, which, I suppose, you have seen.

The WITNESS. I have seen the resolution.

SPREAD OF SOCIALISM

The Socialistic Labor Party is not spread over the United States solely, but also all over Europe. It consists in Germany, for instance, where it took its origin, of perhaps a million voters. In France the number cannot be much less. It is little spread in England, but it is well represented there. It is well represented in the south of Europe—in Spain, Italy, Switzerland, even in the Balkan Peninsula. It is largely spread in Russia and Poland. It has adherents in Denmark and Sweden.

THE SOCIALISTIC LABOR PARTY: WHAT IT IS

The party is two things; that is, it is a scientific propaganda society and has existed as such for about twenty years. It was founded by two remarkable writers and agitators, whose merits are acknowledged by all scientific men who know anything about political economy and political science—Karl Marx, the author of the celebrated work "Das Kapital," or capital, and Ferdinand Lassalle, a pupil of Marx—and several more fellow-writers and agitators.

On the other hand, the party is an evolutionary and revolutionary society. It is evolutionary as long as it can be so, as it is left to itself, and as it has liberty of speech and action; revolutionary—like all natural laws—when it can no longer act freely, but is forced into action. Then it will respond to that call. The political economy which Karl Marx teaches is contrary to all present political economy, or what is called such. I shall, perhaps, need more than an hour to explain it.

The CHAIRMAN. You may have what time you please.

The WITNESS. I will try to make it as clear and concise as possible, and I hope it will interest every one of you gentlemen, since it is a party (and a science at the same time) so very largely represented in Europe and growing in the United States.

POLITICAL ECONOMY NOT ALWAYS THE SAME

Present political economy takes it for granted that its laws, or what it so calls, have existed at all times in the same way; have been the same laws under all forms of civilization and culture.

KARL MARX'S VIEWS

Karl Marx is the first man that says that this is a total error. There have been at varying periods of time different kinds or systems of production. But we may, for the sake of convenience, classify these different periods into three.

THE THREE HISTORIC PERIODS OF PRODUCTION

I. The Slave Period. The earliest of these was the period of Slavery, when all production was carried on by slaves, in a way well known to every one of our contemporaries in the United States. At that time very few riches could exist in the world; production was small, and men were working only for the daily wants of life. There was but little commerce in the world.

II. The Feudal Period. The second period was the Feudal period of production, in which the laborer was no longer enslaved, but was bound to the soil—bound to a certain vocation or calling—bound to a certain market, wherein to sell his merchandise and wherein to buy his merchandise, but otherwise provided for by law; nobody could be entirely helpless. There was provision made for any class of society. The means of labor did not belong at that time, as private property, to anybody, or only very exceptionally so. The land belonged to all the members of a community, or to all the communes within a state or nation. Just so the moneyed capital of the nation belonged more or less, or was, at least, applicable to all the wants of all the people. There was provision made, in short, for everybody within the community. But there was no freedom of movement or of action for the laborer, while, of course, it was always existing for the ruling classes. This period had an end about the time of the Reformation and of the discovery of America.

III. *The Capitalistic Period.* The third is called the Capitalistic period, or kind of production. It began in different countries at different times, but is now spread all over the civilized world.

THE TERM CAPITAL

I must premise here that Karl Marx understands by the term "capital" quite a different thing from what other writers understand. In fact, common writers in political economy use the term in four or five different senses—now in the one and then in the other, and thereby create a confusion of ideas of which it may be said that it is startling that it has not sooner been criticised. The world had to wait for Karl Marx to direct its attention to this very strange proceeding. Capital is, in the sense of Karl Marx (as later on I shall prove), that portion of the proceeds of labor, which is robbed by the employer of labor under the forms of law, and by the aid of which new production is carried on. I break off here on this point because the evidence will come afterward.

HISTORICAL NECESSITY FOR EACH PERIOD

So Karl Marx, by teaching that there are or have been three different kinds of production in the world, and that they may co-exist in the world here and there in remnants of old periods—by teaching this, he exhibits first his whole system as a system of natural laws of evolution.

In the opinion of Karl Marx there is a natural, a historical necessity for each of these developments. They are created by the progress of science and of technical inventions and discoveries, and they are made possible by certain kinds of political forms which are consequences of the kind of production. In fact all ideal forms of society, religion, jurisprudence—technical institutions—education, every ideal interest in society depends upon the kind of production. Each will create its own forms of evolution. It will sometimes create them by revolution, just as forces of nature work usually, slowly and easily, but, at times, will work revolutionarily. And so there has never been a progress from one form of production in society to the other without a forcible revolution. As Karl Marx expresses it, "force has always been the midwife of new forms of society and institutions."

REFORMS NOT THE WORK OF SINGLE MINDS

It is a consequence of this view that a revolution cannot be made or that the world cannot be reformed by the whims and ideas of single discoverers or inventors, or "improvers of the world," as he calls them. You know now-a-days everybody has his own *recipe* for reforming the world—for improving society. We call those, after the precedents of Karl Marx, Utopias. The world cannot be reformed in that way. It must reform itself, it must bide its time, and then it will come forth by its very inborn, inherent necessities by the wants of the people, by the progress of the times in general.

THE CONSERVATIVES ARE THE REAL REVOLUTIONISTS

When it comes in a revolutionary form then it is always conjured up not by the progressive part of society, but by their adversaries—by the conservative part of society. It is they who become the first revolutionists.

In order to make that clear by an example, I will refer to the United States war about slavery. All gentlemen of

your ages must recollect how it came about. It came about
by Mr. Stephen A. Douglas's Kansas and Nebraska bill.
The Abolitionists would never have made a revolution—in
fact they despaired of seeing slavery abolished during their
lives—say within thirty or forty years. When I was part of
the Abolitionist party in Texas—in the den of the lion
—thirty years ago, I despaired of seeing the days of the
abolition of slavery. But Stephen A. Douglas's Kansas and
Nebraska bill, which was a revolutionary act on the part
of the South or in its behalf (for it was taken to mean a
revolution in favor of the South), brought about the reaction not only of the Abolitionist party, but of the whole
North. You see, an evolution was going on for thirty years,
but the revolution was introduced and set into action by
the Conservative party; and it was a necessity which excited, which forced, the North to respond by a war,
which, however, was brought upon the country by the
South itself. By this example you will understand the position in which the socialistic labor party and Karl Marx
stand with regard to evolution and revolution. . . .

HOW, UNDER SOCIALISM, EACH MAN'S SHARE
WOULD BE REGULATED

Q. How, under your communistic system, are you going
to regulate the share which each man is to get for his
production; how could you, as an intellectual laborer—for
you would not be an industrial laborer—get your share?
—A. Our teachers, those to whom I belong, know quite
well what I am worth as a teacher, and they will not value
me at less than my worth. I can trust to them. So you
can trust to the virtue of laborers, that they will of themselves justly estimate the value of every man's work.

Q. That is precisely what I want to know, by what
system of distribution; what authority is there. You say
that the people who employ you as a teacher, will know.
—A. No; not the people that employ me, but other
teachers, I say.

Q. Well, of course, we are speaking of you only as an
example. How are they to do that—by some common form

of action, as a public meeting?—A. Certainly; in their monthly or yearly meetings.

Q. And so as to every other man?—A. And so as to every other man, and every other employment.

Q. Then you would not have any capitalists—you would have no difference between one man and another?—A. Oh, certainly. We acknowledge gradations in work—inferior work, simple work, average work, and superior work, or "qualified" work, as it is called in political economy. And I think laborers, as a rule, will be apt to think more highly of mental labor than what it is really worth.

COMPENSATION OF "DIRECTORS OF LABOR" UNDER SOCIALISM

Q. What do you call a man that is a director of labor and not a laborer himself; a man directing the exchanges of labor?—A. He will, of course, be made a director only because he is more than a common laborer, and he can perform more.

Q. Would you propose to give him a high salary?—A. Either a higher salary or higher "earnings," as we would call it then.

Q. Would you have that arranged by a vote of the people, also?—A. Certainly.

Mr. CALL. It appears to me that you would have a good deal to do.

The WITNESS. That is self-government, and nothing else is.

Q. If you were to regulate the salaries of everybody employed in the country, do you not think it would amount to a great mass of legislation?—A. Well, is not that kind of legislation already carried on in society? Not publicly, but it is carried on in the way of every day business.

Q. But it is done now by individual employers; it would be done, under your plan, by the community.—A. It may come up once a year, perhaps, when the prices of every kind of work and merchandise are regulated, not only of one branch, but of all branches, by common agreement and compromise. Of course nothing would be perfect at the outset.

Q. Once a year you would have a meeting of these different societies to regulate what each man could get?—A. Yes.

Q. And do you think every man would be satisfied with that?—A. Why, certainly; how otherwise would he be? He has no means of helping himself. Every one else is treated just the same way as himself.

Q. That may be your idea; but that is not exactly a free government, is it?—A. It is exactly a free government, and a self-governing government; and it is no longer a corrupt government. Corruption is only possible through representation. It is no longer possible when the people make their own laws and really elect their own officers.

By the CHAIRMAN:

Q. You ignore the potent fact, or at least something that you hear a good deal about—the possibility of corruption of the ballot itself, do you?—A. Oh, I know there are now corrupt voters, depraved men.

Q. Do you think that under the new conditions there would be any less of them?—A. Why, my dear sir, there would be no motive to corruption. How is there to be corruption if capital is not any longer private property? How could it tempt to corrupt? It is impossible.

By Mr. CALL:

Q. What difference does it make about private property when one man wants more than another? Suppose the capital all belongs to the community, and I want more of it, and you less, how would you satisfy the difference?—A. Suppose the difference between the highest and lowest wages will be as one to ten—that will perhaps be the most that will occur—would not that be better than it is now? Now-a-days a poor sewing woman earns from 9 to 11 cents a day if she is very diligent and works all her hours, while Jay Gould, who does not work at all, properly speaking (for he produces nothing), gets paid for every hour of the day, say, $10,000.

Q. Why could you not give the sewing woman more

than 10 cents a day—say, $2 a day—without interfering with Jay Gould?—A. I do not object, but I took that only as an example; that while now-a-days the most enormous differences in the reward are allowed and are legal, there will then be only a very narrow limit, but still limit enough to warrant the individual activity of each in his own way.

Q. Suppose all that to be so. Why not correct that without going into these tremendous changes that you speak of? Why not get to some practical way of rewarding labor?—A. Simply because it is impossible; you have not the power.

Mr. CALL. It strikes me that if those people who pay these sewing people only 10 cents a day would get together and agree to pay them more, that would be sufficient. . . .

WHO ARE LABORERS

By Mr. CALL:

Q. Where do you limit the line of labor? Who is a laboring man and who is not a laboring man, according to your idea?—A. Useful labor, I have already explained, is the only labor. All the rest is wasteful labor.

Q. What is useful labor?—A. That which produces wealth, directly or indirectly.

Q. Take Mr. Vanderbilt, for instance. I do not know Mr. Vanderbilt, and I merely mention him as an example; nor have I any connection with men of such large wealth; but take him as a representative of his class, does not the man that directs the great influences that control industry become a working man?—A. *He* does not direct anything. He pays directors, who do the work.

Q. Is not his brain worth anything?—A. No, not at all, since it is not exercised for the advantage of the country.

Q. Does he not occupy something of the position that you do—your brain and his brain alike directing these movements in the direction of increasing progress? What is he doing but directing the influences at his command to increase production, and what is the difference between your work and his? You are a laborer in your way, and is not he a laborer in his?—A. It is very strange that that must be answered, since he can himself fix the price of what he calls his labor.

Q. I should like you to tell me where is the line of distinction between useful labor and labor that is not useful. Is it in industrial employment—manual labor—or is it in all the exercises of the brain, just such as you have shown us to-day?

LABOR THAT IS NOT USEFUL IS NOT TRUE LABOR

A. I have not for a moment denied that intellectual labor is labor; but this intellectual labor that is exercised to the damage of the whole society and country is not useful labor. Every labor must be useful in order to be true labor. That is the first distinction of political economy.

Q. Then every man who has useful ideas is performing intellectual labor, is he not?—A. Conceding that, yet Mr. Vanderbilt's useful ideas I have never yet seen.

Mr. CALL. Well, he may be a very good man and have some very good ideas.

The WITNESS. Oh, I do not say that he may not be a very good man, after the opinion of the times.

Q. But let us take the question philosophically; you say intellectual labor that is useful is true intellectual labor?—A. Yes.

Q. And the man that you call a capitalist, the man that has got some means and happens to use them, his is not useful labor, but is injurious labor, as I understand you to say?—A. Yes; it is injurious for two reasons: First, because that capital by whose accumulation he spends his mental energy is robbed under legal forms, and he has no right to rob. What he afterwards does with this robbed property is again a detriment to society, because it is meant to accumulate more and more capital; that is to say, to extract from the people (who are, as it were, the soil on which the nation is sustained) more and more of the power to create wealth.

Q. You say that this is "robbed." A gentleman who sat recently in the place where you now sit has some very liberal ideas, and though they do not approach yours they are still very decided in the direction of liberal legislation for the benefit of the people at large, and he has some politico-economic theories like yours. He told us that he knew an instance, indeed several instances, but one special instance, a noted one in New Jersey, where one of those "robbers," as you call them, had acquired very large means by his improvement of the condition of labor in his factories. I suppose you would call that man a very bad man and his labor bad?—A. No.

Q. He testified that this employer had acquired large means by increasing the wages of the laborers, and by providing for them in old age, and administering to their comfort in sickness and showed us a model factory—a kind of paradise on earth. Now, what do you call that?— A. You take the question into an entirely novel department. I am not now talking of morality. I did not speak of morality. I spoke from a politico-economic stand-point.

PRIVATE CAPITAL IMPOVERISHES

Q. But that is not merely morality, but political economy also.—A. I ought to have spoken of the theory of Karl Marx, when he shows that private capital must impoverish every country, and the warning signs of this are now observed over the country in the crises, the great crashes that come now and then over all the trading and mercantile communities. They show that we have a very unsound state of society. Marx' theory is this: That capital must ruin and must abolish itself, just as slavery has abolished itself. We cannot do anything against this natural action of economical and historical causes. It is a historical necessity that the kind of production which now prevails will ruin itself, and that, too, before this century is over.

Q. May it not be that the fault of your theory is simply this: that you assume that capital is a thinking, sentient being, whereas there is no such thing, and capital is nothing but the means by which the workingman, who has developed his brain and capacity for organization, directs the labor of his fellows—nothing but the brain instrumentalities in connection with the opportunity of usefully directing their labor. Now, if that be capital why should it not exist?—A. As soon as you establish a state of society where people are equal and free to compete, as soon as you take away the private property in land, money, and education, as soon as you educate people equally and give them every opportunity in the same manner, according, of course, to the state of their respective gifts, but according to the best development possible for education, as soon as you establish such a society, then you may speak.

Q. Suppose the statistics of this country, and of all other countries, should, in opposition to what you say, show that the great manufacturing and producing interests of the world are in the hands of workingmen who have built up these great businesses themselves, and should show that their power is simply the superior intellectual knowledge of their business by which these workingmen are able to give direction to the combined efforts of their fellows— suppose statistics exhibit this to be a fact in every part of the world, then what becomes of your theory that you must take the land in order to do that which is already done by the workingmen themselves?—A. In former times it might truthfully be said that in the United States every person who was a real workingman and was industrious and diligent, and somewhat parsimonious, might ultimately come to a competency, and among thousands there might perhaps be one or two, or three at most, who might become rich; but the opportunities for this are past. You do not see any such thing now.

Q. Such a thing as what?—A. You must not always interrupt me, my dear sir.

Mr. CALL. I beg your pardon. I only wanted to know what you had said.

ALL BRANCHES OVERCROWDED

The WITNESS. Nowadays everything is very different; wages have gone down, and the wants of life have gone up in prices. Compare only the thirty last years of which I can bear witness, and it is now less possible than ever before to make savings, and still less possible, if you have some few savings, to employ them so as to make them useful, to make capital out of them. The chances are all now gone. The best and most useful land in the United States has been taken up now, or is in the course of being taken up. You have to travel far out into the West if you wish to find a place for pre-emption. And so it is with all branches of manufacture and industry; they are so over-crowded that superfluous men are to be found in every walk of life. Nowadays it is an impossibility, except under very favorable circumstances, to become a Vanderbilt or a rich man. And we know the means by which these men have become so rich. I only know one man, and that was Peter Cooper, who really could say, "I have earned most of my fortune by honest work." All the rest have earned it by means which, if lawful or legal, have at least not been just.

Testimony

SOURCE: R. Heber Newton, Testimony before the Senate Committee on Education and Labor, New York, 18 September 1883 (from *Report of the Committee*, Vol. II, pp. 535–90).

Newton was Rector of All Souls Episcopal Church in New York and a leader in the movement toward social Christianity, although the Co-operative Commonwealth which he advocated was rather vaguely conceived and the means for bringing it into being were even more vaguely stated. His testimony—which runs to more than forty thousand words—embodies the substance of a carefully prepared document later published in Newton's *Social Studies* (New York, 1887). Although he lists "the faults of labor" (inefficiency, lack of interest in its work, thriftlessness, "harmful indulgences" such as "drinking, smoking, excursioning, &c."), his description of the "faults of capital" is much more detailed and bears a much greater weight of thought and emotion. His references to Carlyle, Ruskin, Kingsley, and Morris (in portions of his testimony not reprinted here) indicate the continuity between much American clerical interest in the problems of industrialism and the great Victorian debate that had been in progress for several decades.

[NEW YORK, *September* 18, 1883]
[The Rev. R. HEBER NEWTON sworn and examined.
Mr. NEWTON:]

A LABOR QUESTION COMING

The broad fact that the United States census of 1870 estimated the average annual income of our wage-workers

at a little over $400 per capita, and that the census of
1880 estimates it at a little over $300 per capita, is the
quite sufficient evidence that there is a labor question
coming upon us in this country. The average wages of
1870 indicated, after due allowance for the inclusion of
women and children, a mass of miserably paid labor—that
is of impoverished and degraded labor. The average
wages of 1880 indicated that this mass of semi-pauperized
labor is rapidly increasing, and that its condition has become 25 per cent. worse in ten years. The shadow of the
old world *proletariat* is thus seen to be stealing upon our
shores. It is for specialists in political economy to study
this problem in the light of the large social forces that are
working such an alarming change in our American society.
In the consensus of their ripened judgment we must look
for the authoritative solution of this problem. I am not
here to assume that *rôle*. I have no pet hobby to propose,
warranted to solve the whole problem without failure. I
do not believe there is any such specific yet out.

NATURAL LAWS AND MORAL LAWS

While I await hopefully the broad study of these problems by trained specialists, and while I thoroughly recognize that vast natural laws are driving the world of industry and trade, yet I do not think we ought to make a
fetish of natural law, and sit down before it with the
impotence of despair.

The natural laws which adjust the affairs of man take
up into themselves, as factors in their forces, reason, sentiment, conscience, and will. Man weights these laws by his
ignorance and folly and selfishness, and can weight them
on the other side by his wisdom and conscience and
brotherliness. He can largely command the natural law of
society just as he so largely commands the natural law of
the physical world. My vocation leads me to study natural
law as the expression of mind and will. And so in political
economy I see the laws of man as he is, of the average
existing man, and find at the core of the evils human
fault, the errors and wrongs and imperfections of the be-

ings who are the atoms in this social world, in the correction of which, things will be bettered. Tregarva, in "Yeast," summed up his conclusions of the imbruted state of the peasantry in an English village into one sentence—"Somebody deserves to be whopped for all this." Who ought to be whopped here? Like every other question of which I know anything, there are two sides to this question—as to where the fault lies of the present state of labor. . . .

GOOD RESULTS OF A HUMANE POLICY TOWARD LABOR

Not a few of our manufacturers are already opening their eyes to these facts of the industrial problem, and, with far-seeing generosity and human brotherliness that will, according to the eternal laws, return even the good things of this world unto them, they are providing their workingmen with libraries, reading-rooms, and halls for lectures and for entertainments. They are encouraging and stimulating the formation of literary and debating societies, bands, and clubs and such other things as give social fellowship and mental interest. All this can be done at comparatively small cost. The men in the employ of a great establishment can be taught a new interest in their task as they learn to understand its processes and the relation of these processes to society at large, which can easily be done by lectures, &c. Such work as this is a work that demands the leadership, the organizing power which the employer can best furnish. At the last session of the Social Science Association an interesting paper sketched some of these efforts. In what wiser way could our wealthy manufacturers use a portion of the money won for them by the labor which has exhausted its own interest in its task? . . .

RATIO OF WAGES TO PRODUCTION, 1875–1880

Mr. Carroll D. Wright, in the 14th annual report of the Massachusetts Bureau of Labor (1883), shows that in 1875 the percentage of wages paid to the value of production, in over 2,000 establishments, was 24.68; and that in 1880 it was 20.23. This means that the workingmen's share of the returns of their own labor, so far from increasing, has decreased one-sixth in five years.

The workingman is disposed to believe in the light of such figures that the large wealth accumulated by his employer represents over and above a fair profit the increased wages out of which he naturally regards himself as being mulcted. He may be thick-headed, but he can see that in such a see-saw of profits *versus* wages the superior power of capital has the odds all in its favor. He learns to regard the whole state of the industrial world as one in which *might* makes *right*, and feebleness is the synonym of fault.

How, in the name of all that is reasonable, can the average man take much interest in his employer or identify himself with that employer under such a state of things as the economy sanctioned by the employer has taught him. This is aggravated by the whole character of our modern industrial system.

THE FACTORY SYSTEM A NEW FEUDALISM

The factory system is a new feudalism, in which a master rarely deals directly with his hands. Superintendents, managers, and "bosses" stand between him and them. He does not know them; they do not know him. The old common feeling is disappearing. And—this is a significant point that it behooves workingmen to notice—the intermediaries are generally workingmen who have risen out of the ranks of manual labor and have lost all fellow feeling with their old comrades, without gaining the larger sympathy with humanity which often comes from better culture. The hardest men upon workingmen are ex-workingmen. It is stated, on what seems to be good authority, that the general superintendent of the great corporation which lately has shown so hard a feeling toward its operatives when on strike was himself only ten years ago a telegraph operator.

LACK OF HUMAN RELATIONSHIP BETWEEN CAPITALISTS AND THEIR LABORERS

A further aggravating feature of this problem is the increasing tendency of capital to associated action. What little knowledge of his employés or sympathy with them the individual manufacturer might have is wholly lost in the case of the corporation. To the stockholders of a great joint-stock company, many of whom are never on the spot, the hundreds of laborers employed by the company are simply "hands"—as to whose possession of hearts or minds or souls the by-laws rarely take cognizance. Here there is plainly a case where capital—the party of brains and wealth —the head of the industrial association, should lead off in a systematic effort and renew, as far as may be, the old human tie, for which no substitute has ever been devised. . . .

WAGES: THEIR PURCHASING POWER, 1860–1881

The increase of prices which is going on in our society is imposing a constantly growing burden upon the resources of labor. Mr. Carroll D. Wright, in the Princeton Review for July, 1882, says that from 1860 to 1878 there was an average increase of wages of 24.4 per cent., and of prices of 14.9 per cent.; that from 1878 to December 1881 there was an annual average increase of wages of 6.9, and in prices an average increase of 21 per cent.; and that covering the whole period of 21 years there was an average increase in wages of 31.2 per cent., and in prices 41.3 per cent. In other words, between 1860 and 1881 our workingmen had suffered a reduction of ten per cent. on the purchasing power of wages, and this between a dead level year and one of general prosperity.

Under tendencies thus forcing prices up, the slight increase of wages where it may be found is relatively outdistanced, and the resources of labor are thus steadily diminishing. How hopeless, then, the preachments upon thrift, as the alone salvation of the poor man, become when his resources are steadily decreasing. . . .

SOCIAL FORCES FAVORING CAPITAL AND LAND AS AGAINST LABOR

As I read the problem of society to-day, there are large forces making for the interests of capital and land, as against the interests of labor—these three factors together creating all wealth.

(1.) LEGISLATION WORKS AGAINST LABOR

Legislation has thus far been in the hands of the well-to-do classes, of capital and of land, and it has been shaped in this free country, as in Europe, in the interests of these two classes. There is very little legislation recorded on our statute-books that looks to the care of the rights of labor, while there is a vast body of laws in existence guarding every possible interest of capital. Our legislatures are over-burdened with all sorts of special bills, devised to benefit private parties, but the measures of purely public utility are few and far between. We have in no one of our States any legislation at all comparable with the elaborate factory acts of England. Only a dozen of our States have labor bureaus, and these are all, with one exception, the growth of the last half dozen years. This great State has only just created such a bureau. This metropolitan city has, only within three years, as the result of a long agitation, obtained adequate sanitary laws for the tenement houses which shelter (?) 500,000 human beings, and a proper staff of officers to enforce them. Rich men have all sorts of carefully drawn up acts guarding the loaning and borrowing of money; but the poor man when he wants to borrow, has to go to the pawn-shops, over which, as he finds, to his cost, there is next to no restraint of law; so that after he has once deposited a valuable article, in time of need, and agreed to pay a ruinous rate of interest, he has no security that he will ever get back his property, even though able and anxious to redeem it.

It is the same story everywhere. The men at the top of the heap cry out, whenever an attempt is made to secure legislation for labor, "Hands off; the sacred principle of self-help must not be interfered with; the less legislation the better," and so on to the end of the gamut of stock-phrases which the press and the professors roll off with unctuous glibness.

Meanwhile these very many-millionaires and these very

gigantic corporations, whose counsel are so eloquent upon the danger of over legislation, have climbed to their high prosperity by the helping hand of law through legislation specially enacted to further their schemes. They never could have been what they are but for special legislation. The hypocrisy of the cant of "non-legislation" is sickening to honest minds and must be irritating beyond description to those who are silenced by it. Labor is opening its eyes to see at last that a democratic country which rarely legislates for the *demos*, the people, is something of a fraud. Labor is preparing to enter the political field, and is making tentative essays in this direction. In England the pressure of the trades unions has already wrested solid victories from Parliament; and under the growing mental enlightenment and the deepening moral sentiment, an immense stride is being taken towards a new era of statesmanship; in which the state will look first of all, for its own safety and prosperity, to the rightful ordering of the conditions of life among the vast mass of labor, on which the whole social structure rests. We shall never gain a satisfactory adjustment of the problem until our governments, municipal, State, and national, concern themselves at least as much with the interests of labor as with those of capital. And this will never be until labor takes the field of politics in dead earnest, and compels attention to its long-neglected claims.

(2.) INDUSTRIAL DEVELOPMENT WORKS AGAINST LABOR

There are more puzzling factors than privileging legislation at work to handicap labor. Our century has witnessed a revolutionary change in the character of the industrial system—a change which has been steadily making for capital against labor, except in so far as its own excesses have wrought local and partial protest and reaction. The introduction of the system of aggregated labor in the factory, and the development of the principle of the division of labor, thus made practicable, have gradually reduced the once free artisan to a new serfdom, in which he is completely at the mercy of capital, except as by union he

makes resistance. He no longer is master of a craft. He is
a bit of a process. He does a fraction of a complete job.
Of the rest of the process he knows nothing. Consequently
he cannot stand by himself. If he loses his place he cannot
set up, in a small way, for himself, even if the general
conditions of the business would give him a ghost of a
chance. In losing the home work of the artisan of the olden
time he loses with it the foothold on the soil, though that
soil were but a bit of a garden, which gave him the sense
of freedom. He literally has no base for personal independence. He no longer offers his wares, the products of
his handicraft, for sale in the market. He has neither the
workshop, the tools, nor the knowledge of any complete
process by which to make anything himself.

LARGE WEALTH AND COMBINED LABOR
NOW NECESSARY TO INDUSTRY

Only large wealth commands the means of production,
and only combined labor supplies the power of production.
The workman awaits the offer, on the part of the capitalist
of a workshop, of tools and of the fellows who can complete
his fractional skill. He has become a part of a gigantic
mechanism that is run by capital. He is utterly, absolutely
helpless in himself. He therefore has to enter the "labor
market" and offer for sale—no longer his works, but his
working. He sells himself. Under what is, with grim sarcasm, called "the system of free contract" he engages on
his part to make over to an employer his labor in return
for that employer's finding him the means and conditions,
without which he is no longer able to labor.

A new feudal system is set up, in which, through all the
descending gradations, labor holds its little all by the grace
of the feudal lord. It draws the feoff of life from its master
and suzerain. Of course it is true that under the old home-
workshop system there were journeymen who were in a
certain sense dependent on the master, for whom the master found the workshop, to whom he paid wages, and
whose products he sold; but each man could become a
master of his craft and of his tools, and thus of himself.

Each man looked forward to becoming a master workman, hiring other workmen, an expectation which, while we hear much about its being still a possibility, is becoming increasingly difficult of realization with each fresh turn of the wheel in the evolution of the factory system, and which, to all intents, is practically unrealizable already in most branches of industry.

It is not speaking too strongly to say that such a radical revolution as has thus been wrought in the condition of labor is without a parallel in the previous history of Christendom, and that it is fraught with dangers of the most ominous kind to society at large. Unarrested—or perhaps, let me rather say, led on to no further and higher evolution, in which its present action shall be corrected—this system would crush out the free manhood of the workingman.

MEN BECOMING MERE TENDERS UPON MACHINES

This factory system has been still further aggravated by the introduction of mechanism and of steam. Increasingly, the labor formerly wrought by man is being done by machinery driven by steam. One after another the processes of every old-time handicraft are being transferred to vast and complicated machines, and production is no longer to be called a manufacture, but a machino-facture. The skill which of old lay in the deft fingers of the craftsman is becoming lodged in steely mechanisms. Men become the tenders upon the costly and cunning machine. As such mere tenders, whose work is to feed and wait on the intelligent labors of these giant looms and presses, skilled workmen are no longer requisite. Poorer workmen take their place; women take the place of these inferior men; children at last come into demand in lieu of women. Poor workmen demand less pay than skilled craftsmen, women less than men, and children less than women. Thus wages fall, and a man's foes are they of his own household, very literally. The contrast between the New England operatives of a generation ago and those of to-day is very significant of the change which the factory is steadily working.

Nor is this all of the evil effect of the system. The introduction of mechanism displaces *all* human labor to an ever-increasing extent. One machine does the work of a host of hands. So these hands are thrown out of employment, and thus as mechanism enters one field of production after another men retire. Of course this action is mitigated, to some extent, by the opening up of other lines of occupation. The enormous development of industry in our age, and especially in our country, prevents us from feeling the full force of this tendency. But it is working among us at an alarming rate of speed.

Thus, in these various ways, labor suffers severely from the modern mechanical improvements, and from the monster forces which science has broken in to these engines. Its work is first robbed of interest and educating power, as already pointed out in the early part of this talk, and then taken from it. The labor market is crowded with the dispossessed "hands," who bid against each other and bid their wages mutually down.

The one beneficent effect of mechanism upon labor has been the cheapening of goods. Great as this benefit may be, its value seems to me much overrated when we consider the inferior quality of cheap goods, while it is as largely negatived when we note the lowered wages by which it is generally accompanied.

THE TRUE *versus* THE FALSE FUNCTION OF MECHANISM

Thus far it is questionable whether labor has derived any substantial benefit from the marvelous development of mechanism, at all comparable with the injury it has experienced from this revolution. It was fondly hoped, in the dawning of our era of mechanism, that all servile and exhausting toil was to be lifted from man; that all necessities were to be so multiplied that the poor would cease to want, and that leisure and its opportunities of culture would come to be a common blessing, through the immense increase of production, that is to say, of wealth. What a mockery these dreams seem now!

Yet these dreams were clearly no wild fancies. They

were true visions of what might be, under any just system of controlling these genii whom science has summoned to the service of man; visions which may come true if ever *man* becomes their master instead of *men*—the commonwealth, and not private rich men. In any equitable distribution of the immensely increased wealth which mechanism has created labor would have been much better off. But it is precisely against such equitable distribution that mechanism has worked.

THE INCREASED PRODUCTIVITY ENRICHES THE PARTY IN POSSESSION OF THE PLANT

The party owning the plant and controlling the means of production has found its power multiplied portentously. It has been those means of production which have received the increase of productive power, and he who owns them gains the benefit of their increased productivity. Capital reaps the golden harvest. Capital's yoke takes a new clasp around the neck of labor—more its slave by each new improvement that dispenses with human skill. It is thus that capital—the party possessing the means of production—is becoming ever richer and more powerful, while labor is becoming ever poorer and weaker, save as it combines and, not being as yet wholly superfluous, stays the downward tendency; and save as other factors enter the problem, changing the equation. . . .

THE DUTY OF THE HOUR

Wise men among our capitalists and in our governments, it seems to me, ought to be stirring themselves to prevent such contingencies.

Capital ought to be seriously endeavoring to ally labor with itself, and to train it into capacities for a share in the possession and control of the means of production. The ownership of the means of production by the people and for the people seems to me just as certainly the ultimate form of the social order as government by the people and for the people is the oncoming form of the political order. And in society, as in the state, the choice for men is not that of accepting or rejecting an evolution of nature, but simply of resisting it and blocking its pathway, which means always French revolutions, or of guiding it slowly and peacefully along safe channels. . . .

NEITHER MORAL NOR ECONOMIC RIGHT TO MISAPPROPRIATE ONE'S OWN MONEY

Q. Do you believe that the wealthy man has any moral right to . . . misappropriate his money, any more than to burn it up?—A. No, sir.

Q. You do not believe that he has any more moral right to do that than to destroy his jewels by dissolving them in acid?—A. No, sir; and not only do I believe that he has no moral right to do so, I believe that he has no economic right to do so. There is no such thing as pure private property. No man makes his money by himself alone. Each man makes his money through the co-operating labor and skill of others. The manufacturer has his hands working with him and for him who really produce the goods out of which he makes his fortune. The trader or the carrier has the whole country working with and for him. We see this most clearly in the case of real-estate speculation. Did the first Mr. Astor make his huge fortune by himself? He doubtless had the foresight which others lacked; but what was his foresight? The vision of the hosts who would come here to build up a great city. They came and have kept coming, and *they*—the hosts of men who get a bare living as well as those who get comfortable fortunes; laborers, mechanics, manufacturers, traders, merchants, &c.—have builded up New York, and given to its land the enormous value in which Mr. Astor's lots have shared. The city has built up Mr. Astor's huge wealth. The city has not only a moral claim, it has an *economic* claim, hard and solid as his own land. It holds a first mortgage on every house of the Astor estate, which it is not charity but simple justice to recognize. And so with every other form of private wealth, though we cannot always as clearly trace the connection.

PRIVATE WEALTH A SOCIAL TRUST

Private wealth is literally a social trust. It is a function called into action by society for the good of the body. This matter can even be reduced to an arithmetical statement, which ought to satisfy the hardest-headed millionaire. And, lest I should be put down at once as a "sentimentalist," let me again shelter myself behind so unsentimental an authority as Mr. Edward Atkinson.

I have already quoted his remark, but its substance will bear repetition here. He showed his hearers that the sum total of the divisible amount per annum is a definite and knowable amount, yielding a definite and calculable income, when divided by the population of the land. He showed that the average annual productivity of the country represented an amount which, if distributed equally to every man, woman, and child, would give to each person 50 cents a day. And then he told them in the words which I have already quoted that by as much as any of them had more than this 50 cents per diem, some one or some ones had less, there being no alternative to such an arithmetical problem.

SOCIETY'S RIGHT TO LIMIT PRIVATE FORTUNES

Q. Then this matter of what you call absolute individual ownership is, from necessity, subject to some such limitation as that which may be drawn by the law?—A. So it seems to me. Society has the right to limit the growth of the private fortunes which it really creates. If it finds them becoming excessive and so harmful, it can take measures to limit them. In such action it should, of course, proceed gradually and carefully, and in the light of the various experiments made by other peoples. It could limit the entail, devoting all over a certain amount to the state for public uses; or it could introduce an income tax. Either of these resorts would be better than setting a limit to accumulation. That would be a dangerous experiment. We don't want to kill the goose that lays the golden egg. Indeed, I should deprecate the resort to legislation at all, until a fair experiment has been made of what can be done through the moral forces of public sentiment; an experiment on which we have scarcely entered as yet. Still, I think we might hold this rod of legislation over our great fortunes as an extra incentive to good behavior.

Of one thing I am sure. Society must either teach great wealth its duties, or prevent the handing down of these great fortunes, or even, as a last resort, their accumulation. . . .

Q. This extravagant expenditure in private architecture is everywhere.—A. It is certainly growing rapidly.

Q. I suppose you do not lose sight of the æsthetic effects of that?

GREAT WEALTH A CORRUPTER OF ART

A. Doubtless great wealth has always been a patron of art. There is a good side to this palace-building, I am well aware. Certainly, with the rapid increase of large wealth among us, taste in domestic art has wonderfully improved. And this is altogether good, in so far as the law of restraint is observed and art is prized for its beauty and not for its rarity or costliness. But here comes in the inevitable danger of the art which is fed from great wealth. That art is drawn aside from its simplicity, its high ideals, its just restraint, its purity and seriousness. Great wealth tempts art to work for high pay; to minister to the whims and follies of Crœsus; to pamper pride and ostentation; to stoop to frivolous aims, and to rest content with brilliant tricks; to whet the sensual appetite of its idle and pleasure-loving patrons. I am not drawing on my fancy. This is the story that all history reads. Art has always been seduced and corrupted by wealth; and then, art itself has turned procuress to the lords of hell! Athens and Venice and every other city of art tell the same tale. We have been rarely fortunate in having had in the man* who, more than any other, has guided the domestic decoration of our city,

* The allusion is almost certainly to Richard Morris Hunt (1827–95), architect of the William K. Vanderbilt mansion on Fifth Avenue, New York, described in Document 25.

a noble nature animating great artistic powers. His ideals
have been the highest, and his canons of art the soundest;
and he has done a vast service in starting our æsthetic
progress along right lines. But how long will the early restraint be allowed by men eager to outshine their rivals?
We are only in the first dawn of the art which wealth feeds,
and it is too early to feel much of its corrupting touch. But
this gifted genius to whom I have referred, who knew well
what art was really desired by our very wealthy people,
was anything but sanguine of the tendencies at work. No
more severe judgment on this question have I ever heard
or read than that of the man to whom our city owes so
much. He knew too well with what ignorance, conceit,
pride, ostentation, and folly art has to struggle when it
accepts Crœsus as its patron. What do you think of an
estimable family proposing to decorate a dining-room ceiling with a copy of the paintings to which the *demi-monde*
look up in a celebrated café of Paris? A fine patronship of
art is American shoddy! The one hope is, that it may be
conscious of its own ignorance, and leave to a man who
understands his vocation full liberty to do his best.

DOCUMENT 55

(PLATE 25)

The Strike

SOURCE: Robert Koehler, "The Strike" (wood engraving from a painting), *Harper's Weekly*, XXX (1 May 1886), 280–81.

The composition of this highly emblematic picture shows an almost medieval disdain of literalness, but Koehler employs a conventional genre realism in the rendering of individual figures and objects. (He had studied in Munich under Ludwig von Löfftz and Franz von Defregger.) The result is a condensed image of industrial conflict which states all the essential elements and places them in a relation of crisis. In the background is the hideous monotone of a raw industrial city with smokestacks and a river that is obviously a muddy sewer. In the middle distance stands the factory, where work has stopped: the chimneys are not smoking. The "hands" are gathering before the house of the owner of the factory, who is specified by means of a top hat and the butler at his elbow. (The location of the house overlooking a dump heap is one of the major violations of literalness.) As a spokesman for the workers vehemently presents their demands, one of the men, in the foreground, is picking up a stone—perhaps to break a plate-glass window in the owner's house. The ragged woman standing passively with two children in the left foreground implies the nature of the workers' grievances, but an older woman in the center foreground seems to be remonstrating with her husband as if to oppose the strike.

Perhaps inevitably, the painting represents a state of affairs characteristic of a period twenty or thirty years in the past. It was reproduced in the issue of *Harper's Weekly* which was on the stands when the Haymarket bombing occurred in Chicago. The scale of the industrial operation Koehler depicts is primitive, almost bucolic; the owner lives close to his plant, he meets the workers face to face, and they are so few in number that he might conceivably know all of them, at least by sight. The strike at the McCormick plant which led up to the Haymarket bombing involved some fourteen hundred men. The workers in the painting act as a group; they do not seem to have any formal organization resembling a union. And, at least at this stage, the police and militia are not involved.

Document 56

(Plate 26)

The Great Strike—Scenes of Riot in Chicago

source: C. and A. T. Sears, "The Great Strike—Scenes of Riot in Chicago. Fight between the Military and the Rioters at the Halsted Street Viaduct" (wood engraving), *Harper's Weekly*, XXI (18 August 1877), 640.

The great railroad strike of 1877 was the first industrial conflict on a national scale and it released unprecedented violence. Beginning on 16 July as a protest against reductions in wages on the Baltimore & Ohio railroad, it had spread rapidly to the Pennsylvania system and thence to the Middle West and the Pacific Coast. Governors of several states called out the militia at once, and when these troops were unable to restore order (even in some cases refusing to fire on the strikers), President Rutherford B. Hayes sent in federal troops. Riots in Baltimore, Philadelphia, Pittsburgh, and other cities had preceded the disturbances in Chicago, where the first strike occurred at the Michigan Central freight yards on 24 July. Many workers in factories and shops joined the railway strikers. By 26 July, the date of the fight represented in the drawing from *Harper's Weekly*, the city was being patrolled by the municipal police force, five thousand volunteer deputies mobilized by the Chicago Board of Trade, two regiments of state militia, members of patriotic organizations such as the Ellsworth Zouaves, and more than a regiment of federal regular troops (some hastily recalled from fighting Indians on the Western plains).

On the morning of 26 July police attempting to disperse a crowd estimated to number ten thousand gathered at Turner Hall, near the Halsted Street Viaduct, were forced to retreat when their ammunition gave out, but returned to the attack when they were reinforced by

a body of cavalry and "two companies of regular in-
fantry armed with SPENCER repeating rifles." At least
12 workers were killed; about one hundred of their
leaders were arrested.*

Federal troops and militia succeeded finally in breaking through the strikers' blockades of rights-of-way, and
by the early days of August, after about two weeks of
violence throughout the country, trains were again running on schedule.

Although there was much popular support for the
strikers, metropolitan newspapers were almost unani-
mously hostile to them. The *New York Times,* for example, announced in a headline that Chicago was "in
Possession of Communists" and exhausted its vocabulary
of abuse against those who supported the strike. *Harper's
Weekly* said that the crowd around Turner Hall was
"mainly made up of roughs who never did an honest
day's work." The editorial writer also spoke of "a howling, yelping mob of irresponsible idiots," adding: "They
talked of what they were going to do, and how they had
gotten things all their own way, every language except
Chinese being used. The communistic element was
largely represented, many of the lowest class of Poles
and Bohemians being on hand."†

The incomprehension of the middle-class public is
illustrated in a sermon preached by Henry Ward
Beecher on 22 July 1877, at the height of the disturbance. "Comprehensively," he declared, "this is a rebellion on the part of the railroad operatives against
participating in that shrinkage which the whole country
is undergoing." When he added that the strike "grew
out of a false philosophy which might exist among the
communists of Paris or in the slums of Europe, but
which should be scorned by the educated workingmen
of America!" the congregation applauded.

Earlier in this sermon Beecher had made a remark
that became notorious. The New York *Herald* reported
it as follows: "It was said that $1 a day was not enough
to support a wife and six children. It was not enough if

* Samuel Yellen, *American Labor Struggles* (New York, 1936),
Chap. I, "The Railroad Uprisings of 1877," pp. 3–38.

† Anonymous, "The Great Strike," *Harper's Weekly,* XXI (18
August 1877), 647.

a man smoked, if he drank beer and if he and his family wanted superior clothing, food and shelter. 'But,' said Mr. Beecher vehemently, 'is not $1 a day enough to buy bread? and water costs nothing; and a man that can't live on bread is not fit to live. What is the benefit of a civilization that simply makes a man incompetent to live under existing conditions? Education and civilization are designed to make a man a universal instrument of improvement and to make it possible for him to live under any conditions. . . . A family may live, laugh, love and be happy, that eats bread and good water in the morning, water and good bread at noon and good bread and water at night.' " The reporter added: "The congregation evidently regarded this proposition as a huge joke, for they laughed loudly."‡ The following Sunday, having placed thirty plain-clothes policemen in the church with a squad of detectives in reserve nearby, Beecher announced from the pulpit that he had received many abusive and some threatening letters during the week. He asserted that he had been quoted inaccurately in the press, but his clarification was not very clear: "He said the workmen should call on God, and stop using tobacco and beer, subdue their passions, and try by self-denial to make homes for themselves and families. . . . 'I don't say that $1 a day is enough to support a working man, but it is enough to support a man. He is going through a transition, and a man should be superior to his circumstances.' "§ One could hardly find a more apt illustration of the irrelevance of a decadent cult of "ideality" (for Beecher is uttering a kind of debased version of Thoreau) to the issues being fought out by militia and rioters at the Halsted Street viaduct in Chicago.

‡ New York *Herald*, 23 July 1877, p. 10, col. 5.
§ *New York Times*, 30 July 1877, p. 8, col. 2.

DOCUMENT 57

(PLATE 27)

The Anarchist Riot in Chicago—
A Dynamite Bomb Exploding among the Police

SOURCE: Thure de Thulstrup, "The Anarchist Riot in Chicago—A Dynamite Bomb Exploding among the Police" (wood engraving from sketches and photographs furnished by H. Jeanneret), *Harper's Weekly*, XXX (15 May 1886), 312–13.

The Haymarket incident was the culmination of a series of disturbances growing out of a labor dispute at the McCormick Harvester factory in Chicago which led to a lockout of about fourteen hundred employees on 16 February 1886, and a strike which was called two days after the lockout. There was intermittent violence over a period of weeks, with a particularly acute outburst on 3 May, when strikers attacked scab workers leaving the plant and the police killed one striker and wounded several others. The International Working People's Association called a mass meeting in Haymarket Square for the evening of the following day to protest police brutality. About twelve hundred people gathered for the meeting. They were addressed from a wagon standing near the curb by August Spies (editor of the anarchist *Arbeiter-Zeitung*), Albert R. Parsons (editor of *Alarm,* another anarchist paper), and Samuel Fielden, a teamster who was prominent among Chicago radicals. Shortly after 10 P.M., when the crowd had dwindled to perhaps four hundred because of threatening weather and Fielden was concluding his speech, a column of 180 policemen suddenly appeared and ordered the crowd to disperse. Fielden stopped speaking and those with him on the wagon began to climb down. It was at this moment that the bomb was thrown, by someone who was never identified. It killed one policeman and wounded about seventy. The police opened

fire on the crowd, killing one person and wounding
more than fifty.*

Eight radicals, including the three speakers who had
addressed the meeting on the evening of 4 May, were
convicted of conspiracy to commit murder on the theory
that their inflammatory speeches had incited some unknown person to throw the bomb. Seven were sentenced
to death and one sent to prison for life. Four men were
hanged in November 1887. One of the three who had
been sentenced to death committed suicide in prison;
and the sentences of the other two were commuted to
life imprisonment. The three men who were serving
prison sentences were pardoned by John P. Altgeld after
he became governor of Illinois in 1893.

Public opinion overwhelmingly favored the conviction of the accused men. Theodore Roosevelt, for example, accepting the commonly held belief that the
crowd assembled to hear the radical speakers had attacked the police, said he would have shot down the
"rioters." Organized labor was divided. The New York
Central Labor Union, led by Samuel Gompers, issued
a statement denouncing the verdict. On the other hand,
Terence V. Powderly of the Knights of Labor, deeply
concerned over the hostility toward all labor organizations aroused by the bomb, forbade the Knights to collect
funds for the defence of the condemned men. Even
Henry George, after declaring in January 1887 that the
convictions were "shamelessly illegal," by October had
decided that the verdict was just. Only a few writers
and intellectuals ventured to criticize the legality of the
proceedings—the most conspicuous being Robert Ingersoll, Henry D. Lloyd, and William Dean Howells.
When Altgeld pardoned the convicted men still in
prison, he was subjected to a torrent of public abuse.
The Toledo *Blade*, for example, declared: "Governor
Altgeld has encouraged anarchy, rapine and the overthrow of civilization."† Later that same year Judge

---

* This account of the bombing is based on Henry David, *The
History of the Haymarket Affair: A Study in the American
Social-Revolutionary and Labor Movement* (1936), 2d ed., New
York, 1958.

† Quoted in Raymond Ginger, *Altgeld's America: The Lincoln
Ideal versus Changing Realities* (New York, 1958), p. 86.

Joseph E. Gary, whose conduct of the trial is regarded by historians as highly prejudicial, was re-elected by a landslide vote.

Henry David, author of the standard monograph on the Haymarket incident, calls this drawing in *Harper's Weekly* "imaginative" and cites it among the distorted accounts which appeared in the press throughout the country. The drawing is inaccurate in showing the bomb exploding while Fielden was still speaking, in representing the civilian in the foreground as firing at the police with a pistol, and in the suggestion (in the background at the right) of an attack on the police with sticks. Exhaustive investigation of the incident in subsequent court proceedings failed to establish any acts of aggression against the police except the explosion of the bomb. The inaccuracies in the drawing can be explained in part at least by the fact that de Thulstrup was not an eyewitness of the catastrophe but was working up data furnished by another man. The 15 May issue of *Harper's Weekly* appeared so soon after the event that the data may have been sent from Chicago to New York for actual preparation of the drawing. But the public conception of what had happened was shaped by precisely such distortions in the press.

Documents 58–59

(Plates 28 and 29)

Equal to the Anarchists

Liberty is Not Anarchy

sources: Thomas Nast, "Equal to the Anarchists. They Will Have All the Rope They Want, and More Too" (pen-and-ink drawing), *Harper's Weekly*, XXX (4 September 1886), 571.

Thomas Nast, "Liberty Is Not Anarchy" (pen-and-ink drawing), *Harper's Weekly*, XXX (4 September 1886), 564.

These two drawings by Nast, which appeared in the same issue of *Harper's Weekly*, illustrate the almost unanimous public reaction to the trials being carried on in Chicago. It is significant that although the defendants were accused of conspiracy to commit murder, the crime for which Nast advocates hanging them in the crude drawing of the gallows is their political doctrine. The other cartoon, more elaborate and carefully finished, portrays the seven defendants as Lilliputian vermin being squeezed in the majestic hand of Columbia—creatures too contemptible to be attacked by the sword of justice.

PART VII

The Conservative Position

Ideologies are polemic: they are constructed either for attack or defense. The business leaders of the United States in the post-Civil War period did not feel insecure enough on the whole to devote much energy to rationalizing their position of power in the management of the economy. As Edward C. Kirkland has pointed out, the captains of industry tended to be inarticulate. They read few books, they were not interested in ideas, they did not have the impulse to relate their day-to-day decisions to any general principles.* Nevertheless, the growing extent and violence of strikes and the challenge of left-wing protests during the 1880s demanded some reasoned defense of the established order—or disorder, if one accepted the charges of dissident critics. The hearings conducted in 1883 by the Senate Committee on Education and Labor, having for their immediate occasion a national telegraphers' strike, illustrate the way in which public concern over a palpable breakdown in the functioning of a major industry could compel a long-overdue examination of the premises of the new industrialism. In the present section are gathered selections from the testimony of four spokesmen for business. Together with the statements in the previous section, this testimony embodies the materials for a debate be-

* Edward C. Kirkland, *Dream and Thought in the Business Community, 1860–1900*, Ithaca, N. Y., 1956.

tween challengers and defenders of the industrial system. But as might be expected, the transcript of the
hearings lacks the neat structure of an organized debate.
The issues are not clearly analyzed; there is seldom an
explicit confrontation between affirmative and negative
propositions; and since the conservative witnesses appeared as individuals, without even a rudimentary pre-
arrangement comparable to that made by the Central
Labor Union of New York, their testimony seems on
the surface even more rambling and incoherent.

Nevertheless, the conservative defense has at bottom
a greater consistency than does the radical attack. This
was doubtless inevitable, since the spokesmen for business were all taking for granted an existing policy and
in order to make their case had only to refute the varied
propositions of their critics. The general principles that
control their thought appear as a rule only in aphoristic
dicta felt to be self-evident and therefore in no need of
elaborate demonstration. To all proposals for reform
through legislation, the conservatives replied simply that
man can create nothing by statute, that governmental
interference in economic processes can cause only harm
in the short run, and in the long run can change nothing. To leftist assertions that mechanization was alien-
ating workers from their employers, the business leaders
replied blandly that since the true interests of labor
and capital were identical, organization of workers into
unions was anomalous and potentially harmful to both
employee and employer. The charge that capitalists were
exploiting the workers was met with the flat assertion
that labor always gets its fair share of profits, or the
more restricted *argumentum ad hominem* to the effect
that American workers were better off by far than those
in Europe. (Else how explain the stream of immigration
westward across the Atlantic?) If railways were charged
with being rapacious monopolies, the answer could be
made that they had settled Western lands and had
steadily reduced freight rates.

In framing positive proposals the conservative spokesmen had a more difficult task, for their deepest belief
was that the resolution of all difficulties must be left
to the operation of natural forces. Two main contentions
tend to recur in their testimony. One of these is the

idea of the West as a safety valve—developed here
most fully by Jay Gould, manipulator of Western railways. The other, propounded by Edward Atkinson and
Dexter A. Hawkins, was that any relief from poverty
among the workers must come from greater productivity,
which would augment the fund available for distribution as wages. Atkinson emphasizes the elimination of
waste, especially through improved technology; Hawkins
emphasizes increased efficiency through education of
the labor force (even though the use of public funds
for this purpose, which he advocates, seems to violate
the doctrine of the minimal state which in principle all
the conservative spokesmen supported).

Except for Jay Gould, the men whose views are collected in this section were not themselves among the
real masters of the American economy. Furthermore,
Danford Knowlton and Atkinson were unrepresentative
of Republican orthodoxy because they opposed the protective tariff. But what we are concerned with is the
rationale of industrialism that was made available to the
general public, particularly the logical or rhetorical devices by means of which the imperatives of business
activity were accommodated to the system of values
cherished by the community. Here the utterances of
apologists are more significant than the actual concepts
and motives of the men in control of the industrial and
financial system.

The logical, or at any rate the conceptual bridge between the official value system of American society in
the 1880s and the contours of large-scale mechanized industry with its typical financial institutions (the corporation, the trust, Wall Street, and so on) was the venerable notion of natural law. This connection is implicit
in all the testimony of spokesmen for business before
the Senate Committee, but the best systematic exposition
of the principle is contained in a little book published in
1887 by Henry Wood (1834–1909), a professional
writer. Wood was a native of Vermont who had entered
business in Iowa and then Chicago, and by the time he
was forty had earned enough money to retire. After a
serious illness drew his interest to mental healing, he
began the production of a long series of books devoted
to the New Thought movement. He carried on a vast

correspondence with readers who sought his guidance in their personal problems. In 1893 Benjamin O. Flower, editor of *The Arena* (a journal that opened its pages to many unconventional ideas, including for example Hamlin Garland's early fiction under the influence of Henry George), said that Wood was "the Emerson of the new metaphysical thought."†

Wood's thought was not new but it was very metaphysical. His *Natural Law in the Business World* is a homily on the Emersonian text, "The moral law lies at the center of nature and radiates to the circumference." In essays such as "Wealth" Emerson had long ago deduced from this Neoplatonic proposition the maxims of laissez-faire economic theory. Wood had only to bring the argument up to date by adding references to labor unions: "Their conflict is not with employers or capitalists, but with the law of supply and demand. They are, apparently, not aware that their contest is with nature, and that it is impossible to overcome or repeal a Natural Law." The very conception of "labor combinations" is erroneous because it has for its foundation "the idea of a necessary and natural antagonism towards employers." The truth is that the universe is one integrated, harmonious system; its constituent principles, the laws of nature, are "the methods of the Creator"—the most "fundamental and universal" being "the law of supply and demand." The regulation of economic processes by "price and competition" is therefore the divine will, and man opposes these forces at his peril. It follows also that "extra legislation [i.e. human statutes supplementing Natural Law] is no cure for the ills of society." The conclusion is obvious: "We would like, most heartily, to see every laboring man in America have high wages, and steady work; but *nothing* can bring this desirable condition about, but industry, patience, providence, temperance, and public confidence."‡

While it is true that Emerson's varied and restless thought embodied a strain of economic conservatism,

† DAB, *s.v.* Henry Wood.

‡ *Natural Law in the Business World* (Boston and New York, 1887), pp. 215–22.

Wood's use of Emersonian ideas involves an oversimplification and vulgarization closely paralleling Henry Ward Beecher's operations in the realms of theology and ethics. The process by which the challenging and often disturbing insights of pre-Civil War transcendentalism were converted into a bland genteel tradition has been noted by George Santayana in general terms,§ but it is important to realize how pervasive this diluted transcendentalism became in the official culture of the late nineteenth century. The concept of Natural Law, with a minimum of interpretation, could be used and was used to confer on Big Business the faded glamor of Ideality; it gave to Protestant clergymen at least a pseudointellectual argument in support of the new capitalism. This pattern of ideas makes clear why a theological reorientation had to accompany the growing concern of clergymen like R. Heber Newton and Washington Gladden with social problems. They had to work themselves free of the inhibitions imposed on serious theological thought by post-Emersonian optimism.

§ "The Genteel Tradition in American Philosophy," in *Winds of Doctrine*, New York, 1912.

DOCUMENT 60

Views

SOURCE: Dexter A. Hawkins, "Views" (a written communication to the Senate Committee on Education and Labor, New York, dated 10 September 1883, in *Report of the Committee*, Vol. II, pp. 151–55).

Hawkins' statement is a compendium of standard conservative maxims: free land is a safety valve, equality is unnatural, efforts to legislate economic reforms are attempts to be wiser than the Creator, and so on. Two of his contentions, in particular, echo ideas already expressed in cartoons by Thomas Nast: the notion that dues paid by a worker to a union are wasted, and the assertion that strikers are killing the goose that laid the golden egg. It should be pointed out, however, that Hawkins was serious in his advocacy of education as a means of improving the lot of the laborer; he was a conspicuous advocate of free public schools. Although at the time of his testimony he was a lawyer practicing in New York, he spoke for a solid New England tradition: he was descended from colonial stock and was a graduate of Bowdoin.

[NEW YORK, *September 19, 1883*]

The CHAIRMAN presented the following communication from Col. Dexter A. Hawkins, which was read and ordered to be printed with the testimony:

111 BROADWAY, NEW YORK,
September 10, 1883.

To the honorable Senate Committee on Education and Labor:

In compliance with your invitation I submit the following facts and views:

Every person who performs a reasonable amount of daily labor during the period that he is competent to work is entitled, as the fruits of that labor, to a reasonable support for life for himself and for those who cannot labor that are dependent upon him. Those who can labor but won't are not entitled to any support at all out of the fruits of the labor of their fellows.

Whenever the natural conditions in a country are such that it will not produce this support when intelligently worked that fact may safely be taken as a hint from Providence to emigrate. But whenever the laws or social organism in a country is such that their legitimate effect is to prevent any portion of society from obtaining such support from such labor it is clear proof that the laws or social organism should be modified. In the end they are modified always in such cases, either peaceably and wisely, through such investigations as your committee is making, or blindly and by violence.

The face of the earth is not a dead level; rivers are not of equal size; trees are not of a uniform height or bigness, and men are no exception to this universal law of nature; they differ in capacity, physical and intellectual. Under any just and equal laws some must become and will become rich and others poor, but the poorest, to the extent that they are willing to work, are entitled to food, clothing, shelter, and education—a livelihood; and the wealthiest, so far as they comply with the laws, are entitled to the full and complete protection and enjoyment of all their possessions.

The function of human laws in this regard is fully performed when they enable the individual, if he makes the best use of his faculties, to acquire and enjoy the same proportion of the goods of this world, in relation to his fellows, that his faculties and the use he makes of them bear to those of his fellows. All beyond this is outside of the function of human laws. This necessarily gives the fullest and widest scope for the legitimate exercise of individual powers of acquisition, possession, enjoyment, and disposition.

Thirty years ago I made a careful study of the condition of labor in the various countries of Europe and of the British Kingdom. Food there was no cheaper than at that time in this country. Clothing was about thirty per cent. cheaper. Shelter was about twenty-five per cent. cheaper. But wages were not more than one-half what they were here, and the education of the laborers was far below that of those in our then free States. (Our slave labor was far more ignorant than their labor.)

But a social organism existed there, the offspring of the feudal system, that imposed heavy burdens upon labor, and made it abnormally difficult for labor to improve its condition; hence "labor organizations" or "unions" and a social war between these organizations on the one side and capital and the ruling classes on the other.

The condition of free labor in this country then was, on the whole, nearly twice as good as there. The great emigration from Europe in the last thirty years, and the addition in that period of some thirty per cent. from the mines to the stock of silver and gold money in the world, has raised the rate of wages all over Europe. But the price of food, of clothing and of shelter has risen there almost equally as much, so that the condition of the laborer there is not much improved in those three items. But in the education of the laborer there it has greatly advanced. England, Scotland, Ireland, Wales, France and Italy then did not recognize the duty of the property in the State, whoever owned the property, to provide for the education of all children in the state, no matter to whom the children belonged. Those countries do now each recognize this duty, and have provided by law for its performance; and in the interest of society they require every child to be educated at least in the elementary branches of both knowledge and industry. This has improved and is fast improving and elevating the character and condition of labor in those countries.

The vast immigration to this country of the last thirty

years would have tended to reduce wages and lower the condition of labor here, had not the addition of 90,000 miles to our railways in that time opened up, as it were, a new continent to labor, nearly as large as the whole of Europe; and had not the stimulus of a protective tariff in the last twenty years, by giving our own market to our own people instead of to Europeans, doubled the product of our manufacturers.

These two things have in this country as a whole made the demand for labor keep pace with the supply, though increased from abroad now at the rate of three-quarters of a million emigrants per year. The distribution by means of the railroads of this increase from without of two thousand a day speedily draws off any temporary excess of laborers in any locality. Aided by the above favorable conditions, the price of labor in this country instead of declining for the last thirty years has, as a whole, steadily advanced; while the price of nearly every thing that the laborer needs to consume or to use has, owing to the development of machinery and home manufactures, steadily declined. Scarcely anything except rum and tobacco has increased in price; and the laborer is on the whole better off without these than with them. Food products are cheaper in this country than in Great Britain, France and Germany, for of our surplus we export to them nearly five hundred million dollars' worth per year. Shoes and hats are cheaper, and also clothing of all kinds, except the finer and higher grades, which are not necessaries, but luxuries. Shelter is dearer, because we require new houses for at least two millions of people per year, and nineteen-twentieths of the cost of a house is in some form labor; and the price of labor is still on the average about double what it is in Great Britain, France, Germany, and Italy. The investigations made this year by Mr. Porter and reported from week to week in the Tribune demonstrate this.

It follows from the above facts that the relations of labor to capital are more favorable to labor in this country on the whole than in any other.

In many countries a laborer, discharged without a recommendation or certificate, cannot get employment from any other capitalist. Where such is the rule there would seem to be a propriety in allowing labor unions to dictate to some extent who should be discharged and who employed. But when, as in this country, capital does not possess, or exercise any such prerogative, such dictations are injurious to labor. In some countries no one can exercise a trade till he has served an apprenticeship and obtained his certificate as journeyman or master-workman. In those countries there would seem to be some reason in allowing trades unions to dictate the number of apprentices, so as not to have the trades overcrowded; but in this country as a rule no such apprenticeship or certificate is required. The only effect, then, here of trades unions dictating the number of apprentices a mechanic may take and instruct is to lower the grade and number of our skilled workmen and reduce the ability of labor to compete with capital and to gain a livelihood.

The trades unions were very proper and necessary in Europe under a state of society very different from ours. But in this country they are introducing and enforcing foreign and despotic rules and regulations not in harmony with the condition of affairs here, and that amount often to a positive tyranny over labor; and, besides, they deprive the laborer of a percentage of his earnings.

I will state an instance: The Cumberland coal miners a few years ago were induced to join one of these organizations, and each one paid a portion of his wages into its treasury. The managers, who were not themselves laborers, selecting a time when the companies had entered into large contracts to deliver coal, ordered the miners to strike unless an increase of 30 per cent. on their wages was granted. To save a greater loss from breach of contracts the companies yielded to this extortion; but as soon as their contracts were filled they explained to these managers that the price must go back to the former rate on a certain day or the mines would be closed, for every ton mined at the extortionate rate brought a loss. When the day arrived these managers ordered the whole three thousand miners to strike, and for nearly five months they did not mine a ton of coal, and they and their families were reduced to the greatest straits for their daily bread. Then the managers allowed them to go to work at the old rate all the time offered by the companies. Here was a positive immediate loss to the laborers of nearly a million dollars of wages, a large loss to the capitalists, and a driving away of business to other coal regions, which will decrease labor for many years in that region, thus bringing a large future loss upon these laborers.

This is but one of many similar cases that I could name. Labor unions frequently demand that the length of a day's work and the price of it should both be regulated by statute. This is the same thing in principle as fixing by law the price the laborer should pay for everything he consumes or uses, and the quantity he should consume or use each day, without any regard to his ability or needs. Such things are outside of and beyond the sphere and province of statute law. They are, and, from the very inherent nature of things, must be, regulated by supply and demand, and not by statute. To regulate both the length and price or quantity and price of a day's work by statute is as absurd as to enact that water should of its own accord run up hill. One laborer may be able to do twice as much work in a day as another. To restrict all to the same amount (which is necessarily that of the least efficient), as some of these organizations do, is as absurd as to give only the same amount of food for a meal and cloth for a suit to a giant as is required for a pigmy. It is attempting to be wiser than the Creator. Labor organizations in harmony with our free institutions and social conditions may do much good; but those thus far imported from Europe are quite as much out of place here as would be European governments and methods of administration. They mean well, but lack knowledge of American affairs and free institutions. The chief cause of strikes is ignorance on the part of laborers of the mutual exigencies of capital and labor. Capital requires safety and a reasonable increase; labor requires constant employment at reasonable wages and sure payment. It is for the interest of the laborer that his employer, whether an individual or a corporation, should have ample capital and that this capital should increase from year to year from the proceeds of the business. This secures sure pay and steady employment and a prospect of a rise of wages. If the capital is not ample the payment is uncertain; and if the business does not increase the capital, wages cannot rise; in fact they will fall or the capital will seek other and more profitable investment. The strikers sometimes, as at Pittsburgh a few years ago, destroy capital; this is killing the goose that otherwise could lay the golden egg for them, and results from ignorance of the mutual interest and relations of capital and labor. Educated labor would never, to raise wages, resort to the destruction of capital, any more than a hungry crowd would destroy food in order to increase their supply of it.

The better provision made by law in Europe for the universal education of labor there is steadily but surely putting labor here at a disadvantage. If we do not soon bestir ourselves, the superior training they are now giving their people will leave ours in the competitive race with them handicapped with a backload of ignorance. Intelligence in the laborer is to-day essential to a high productive capacity. Formerly, where little or no machinery or scientific processes were used, it was not. We must enable our labor to keep abreast of the progress of the world, or our country will fall to the rear. Ignorance begets ignorance, and it is a long, slow, and painful struggle to rise from it when kept down by competition with foreign intelligence. The labor unions and friends of labor throughout this country see this; and they are making a wise and just demand upon the Government for laws that shall secure to every child in this country a good elementary education. Careful experiment and examination and comparison of results has demonstrated that a good elementary education, such as should be given to every youth in the free common school, adds 50 per cent. on the average, to his capacity as a mere productive machine over what it would be if he remained illiterate. Pauperism and crime add heavy burdens to labor, as the paupers must be supported, and crime detected and punished, and society protected against criminals; all at the expense of labor or the fruits of labor. The illiterates in this country produce nine times as many criminals and thirty times as many paupers, according to their number, as do the literates.

In the United States there were, according to the census of 1880, 4,404,362 illiterate adults. The minimum *annual* loss to the country on the labor of these by reason of their illiteracy is not less than $50 each, or $210,219,100; or more than twice as much as the *annual* cost of our whole system of public education in the entire country.

If special provision is not made by law to secure general education, this gigantic army of ignorance will by 1890 be increased to five millions of human beings; enough not only to prostrate industry in this country, but to destroy in fact, if not in name, all free government. Free government and ignorant citizens are no more compatible than fire and water. One or the other must cease to be. If free government takes hold of illiteracy in season it can extinguish it; but if it delays too long it will itself be tumbled into the grave.

Labor is in favor of free government and prosperity; hence it demands universal education. All intelligent capital joins in this demand. The National Treasury is overflowing; the National Government is responsible for precipitating upon the country four millions of illiterate citizens. Self-preservation is the first law of governments as well as of nature. There cannot be a reasonable doubt of the power of the Government to appropriate the money from the National Treasury sufficient to eliminate this illiteracy and to supervise its proper expenditure.

Labor thus made intelligent will harmonize itself with capital, and will in any event be amply able, wisely and peacefully, to assert and maintain its just rights.

It is my deliberate judgment that your honorable committee could not do a wiser thing than to give your influence to secure from the National Government the demand of labor for universal education in the elementary branches of knowledge and industry. After the nation has done what is asked, then the States will be able to preserve, support, and enforce universal education.

Very respectfully,

DEXTER A. HAWKINS.

DOCUMENT 61

Testimony before the Senate Committee on Education and Labor

SOURCE: Edward A. Atkinson, Testimony before the Senate Committee on Education and Labor, New York and Boston, 6 September and 17 October 1883 (in *Report of the Committee*, Vol. II, pp. 230–32; Vol. III, pp. 342–44).

Like Dexter A. Hawkins, Atkinson was a descendant of colonial New England ancestors, but he was not a college graduate. He began at fifteen sweeping floors in textile mills and rose to the position of treasurer of several manufacturing concerns by the time he was twenty-one. Later he headed a mutual insurance company in Boston. He was an indefatigably public-spirited citizen, a kind of lesser Benjamin Franklin. He invented an oven that economized fuel and published a treatise on *The Science of Nutrition* (1896); he was a pioneer in the collection and use of statistics for the study of social and economic problems; he wrote books and pamphlets about industrial architecture, banking, the level of real wages, various kinds of economic legislation, and a dozen other subjects. An advocate of sound money, a free-trader, a pacifist and anti-imperialist, he was a particularly articulate mouthpiece for enlightened conservative opinion during the last quarter of the nineteenth century. His most characteristic proposal for the solution of economic problems was the elimination of waste in agriculture and industry, and the use of advanced technology. This proposal was derived from an implied wages-fund theory which maintained that the only significant increase in wages must come from increased productivity rather than from legislative interference with the distribution of the national income or from demands by labor unions.

[From an Address, "The Elements of National Prosperity," delivered at the opening of the Second Annual Fair of New England Manufacturers' and Mechanics' Institute, Boston, 6 December 1882, and read into the transcript of testimony before the Senate Committee on Education and Labor, New York, 6 September 1883.]

What, then, can we do to make the struggle for life easier? The only answer is, "Give such instruction as will develop brain and hand together, so that the purchasing power of each dollar may be increased. Save the waste of labor and the waste of product. We are the most wasteful nation in the world; and one reason is that even at our present measure of product there is vastly greater abundance here than there is anywhere else.

What margin is there for increase or for saving, do you ask? The answer is plain. Our general methods of agriculture are poor and shiftless; our crops are not one-half what a reasonably good system would bring forth. The potentiality of a single acre of land is still almost an unknown quality. If I were to say to you that, next to the abolition of slavery and the use of the railway and the steamship, the re-discovery of the method of saving green crops—called *ensilage*—was the most important event in its effects on material welfare of the present century, you might suggest that a commission of lunacy should be appointed to examine the condition of my brain. Consider the waste of fencing, because one man cannot trust his neighbor to keep his cattle where they belong. Witness the waste of sheep, because the cur dog is tolerated while the farmer suffers.

Marvelous as the machinery in this great building may be, science has work to do vastly greater than any thing yet accomplished. Almost the only tools yet perfected are the water-wheel and the dynamo-electric machine. Look at that seemingly perfect steam-engine and boiler; it wastes nine-tenths of the fuel with which it is supplied. Examine that costly and clumsy locomotive and heavy train of cars; only one pound in a hundred of the fuel used is actually applied to the movement of the load. Observe that almost self-operating carding-engine, spinning-frame, and loom; are they perfect? Four-fifths of the power is wasted in operating them; and when you have put your cotton fiber into cloth you have lost three-fourths of its original strength by your rough treatment.

Your builders cut up your timber so as to lose or waste one-half its strength; most of your architects plan your buildings so as to assure the most perfect combustion. You make a clumsy effort to distribute your fire-loss of nearly a hundred millions a year through insurance companies, and you waste 40 per cent. of your premiums in the mere expense of making the attempt. You cannot even start a horse-car without wasting the knees of your horses by the excessive strain.

I might go on in this line indefinitely, but the greatest waste of all is the waste of food and fuel.

The grain, root, and hay crops of this country weigh over 150,000,000 tons—300,000,000,000 food pounds to be harvested, sorted, distributed, converted into meat, butter, cheese, bread, and the like, in order that each one of us may have our daily ration of about three pounds—a pound each for our breakfast, dinner, and supper.

Seventy million tons of coal are mined and converted. Are we not all aware that half our food is wasted, and perhaps more than half our fuel, especially in cooking?

How shall we save this waste? Must we not save it if each man, woman, and child can earn, on the average, only what 50 cents a day will buy? Try for yourselves what you can get in the little shops on the South Cove or at the North End, where the poor must buy their food, and then you will know why so many suffer want, even in the midst of plenty, for the lack of instruction in the commonest arts of life. Must not our common schools be somewhat common in quality when they qualify their pupils so little in the practical arts of life?

And here let me call your attention to the importance

of the smallest fraction saved. In order to do this I must repeat myself. The average charge upon the New York Central and Hudson River Railroad in 1866–'69, inclusive, was 1.9567 cents in gold—say 2 cents per ton per mile. From 1870–'79, inclusive, it was 1.1123 cents. The difference was only .8444, say eighty-five hundredths of a cent per ton per mile. Yet in the ten years last named this difference saved the consumers of the goods carried over this one line 121,000,000 gold dollars.

The average charge over this line has been again reduced, and was last year only seventy-eight hundredths of a cent per ton per mile.

This line performs one twenty-sixth part only of the railway service in moving merchandise of the United States. If all the other railways have reduced their rates since 1869 only one-half as much as this corporation has reduced theirs—which is far within the fact—the saving on the moving of merchandise in the year 1881, as compared to the rates prevailing from 1866 to 1869, only twelve to fifteen years since, was over $400,000,000. Let us be conservative, and call it only $300,000,000, and then we have a sum more than sufficient to pay the first cost of the 9,400 miles of new railroad which we added to our service in that year.

Eighty-five hundredths of a cent a ton a mile is equal to $8.50 per ton from Chicago to Boston, or less than a dollar on a barrel of flour carried a thousand miles; yet this little fraction, applied only in part to the total traffic of all the railroads of the United States, worked a saving of over $200,000,000 a year for ten years to 1879, inclusive; and at the yet lower rates of 1880 and 1881, as compared to 1866–'69, inclusive, this saving has been, at the very least, $300,000,000 a year, or 33⅓ per cent. of the estimated amount of our possible annual addition to our wealth or capital. It has not been added to capital, however; by far the larger part has gone to the benefit of consumers, and has been saved by them in the work of gaining their subsistence. This is the function of capital in the form of a railroad. . . .

The fortunes which the railway magnates have secured to themselves, and which they are now applying in part to an extension of the railway service by at least 10,000 miles in the year 1882, constitute but a small part of this saving; the greater part has been secured by consumers, and has to that extent reduced the cost of subsistence.

Upon this basis the computation of an actual saving to consumers of $300,000,000, as given in the body of the address, may be considered a very safe and cautious one.

In fact, the effect of the construction and extension of our railway service, and the progress made since the panic of 1873 in the reduction of its cost, almost transcends comprehension; and all computations and forecastings based upon these changes have a visionary aspect even to the most careful student. The gain in this respect more than compensates for the waste of public money and the abuses of the powers of taxation, and thus even retards the progress of economic reform by obscuring the evil effects of excessive taxation.

In this address it is therefore made apparent, on the one hand, that the average measure of comfort which each man, woman, and child can enjoy must come within the substance of what half a dollar a day will buy; while, on the other hand, this analysis of the results of science applied to the construction of railways proves that, after making due allowance for the fluctuations of the seasons and the variation of the crops, the purchasing power of each half dollar has been increased at least 5 per cent., perhaps more, since 1870. . . .

[From oral testimony before the Senate Committee on Education and Labor, Boston, 17 October 1883.]

WHAT LEGISLATION CAN, AND WHAT IT CANNOT DO

I have no special plan or patent method to submit to you for abating want or abolishing poverty by statute; nor for rendering every man, woman, and child capable of obtaining a good subsistence without working for it. None

of these benefits can you confer. You can create nothing
by statute; if you could we would all elect ourselves legislators. All that you can do by statute is to alter the
distribution of our annual product. You can take from one
and give to another, either directly or indirectly. You can
alter the legal-tender acts, or you can maintain the coinage of silver dollars worth only 83 cents. If you do maintain this base coinage you will soon make the rich richer,
but you will also make the poor so much poorer that even
in this land of rich abundance poverty will abound. It is
within the easy power of legislators, however, to make the
fortunes of the few and to mar the fortunes of many persons. You can render subsistence more difficult than it
would be if good judgment only were applied to the framing of laws. One has said that "the chief function of
modern law-makers has been to remove legal obstructions
created by the legislators of the past." A good subsistence
consists in an abundant supply of food, fuel, clothing, and
shelter. Can you increase this abundance? . . .

LABOR BECOMING MORE EFFECTIVE YEARLY

. . . in a civilized State, which has been long endowed
with common schools, in which services are exchanged, in
which justice is assured, and in which men respect each
other's rights, but leave each other free, not because it is
lawful to do so, but because the vast majority intend to
live rightly and justly and to govern themselves, an annual
product more than ample to save every man, woman, and
child within the State from want is easily assured by the
co-operation of capital and labor working freely together.
As time has passed during the last fifty years such an
ample subsistence has been and can be assured to each
and all with less hours of work and less exhaustive labor
as each year passes, if instruction and intelligence keep
pace with capital. I am inclined to think that every intelligent workingman in the State of Massachusetts has become a third more effective than he was twenty or thirty
years ago by the application of larger capital to production,
if his power be measured by the quantity as much as by

the price of the things upon which he exerts his labor or for which he can exchange his wages. . . .

EQUALITY OF SUBSISTENCE A QUESTION OF DISTRIBUTION

The whole question of substantial equality, not in property, which is secondary, but in subsistence, which is the main thing, is therefore today a question of distribution rather than of production. Now, although there may be this almost measureless quantity of the things which men need to supply their material wants each and every year, yet the poor we have always with us, and the pauper is to be found in all our cities and in many of our towns, and although we in Massachusetts have imported most of our poor, it behooves us to remove the causes of want if we can do it by legislation or otherwise.

HENRY GEORGE'S THEORY

It is alleged by Henry George that these bad conditions have arisen merely because the rich have grown richer, and that, as a necessary consequence, the poor have become poorer. I venture to deny the premises on which the allegation is made, and to pronounce this conclusion utterly false. Nay, in order to present the case with the most startling clearness, I may venture to affirm that the late Cornelius Vanderbilt was the greatest and most useful communist of his day, and I mean by that that he may be taken as the exponent of a small class of men who have achieved enormous fortunes in a single life, and yet have done more than any other men to bring an ample subsistence within the easy reach of all at a less and less cost, whether cost be measured in labor, in price, in wages, or in purchasing power of the laborer.

CAUSES OF POVERTY

If poverty has appeared to increase alongside this accumulation of wealth it has not been because of the wealth, but for want of such intelligence on the part of those who are poor as would enable them to grasp the benefits which the great masters in the application of capital to useful purposes have brought within their easy reach.

If men are poor to-day in this land it is either because they are incapable of doing the work which is waiting to be done, or are unwilling to accept the conditions of the work. There are twice as many clerks as are needed, and not half enough skilled mechanics; twice as many poor sewing women who can only sew in the poorest way, and not half enough skilled seamstresses; twice as many men trying to live by their wits, and failing in it, as there are capable of applying their heads and hands together to useful arts; twice as much capital waiting to be used as there are men capable of using it profitably to themselves and safely for those of whom they borrow it.

DOCUMENT 62

Testimony

SOURCE: Danford Knowlton, Testimony before the Senate Committee on Education and Labor, New York, 27 September 1883 (from *Report of the Committee*, Vol. II, pp. 1071–72).

Knowlton, a New York merchant, devoted most of his testimony to arguments against protective tariffs. But he prefaced his remarks with a brief statement of the doctrine of laissez-faire that probably approximates the view most widely current among run-of-the-mill businessmen.

[NEW YORK, *September 27, 1883*]
[DANFORD KNOWLTON sworn and examined.
Mr. KNOWLTON:]

WAGES BEST SETTLED BY ARRANGEMENT BETWEEN INDIVIDUAL EMPLOYERS AND EMPLOYÉS

As a general remark I would say that the reward of labor is more satisfactorily determined between the employer and the employed by mutual agreement or arrangement between them than it can, in my opinion, be effected by legislation. The laborer has, and should always maintain, the right to sell his labor to the best advantage. And the employer has, and should always maintain, his right to employ labor as he pleases, under such agreements as he is able to make with the employed. Any combination of employers to depress the price of labor or combinations of laborers to increase beyond a proper limit the reward for their labor is fraught with injury to both parties, because it violates a general law on which society is based, namely, freedom of action, whether for employer or employed. There are periods, no doubt, of great prosperity, in which the laborer may not obtain the full reward of his labor, or the amount which the product he produces would warrant. There are, on the other hand, periods of great depression, in which the wages of the laborer may exceed his fair proportion of the value of the product which he turns out. And therefore it will be seen that any attempt by legislation to fix the price of labor is absurd and impracticable. The value, for instance, of cereals may be largely enhanced by a short crop; the value again may be very much depressed by a superabundant crop, and it would be just as absurd to attempt to regulate the prices of those cereals or other products of the earth by legislation as it would be to regulate the prices of the labor which produces them. Any class of laborers in this country who find the employment of the labor in which they are engaged unremunerative are at liberty to change to any other employment, or to seek homes on our vast territory presented to them by the Government for settlement, and make themselves happy homes there, so that no great hardship can come to the laborer from any misfortune in the circumstance of the times which reduces the price of labor for the moment.

Capital, we must all admit, gives great advantages to its possessor. It is generally the result of industry and economy—it may not always be—but these advantages inhere in ownership of capital. Now, when in addition to that you add to the power of capital by legislation in the creation of monopolies you are doing a very great injury to the laborer. Legislation should neither put the capitalist in a position to grind the face of the poor or the laborers in a position to overthrow all the just rights of the employers, and to thus disturb the regular course of business.

SUPPLY AND DEMAND MUST GOVERN

In other words, supply and demand is the unavoidable and inevitable rule which must govern all things in the end. You may throw things out of joint a little for the time being by legislation or by combinations of men as against capital in trades unions, &c., but ultimately you will come back to the fact that supply and demand must govern prices of products or of labor. So that if you are overburdened with products you must expect low prices. If you have for the time too much labor the price of the labor must suffer; but in this country there need be no great suffering, from the fact that I have before stated, that there are open to all men such varieties of employment and so much virgin soil on which to raise the necessaries of life. The power of capital being doubled, and sometimes more than doubled, by legislation, produces monopolies which are becoming very odious to the people of this country. When the laborer finds that those monopolies are exercised not only by the power of capital but by the power of legislation to his injury he becomes discouraged and disgusted, and perhaps may resort to brute force to overcome his oppressors. That is one point which, in our country, should not be forgotten.

NO ANTAGONISM BETWEEN CAPITAL AND LABOR

There is no real antagonism between capital and labor rightly understood. The capital cannot build a house or a ship without a laborer. The laborer cannot build a house or a ship without capital. They are interdependent upon each other, and that interdependence is the great safety-valve of our political affairs.

THE LEGITIMATE FUNCTIONS OF GOVERNMENT

Let us inquire for a moment what are the proper functions of government, and how far, if at all, it may interfere with the natural laws governing commerce, manufactures, and agriculture. The legitimate functions of government I conceive to be to maintain domestic tranquillity, defend the people from invasion, and protect them when traveling abroad, or upon the ocean, the great highway of nations, to which may be added a few other functions of kindred nature, leaving the individual enterprise untrammeled. For that purpose we maintain an Army, Navy, and civil courts. When these general functions are exceeded the result is generally injurious to the Government. It is better always to leave individual enterprise to do most that is to be done in the country. . . .

DOCUMENT 63

Testimony

SOURCE: Jay Gould, Testimony before the Senate Committee on Education and Labor, New York, 5 September 1883 (from *Report of the Committee*, Vol. I, pp. 1084–90).

The members of the Senate Committee evidently wished to take full advantage of the opportunity to elicit Gould's opinions about a wide range of topics discussed by earlier witnesses. Because he was closely identified both with Western railroads and with the Western Union Telegraph Company, his views on land grants and monopolies were particularly significant. His answers provide an unusual insight into the off-the-cuff thinking of one of the most powerful men in the United States. His tone is bland and reassuring; he is aware of minor difficulties in the workings of a complex and rapidly expanding economic system, but refuses to recognize the existence of really serious problems or conflicts. The West offers a great field for labor, and education of the workers will resolve any difficulties not remedied by the operation of the safety valve of Western lands. Conflict between workers and employers is due to the intrusion of outside influences—presumably European radical theories or the mischief-making of parasitic labor organizers who are not themselves workers.

[NEW YORK, *September* 5, 1883]

[JAY GOULD sworn and examined.]

STRIKES, THEIR CAUSES AND RESULTS

Q. What is your observation and opinion in regard to strikes, their causes, and their results.—A. Strikes, of course, come from various causes, but they generally come from a class of dissatisfied men—the poorest part of your labor generally are at the bottom of a strike. Your best men do not care how many hours they work, or anything of that kind; they are looking to get higher up; either to own a business of their own and control it, or to get higher up in the ranks.

Q. But from the necessity of the case only a very small number can expect that.—A. Well, there are a great many who have places in view all the time. Of course there are only so many places to be filled, but there are a great many that are looking after those places. There may be only one place to be filled, but there may be five hundred nice, industrious fellows who are all working for it.

Q. That keeps them quiet?—A. Yes, sir.

Q. And may they not, for that very reason, be willing to put up with hardships and insufficient compensation for the time being?—A. They may.

Q. So the fact that these men were contented, or, at all events, were quiet, might be no reason for believing that the mass of the laborers were receiving fair pay. Now, don't you think, when you come to treat of the labor of the country in that broad way, and to consider that most of the laborers must always necessarily be in the ranks, so to speak—privates—and can never reasonably expect to become officers or to be promoted, do you not think their dissatisfaction may oftentimes be based on the fact that they do not receive compensation enough to keep them from suffering?—A. Is it not true that they get better pay here than in any other country? That is why they come here, I believe.

Q. I believe so.—A. And is it not true also that capital, if it gets better remuneration in some other country than it gets here, will go there? You cannot transfer your house, but you can transfer your money; and if labor is put up too high here, all the manufacturing will be done abroad, because the capitalists will go where they can get cheaper labor. So that when you sit down and try to get a panacea for a particular evil you run against a great many obstacles that come in the way of putting it in practice, and my observation has been that capital and labor, if let alone, generally come together and mutually regulate their relations to each other. There are some of these people who think they can regulate the whole of mankind, but they generally get wrong ideas into the minds of the public.

Q. Notwithstanding the fact that labor is better paid in this country than elsewhere, capital is also very much better paid in this country, and is likely to be so, at least for the present, and capital, like labor, is coming here from the older countries; and yet we find labor here dissatisfied to a great extent. Is not that so?—A. I think not. I think there is a far greater satisfaction here among the workingmen generally than anywhere else in the world, far greater than among the laboring classes that I have seen abroad. I only speak of what I have seen myself. I have traveled through Ireland, and the north of Ireland, you know, is a great manufacturing region. I saw the condition of labor there, and in Scotland, England, France, Germany, Holland, and Belgium, and I found everywhere among the masses a burning desire to get to America. They said, "We would get better wages there. So-and-so has written to us that we can get better wages there, and if we do not like one thing there we can turn to another. There are broad acres in the West." That is the sentiment that I found generally existing among those people.

LABOR GETS ITS FAIR SHARE

Q. Of the strikes which you have observed in this country, many, you say, have originated with dissatisfied and complaining working people; dealing with the question in the mass, as you have observed it, do you think that the working element of the country gets as much of the accumulated wealth that it and capital together produce as it ought to get?—A. Yes, sir.

Q. Labor, you think, gets its fair share?—A. Yes, sir. The returns of capital are not high; they are going lower. Manufacturers, for instance, do not expect to make the profits that they made some years ago; they expect to make a less profit, and make it up by larger sales. Now, labor gets the difference; because, after all, it is the great integral part that goes into every manufactured article. The raw material is comparatively a small element. Take iron; the mountains are full of the ore; it is labor that takes the ore out, that moves it to the furnace, that makes the pig-iron, and it is labor that converts that iron into the manufactured product; and when it is finally sold all that accumulated labor in all the different stages of production has to go in, and that plus the raw material, makes up the cost of the article. The balance, the difference between the cost and the selling price, whatever it is, is profit, and that profit does not average in this country to manufacturers as much, I think, as it does abroad. The profit here is less than elsewhere; the cost of the labor is more.

A SURPLUS OF LABOR

Q. Yet there seem to be numerous strikes in the country this present season. For some reason labor is restless, uneasy, and to some extent unemployed.—A. Well, there is a little overplus of labor. In the first place, we have been importing an enormous amount of new material in the way of immigration; all those people had to be placed. Then we were building railroads too rapidly, and now we have stopped. That leaves a surplus of labor. The manufacturers, too, have been going on and manufacturing more than the consumption of the country required, and they are reducing their production. This, with the fact that we have stopped building railroads, has left a surplus of labor here for the time being which has got to place itself.

Q. In your judgment, in what way can that labor be best placed?—A. Well, the people soon place themselves; they go to the West; they go into the Northwest and into the Southwest. Everywhere you travel you will find parties of them going and seeking homes in the new country.

Q. What opportunities are there for obtaining homes in that new country?—A. Splendid opportunities.

LAND GRANTS TO RAILROAD COMPANIES

Q. My question is designed to lead you to this matter of the land grants, the absorption of the public lands by railroad corporations and other parties, and their dealings with this land and with the laborers of the country who seek to become its possessors.—A. The giving of these land grants to railroads has not been an unmixed evil. The Government very wisely kept every alternate section, and the construction of the railroads by those parties that had the grants made the alternate sections worth more than the whole was worth before the railroads were started. Besides, the railroads have gone to work and instituted a system of settlement on those lands. They have advertised them—and the Government would never have done that. They have gone and brought emigrants from the Eastern States and from foreign countries; and they have given the purchasers of their lands credit, and in many cases, in hard times, they have even furnished them a little capital. We have done a great deal of that. Where the settlers lost their wheat, we would furnish them wheat to sow the next year, and if a settler gets one good crop it pays for his farm. So that though the Government seems to have given away enormous grants of land, yet if I as an individual had been the owner of that land, I would have been very glad to have done the same thing. . . .

Q. There has been testimony before us in regard to those lands being taken up in enormous quantities in single ownerships, sometimes several thousand acres. Do you know of such cases?—A. No, sir. It is not to the interest of railroads to sell their lands to speculators. They want to get actual settlers on them so as to get the products to carry.

Q. There has been testimony in regard to "bonanza" farms, which are carried on like large factories. What do you know or think of them?—A. I have discouraged them. I like to sell the land in small farms and have the families on them.

Q. Farms of about how many acres?—A. From 80 to

160 acres. But if they have a lot of boys growing up they will take probably double that. They want to lay a foundation so as to have land enough around them when their sons grow up and marry. . . .

A GREAT FIELD FOR LABOR IN THE WEST

Q. Is there any difficulty, either by reason of the fact that they cannot get there or that they cannot maintain themselves when they are there, in finding an outlet at the West for the laborers who are a surplus in these Eastern States?—A. No, sir; there is a great field there for that surplus labor.

Q. How can a laboring man here in New York City, with a family and nothing else but his hands and his health, get out West on a piece of land?

"BETTER A BEGGAR IN NEW YORK THAN A NABOB OUT WEST."

A. Well, he can get out easily enough if he makes up his mind to go. Most of those parties here won't go; they say they would "rather live in New York and be a beggar, than live out West and be a nabob." I have had lots of them tell me that.

Q. If a good, decent, healthy man, such a man as ought to have a chance to live somewhere, wanted to go out West to live, how could he get there?—A. He could go to the agent of any of these railroads——

Q. [Interposing.] Mind, he is a man who has no money, nothing but health and a family.—A. A man who had no money would have to do like the man who wanted to go West on the canal, before the railroads were built, and thought he might "work his passage." The canalboat man told him "all right," he would take him; so he set him to driving the horses on the tow-path. In like manner a man such as you describe going West would probably have to go afoot if he hadn't any money to pay his fare, unless he could find some man to buy his ticket.

Q. I didn't know but there might be some provision made to advance to such a man the expense of going out

there.—A. Well, that would be a fair subject for our legislators to take up and deal with.

Q. We have had a man six feet high, who has driven
a truck team, and who has more intellectual capacity than
half, or perhaps any, of the members of Congress, offering
here before this committee to agree under contract to work
diligently and faithfully for the next twenty years for anybody who would give him employment and agree to maintain himself and his family. That man said he had been
unable to get anything ahead, and could not find a chance
to work; that he was hungry, and his family were hungry,
and that he didn't know what to do; and it was represented
to us here that he was one of a large class. He said that
folks told him to go West; but such a man cannot go
West, if he tells the truth about his situation, and even if
he were to adopt the plan you suggest, his family certainly could not accompany him, driving a mule on the
canal tow-path.—A. That man, I take it, was not a telegraph operator.

Q. He was not a telegraph operator. He was not a man
that the Western Union Company is responsible for in any
way. He told us he was a truckman.—A. Well, I know
there are a great many cases of actual suffering in a
large city like this, and in all large cities. It is a very difficult thing to say exactly how you are to ameliorate everybody's condition. I have noticed, though, that generally
if men are temperate and industrious they are pretty sure
of success. In cases such as the one you describe I could
almost always go back behind the scenes and find a cause
for such a person's "misfortunes." . . .

THE FEELING BETWEEN EMPLOYERS AND EMPLOYÉS

Q. There has been testimony before us that the feeling
generally between employers and employés throughout the
country is one of hostility, especially on the part of the
employés toward those whom they designate as monopo-
lists. From your observation, what do you think is really
the feeling as a general rule between those two classes?—A.
I think that if left alone they would mutually regulate

their relations. I think there is no disagreement between the great mass of the employés and their employers. These societies that are gotten up magnify these things and create evils which do not exist—create troubles which ought not to exist.

Q. Of the men who conduct business enterprises and wield the power of capital in this country to-day, what proportion do you think are what are called "self-made men"?—A. I think they are all "self-made men"; I do not say *self*-made exactly, for the country has grown and they have grown up with it. In this country we have no system of heirlooms or of handing down estates. Every man has to stand here on his own individual merit.

Q. What is the proportion of those men who have made their own fortunes pecuniarily, such as they are?—A. I think they are nearly all of that class. I think, that according to my observation in the field that I have been in, nearly every one that occupies a prominent position has come up from the ranks, worked his own way along up.

NO DANGER OF
AN AMERICAN ARISTOCRACY OF WEALTH

Q. There is talk, too, from time to time, of the danger that our people in this country may subdivide into classes based upon pecuniary distinctions, and that we shall have an aristocracy of wealth saddled upon us like the aristocracy of rank in the old countries. What do you think of that?—A. That is not in accordance with my observation at all.

Q. But this fear is with reference to the future. Large fortunes have been accumulated in this country. Now, what do you think of the probability of their dispersion in succeeding generations under the operation of natural laws? Or are they likely to be consolidated, and are we likely in that way to have permanently wealthy families fastened upon the community?—A. They could not be perpetuated unless we had some system of legislation which would allow it. Our laws do not encourage entailed estates—do not permit them. You can only will to your

PLATES 20 THROUGH 37

PLATE 20. Anonymous, "Land, Ho!—Scene on Board an Emigrant Ship" (wood

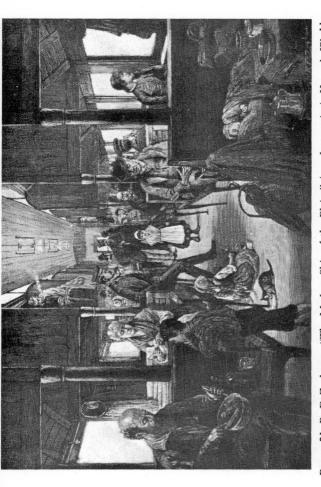

PLATE 21. R. F. Zogbaum, "The Modern Ship of the Plains" (wood engraving), *Harper's Weekly*, XXX (13 November 1886), 728.

PLATE 22. W. A. Rogers, "Immigrants Waiting to be Distributed in the Coal Regions of Pennsylvania" (pen-and-ink drawing), Harper's Weekly, XXXII (28 July 1888), 557.

PLATE 23. W. A. Rogers, "A Question of Labor" (pen-and-ink drawing), *Harper's Weekly*, XXXII (29 September 1888), 721.

PLATE 24. Graham and Durkin [first names unknown], "A Riot on Forty-Second Street, Near Broadway" (wood engraving), Harper's Weekly, XXXIII (9 February 1889), 105.

PLATE 25. Robert Koehler, "The Strike" (wood engraving from a painting), *Harper's Weekly*, XXX (1 May 1886), 280–81.

PLATE 26. C. and A. T. Sears, "The Great Strike—Scenes of Riot in Chicago. Fight between the Military and the Rioters at the Halsted Street Viaduct" (wood engraving), *Harper's Weekly*, XXI (18 August 1877), 640.

PLATE 27. Thure de Thulstrup, "The Anarchist Riot in Chicago—A Dynamite Bomb Exploding among the Police" (wood engraving from sketches and photographs furnished by H. Jeanneret), *Harper's Weekly*, XXX (15 May 1886), 312–13.

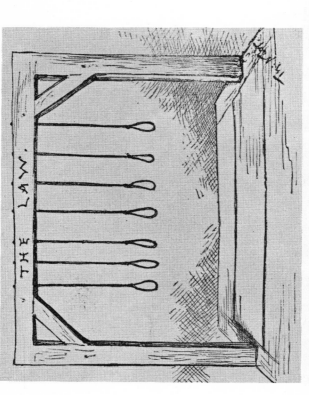

PLATE 28. Thomas Nast, "Equal to the Anarchists. They Will Have All the Rope They Want, and More Too" (pen-and-ink drawing), *Harper's Weekly*, XXX (4 September 1886), 571.

PLATE 29. Thomas Nast, "Liberty Is Not Anarchy" (pen-and-ink drawing), *Harper's Weekly*, XXX (4 September 1886), 564.

PLATE 30. Thomas Nast, "The Workingman's Mite" (wood engraving), *Harper's Weekly*, XV (20 May 1871), 468.

PLATE 31. James H. Whitehouse, "The Bryant Vase" (in silver), from an engraving in *The Masterpieces of the Centennial International Exhibition*, Vol. II, *Industrial Art*, by Walter Smith (Phila., 1878), 276.

PLATE 32. F. E. Palmer, "Across the Continent. 'Westward the Course of Empire Takes Its Way.'" (Currier & Ives lithograph, 1868, from a painting by J. M. Ives). Courtesy of the Bancroft Library, Robert B. Honeyman, Jr., Collection, University of California, Berkeley.

PLATE 33. Archibald M. Willard, "The Spirit of '76" (painting). Courtesy of the Western Reserve Historical Society, Cleveland, Ohio.

PLATE 34. John Mulvany, "Custer's Last Rally" (chromolithograph c. 1890 by D. C. Fabronius, in the library of the Kansas State Historical Society, Topeka; from a painting, 1881).

PLATE 35. John Rogers, "Weighing the Baby" (sculpture, cast plaster of Paris), March 1877. Courtesy of The New-York Historical Society, New York City.

PLATE 36. John Rogers, "Checkers up at the Farm" (sculpture, cast plaster of Paris), December 1875. Courtesy of The New-York Historical Society, New York City.

PLATE 37. Anonymous, "The Revivalists in Brooklyn—Opening Service of Messrs. Moody and Sankey in the Rink" (composite steel engraving and wood engraving?), *Harper's Weekly*, XIX (6 November 1875), 900–1.

children, or to their children at the furthest, and they generally dissipate their fortunes; so that your hired man to-day may come to be the master of your son's children. You can't tell. That process does go on all the time.

Q. The danger that might be apprehended from corporate wealth and its perpetuation, how is that affected by this fact that you now speak of, the general distribution of inherited estates?—A. The ownership is changing all the time.

WHAT A CORPORATION IS

Q. Every corporate property is owned by individuals, is it not?—A. Yes; a corporation is only another name for the means which we have discovered of allowing a poor man to invest his income in a great enterprise. In other words, instead of one man owning any of these great properties in bulk, they are divided into small shares, so that the man who has got only $200 or $500 or $5,000, or whatever it may be, can own an interest in proportion to his capital. That is what a corporation means.

Q. Then, in your opinion, the natural operation of the laws of descent as they exist in this country is to guard the community against any danger from the perpetuation of associated corporate wealth, or of great individual fortunes in the future?

OUR FUTURE MENACED NOT BY CAPITAL, BUT BY IGNORANCE

A. Yes, sir; I do not think there is any need to be afraid of capital; capital is scary. What you have got to fear is large, ignorant masses of population; I don't think the liberties of the people have anything to fear from capital. Capital is conservative and scary; but what you have to fear in a republican government like ours, where there is no military control, is large masses of uneducated, ignorant people.

Q. Do you think there is any danger to this country in that direction?—A. I think we are accumulating great masses of such people from abroad. Whether we have a system that will educate them up rapidly enough I do not know.

Q. If there was to be any legislation in any direction on this general question, don't you think that it might as well be in the direction of educating the people as in any other?

EDUCATE THE MASSES

A. I think that is what we should do—educate the masses, elevate their moral standards. I think that is the only protection we can have for a long period in the future. When the people are educated and intelligent you have nothing to fear from them.

Q. Do you think that to do that would accomplish more for labor than anything else we could do?—A. Yes, sir; because education fits a man so that if he does not like one field of labor he can go to another. Business is constantly changing, and where there is an excess of one class of labor there is very likely to be a lack of another class, and if a man is properly educated he can turn his hand to a great many different things.

LABOR UNIONS—ARE THEY GOOD OR BAD?

Q. Do you think the labor unions of the country are an injury or a benefit to the laborers and the country generally?—A. Well, I cannot say about that. I have not paid much attention to those unions. I think that anything that tends to elevate the working classes or to educate them, or that provides for those who are in want, provides a fund for the widows and orphans in any particular business, I think anything of that kind is the legitimate object of such societies. But when they get beyond that I think they get into a broad sea that they cannot control, because labor, like everything else, is regulated by the law of supply and demand. "You can lead a horse to water, but you cannot make him drink." . . .

DOCUMENT 64

(PLATE 30)

The Workingman's Mite

SOURCE: Thomas Nast, "The Workingman's Mite" (wood engraving), *Harper's Weekly*, XV (20 May 1871), 468.

In this cartoon Nast is less successful than usual in finding a way to state abstract ideas in a non-verbal medium; he has to resort to labels so extensive that they add up to a sizable discourse. But the propagandist's cunning is evident in the device of directing emotions about the sanctity of the home, the breadwinner's duty to provide for wife and babes, against trade unions. As the father drops his dues into the union box, the wife pleads with him as if he were a drunkard squandering his wages on drink. The proposed alternative of the savings bank was a special project of conservative spokesmen like Edward A. Atkinson. The charge that labor unions subject workers to the tyranny of union officials and drain away in dues a part of the weekly paycheck that should go into support of the laborer's family is advanced by Dexter A. Hawkins in Document 60.

DOCUMENT 65

Seed That Bears Fruit

SOURCE: Thomas Nast, " 'Seed That Bears Fruit.' Capital the Result of Labor and Labor the Result of Capital" (wood engraving), *Harper's Weekly*, XXII (18 May 1878), 385.

This cartoon exhibits Nast's remarkable power to state abstract ideas in visual terms. It is true that he has to rely on a subtitle setting forth one of the platitudes of prevalent economic theory. (Henry Ward Beecher, for example, remarked in a sermon, "Now Capitalism is nothing more nor less than condensed labor.")* And Nast's phrasing ("Capital the result of labor and labor the result of capital") involves a sophistical pun on "result." But the feat of clothing this syllogism in agrarian garb is truly inventive. The capitalist stands in the foreground in the costume of a farmer and performs the mythically sanctified act of sowing seed by hand. Transactions in Wall Street (for capital is equated with credit) are invested with favorable emotions associated with agriculture from an antiquity stretching far back of mechanization: the horse-drawn plow in the background was one of the most reassuringly archaic symbols available to the later nineteenth century.

* *New York Times*, 30 July 1877, p. 8, col. 1.

Thomas Nast, " 'Seed That Bears Fruit.' Capital the Result of Labor, and Labor the Result of Capital" (wood engraving), *Harper's Weekly*, XXII (18 May 1878), 385.

PART VIII

The Arts in Popular Culture

A. IDEALITY, REVERENCE, AND THE MAN OF LETTERS

Serious literature was in a state of confusion during the post-Civil War decades. Toward the middle of the century New England had developed a clearly defined role for the Man of Letters—a partly secularized version of the role formerly assigned to the Puritan clergyman. Writers as diverse as Emerson, Hawthorne, Lowell, and Longfellow passed from the inner conflicts and radicalisms of their youth to the secure status of lawgivers, custodians of ideal values for the region and for the nation at large wherever the moral authority of New England was acknowledged. But the shock of the war and of economic expansion weakened the claim of New England to cultural dominance and undermined the relatively stable social system within which the conception of the Man of Letters had meaning. Writers of the generation that came of age during and after the war, the generation of William Dean Howells, were grievously handicapped by uncertainty about their relation to their society. Because they could not be sure what audience they were addressing, they had little sense of direction. The local-color movement of the 1870s and 1880s explored new subject matter but achieved little real innovation because it could not escape from conventional notions of ethics and methods of characterization. Howells' campaign to define "realism" as a literary mode, which he carried on through the pages of the *Atlantic Monthly* and other periodicals from the later 1860s onward, was essentially an effort to define a new role for the American writer. Howells, however, was hampered by divided loyalties. His Emersonian belief in the moral order of the universe was not ultimately congruous with the doctrine of objectivity in literature. Realism could not be fully tested as a fictional technique until a generation of writers appeared who were indifferent or hostile to the tradition of Emerson—men like Stephen Crane and Harold Frederic and, somewhat later, Theodore Dreiser.

Producers of popular literature were undisturbed by such difficulties. They simply exploited the archaic conventions of "sensation" fiction to provide a staple commodity for a constantly widening market. The problem of production was solved; the focus in the 1870s and 1880s was on distribution, and the dominant figures were those marketing experts, the editors of mass-circulation periodicals.

DOCUMENT 66

(PLATE 31)

The Bryant Vase

SOURCE: James H. Whitehouse, "The Bryant Vase" (in silver), from an engraving in *The Masterpieces of the Centennial International Exhibition*, Vol. II, *Industrial Art*, by Walter Smith (Philadelphia, 1878), p. 276.

The best commentary on this emblematic representation of the traditional role of the Man of Letters is the explanatory note by the designer of the vase, James H. Whitehouse, "chief artist of Messrs. Tiffany & Co., of New York." The allegorical mode in which the vase is conceived, the presuppositions about the poet's relation to Nature, and the assumption that his career is harmoniously related to the mainstream of American history are equally anachronistic and equally ironic in the context of post-Civil War industrialism. The vase, wrote Whitehouse,

> is intended to symbolize Mr. Bryant's life and character through the medium of a classic form, covered with ornamentation drawn from nature, and suggested by his works. As in Mr. Bryant's career there has been nothing inharmonious, all the details of this design are made subordinate to the simple classic outline which is preserved unbroken. The heavier lines of the fretwork are derived from the apple-branch, which suggests that while Mr. Bryant's writings are beautiful, they also bear a moral: as the apple-tree blooms with a beautiful flower in the spring, and in the autumn bears fruit. Poetry is symbolized by the eglantine, and immortality by the amaranth, which is said never to lose its fragrance, and these are blended with the lines formed of the apple-branch.

The primrose, for early youth, and ivy for age, form a border directly above the handles. Encircling the neck at the narrowest part, the immortal line, "Truth crushed to earth shall rise again," is rendered verbatim, the beginning and end being separated by a representation of the fringed gentian, which Mr. Bryant remembers in one of his poems as always pointing to heaven. Eras in the poet's life are illustrated by a series of bas-reliefs. In the first, as a child, looking up with veneration at a bust of Homer, to which his father points as a model. The second shows him in the woods, reclining in a meditative attitude under the trees. Between the first and second of these medallion pictures is a portrait of the poet, laurel-crowned. Above this, the lyre for Mr. Bryant's verse; and beneath, the most primitive printing-press, for his connection for over half a century with the "New York Evening Post." In a smaller medallion is the waterfowl, used by Mr. Bryant as an emblem of faith, and introduced for that reason as the key-note of his writings. The ornament around the lower part of the vase is of the Indian corn, with a single band of cotton-leaves, and at the foot is the water-lily, emblematic of eloquence, for Mr. Bryant's oratory. The handles are in harmony with the general outline, but subordinate to it, and as humor is a subordinate element in Mr. Bryant's writings, it is suggested here by the American bob-o'link for the humorous poem of "Robert of Lincoln." The two great American staples are introduced to complete the ornamentation of the handles—the stalk, leaf and grain of the Indian corn on the inside, and the bud, flower and ripened boll of the cotton on the outside. On the base which supports the vase is the lyre for verse, which with the broken shackles point to Mr. Bryant's services in the cause of Emancipation.

The designer has introduced symbols from nature, as the fittest means of illustrating the life of an author whose writings teem with symbols drawn from the same source, and has intended to bring unity out of elaborate detail.*

* *The Masterpieces of the Centennial International Exhibition*, Vol. II, *Industrial Art*, by Walter Smith, pp. 275–77.

DOCUMENT 67

Memorable Ghosts

SOURCE: Rebecca Harding Davis, ["Memorable Ghosts"], from *Bits of Gossip* (Westminster [London], 1904), pp. 32–47.

Looking back after more than forty years upon her pilgrimage from what she calls "the backwoods" of West Virginia to Boston and Concord in 1862, Mrs. Davis speaks with an ironic detachment about her youthful awe in the presence of the New England Men of Letters. The contrast between what she felt as an aspiring writer in the 1860s and her later conclusion that these men stood outside the real world, unable to "see it as it was," represents accurately a major transition during the post-Civil War period. Her emphasis on the remoteness of the New England writers from "humanity" is an indirect way of calling attention to the irrelevance of the pre-Civil War literary creed to post-Civil War society. Her use of the phrase "commonplace world" is a shorthand statement of Howells' contention that the doctrine of ideality was outmoded, and that literature should concern itself with everyday reality. Particularly interesting is Mrs. Davis's insistence on the contrast between the exalted view of the war expounded by Bronson Alcott and the "filthy spewings" that she had seen at firsthand near the battlefront. Her generation of writers had attempted to substitute the "back-bone of fact" for ideality as the substance of literature.

I wish I could summon these memorable ghosts before you as I saw them then and afterward. To the eyes of an observer, belonging to the commonplace world, they did not appear precisely as they do in the portraits drawn of

them for posterity by their companions, the other Areopa-
gites, who walked and talked with them apart—always
apart from humanity.

That was the first peculiarity which struck an outsider
in Emerson, Hawthorne, and the other members of the
"Atlantic" coterie; that while they thought they were guiding the real world, they stood quite outside of it, and
never would see it as it was.

For instance, during the Civil War, they had much to
say of it, and all used the same strained high note of
exaltation. It was to them "only the shining track," as
Lowell calls it, where

> . . . "heroes mustered in a gleaming row,
> Beautiful evermore, and with the rays
> Of morn on their white shields of expectation."

These heroes were their bravest and their best, gone to
die for the slave or for their country. They were "the army"
to them.

I remember listening during one long summer morning
to Louisa Alcott's father as he chanted pæans to the war,
the "armed angel which was wakening the nation to a
lofty life unknown before."

We were in the little parlor of the Wayside, Mr. Hawthorne's house in Concord. Mr. Alcott stood in front of
the fireplace, his long gray hair streaming over his collar,
his pale eyes turning quickly from one listener to another
to hold them quiet, his hands waving to keep time with
the orotund sentences which had a stale, familiar ring as
if often repeated before. Mr. Emerson stood listening, his
head sunk on his breast, with profound submissive attention, but Hawthorne sat astride of a chair, his arms folded
on the back, his chin dropped on them, and his laughing,
sagacious eyes watching us, full of mockery.

I had just come up from the border where I had seen
the actual war; the filthy spewings of it; the political job-
bery in Union and Confederate camps; the malignant
personal hatreds wearing patriotic masks, and glutted by
burning homes and outraged women; the chances in it,

well improved on both sides, for brutish men to grow more brutish, and for honorable gentlemen to degenerate into thieves and sots. War may be an armed angel with a mission, but she has the personal habits of the slums. This would-be seer who was talking of it, and the real seer who listened, knew no more of war as it was, than I had done in my cherry-tree when I dreamed of bannered legions of crusaders debouching in the misty fields.

Mr. Hawthorne at last gathered himself up lazily to his feet, and said quietly: "We cannot see that thing at so long a range. Let us go to dinner," and Mr. Alcott suddenly checked the droning flow of his prophecy and quickly led the way to the dining-room.

Early that morning when his lank, gray figure had first appeared at the gate, Mr. Hawthorne said: "Here comes the Sage of Concord. He is anxious to know what kind of human beings come up from the back hills in Virginia. Now I will tell you," his eyes gleaming with fun, "what he will talk to you about. Pears. Yes. You may begin at Plato or the day's news, and he will come around to pears. He is now convinced that a vegetable diet affects both the body and soul, and that pears exercise a more direct and ennobling influence on us than any other vegetable or fruit. Wait. You'll hear presently."

When we went in to dinner, therefore, I was surprised to see the sage eat heartily of the fine sirloin of beef set before us. But with the dessert he began to advocate a vegetable diet and at last announced the spiritual influence of pears, to the great delight of his host, who laughed like a boy and was humored like one by the gentle old man.

Whether Alcott, Emerson, and their disciples discussed pears or the war, their views gave you the same sense of unreality, of having been taken, as Hawthorne said, at too long a range. You heard much sound philosophy and many sublime guesses at the eternal verities; in fact, never were the eternal verities so dissected and pawed over and turned inside out as they were about that time, in Boston, by Margaret Fuller and her successors. But the discussion

left you with a vague, uneasy sense that something was
lacking, some back-bone of fact. Their theories were like
beautiful bubbles blown from a child's pipe, floating
overhead, with queer reflections on them of sky and earth
and human beings, all in a glow of fairy color and all a
little distorted.

Mr. Alcott once showed me an arbor which he had built
with great pains and skill for Mr. Emerson to "do his
thinking in." It was made of unbarked saplings and
boughs, a tiny round temple, two storied, with chambers
in which were seats, a desk, etc., all very artistic and complete, except that he had forgotten to make any door.
You could look at it and admire it, but nobody could go
in or use it. It seemed to me a fitting symbol for this
guild of prophets and their scheme of life. . . .

I went to Concord, a young woman from the backwoods, firm in the belief that Emerson was the first of
living men. He was the modern Moses who had talked
with God apart and could interpret Him to us.

When I heard him coming into the parlor at the Wayside my body literally grew stiff and my tongue dry with
awe. And in ten minutes I was telling him all that I had
seen of the war, the words tumbling over each other, so
convinced was I of his eagerness to hear. He was eager. If
Edison had been there he would have been just as eager
to wrench out of him the secret of electricity, or if it had
been a freed slave he would have compelled him to show
the scars on his back and lay bare his rejoicing, ignorant,
half-animal soul, and an hour later he would have forgotten that Edison or the negro or I were in the world—having
taken from each what he wanted.

Naturally Mr. Emerson valued the abnormal freaks
among human souls most highly, just as the unclassable
word and the mongrel beetle are dearest to the grammar-
ian or the naturalist. The only man to whose authority he
bowed was Alcott, the vague, would-be prophet, whose
ravings he did not pretend to fathom. He apparently
shared in the popular belief that eccentricity was a sign
of genius. . . . His interest in his Ego was so dominant

that it probably never occurred to him to ask what others thought of him. He took from each man his drop of stored honey, and after that the man counted for no more to him than any other robbed bee. I do not think that even the worship which his disciples gave him interested him enough to either amuse or annoy him.

It was worship. No such homage has ever been paid to any American. His teaching influenced at once the trend of thought here and in England; the strongest men then living became promptly his disciples or his active antagonists.

But outside of this central circle of scholars and original thinkers, there were vast outlying provinces of intelligence where he reigned absolutely as does the unseen Grand Llama over his adoring votaries. New England then swarmed with weak-brained, imitative folk who had studied books with more or less zeal, and who knew nothing of actual life. They were suffering under the curse of an education which they could not use; they were the lean, underfed men and women of villages and farms, who were trained enough to be lawyers and teachers in their communities, but who actually were cobblers, mill-hands, or tailoresses. They had revolted from Puritanism, not to enter any other live church, but to fall into a dull disgust, a nausea with all religion. To them came this new prophet with his discovery of the God within themselves. They hailed it with acclamation. The new dialect of the Transcendentalist was easily learned. They talked it as correctly as the Chinaman does his pigeon English. Up to the old gray house among the pines in Concord they went —hordes of wild-eyed Harvard undergraduates and lean, underpaid working-women, each with a disease of soul to be cured by the new Healer.

It is quite impossible to give to the present generation an idea of the devout faith of these people. Keen-witted and scholarly as some of them were, it was as absolute as that of the poor Irishman tramping over the bogs in Munster to cure his ailments by a drink of the water of a holy well.

Outside of these circles of disciples there was then

throughout the country a certain vague pride in Emerson
as an American prophet. We were in the first flush of our
triumph in the beginnings of a national literature. We
talked much of it. Irving, Prescott, and Longfellow had
been English, we said, but these new men—Holmes and
Lowell and Hawthorne—were our own, the indigenous
growth of the soil. In the West and South there was no
definite idea as to what truth this Concord man had
brought into the world. But in any case it was American
truth and not English. Emerson's popularity, therefore,
outside of New England was wide, but vague and imper-
sonal. . . .

DOCUMENT 68

Speech at the Whittier Birthday Dinner

SOURCE: Samuel L. Clemens (Mark Twain), ["Speech at the Whittier Birthday Dinner"] (1877), *Harvard Library Bulletin,* IX (Spring 1955), 177–80.

"The 'Atlantic' coterie," as Mrs. Rebecca Harding Davis called it—Emerson, Longfellow, Whittier, Holmes, Lowell—comprised the most eminent among the men of letters who had survived from the Golden Day before the Civil War. When Henry O. Houghton, publisher of the *Atlantic Monthly,* gave a dinner in December 1877 to celebrate the seventieth birthday of Whittier, the occasion inevitably took on an air of ceremony and even of ritual.* But times were changing. The editorial chair of the magazine had been occupied since 1871 by a young writer from the West named William Dean Howells, whose sincere veneration for the New England great had not prevented him from opening the pages of the *Atlantic* to such representatives of the new era in literature as Bret Harte and Mark Twain. In order to provide a lighter touch in a program that could hardly fail to verge on the lugubrious, Howells had invited Mark Twain to make a short speech. The reader should keep in mind the context of the skit which the humorist prepared for this challenging occasion. The first speaker on the program had been Emerson, still greatly venerated in spite of a failing memory that had all but isolated him from his surroundings. Emerson had recited, "with much feeling," Whittier's "Ichabod," a poem written almost thirty

* This account of the dinner is based on Henry N. Smith, "That Hideous Mistake of Poor Clemens's," *Harvard Library Bulletin,* IX (Spring 1955), 145–80.

years before in the white heat of moral outrage over
Daniel Webster's vote for the Fugitive Slave Act. Among
many congratulatory letters read to the company was
one from Josiah G. Holland, editor of *Scribner's
Monthly*, asking the following question: "I wonder if
these old poets of ours—Mr. Dana, Mr. Bryant, Mr.
Emerson, Mr. Longfellow and Mr. Whittier—appreciate
the benefit they confer upon their fellow-citizens by
simply consenting to live among them as old men? Do
they know how they help to save the American nation
from the total wreck and destruction of the sentiment
of reverence?" In reporting the dinner, *Harper's Weekly*
quoted Holland's letter with approval—and, incidentally, made no reference to Mark Twain's part in the
program.

On the surface Mark Twain's speech is perfectly
proper: he characterizes Emerson, Holmes, and Longfellow as "the gracious singers to whom we & the world
pay loving reverence & homage." The guests at the
dinner took his little burlesque in good part. But when
it was reported in the press, many newspapers outside
Boston, particularly in the Middle West, were outraged by what they took to be an act of aggression
against the almost sacerdotal cult of the man of letters.
The twentieth-century reader wonders whether Mark
Twain had not touched a sensitive nerve in suggesting
that the venerable literary giants of New England were,
as he subtly and perhaps unwittingly implies, imposters.

Mr. Chairman—This is an occasion peculiarly meet for
the digging up of pleasant reminiscences concerning literary folk; therefore I will drop lightly into history myself.
Standing here on the shore of the Atlantic & contemplating
certain of its biggest literary billows, I am reminded of
a thing which happened to me fifteen years ago, when
I had just succeeded in stirring up a little Nevadian literary ocean-puddle myself, whose spume-flakes were beginning to blow thinly California-wards. I started on an
inspection-tramp through the Southern mines of California. I was callow & conceited, & I resolved to try the virtue

of my nom de plume. I very soon had an opportunity. I knocked at a miner's lonely log cabin in the foot-hills of the Sierras just at nightfall. It was snowing at the time. A jaded, melancholy man of fifty, barefooted, opened to me. When he heard my nom de plume, he looked more dejected than before. He let me in—pretty reluctantly, I thought—& after the customary bacon & beans, black coffee & a hot whisky, I took a pipe. This sorrowful man had not said three words up to this time. Now he spoke up & said in the voice of one who is secretly suffering, "You're the fourth—I'm a-going to move." "The fourth what?" said I. "The fourth littery man that's been here in twenty-four hours—I'm a-going to move." "You don't tell me!" said I; "Who were the others?" "Mr. Longfellow, Mr. Emerson, & Mr. Oliver Wendell Holmes—dad fetch the lot!"

THE MINER'S STORY

You can easily believe I was interested.—I supplicated —three hot whiskies did the rest—& finally the melancholy miner began. Said he—

They came here just at dark yesterday evening, & I let them in, of course. Said they were going to Yo Semite. They were a rough lot—but that's nothing—everybody looks rough that travels afoot. Mr. Emerson was a seedy little bit of a chap—red headed. Mr. Holmes was as fat as a balloon—he weighed as much as three hundred, & had double chins all the way down to his stomach. Mr. Longfellow was built like a prize fighter. His head was cropped & bristly—like as if he had a wig made of hair-brushes. His nose lay straight down his face, like a finger, with the end-joint tilted up. They had been drinking—I could see that. And what queer talk they used! Mr. Holmes inspected this cabin, then he took me by the button-hole, & says he—

"Through the deep caves of thought
I hear a voice that sings:
Build thee more stately mansions,
O my Soul!"

Says I, "I can't afford it, Mr. Holmes, & moreover I don't want to." Blamed if I liked it pretty well, either, coming from a stranger, that way! However, I started to get out my bacon & beans, when Mr. Emerson came & looked on a while, & then *he* takes me aside by the button-hole & says—

> "Give me agates for my meat;
> Give me cantharids to eat;
> From air & ocean bring me foods,
> From all zones & altitudes."

Says I, "Mr. Emerson, if you'll excuse me, this ain't no hotel." You see it sort of riled me—I warn't used to the ways of littery swells. But I went on a-sweating over my work, & next comes Mr. Longfellow & button-holes me, & interrupts me. Says he—

> "Honor be to Mudjekeewis!
> You shall hear how Pau-Puk-Kee-wis—"

But I broke in, & says I, "Begging your pardon, Mr. Longfellow, if you'll be so kind as to hold your yawp for about five minutes, & let me get this grub ready, you'll do me proud." Well, sir, after they'd filled up, I set out the jug. Mr. Holmes looks at it, & then he fires up all of a sudden & yells—

> "Flash out a stream of blood-red wine!—
> For I would drink to other days."

By George, I was getting kind of worked up. I don't deny it, I was getting kind of worked up. I turns to Mr. Holmes, & says I, "Looky-here, my fat friend, I'm a-running this shanty, & if the court knows herself, you'll take whisky-straight or you'll go dry!" Them's the very words I said to him. Now I didn't want to sass such famous littery people, but you see they kind of forced me. There ain't nothing onreasonable 'bout me; I don't mind a passel of guests a-tread'n on my tail three or four times, but when it comes to *standing* on it, it's different. & if the court knows herself, you'll take whisky-straight or you'll go dry!" Well, between drinks they'd swell around the cabin & strike attitudes & spout. Says Mr. Longfellow—

"This is the forest primeval."

Says Mr. Emerson—

"Here once the embattled farmers stood,
And fired the shot heard round the world."

Says I, "O, blackguard the premises as much as you want to—it don't cost you a cent." Well, they went on drinking, & pretty soon they got out a greasy old deck & went to playing cut-throat euchre at ten cents a corner—on trust. I begun to notice some pretty suspicious things. Mr. Emerson dealt, looked at his hand, shook his head, says—

"I am the doubter & the doubt—"

—& calmly bunched the hands & went to shuffling for a new lay-out. Says he—

"They reckon ill who leave me out;
They know not well the subtle ways
I keep.   I pass, & deal *again!*"

Hang'd if he didn't go ahead & do it, too! O, he was a cool one! Well, in about a minute, things were running pretty tight, but all of a sudden I see by Mr. Emerson's eye that he judged he had 'em. He had already corralled two tricks, & each of the others one. So now he kinds of lifts a little, in his chair, & says—

"I tire of globes & aces!—
Too long the game is played!"

—and down he fetches a right bower. Mr. Longfellow smiles as sweet as pie, & says—:

"Thanks, thanks to thee, my worthy friend,
For the lesson thou hast taught!"

—and dog my cats if he didn't down with *another* right

bower! Well, sir, up jumps Holmes, a-war-whooping, as usual, & says—

> "God help them if the tempest swings
> The pine against the palm!"

—and I wish I may go to grass if he didn't swoop down with *another* right bower! Emerson claps his hand on his bowie, Longfellow claps his on his revolver, & I went under a bunk. There was going to be trouble; but that monstrous Holmes rose up, wobbling his double chins, & says he, "Order, gentlemen; the first man that draws, I'll lay down on him & smother him!" All quiet on the Potomac, you bet you! They were pretty how-come-you-so, now, & they begun to blow. Emerson says, "The bulliest thing I ever wrote, was Barbara Frietchie." Says Longfellow, "It don't begin with my Biglow Papers." Says Holmes, "My Thanatopsis lays over 'em both." They mighty near ended in a fight. Then they wished they had some more company—& Mr. Emerson pointed at me & says—

> "Is yonder squalid peasant all
> That this proud nursery could breed?"

He was a-whetting his bowie on his boot—so I let it pass. Well, sir, next they took it into their heads that they would like some music; so they made me stand up & sing "When Johnny Comes Marching Home" till I dropped—at thirteen minutes past four this morning. That's what I've been through, my friend. When I woke at seven, they were leaving, thank goodness, & Mr. Longfellow had my only boots on, & his own under his arm. Says I, "Hold on, there, Evangeline, what you going to do with *them*?"—He says: "Going to make tracks with 'em; because—

> 'Lives of great men all remind us
> We can make our lives sublime;
> And departing, leave behind us
> Footprints on the sands of Time.' " . . .

As I said, Mr. Twain, you are the fourth in twenty-four

hours—and I'm going to move; I ain't suited to a littery atmosphere.

I said to the miner, "Why my dear sir, *these* were not the gracious singers to whom we & the world pay loving reverence & homage: these were impostors." The miner investigated me with a calm eye for a while, then said he, "Ah—impostors, were they? are *you?*" I did—not pursue the subject; and since then I haven't traveled on my nom de plume enough to hurt. Such is the reminiscence I was moved to contribute, Mr. Chairman. In my enthusiasm I may have exaggerated the details a little, but you will easily forgive me that fault since I believe it is the first time I have ever deflected from perpendicular fact on an occasion like this.

DOCUMENT 69

Mark Twain's Mistake at the Whittier Dinner

SOURCE: Anonymous, "Mark Twain's Mistake at the Whittier Dinner," Springfield (Mass.) *Republican*, 27 December 1877, p. 8.

For reasons not entirely clear, although bad feeling between Mark Twain and Samuel Bowles, editor of the Springfield *Republican*, may have been involved, that paper was particularly rancorous in its criticism of the Whittier Dinner speech. This unsigned letter to the editor of the *Republican*, published ten days after the banquet, is valuable for its capsule summary of the cult of ideality which was central to the Genteel Tradition.

To the Editor of The Republican:—

No one caring in the least for the "fitness of things" can read without a sense of pain the words of "Mark Twain" at the late Atlantic-Whittier dinner. Imagine the scene, the really brilliant company, bright in the best sense of that suggestive word—"shedding much light, opposed to dark," as Webster has it—gathered to celebrate with sober joy and good cheer the 70th anniversary of a man of the most singular delicacy and refinement, combined with a strength, simplicity and sturdiness not always found with so much gentleness! Fit combination of events, the celebration of the progress of a life, which has had for its object the making of to-morrow better than today; and the speeding of an enterprise, which having passed its teens, looks forward to an earnest, ever broadening life. Gathered about the charming board with the gentle poet and the friend whose skill and enterprise enable them to sing to the whole round world, we see him who thinks that "life is not an empty dream," but that it holds high and holy, bright and gladsome things, of which he who has clean hands and a pure heart may taste. Beside him sits the philosopher who has dug deep and brought to light much that makes us think and hope, even if the mines *have* encroached on what are sometimes considered pre-empted claims. Then, also, if wit and fun were wanted, and keen thrusts at sham and pretense, accompanied with a sincere reverence for the beautiful and true, he who sits at the left is able and willing, and there are two others, who, were quiet, delicately delicious humor cared for, could bring it forth. Into this China shop bursts a wild Californian bull. True gentlemen bear insult in silence, and let such things dash on to their own destruction. But there is food for reflection in the incident. The songs, the literature, the wit and humor of a land tell tales, and when a bright, clever man, who does possess genuine humor, and has really discovered a new and curious vein, instead of fitting it to something that will amuse and relax the mind, without polluting it, finds his greatest glory in embellishing with his gift the low, poor, weak parts of our nature, and dressing in the garb of bar-room habitues the men who stand at the other end of life,—is it not well to inquire whether the popularity of this man ought not to have already reached a climax? Literary men in America, where so much is tolerated, ought to aim higher than the gutter, no matter what they have of talent, or even genius. American social life, upon which, by God's aid, must be built the mighty fabric of the future state, is in the formative period, and, jealous as we might have been of our political honor, a thousand times more jealous must we be of that most precious possession—reverence for that which is truly high. According to England's laureate, the good things of time are ours:—

> "To shape and use; arise and fly
>   The reeling Faun, the sensual feast!
>   Move upward, working out the beast,
> And let the ape and tiger die!"

Springfield, December 19, 1877.

DOCUMENT 70

Letter to Andrew Lang

SOURCE: Samuel L. Clemens (Mark Twain), ["Letter to Andrew Lang"], [Hartford, 1889], in *Mark Twain's Letters*, ed. Albert B. Paine, 2 vols. (paged continuously) (New York, 1917), pp. 525–28.

This letter, of which the first page has been lost, is the nearest Mark Twain ever came to an apologia for his career, and as such should be considered together with the technical precepts set forth in "How to Tell a Story" (Document 73). The immediate occasion of the letter to Lang was harsh treatment of *A Connecticut Yankee* in the English press, but Mark Twain was also aiming at a target that could not be acknowledged explicitly; to wit, Matthew Arnold. His resentment against Arnold had been mounting since the Englishman's lecture tour in the United States in 1883–84 and had reached a peak with the publication of Arnold's "Civilisation in the United States" in the *Nineteenth Century* for April 1888, which emphasized the lack of "distinction" in American civilization and cited as evidence the general vulgarity of the newspapers and the "addiction to 'the funny man,' who is a national misfortune there." Mark Twain was doubtless influenced also by the general wave of Anglophobia in this country in the 1880s. But while he was in the process of gathering materials in his notebooks for a vitriolic counterattack, Arnold died, and the project had to be abandoned.

Mark Twain's political emotions, together with his habitually exaggerated reaction to criticism of his work, impelled him on this occasion toward a much more emphatic and uncritical identification with popular culture than he normally felt. Within a few years he would veer in the opposite direction toward a condemnation of

American attitudes in *The American Claimant* (1892). Nevertheless, the inventory of what constitutes popular culture contained in the letter is unusually interesting. It will be observed that the literary items are Kipling, James Whitcomb Riley, and "the little everybody's poet" —perhaps Will Carleton, the prolific dialect rhymster whose effusions were featured during the 1880s in *Harper's Weekly* and other widely circulated magazines. Music is represented by the hurdy-gurdy, the melodeon, and the village singing society; graphic art by chromolithographs—which Hank Morgan had pointedly preferred to medieval tapestries in *A Connecticut Yankee;* and sculpture by "the plaster cast," evidently a reference to the John Rogers statuary groups that were being sold in great numbers (see Documents 79 and 80). A tantalizing vista is opened up by the inclusion of the Salvation Army in the list, but Mark Twain does not develop this suggestion of brow levels in religion.

Since Mark Twain was himself a writer of humor and of fiction and a star of the lecture platform, his failure to mention either the humorists (who were immensely popular in the newspapers and on the lecture circuit) or the voluminous output of "sensation fiction" in the 1870s and 1880s is surprising and significant. If he had listed humor as one of the components of popular culture he would have had to define his own relation to this culture more precisely; his failure to do so suggests that he is indeed engaging in polemics rather than setting forth a carefully considered analysis of his role as an artist. On the other hand, his many burlesques of sensation fiction (such as the account of the "fearful and wonderful novel" in *Roughing It*) had made clear his amused scorn of the genre, and he would have weakened his case for popular culture if he had acknowledged the dominant position of this kind of fiction among the commercialized popular arts.

[First page missing.]

They vote but do not print. The head tells you pretty promptly whether the food is satisfactory or not; and everybody hears, and thinks the whole man has spoken. It is a delusion. Only his taste and his smell have been heard from —important, both, in a way, but these do not build up the man, and preserve his life and fortify it.

The little child is permitted to label its drawings "This is a cow—this is a horse," and so on. This protects the child. It saves it from the sorrow and wrong of hearing its cows and its horses criticized as kangaroos and work-benches. A man who is white-washing a fence is doing a useful thing, so also is the man who is adorning a rich man's house with costly frescoes; and all of us are sane enough to judge these performances by standards proper to each. Now, then, to be fair, an author ought to be allowed to put upon his book an explanatory line: "This is written for the Head;" "This is written for the Belly and the Members." And the critic ought to hold himself in honor bound to put away from him his ancient habit of judging all books by one standard, and thenceforth follow a fairer course.

The critic assumes, every time, that if a book doesn't meet the cultivated-class standard, it isn't valuable. Let us apply his law all around: for if it is sound in the case of novels, narratives, pictures, and such things, it is certainly sound and applicable to all the steps which lead up to culture and make culture possible. It condemns the spelling book, for a spelling book is of no use to a person of culture; it condemns all school books and all schools which lie between the child's primer and Greek, and between the infant school and the university; it condemns all the rounds of art which lie between the cheap terra cotta groups and the Venus de Medici, and between the chromo and the Transfiguration; it requires Whitcomb Riley to sing no more till he can sing like Shakespeare, and it forbids all amateur music and will grant its sanction to nothing below the "classic."

Is this an extravagant statement? No, it is a mere statement of fact. It is the fact itself that is extravagant and grotesque. And what is the result? This—and it is sufficiently curious: the critic has actually imposed upon the world the superstition that a painting by Raphael is more valuable to the civilizations of the earth than is a chromo; and the august opera than the hurdy-gurdy and the villagers' singing society; and Homer than the little everybody's-poet whose rhymes are in all mouths to-day and will be in nobody's mouth next generation; and the Latin classics than Kipling's far-reaching bugle-note; and Jonathan Edwards than the Salvation Army; and the Venus de Medici than the plaster-cast peddler; the superstition, in a word, that the vast and awful comet that trails its cold lustre through the remote abysses of space once a century and interests and instructs a cultivated handful of astronomers is worth more to the world than the sun which warms and cheers all the nations every day and makes the crops to grow.

If a critic should start a religion it would not have any object but to convert angels: and they wouldn't need it. The thin top crust of humanity—the cultivated—are worth pacifying, worth pleasing, worth coddling, worth nourishing and preserving with dainties and delicacies, it is true; but to be caterer to that little faction is no very dignified or valuable occupation, it seems to me; it is merely feeding the over-fed, and there must be small satisfaction in that. It is not that little minority who are already saved that are best worth trying to uplift, I should think, but the mighty mass of the uncultivated who are underneath. That mass will never see the Old Masters—that sight is for the few; but the chromo maker can lift them all one step upward toward appreciation of art; they cannot have the opera, but the hurdy-gurdy and the singing class lift them a little way toward that far light; they will never know Homer, but the passing rhymester of their day leaves them higher than he found them; they may never even hear of the Latin classics, but they will strike step with Kipling's drum-beat, and they will march; for all Jonathan Edwards's help they would die in their slums, but the Salvation Army will beguile some of them up to pure air and a cleaner life; they know no sculpture, the Venus is not even a name to them, but they are a grade higher in the scale of civilization by the ministrations of the plaster-cast than they were before it took its place upon their mantel and made it beautiful to their unexacting eyes.

Indeed I have been misjudged, from the very first. I have never tried in even one single instance, to help cultivate the cultivated classes. I was not equipped for it, either by native gifts or training. And I never had any ambition in that direction, but always hunted for bigger game—the masses. I have seldom deliberately tried to instruct them, but have done my best to entertain them. To simply amuse them would have satisfied my dearest ambition at any time; for they could get instruction elsewhere, and I had two chances to help to the teacher's one: for amusement is a good preparation for study and a good healer of fatigue after it. My audience is dumb, it has no voice in print, and so I cannot know whether I have won its approbation or only got its censure.

Yes, you see, I have always catered for the Belly and the Members, but have been served like the others—criticized from the culture-standard—to my sorrow and pain; because, honestly, I never cared what became of the cultured classes; they could go to the theatre and the opera, they had no use for me and the melodeon.

And now at last I arrive at my object and tender my petition, making supplication to this effect: that the critics adopt a rule recognizing the Belly and the Members, and formulate a standard whereby work done for them shall be judged. Help me, Mr. Lang; no voice can reach further than yours in a case of this kind, or carry greater weight of authority.

B. STORY-PAPER FICTION

The most important effect of industrialism on popular culture was the proliferation of weekly "story papers" devoted mainly to serialized "sensation" novels. These story papers and the closely related dime novels were recognized by many observers as a significant phenomenon. The Reverend Jonathan B. Harrison, for example, after a systematic investigation of social conditions in a New England factory town, had the following report to make in 1880:

> The young people of the mills generally read the story papers, published (most of them) in New York city, and devoted to interminable "continued" narratives, of which there are always three or four in process of publication in each paper. I have read some of these stories. They have usually no very distinct educational quality or tendency, good or bad. They are simply stories,—vapid, silly, turgid, and incoherent. As the robber-heroes are mostly grand-looking fellows, and all the ladies have white hands and splendid attire, it may be that some of the readers find hard work more distasteful because of their ac-

quaintance with the gorgeous idlers and thieves, who, in these fictions are always so much more fortunate than the people who are honest and industrious. But usually, as I am convinced by much observation, the only effect of this kind of reading is that it serves "to pass away the time," by supplying a kind of entertainment, a stimulus or opiate for the mind, and that these people resort to it and feel a necessity for it in much the same way that others feel they must have whisky or opium.*

Mrs. Jennie C. Croly, a veteran of humanitarian efforts to help working girls in New York, contributed further data concerning the audience for story papers in her testimony before the Senate Committee on Education and Labor in 1883:

By the Chairman:
Q. As to the large numbers of these poor girls that you speak of, what opportunities are there for them in the way of recreation, in the way of reading or any of the ordinary pleasures or relaxations in life— what is a girl going to do if she has half a day of spare time?—
A. Well, in the first place, such girls do not care much about sitting down to read. If they have half a day of spare time they want to get out of doors, they want air. . . . as for reading they want something very different from what they have in their daily lives, and so they run to the story papers that contain flashy stories; that tell about the fine ladies and how many dresses they have, and that tell about the worst murders and the most exciting incidents that they can get. And I do not blame them for it. They are crazy for something that is outside of themselves, and which will make them forget the hard facts of their daily lives.†

The formulas for sensation fiction had been perfected in the 1840s by drawing upon English sentimental and

* *Certain Dangerous Tendencies in American Life, and Other Papers* (Boston, 1880), pp. 167–68.
† *Report of the Senate Committee on Education and Labor,* II, pp. 613–14.

Gothic fiction of the eighteenth century, with some features, such as occasional use of historical settings, taken over from Scott, and even a few touches from Dickens—although not, alas, his humor. George Lippard's overblown novel *The Quaker City; or, The Monks of Monk Hall,* published in 1844, may stand as an encyclopedia of the genre. By the 1870s techniques of production had been standardized. Although there is not enough space in an anthology to accommodate actual samples, the flavor of this fiction is accurately conveyed by the following letter written to Robert Bonner of the *New York Ledger* in 1872 by Leon Lewis who, with his wife, had undertaken to produce weekly installments of two serials for $150 a week:

> We send herewith No. 10 of the Girl Hermit. This is now the situation:
> 1. The hero and his comrade are adrift at night on two planks in the middle of Lake Huron.
> 2. The heroine, "the Girl Hermit"—is being carried away from her island home by Indians.
> 3. The heroine's mother is shut up in a rock-bound dungeon with prospect of starving to death, having only 10 days' food.
> 4. The heroine's father is in a similar striking fix, having the villain in custody, and great things depending upon his actions.
> To this point the interest of the tale has been deepening from the beginning, and it will continue to deepen from this point to the end, making it
> THE GREATEST STORY of the 19TH CENTURY!
> This would be egotistical, of course, if said to anybody but you, but you will understand us.
>
> Ever affectionately yours,
> Leon and Harriet Lewis.‡

Mechanization was clearly the principal stimulus to the development of story papers devoted to this kind of reading material. The process began in the 1830s with the introduction of the steam rotary press, which

‡ Mary Noel, *Villains Galore: The Heyday of the Popular Story Weekly* (New York, 1954), p. 77.

drastically lowered the cost of printed matter and made
possible the publication of five-cent daily newspapers.
In the following decade enterprising publishers in Boston, Philadelphia, and New York discovered there was
an even larger audience for fiction than for the news
and political discussion of the dailies. The story paper,
however, could not reach its full development until new
techniques of marketing as well as of production had
been developed. In the 1850s the consolidation of trunk
railway lines placed markets as distant as New Orleans
and St. Louis and Chicago within reach of New York
publishers. By appealing to the national audience thus
made accessible, Bonner built up the *Ledger* to a circulation of some four hundred thousand in the 1870s.
Several competing journals had circulations of more
than two hundred thousand each.

DOCUMENT 71

Story-Paper Literature

SOURCE: W. H. Bishop, "Story-Paper Literature," *Atlantic Monthly*, XLIV (September 1879), 383–93.

Bishop, a young novelist from Wisconsin, was one of the newer generation of writers whom Howells made it a point to encourage. Although he was only a mediocre writer, his blandly ironic attitude toward boiler-plate fiction was presumably characteristic of highbrows within the orbit of the *Atlantic Monthly*.

The description of New York boys fascinated by bloodcurdling tales about pirates and avengers shows that Tom Sawyer's addiction was not confined to the Mississippi Valley in the 1840s.

The Yates boy, aged fifteen, desired to run away. He confided the intention to his sister, and she naturally conveyed it to his parents. His father summoned him before him, and said, "There is no need of your running away. If you will let me know any town or village in the country to which you desire to go, you shall be set down there with your trunk. I will give you a sum of money, furthermore, to find some kind of occupation, so that you may know by actual experience the value of the good home you have left." The offer was declined, with abashed thanks. It was not what his imagination pictured. He waited, and after a little time turned up missing, as the saying is, with two guns and a pointer dog. He returned from Chicago broken with ague, but departed again for the Cuban war, and has not since been heard of. His escapades were laid, with a show of reason, to the sensational romances, in which it appeared he was much absorbed.

Such stories are common. One day, it is three boys who are arrested at Paterson on their way to Texas, on the proceeds of a month's rent they have been sent to pay, but have appropriated instead. Another, three Boston boys do us the honor to believe that more adventures are to be found in New York than at home, and arrive with a slender capital of four dollars and a half to seek them; are robbed of even this by more knowing gamins of the place, and spend several nights in the station-house before they can be reclaimed. Again, a group of runaways is found behind a New Jersey haystack playing poker, with a knife and a revolver before each one, as the custom is with all well-regulated desperadoes. A late boy-murderer confessed that he had wanted to hide in a cave and prowl and kill, and that he believed he got the idea from his reading.

This last extreme is rare, and the imaginations which go to the others are of an unwaveringly logical kind, which amounts to want of balance. A grain of common sense keeps down the imitative impulse in the majority of cases. They feel that, fine, and possibly veracious, as it all is, it is not, somehow, exactly adapted to their personally taking a part in it. We outgrow it,—for I make no doubt there are those who read this who have known something of the feeling from their own experience; and it would be a poor reader indeed who had had no amicable relations with pirates, avengers, dead-shots of the plains, and destroyers in his youth. We go to our counting-room, our machine-shop, our corner grocery, our law office, as the case may be. We shoot nobody at all, and do our plundering, if plunder we must, within the law, decorously, by light weights and short measures, by managing a company or borrowing of a friend. The remembrance alone survives as a source of the very general enjoyment that is got out of mock heroics.

But let notice be given that it is not an especially humorous point of view that is sought for the story-paper literature. It is an enormous field of mental activity, the greatest literary movement, in bulk, of the age, and worthy of very serious consideration for itself. Disdained as it may be by the highly cultivated for its character, the phenomenon of its existence cannot be overlooked.

The taste for cheap fiction is by no means confined to this country. America leads in this form of publication in the kind of papers mentioned; but romances that do not appear to be of a greatly higher order are almost as profuse with the venders of reading matter at Paris, Turin, or Cologne as here, and not a daily paper on the continent of Europe, in any language, but has its scrap of a continued story, its *feuilleton,* in every issue.

Our story papers, damp from the press and printed very black, upholster all the news-stands, but we shall study them in a more leisurely way at a stationer's. Shall we choose this dingy one at the Five Points, where the grocery and wood and coal business is combined with the other; or this pretentious store under a lofty new tenement house in the German quarter, with the joints already warping apart, the paint blistered, and a plate-glass window cracked by uneven settling? Let it be rather one of the stuffy little, but more prosperous, ones of the up-town avenues. Some late numbers dangle from the edge of the low awning, under which it is necessary to stoop. A bell attached to the door jingles sharply. The interior is festooned with school satchels and jumping-ropes. Mother Carey's, Mother Shipton's, the Egyptian, the Hindoo, and the Golden Wheel of Fortune dream books, the Wild Oats, the Larry Tooley, the Eileen Alanna, the Love Among the Roses, song and dance books, in gaudy covers, ornament the window, among the tops and marbles.

The story papers, the most conspicuous stock in trade, are laid out on the front counter, neatly overlapped, so as to show all the titles and frontispieces. Ten are already in, and more to come,—the Saturday Night, the Saturday Journal, the Ledger, the Weekly, the Family Story Paper, the Fireside Companion. Near them on the glass case, in formidable piles, are the "libraries." These are, omitting the prominent examples which do the same sort of service for standard works, pamphlets reprinting at a dime and a half dime the stories which have appeared as serials in the papers. There are papers which, finding this practice a diversion of interest, distinctly announce that their stories will not reappear, and that their fascinations can be enjoyed only at original sources.

No far-reaching memory is needed to recall when the Ledger was the only journal of this kind. Its notorious prosperity gave rise to a swarm of imitators, eager to share the profits of so good a field. New York is still the great point of supply, but Chicago and some other Western cities have begun to find their account in similar publications for their tributary territories. As the new aspirants arose, it was necessary for each to set up its own peculiar claim to favor. One assumes to be the exclusive family story paper; another offers its readers microscopes, chromos, and supplements; others provide the fullest contents; others go upon the reputations of writers whose abilities to captivate are known: Colonel Tipton Slasher will write—Mrs. Jennie Sarah Ringwood, whose power of passion development—Max Shorthorn, without a peer for pungent humor and drollery—A brilliant corps conceded to be, etc., etc. It would be a mistake to suppose there are not distinctions of reputation here, as among their betters.

But that was a splendid new department opened when it was observed where the most ardent class of patrons came from. They are boys. We may observe it ourselves, if we will give a little heed to the progress of the traffic on publication days. A middle-aged woman, with a shawl over her head and a half peck of potatoes in a basket, stops in for one; a shop-girl on her way home from work; a servant from one of the good houses in the side streets, come on her own account, or possibly for a schoolgirl mistress. But with them, before them, and after them come boys. They begin to read already as they walk away, and thread the streets without heeding their bustle. To-morrow the elevator boy will have the latest number of Cloven-Hoof the Demon, as he rides you up and down at the hotel or the business block. It will be hidden under many a jacket in school-hours. A shock-headed boy from the streets—his case has not heretofore been made public—set by a family to tidy up their cellar for the spring, was found perusing it, seated on a broken stool, and reaching vaguely for such things as might be in the neighborhood in the mean time.

The adventures in the adult papers were not beyond the capacity of the boys; but one, and then another, conceived the idea of conciliating their especial interest by making a paper for them, till this branch, with its Boys' Journal, Boys of New York, Boys of America, Boys of the World, Young Men of New York, Young Men of America, has become rather the larger of the two. The heroes are boys, and there are few departments of unusual existence in which they are not seen figuring to brilliant advantage. They are shown amply competent as the Boy Detective, the Boy Spy, the Boy Trapper, the Boy Buccaneer, the Boy Guide, the Boy Captain, the Boy Robinson Crusoe, the Boy Claude Duval, and the Boy Phœnix, or Jim Bludsoe, Jr., whose characteristic is to be impervious to harm in burning steamboats and hotels, exploding mines, and the like. . . .

The lesson of the necessity of a complete armament is so well impressed that it is not strange it is remembered by any setting out on their adventures. The whole vast action pivots, as it were, around the muzzle of an extended revolver. Every frontispiece shows a combat. Here is a milder one, however, in which a pirate, with a curious taste in bricabrac even for his class, is quaffing a draught from a goblet made of a jeweled skull.

"With a well-directed blow Remington stretched the villain at full length upon the floor."

"With a grating curse, the dying wretch thrust a revolver against the Avenger's breast, and fired."

So the legends read, and so, by hecatombs, goes the carnage on. I estimate that in this pile of dime and half-dime libraries under my hand there are not less than ten thousand slain. It is in detail, too, and not mere generalizing with grape and canister. It is a low estimate, no more than fifty to a book. In this first random chapter come rid-

ing seventy road agents into a town. They slay eighteen of
the residents, and are then slain themselves,—all but one,
who is, by the orders of a leader named Old Bullwhacker,
immediately strung up to a tree, and pays the earthly
penalty of his crimes. And in the next—it is a romance
called Deadwood Dick on Deck; or, Calamity Jane, the
Heroine of Whoop-Up—we find a young man, named
Charley Davis, dashing around a bend, bestriding his horse
backwards, and firing at five mounted pursuers. They were
twelve originally, but he has gradually picked off the rest.
He is joined by Calamity Jane, a beautiful young woman,
who carries a sixteen-shot Winchester rifle, a brace of pis-
tols in her belt and another in her holsters, and between
the two the pursuing five are easily disposed of. Here are a
hundred dead in two chapters only, and the list of the
doomed—amongst them a character named Arkansas Alf,
the Danite Ghoul, who richly deserves it—is far from
exhausted.

The fierce rivalry between numerous competitors tends
to two results. The first is an increase in the number of
the serial stories. Two are found to be carrying *eight serials*
each at a time. Two others have seven each; another six.
None have less than five. What an enormous voracity is
here! Overlapping as they do, a new one commencing as an
old one finishes, how does the subscriber ever escape from
their toils? It seems as if, unless he would forego from one
to seven eighths of the value of his money, which is not a
pleasant thing to do in the most prosperous circumstances,
he must be interlocked with his journal as fast as if in the
arms of an octopus.

The second is the increase in sensationalism. The earlier
stories were more honest and simpler. Here, now, is a
unique combat,—marine divers fighting over a corpse, with
knives, under water. But does anything else that is new remain? It would seem as if the last limit had been reached.
After the enormous carnival of red brotherhoods, border
phantoms, ghouls, demons, sleuths, ocean blood-hounds,
brotherhoods of death, masked terrors, and reckless rangers,
all done with the poor facilities that poverty-stricken hu-

man language affords, one could well expect to find these authors in a gasping state, reduced to the condition of the cannibals of the Orinoco, who could only go up to the hills, and say to their deities, "Oh!"

The same is true of the illustrations. From the point of view of art, so far as art can be considered in them, the earlier were the best. The older representations, sometimes lightly and sketchily printed, of life on the plains and spirited combats, the bold young scouts in their fringed leggings, the lithe heroine, captured or saved, twisted across the back of a galloping steed, were not always without a certain grace in the attitudes. The modern vie with one another in lurid horror and repulsiveness. The Boys of New York has a great cut occupying three fourths of its folio page. It is done in harsh ruled lines, like the most frigid kind of mechanical drawing, and printed black, black, to be visible from the longest possible distance. Coarse as it is, it breathes the essence of madness and murder. The artist should draw none henceforth but demons. Two frightful desperadoes, dark like negroes, with gleaming eyeballs and mustaches of the stubby, thick, jet-black, gambler pattern, are fighting with knives (having fallen out between themselves) in a moving hotel elevator, in which they have taken refuge to escape two detectives in chase. One detective, bounding up the stairs, appears, with a ghastly face and cocked revolver in hand, at one of the openings, as they go by. The other—the boy hero, who is not like a boy, but some strange, brawny ape—is seen clinging, with shrieks, to a ring in the bottom of the elevator, which he has clutched the better to follow them, in danger, now that he has mounted, of falling from exhaustion into the black abyss below. It haunts one. It is a nightmare.

The means taken to bring the papers to notice are often as enterprising as their contents. Copies of the opening chapters are thrown in at the area railings, and printed, regardless of expense, to pique curiosity, in the daily papers. The attention of the households of upper New York was widely awakened recently by an invitation telegram, sealed and addressed, the envelope and message-blank exact, saying, "*The child is still alive. You are personally interested in all the details of A Sinless Crime, to appear in tomorrow's ——.*"

The villain in the story papers, as often as it is indicated clearly who he is, has no redeeming traits. The idea of mixed motives, still less the Bret Harte idea of moral grandeur illuminating lives of continuous iniquity, through their sharing a blanket or a canteen at the end with emigrants delayed in a snow-storm, has not penetrated here. It is no ordinary crimes the villains meditate, either. Murder might almost be called the least of them. The only merciful drawback to their malignity is their excessive simplicity. They go about declaring their intentions with a guilelessness often worthy of positive sympathy. . . .

The good, on the other hand, are known to be good by a constant insistence upon it. We cannot doubt what we are so often assured of. It is generally necessary for the proper complication of incidents that appearances should for some time be much against them; but how immaculate they shine out in the end! The authors are often put to severe straits to bring this about. It is the difficult point of plot-making. How can it be that they seem bad enough to lay themselves open to all this tribulation, when they are in fact so good? Credulity and gentlemanly indulgence are much needed to accept the explanations vouchsafed. . . .

The heroines have for the most part, like full-private James, no characteristic trait of any distinctive kind. She is very beautiful; she often has hair "purple-black" in color, and always "great" eyes of some of the desirable shades; but generally she is simply a precious bundle of goods to be snatched out of deadly perils, and plotted and fought about. She has little actively to do but clasp her hands together, and little to say except "Oh, how can I repay you, my noble, my generous preserver!" She dispenses with chaperonage in a way the first society can never be brought to approve of.

Vast ingenuity is used in supplying motives to the "sleuth-like" personages so numerously engaged throughout the narratives in persistent schemes of vengeance. The original grievance is often found to be very slight. Nor can we believe that the following is always so seriously meant as it is said to be. The "human blood-hound" and "destroying angel"—there is the remarkable phenomenon in one case where "his heart was as white as his face with rage, as he grasped his bowie and followed on the stranger's track" —is continually letting his victim give him the slip without reason. "See here! if you do that again," he seems to be saying, or, "If ever I set eyes on you once more, it will be the worse for you." The plots in fact do not hasten to their conclusion, but are dragged back and detained from it. Time after time the occasion for the avenger to do whatever he is going to is flagrantly then and there, but he does not do it.

As to their constructions, vast as the ground the stories now cover, they are few and simple. This is constant: that the villain gets himself into trouble by loving the heroine, who cares nothing about him. The hero lays himself open by stepping in, in the nick of time, to protect her from consequent schemes of vengeance. Now it is in a Fourteenth Street tenement house, now in a palace in Russian Moscow, now in mediæval Venice, and again at ancient Palmyra; but the repulsing with scorn, the protection, the schemes of vengeance, and their coming to naught are everywhere the same. It sometimes seems hard upon the villain. Everything is against him from the first. She very often has no cause of complaint in the world, to begin with, but an "instinctive repulsion." But once rejected, he has cause enough, it may well be believed.

The "woman scorned" is his counterpart, and the second great source of trouble. She appears in the midst of marriages, in the stories in which she takes part, and forbids the bans, so sure as the marriages are set to take place. With the unscrupulous guardian, who has the keepers of insane asylums to aid him in his projects; the persons changed at birth, or returning thirty years after they were supposed to be lost at sea; the reprobate father or brother arousing acute jealousies by being taken on his clandestine visits after money for a lover, I have mentioned most of the essential elements. Generally, in the shorter stories, of which each paper contains a number besides its serials, there is a great deal of Cinderella business. Poor and plain nieces or wards marry the fine gentleman, in spite of the supercilious daughter, after all.

It is not exalted game to pick to pieces works from which not too much is expected at the best, and the plain road has by no means been abandoned in search of absurdities. But the surprising thing to learn is that there is really so much less in them than might be expected. The admiration grows for the craving which can swallow, without misgiving, so grand a tissue of extravagances, inaneness, contradictions, and want of probable cause. The stories are not ingenious, even, and ingenuity was perhaps supposed to be their strong point.

It is not that they do not give epigrams, bright conversations, penetrating reflections. We can recollect when we skipped all that in the best of books, and desired only to rush headlong on with the movement. Poe, Cooper, Féval, Collins, Charles Reade, have written stories in which what the people do is of very much more interest than what they are; but in these is a kind of fatality; events hold together; they could not have been otherwise.

Though written almost exclusively for the use of the lower classes of society, the story papers are not accurate pictures of their life. They are not a mass of evidence from which, though rude, a valuable insight into their thoughts, feelings, and doings can be obtained by others who do not know them. The figures are like to nature only as much as those drawn without models by an inferior artist are. The product is dried and hectic. The writers do not seem to be telling anything they have seen and known, but following, at third and fourth hand, traditions above them which they have read. The most enlightened field of the novel is social history,—to portray James K. Jackson and Elizabeth May Johnson in relation to their surroundings and times, as the formal historians do Napoleon Bonaparte and Katharine of Aragon. This is a field into which they very superficially enter. Perhaps they consult their popularity in not doing so. A considerable part of their audience is not reflective. It has rather simple wants and aspirations. Lack of culture is a continuous childhood. A statement is enough; a demonstration is not necessary. It is only a tyrannical employer or an unprincipled guardian who prevents the attainment of perfect happiness. Do readers wish for profound and intimate observations made about them which they never think of making about themselves? George Eliot says of a heroine that she is "ardent, theoretic, and intellectually consequent;" Mrs. Ringwood, that she had a blue silk dress and a perfect form. . . .

There are a great many poor persons in the narratives, and the capitalist is occasionally abused, showing that an eye is kept on the popular movements of the day; but poverty is not really glorified. The deserving characters are almost sure to be secretly of good families, and in reduced circumstances only for a short time. Ordinary origin and a humdrum course of life at honest, manual labor are not much wanted even here. The names are selected for their distinction with as much care as those of fashionable New York up-town hotels. The responsiveness of the faces of the characters, particularly the bad ones, who ought to be more hardened, to their emotions is one of the points to note. They turn "sickly yellow," "ghastly pale," and "white, rigid, and haggard" with extraordinary frequency.

The literary influences descending from above are chiefly those of G. P. R. James, Lever, Captain Marryat, Bret Harte (for material), Ouida, Miss Braddon, the books Handy Andy, Verdant Green, Valentine Vox, and the Memoirs of Vidocq,—all of course immensely diluted and deteriorated. Dickens, too, is discernible in names and a whole ragged school of characters whose aspiration is to get something to eat. The faults of style are a superabundance of adjectives and bad grammar. There is the general merit, on the other hand, of short and clear sentences, in deference to readers who wish the fewest possible obstacles between themselves and a direct comprehension of what is going on. If any one expression of those that are popular is more common than another, it is the word "erelong" in concluding paragraphs. Its use helps to give a kind of rhythmic flow to the long-continuing movement of the narratives: "And erelong Reginald DeLacey Earlscourt [or Cuthbert Ravenwood Leigh] was on his way to Grangerfield Manor." . . .

There is a popular impression among people who attach weight to the expression, "truth stranger than fiction" (as though it were not truer, of course), and appreciate too little the difficulty of making something out of nothing, that the material is chiefly matter of pure invention. Such is not the case. The writers keep scrap-books of all the horrible circumstances coming under their notice, and put them together to suit. It is all in the papers. The liveliest ingenuity cannot stimulate the novelist to the desperate inventions of beings whose whole existence is at stake. . . .

And now, having begun to say something in their favor, let us see if anything more can be said. There are story papers and story papers. It may be that those of the cheapest and flashiest order have been too exclusively dwelt upon. Those popular novelists, Mrs. E. D. E. N. Southworth, Mrs. Ann H. Stephens, and May Agnes Fleming contribute Heart Histories, Deserted Wives, and Brides of an Evening to the story papers, and shall one disparage what is found on the table of so many boudoirs, far indeed removed from the lower classes? Some reprint as serials, with their own matters, standard productions, like the Count of Monte Cristo, the Memoirs of Houdin the Conjurer, and Tom Cringle's Log. Others give away Shakespeare's Sonnets and the Bab Ballads for supplements. In general, in the libraries good literature is beginning to mingle among the bad in a very curious way. Robinson Crusoe, very much mangled, it is true, at half a dime, may be found in the Wide-Awake Library, sandwiched between Bowie Knife Ben and Death Notch the Destroyer.

This is a phase of the subject which would bear working out by itself. Perhaps it offers a solution of the problem how the literature of the masses is to be improved. Would the adults take Charles Reade, Hardy, Wilkie Collins,

Dickens, Victor Hugo, and the boys Scott, Bulwer, Manzoni, G. P. R. James, Irving's brigand tales and Conquest of Granada, Poe's Gold Bug and Adventures of Arthur Gordon Pym, if they were as cheap as the others? Is it simply and only a question of cheapness, and has the taste of the audience of story-paper buyers been maligned?

These papers have editorial pages in which a variety of good advice is printed, calculated to counteract, if attended to, though it may possibly be neglected by those whom it could most serve, the unsettling influence of the body of the contents. They aim at the good graces of the family. There is a department of "answers to correspondents," embodying information on manners, morals, dress, education, the affections. Edith F. is informed that too many rings on the fingers are vulgar; Emma D. that pie should be eaten with a fork; and L. M. that there is no such thing as love at first sight. Any young lady, it is tartly said, to whom a young man should propose marriage at first sight would endeavor to restrain his impetuosity for a day or two, so as to discover from what lunatic asylum he had escaped, and have him returned to his keepers. There are short essays and reflections on housekeeping; the care of children; the advisability of cheerfulness and economy; of going early to bed and of rising early; even, somewhat strangely, on moderation and taste in reading. They are trite and Tupperish, but one learns these things somewhere for the first time, and then they are strikingly novel. Who was the profound writer in whom they were new to us? How could we know he took them from predecessors who originated them not far from January 1st of the year One?

In considering the real influence of these papers it must be reckoned, not upon those who have outgrown them, and been led by the study of better things to see their absurdity, but on those who remain immersed in them for lack of better ideals, or leave them only to read nothing at all. They are by no means needed to account for an adventurous spirit in human nature. Robinson Crusoe ran away to sea in the year 1632, when this kind of literature could have been very little prevalent. But they certainly foment it to the utmost. The first condition of a happy existence is the ability to support *ennui*. But the personages here are never exhibited attending to the ordinary duties of existence. Embarked in the chase for some lost child, abducted heiress, or secreted will, they rush hither and thither, without ever stopping, around the world, and around again, if need be; and when it is done they fall into a state of inanition, or at least they would, only at that very moment the story is done, also. The labors and sacrifices demanded are of too extreme a type to be valuable as examples. The heroes and heroines would die for each other at any time, but which would curb his temper in a provoking moment; which would get up first and make the fire, in case there were no servants?—but there always are servants, in troops.

Still, the best of the story papers reward virtue and punish vice. Their dependence upon the family keeps them, as a rule, free of dangerous appeals to the lower passions. Ranging over all countries and periods, they convey considerable information about history and foreign parts into quarters where very little would otherwise penetrate. They encourage a chivalrous devotion to woman, though they do not do much towards making her more worthy of it. The story papers, then,—it is not here a question of those that have been said to be positively bad,—are not an unmixed evil. The legitimate charge against them is not that they are so bad, but only that they are not better.

The great question is, Are they better than nothing? There are persons who read neither story-papers nor anything else. They are no doubt exemplary and superior in many relations of life, prudent in matters of sentiment, cool in business, with the extra time for use that might otherwise have been expended in flights of the imagination; but let us believe that they have secretly their follies, too, as much as if they believed in pirates, hidden treasures, and destroyers.

The taste for reading, however perverted, is connected with something noble, with an interest in things outside of the small domain of self, with a praiseworthy curiosity about the great planet we inhabit. One is almost ready to say that, rather than not have it at all, it had better be nourished on no better food than story papers.

But it is a pity it is no better. This is the last, as it was the first and the continuous reflection from a view of the enormous extent of this imaginative craving, and the means by which it is ministered to. There ought to be in it information of worth; a separation of sense from nonsense; characters which, without preaching, should remain in the memory, as a stimulus to better things in trying times.

DOCUMENT 72

Half-Dime Novels and Story Papers

SOURCE: Anthony Comstock, "Half-Dime Novels and Story Papers," in *Traps for the Young* (New York, 1883), 2d ed. (1884), pp. 20–25.

The name of Anthony Comstock has become a by-word for all that is ridiculous in efforts to enforce morality by censorship, but his lifelong crusade to suppress what he considered obscenity in print was a perfectly logical application of traditional moral and esthetic standards to the sensationalism of the reading matter produced for a mass audience. When Comstock exclaims, "Oh, Infidelity and Liberalism, ye great defenders of obscenity and crime! Ye are mighty in your own conceit, in attempting to defame the mighty God,"* his tone is shrill because he is merely echoing the thunders of clergymen of an earlier period who could speak with real authority. But Cotton Mather or Jonathan Edwards could hardly have said anything very different if they had been confronted by the subliterary fiction of the later nineteenth century. Given the psychological and ethical assumptions which prevailed in Comstock's day, he was justified in regarding his New York Society for the Suppression of Vice as an obviously necessary organization.

And it came to pass that as Satan went to and fro upon the earth, watching his traps and rejoicing over his numerous victims, he found room for improvement in some of his schemes. The daily press did not meet all his require-

* *Traps for the Young*, p. 205.

ments. The *weekly* illustrated papers of crime would do for young men and sports, for brothels, gin-mills, and thieves' resorts, but were found to be so gross, so libidinous, so monstrous, that every decent person spurned them. They were excluded from the home on sight. They were too high-priced for children, and too cumbersome to be conveniently hid from the parent's eye or carried in the boy's pocket. So he resolved to make another trap for boys and girls especially.

He also resolved to make the most of these vile illustrated weekly papers, by lining the news-stands and shop-windows along the pathway of the children from home to school and church, so that they could not go to and from these places of instruction without giving him opportunity to defile their pure minds by flaunting these atrocities before their eyes.

And Satan rejoiced greatly that professing Christians were silent and apparently acquiesced in his plans. He found that our most refined men and women went freely to trade with persons who displayed these traps for sale; that few, if any, had moral courage to enter a protest against this public display of indecencies, and scarcely one in all the land had the boldness to say to the dealer in filth, "I will not give you one cent of my patronage so long as you sell these devil-traps to ruin the young." And he was proud of professing Christians and respectable citizens on this account, and caused honorable mention to be made of them in general order to his imps, because of the quiet and orderly assistance thus rendered him.

Satan stirred up certain of his willing tools on earth by the promise of a few paltry dollars to improve greatly on the death-dealing quality of the weekly death-traps, and forthwith came a series of new snares of fascinating construction, small and tempting in price, and baited with high-sounding names. These sure-ruin traps comprise a large variety of half-dime novels, five and ten cent story papers, and low-priced pamphlets for boys and girls.

This class includes the silly, insipid tale, the coarse, slangy story in the dialect of the barroom, the blood-and-thunder romance of border life, and the exaggerated details of crimes, real and imaginary. Some have highly colored sensational reports of real crimes, while others, and by far the larger number, deal with most improbable creations of fiction. The unreal far outstrips the real. Crimes are gilded, and lawlessness is painted to resemble valor, making a bid for bandits, brigands, murderers, thieves, and criminals in general. Who would go to the State prison, the gambling saloon, or the brothel to find a suitable companion for the child? Yet a more insidious foe is selected when these stories are allowed to become associates for the child's mind and to shape and direct the thoughts.

The finest fruits of civilization are consumed by these vermin. Nay, these products of corrupt minds are the eggs from which all kinds of villainies are hatched. Put the entire batch of these stories together, and I challenge the publishers and venders to show a single instance where any boy or girl has been elevated in morals, or where any noble or refined instinct has been developed by them.

The leading character in many, if not in the vast majority of these stories, is some boy or girl who possesses usually extraordinary beauty of countenance, the most superb clothing, abundant wealth, the strength of a giant, the agility of a squirrel, the cunning of a fox, the brazen effrontery of the most daring villain, and who is utterly destitute of any regard for the laws of God or man. Such a one is foremost among desperadoes, the companion and beau-ideal of maidens, and the high favorite of some rich person, who by his patronage and indorsement lifts the young villain into lofty positions in society, and provides liberally of his wealth to secure him immunity for his crimes. These stories link the pure maiden with the most foul and loathsome criminals. Many of them favor violation of marriage laws and cheapen female virtue.

One day while riding on the cars I purchased a copy of one of these papers. It is claimed to be "high-toned." The reader may judge of the *tone* when he learns that the copy now before me contains made-up stories with the following crimes woven into them. It must be premised that the following is taken from a single issue, and from parts of continued stories. To complete the grand total of infamies it would be necessary to commence at the beginning and go to the end of the fractional parts of the tales from which these extracts are taken.

The gist of these stories consists of—

A conspiracy against a school-girl.

One girl hired to personate a rich girl and marry a villain in her stead.

A man murdered by being blown up by explosives.

A beautiful girl, by lying and deceit, seeks to captivate one whom she loves.

Six assaults upon an officer while resisting arrests.

A conspiracy against an officer to prevent the arrest of a criminal.

A burglary.

An illegitimate child.

A woman murdered by masked burglars.

An attempt to force a beautiful girl to marry a scoundrel to save her benefactor.

Two attempts to coerce a girl to marry against her wishes.

One woman who died in New York comes to life in Italy.

Two attempted assassinations.

One confidence operator at work to swindle a stranger.

An assault on the highway.

A hired assassin.

A massacre by Indians.

One babe stolen to substitute for another.

An attempt to murder a child.

Two women concealing their secretly-born babes.

A rich man is confronted in a castle by a woman he has ruined, who raises such an outcry that he becomes purple and rigid, while blood gushes from his mouth. The woman takes a vial from her pocket and instantly cures him.

One case of clandestine correspondence and meetings between a girl and her lover. This results in the girl running away at night and getting married to hide her shame. This is followed by a scene in their room, where the husband refuses to acknowledge his wife publicly; she being in a delicate condition pleads to have the marriage made public. The husband dares not do this for fear of arrest for other crimes. . . .

. . . these stories give utterly false and debasing ideas of life. All high moral purposes are made to give way to self-gratification. The great safeguard of human society—reverence to law—is broken down. Disobedience to parents is encouraged. The healthful restraint of parental authority is treated as a species of tyranny which the hero first chafes under, then resists, and lastly ignores.

The boy cheats himself by imagining he is doing a manly thing when he naturally follows a base example. To the child that chafes under home restraint, having taken the initiative step to ignore proper authority, a dangerous and lawless life comes easy.

Again, these stories breed vulgarity, profanity, loose ideas of life, impurity of thought and deed. They render the imagination unclean, destroy domestic peace, desolate homes, cheapen woman's virtue, and make foul-mouthed bullies, cheats, vagabonds, thieves, desperadoes, and libertines. They disparage honest toil, and make real life a drudge and burden. What young man will serve an apprenticeship, working early and late, if his mind is filled with the idea that sudden wealth may be acquired by following the hero of the story? In real life, to begin at the foot of the ladder and work up, step by step, is the rule; but in these stories, inexperienced youth, with no moral character, take the foremost positions, and by trick and device, knife and revolver, bribery and corruption, carry everything before them, lifting themselves in a few short weeks to positions of ease and affluence. Moral courage with such is a thing to be sneered at and despised in many of these stories. If one is asked to drink and refuses, he is set up and twitted till he yields or is compelled to by force. The idea of doing anything from principle is ridiculous in the extreme. As well fill a kerosene-oil lamp with water and expect a brilliant light. And so, in addition to all else, there is early inculcated a distaste for the good, and the piercing blast of ridicule is turned upon the reader to destroy effectually all moral character. . . .

C. ORAL DISCOURSE AS A POPULAR ART

During the three or four decades before the Civil War, one of the most conspicuous features of American culture at all levels had been an enthusiasm for oratory. Both Edward Everett and Daniel Webster seemed godlike to the young Emerson in the 1820s and 1830s, primarily because of their eloquence. The speeches of men like Henry Clay and Thomas Hart Benton in the Senate were national events; and even a lesser figure such as Anson Burlingame could launch his career with an oratorical performance on the floor of Congress. In the later 1840s Whitman planned to convey his prophetic message to the American people as an itinerant orator rather than through the pages of a book. But in the course of the 1860s oratory had ceased with surprising suddenness to be a significant factor in national politics. Lincoln's Gettysburg Address was a drastic departure from the tradition of long and ornate discourses of the sort represented by Edward Everett's oration on the same occasion. General Grant, the national hero of the postwar decades, was ill at ease on the platform; and of the politicians who managed the federal government in the 1870s and 1880s, only James G. Blaine was notable for eloquence.

On the other hand, three kinds of non-political oral discourse enjoyed an unprecedented vogue in this period:

(1) Lyceum lectures. The heyday of the lyceum as an educational institution had come in the fifteen years before the Civil War. After the war both lecturers and audiences increased in number, but the emphasis shifted from instruction to entertainment. The platform career of Robert G. Ingersoll was reminiscent of an earlier day: he was a political force and, with his shocking views of the Bible, a kind of anti-preacher.

(2) The oral performances of the vernacular humorists. Most of these men are now forgotten, but they were celebrities in their day. The first of them to achieve a national reputation was Artemus Ward, who died in 1867. The most popular over an extended period was Mark Twain. But there were many others, all known by pseudonyms: Petroleum V. Nasby, Bill Arp, Josh Billings, Eli Perkins, Bill Bye, and the cumbersomely titled Burlington Hawkeye Man (Robert J. Burdette).

(3) The new vernacular style of preaching variously represented by Henry Ward Beecher, T. De Witt Talmage, and Dwight L. Moody.

The leading occupants of metropolitan pulpits were national figures. They were favorites of the lyceum circuit; their sermons were reported in the daily press, were regularly distributed as pamphlets, and were then collected for publication as books. The following description of Henry Ward Beecher's pulpit manner, sent by Mark Twain to the San Francisco *Alta California* in 1867, indicates the news value of big-league preaching even for a California audience. Mark Twain's reference to "the language of the worldly" hints at the vernacular tone that made Beecher so unlike the pulpit giants of an earlier generation:

He has a rich, resonant voice, and a distinct enunciation, and makes himself heard all over the church without very apparent effort. His discourse sparkled with felicitous similes and metaphors (it is his strong suit to use the language of the worldly) and might be called a striking mosaic work, wherein poetry, pathos, humor, satire and eloquent declamation were happily blended upon a ground work of earnest exposition of the great truths involved in his text.

Whenever he forsook his notes and went marching up and down his stage, sawing his arms in the air, hurling sarcasms this way and that, discharging rockets of poetry, and exploding mines of eloquence, halting now and then to stamp his foot three times in succession to emphasize a point, I could have started the audience with a single clap of the hands and brought down the house. I had a suffocating desire to do it.*

* *Mark Twain's Travels with Mr. Brown*, eds. Franklin Walker and G. Ezra Dane (New York, 1940), pp. 93–94.

DOCUMENT 73

How to Tell a Story

SOURCE: Samuel L. Clemens (Mark Twain), "How to Tell a Story" (first published in *Youth's Companion*, 3 October 1895; collected in *How to Tell a Story and Other Essays*, New York, 1897).

The platform performances of the literary comedians in the post-Civil War decades illustrate the difficulty of distinguishing between folk art and popular art. All these men drew heavily upon the tradition of oral humor that had developed in backwoods America during the first half of the century; yet in becoming professional "lecturers" they entered a highly organized and commercialized world of show business, in which individual performers acquired a status resembling that of famous actors.

As Walter Blair points out, Mark Twain conceives of the American humorous story as a dramatic monologue: it depicts a character other than the actual teller of the story. Furthermore, he takes it for granted that the primary medium of the storyteller is oral, for he stresses facial expression and, above all, timing. That is, the storyteller's art is like that of the actor.* But the storyteller is not a mere performer; he composes the story he tells, even though he may be depending on a "source," usually in folklore, for his raw material. The role thus defined has all but disappeared; the closest equivalents in our day are the stand-up comedians of night clubs and television.

Although Mark Twain was a master of the oral anecdote, his real distinction lay in his ability to simulate the effect of oral story-telling in writing. This is the

* Introduction to *Selected Shorter Writings of Mark Twain* (Boston, 1962), p. xv.

origin of his celebrated vernacular style, which has exerted a formative influence on American literary prose of the twentieth century.†

I do not claim that I can tell a story as it ought to be told. I only claim to know how a story ought to be told, for I have been almost daily in the company of the most expert story-tellers for many years.

There are several kinds of stories, but only one difficult kind—the humorous. I will talk mainly about that one. The humorous story is American, the comic story is English, the witty story is French. The humorous story depends for its effect upon the *manner* of the telling; the comic story and the witty story upon the *matter*.

The humorous story may be spun out to great length, and may wander around as much as it pleases, and arrive nowhere in particular; but the comic and witty stories must be brief and end with a point. The humorous story bubbles gently along, the others burst.

The humorous story is strictly a work of art—high and delicate art—and only an artist can tell it; but no art is necessary in telling the comic and the witty story; anybody can do it. The art of telling a humorous story—understand, I mean by word of mouth, not print—was created in America, and has remained at home.

The humorous story is told gravely; the teller does his best to conceal the fact that he even dimly suspects that there is anything funny about it; but the teller of the comic story tells you beforehand that it is one of the funniest things he has ever heard, then tells it with eager delight, and is the first person to laugh when he gets through. And sometimes, if he has had good success, he is so glad and happy that he will repeat the "nub" of it and glance around from face to face, collecting applause, and then repeat it again. It is a pathetic thing to see.

Very often, of course, the rambling and disjointed hu-

† Richard M. Bridgman, *The Colloquial Style in America* (New York, 1966).

morous story finishes with a nub, point, snapper, or whatever you like to call it. Then the listener must be alert, for in many cases the teller will divert attention from that nub by dropping it in a carefully casual and indifferent way, with the pretence that he does not know it is a nub.

Artemus Ward used that trick a good deal; then when the belated audience presently caught the joke he would look up with innocent surprise, as if wondering what they had found to laugh at. Dan Setchell used it before him, Nye and Riley and others use it to-day.

But the teller of the comic story does not slur the nub; he shouts it at you—every time. And when he prints it, in England, France, Germany, and Italy, he italicizes it, puts some whooping exclamation-points after it, and sometimes explains it in a parenthesis. All of which is very depressing, and makes one want to renounce joking and lead a better life.

Let me set down an instance of the comic method, using an anecdote which has been popular all over the world for twelve or fifteen hundred years. The teller tells it in this way:

THE WOUNDED SOLDIER

In the course of a certain battle a soldier whose leg had been shot off appealed to another soldier who was hurrying by to carry him to the rear, informing him at the same time of the loss which he had sustained; whereupon the generous son of Mars, shouldering the unfortunate, proceeded to carry out his desire. The bullets and cannon-balls were flying in all directions, and presently one of the latter took the wounded man's head off—without, however, his deliverer being aware of it. In no long time he was hailed by an officer, who said:

"Where are you going with that carcass?"

"To the rear, sir—he's lost his leg!"

"His leg, forsooth?" responded the astonished officer; "you mean his head, you booby."

Whereupon the soldier dispossessed himself of his

burden, and stood looking down upon it in great perplexity. At length he said:

"It is true, sir, just as you have said." Then after a pause he added, "*But he* TOLD *me* IT WAS HIS LEG!!!!!"

Here the narrator bursts into explosion after explosion of thunderous horse-laughter, repeating that nub from time to time through his gaspings and shriekings and suffocatings.

It takes only a minute and a half to tell that in its comic-story form; and isn't worth the telling, after all. Put into the humorous-story form it takes ten minutes, and is about the funniest thing I have ever listened to—as James Whitcomb Riley tells it.

He tells it in the character of a dull-witted old farmer who has just heard it for the first time, thinks it is unspeakably funny, and is trying to repeat it to a neighbor. But he can't remember it; so he gets all mixed up and wanders helplessly round and round, putting in tedious details that don't belong in the tale and only retard it; taking them out conscientiously and putting in others that are just as useless; making minor mistakes now and then and stopping to correct them and explain how he came to make them; remembering things which he forgot to put in in their proper place and going back to put them in there; stopping his narrative a good while in order to try to recall the name of the soldier that was hurt, and finally remembering that the soldier's name was not mentioned, and remarking placidly that the name is of no real importance, anyway—better, of course, if one knew it, but not essential, after all—and so on, and so on, and so on.

The teller is innocent and happy and pleased with himself, and has to stop every little while to hold himself in and keep from laughing outright; and does hold in, but his body quakes in a jelly-like way with interior chuckles; and at the end of the ten minutes the audience have laughed until they are exhausted, and the tears are running down their faces.

The simplicity and innocence and sincerity and unconsciousness of the old farmer are perfectly simulated, and
the result is a performance which is thoroughly charming
and delicious. This is art—and fine and beautiful, and only
a master can compass it; but a machine could tell the
other story.

To string incongruities and absurdities together in a
wandering and sometimes purposeless way, and seem in-
nocently unaware that they are absurdities, is the basis of
the American art, if my position is correct. Another feature is the slurring of the point. A third is the dropping of a
studied remark apparently without knowing it, as if one
were thinking aloud. The fourth and last is the pause.

Artemus Ward dealt in numbers three and four a good
deal. He would begin to tell with great animation something which he seemed to think was wonderful; then lose
confidence, and after an apparently absent-minded pause
add an incongruous remark in a soliloquizing way; and
that was the remark intended to explode the mine—and it
did.

For instance, he would say eagerly, excitedly, "I once
knew a man in New Zealand who hadn't a tooth in his
head"—here his animation would die out; a silent, reflective pause would follow, then he would say dreamily, and
as if to himself, "and yet that man could beat a drum
better than any man I ever saw."

The pause is an exceedingly important feature in any
kind of story, and a frequently recurring feature, too. It is
a dainty thing, and delicate, and also uncertain and treach-
erous; for it must be exactly the right length—no more and
no less—or it fails of its purpose and makes trouble. If the
pause is too [long] the impressive point is passed, and the
audience have had time to divine that a surprise is intended—and then you can't surprise them, of course.

On the platform I used to tell a negro ghost story that
had a pause in front of the snapper on the end, and that
pause was the most important thing in the whole story. If
I got it the right length precisely, I could spring the finishing ejaculation with effect enough to make some impressi-

ble girl deliver a startled little yelp and jump out of her seat—and that was what I was after. This story was called "The Golden Arm," and was told in this fashion. You can practise with it yourself—and mind you look out for the pause and get it right.

THE GOLDEN ARM

Once 'pon a time dey wuz a monsus mean man, en he live 'way out in de prairie all 'lone by hisself, 'cep'n he had a wife. En bimeby she died, en he tuck en toted her way out dah in de prairie en buried her. Well, she had a golden arm—all solid gold, fum de shoulder down. He wuz pow'ful mean—pow'ful; en dat night he couldn't sleep, caze he want dat golden arm so bad.

When it come midnight he couldn't stan' it no mo'; so he git up, he did, en tuck his lantern en shoved out thoo de storm en dug her up en got de golden arm; en he bent his head down 'gin de win', en plowed en plowed en plowed thoo de snow. Den all on a sudden he stop (make a considerable pause here, and look startled, and take a listening attitude) en say: "My *lan'*, what's dat!"

En he listen—en listen—en de win' say (set your teeth together and imitate the wailing and wheezing singsong of the wind), "Bzzz-z-zzz"—en den, way back yonder whah de grave is, he hear a *voice!*—he hear a voice all mix' up in de win'—can't hardly tell 'em 'part—"Bzzz-zzz—W-h-o—g-o-t —m-y—g-o-l-d-e-n *arm*?—zzz—zzz—W-h-o g-o-t m-y g-o-l-d-e-n *arm*?" (You must begin to shiver violently now.)

En he begin to shiver en shake, en say, "Oh, my! *Oh*, my lan'!" en de win' blow de lantern out, en de snow en sleet blow in his face en mos' choke him, en he start a-plowin' knee-deep towards home mos' dead, he so sk'yerd —en pooty soon he hear de voice agin, en (pause) it 'us comin' *after* him! "Bzzz—zzz—zzz—W-h-o—g-o-t—m-y— g-o-l-d-e-n—*arm*?"

When he git to de pasture he hear it agin—closter now, en a-*comin'!*—a-comin' back dah in de dark en de storm— (repeat the wind and the voice). When he git to de house he rush upstairs en jump in de bed en kiver up, head and years, en lay dah shiverin' en shakin'—en den way out dah he hear it *agin!*—en a-*comin'*! En bimeby he hear (pause— awed, listening attitude)—pat—pat—pat—*hit's* a-*comin'* *up-stairs!* Den he hear de latch, en he *know* it's in de room!

Den pooty soon he know it's a-*stannin'* *by de bed!* (Pause.) Den—he know it's a-*bendin'* *down* *over* *him*—en he cain't skasely git his breath! Den—den—he seem to feel someth'n *c-o-l-d*, right down 'most agin his head! (Pause.)

Den de voice say, *right at his year*—"W-h-o—g-o-t—m-y—g-o-l-d-e-n *arm?*" (You must wail it out very plaintively and accusingly; then you stare steadily and impressively into the face of the farthest-gone auditor—a girl, preferably— and let that awe-inspiring pause begin to build itself in the deep hush. When it has reached exactly the right length, jump suddenly at that girl and yell, "*You've* got it!"

If you've got the *pause* right, she'll fetch a dear little yelp and spring right out of her shoes. But you *must* get the pause right; and you will find it the most troublesome and aggravating and uncertain thing you ever undertook.)

DOCUMENT 74

Sensation versus Stagnation

SOURCE: T. De Witt Talmage, "Sensation versus Stagnation," from *The Masque Torn Off* (Chicago, 1882), pp. 514–26.

In 1880 the Reverend Jonathan B. Harrison, a clergyman of conservative tendencies whose tolerant comments on story-paper fiction have already been quoted (above, p. 403), asserted that one of the most important among the "dangerous tendencies in American life" was the effort to render preaching "more interesting and attractive to the masses" by making it "dramatic and entertaining, but, in large measure, unspiritual." Despite a general decline in piety, he said, there was a "popular liking for oratory in the pulpit," a "demand for what is called eloquent preaching." Unfortunately, however,

> The common American idea of pulpit eloquence is low and sensational. It means chiefly a rapid and emphatic utterance of sonorous sentences, with something extreme, paradoxical, and violent in the thought presented, though not much thought is required. People demand of the preacher that he shall arouse and excite them, and they enjoy with a kind of voluptuousness the temporary stimulus and thrill of emotion which the preaching causes.*

Henry Ward Beecher was perhaps the most celebrated master of this emergent style of preaching, but he had many imitators and a few rivals of almost equal renown. The principal one of these was T. De Witt Talmage, whose base of operations was also Brooklyn. (He was pastor of the Central Presbyterian Church

* *Certain Dangerous Tendencies in American Life* (Boston, 1880), pp. 213–14.

and held services in a tabernacle specially built for his use in 1874 that could seat forty-six hundred in "comfortably cushioned and carpeted pews.") Like Beecher, Talmage reached thousands of readers through regular weekly publication of his sermons; they appeared in London as well as in New York and Chicago.

The kind of pulpit eloquence practiced by Beecher and Talmage was quite different from the sedate theological treatises of old-fashioned clergymen or the sociological discourses presented by proponents of the social gospel. Both men were regularly trained in theological seminaries, but Beecher had greater intellectual pretensions than Talmage, for by means of his watered-down transcendentalism he attempted to accommodate such new concepts as the evolutionary philosophy of Herbert Spencer. Talmage, on the other hand, treated learned discussions of theology with scorn and preached "the most old-fashioned and literal Gospel constantly. . . ."† Unlike Beecher, Talmage was a noted evangelist, fully in sympathy with Dwight L. Moody's revivalism at a time when many conservative clergymen were hostile to it. He sat on the platform at Moody's first service in a remodeled skating rink in Brooklyn in 1875, and meetings were held in Talmage's Brooklyn Tabernacle to accommodate the overflow from Moody's revival.

Talmage's speciality, however, was the denunciation of metropolitan vice on the basis of information gathered on midnight tours in the company of police officers through the saloons and brothels in New York slums. Collected in books with titles of which the earliest is characteristic (*The Abominations of Modern Society*, 1872), and published both in this country and in England in large editions, Talmage's exposés belong to the lurid Matter of the City which George Lippard had domesticated in the United States a generation earlier. Marcus Cunliffe has demonstrated that Stephen Crane drew upon Talmage's writings about New York slum life in composing *Maggie, A Girl of the Streets* (1892).‡

† *Harper's Weekly*, XVI (3 February 1872), 101.
‡ "Stephen Crane and the American Background of *Maggie*," *American Quarterly*, VII (Spring, 1955), 31–44.

There arose no small stir about that way.—Acts xix:23.

What was the matter? Paul had been preaching some sermons that seemed to upset everything. People wondered what he would do next. What is that great bonfire in the streets of Ephesus? Why, Paul has been preaching against the iniquities of the day until the people have brought out nine thousand dollars' worth of bad books and tumbled them into the fire. There seemed to be no end to his impertinence, for now he is assaulting the Temple of Diana, a building twice as large as St. Paul's Cathedral, London; its roof supported by columns of green jasper; its sculptured altars of Praxiteles; its paintings [by] Parthasius, and its audience-room capable of holding fifty thousand idolators. In the month of May, when there were a great many strangers in the city, come there to buy medallion representations of that temple, Paul is thundering against it, until he completely ruins the stock of trinkets and spoils the medallion business, and the merchants gather together in a great indignation mass-meeting to denounce him, and say this thing must stop. Never before or since was there such a sensation. Paul was the great disturber of the day. He went to Iconium, and made a sensation. He went to Corinth, and made a sensation. He went to Jerusalem, and made a sensation. In other words, wherever he went, "there was no small stir about that way."

What is a sensation? Noah Webster says it is "an excited state of thought or feeling," and I cannot see anything more valuable than that, if the excitement of thought and feeling be in the right direction. But as the word "conservatism" has been twisted from its noble sense to mean a stupid do-nothingism, and as "liberalism" has been twisted from meaning generous treatment of opinions of others to mean a surrender of Christianity, so the word "sensation" has sometimes been twisted to mean everything erratic and reprehensible. But this I do declare: No one ever accomplished any good for church or State without exciting a sensation. Sensation is life. Stagnation is death. When sometimes I have been charged with making a sensation I have taken it as complimentary, and I have wished that the charge were more thoroughly true, and I promise, if God will help me, in the future I will make it more accurate!

I go on in this anniversary discourse, begun last Sabbath, and to-day speak to you chiefly of sensation versus stagnation. When I was a layman, worshiping in the pews, I noticed that religion was very often associated with dullness. . . . I noticed what every layman notices and remarks, that there is something radically wrong in the church of God at this day. In our boyhood days we tried every kind of art to keep awake in church. We ate caraway-seed, and cloves, and cinnamon, and held up one foot until it began to ache, and pinched ourselves until we were black and blue, or got stimulus from an older brother who stuck us with a pin, or saw the reproving look of some older sister that filled us with a sense of self-abnegation, until we looked up to the elders' and deacons' pew in the old Dutch church, and saw the seven sleepers (!) these consecrated men having lost their hold at the end of the second head of the discourse, and then we felt encouraged to think that, after all, there might be some chance for us when such very good men got asleep. What is the use of hiding the fact that there is more sleeping done in the churches than in any other kind of buildings? . . .

I put the complaint that the people do not like to come to church where it belongs. I say to the young men who are entering the ministry, if you want an audience, do as Paul did in my text—make a big stir. "There arose no small stir about that way." Men want help. Give them help, and they will come again. What do they care about the conventionalities of religion. How much of your Latin do they understand? What do they know about those sesquipedalion words that crawl through your senses like thousand-legged worms? They know that your chief anxiety is lest you lose your place in your notes. They know it is all a matter of calculation that the soap-lock curl comes down half way on your forehead, so that at the right moment you may brush it away with a hand delicate and diamonded. What do they care about your Arian controversy, when the controversy with them is how they can pay a note of $500 with $200, and how they can get comfort for the child they buried yesterday in Greenwood. . . . As long as we stick to the mere technicalities of religion in our churches, a few people may come because it has been eternally decreed that they should come; but the great masses of the people will not come any more than they would come and sit down in an ice-house, or accept an invitation to spend an evening in the vault of a cemetery. My friends, the great battle in this country is to be fought, not between Christianity and infidelity, but it is to be fought between honest Christian sensation and putrid stagnation. Let the churches of God wake up, hoist their banners, blow the trumpet, give the battle-shout, and in twenty years the earth will be the Lord's. It is high time we brought up the cavalry. The big guns are stuck in the mud. The great danger for the church of God in this day is not sensation, but stagnation. Sensation is life. Stagnation is death. As I told you in the beginning of this discourse last Sabbath, that my first resolution had been to preach a religion six thousand years old appropriate to the present time, so I now tell you, in the second place, that it has been my resolution, God helping me, never to be dull. . . . There is not anything that is available, in a parlor, or on a lecturing platform, in the art of persuading people to right feeling and right action that is not appropriate for the pulpit. I shall before long preach a sermon on the sarcasm of the Bible. Elijah used it. Paul used it. Christ used it. If a man say a thing in church merely to make people laugh, he is reprehensible; but if he say a thing so strikingly true that people do laugh, that is another thing. I do not care whether they cry, or laugh, or hiss, or applaud, or get up and go out, or what they do, if they only quit sin and with fleet foot start for heaven. For this purpose we must ransack the mineral, the botanical, the agricultural, the æsthetic, the scientific, the poetic, the literary, the historical, the astronomical worlds for illustration. If we cannot get anything better than two flints, we must smite them together and strike fire. In vain the gold chasing on the hilt of the sword, if the edge of it is not sharp enough to cut. In vain the $100 rod and reel from Conroy's, with fly of gold pheasant or gray drake, if we cannot catch anything. In vain the expense of the collegiate and theological education of seven or ten years, if we get hopelessly buried in our own armor. During the last war I was chaplain for a few weeks in a Pennsylvania regiment, and I was told one day that there was a cavalryman sick and wounded, and perhaps dying, in a barn four or five miles away. I walked over to see if I could be of any service to him. He asked me to take his horse, which was suffering from lack of attention, and his entire equipment up to headquarters at Hagerstown. I consented, but knew not what I was undertaking, for I had on and around me on the horse a heavy sword, a carbine, pistols, saddle-bags, and a great many other things I knew not the names of, and I was so overloaded I had to go on a slow walk and hold fast to the pommel of the McClellan saddle, and when I got half way up to headquarters the girth broke, and I went off, and it was a great job to get loaded up again. In the woods all around about there were stragglers from the Confederate army, but they did not seem at all affrighted at my warlike appearance! When I rode up to the encampment, and the boys gave three cheers for the chaplain who had been so brave as to capture a horse, my embarrassment exceeded my exhilaration. But I was then in the condition in which a multitude of us are in the ministry to-day—loaded up with equipment enough to slay Apollyon, yet we cannot wield it, and we go along on a slow walk, afraid that our system of didactic theology will fall off on one side, or our church history or homiletics will fall off on the other side—carefully guarding to keep our theology right side up, while David felled Goliath with a shepherd-boy's sling, and Shamgar slew six hundred men with an ox-goad. I believe in the day of eternity it will be found out that some backwoods Methodist minister who never had but three months' education in his life, but set all the prairies on fire with zeal for God, and in the summer preached to his audience in his shirt-sleeves, will be found to have done more for the race than some of us who have all the titles of the schools, and who wrap around us the gowns and the bands and the surplices, which are not enough to keep us from freezing to death in an ecclesiasticism twenty degrees below zero!

But I go further, and tell you in this anniversary sermon that in the decade through which we have passed I have tried to carry out the resolution of never explaining to you what I do not understand myself. I believe in God's sovereignty and man's free agency. Harmonize them I cannot. I believe God is one, and yet in three persons. How that can be I know not. I believe that Christ had in his nature the divine and the human. How they were interjoined I cannot explain. For years I tried to explain these things, but I found that the greatest undertaking of my life was to make other people understand that which was beyond my comprehension. Sometimes when I had preached on the subject and hoped that it was plainer to the people than it was to myself, and pronounced the benediction, some plain man at the foot of the pulpit would ask me a question which would confound me, and I would have to tell him I would see him some other time! Now, there are some things that I do know. Sin is wrong; that I know. Christ came to help us out of it; that I know. Christ has a sympathy compared with which fatherly and motherly compassion is cruelty; that I know. His grace is mighty for mightiest calamity; that I know. The religion of Jesus Christ kindles in the soul great expectations amounting to a supernatural glee; that I know. That religion is a sedative to soothe all nervous perturbation, that [it] is a stimulus to arouse inertia, that it pulls up by the root the red dahlia of war, and plants instead thereof the white lily of peace; that I know. That it hangs around the dying couch of the Christian the saffron, and orange, and purple clouds of a heavenly sunrise, and swings back the gates of glory so wide that they shiver the gates of the sepulcher; that I know. Now, knowing these things beyond all controversy, knowing them beyond all mistake, knowing them from my own experience, or from my own observation, what is the use of my taking your precious time and my precious time in telling you what I do not know? We had a great fire at my house the other day. I burned up five hundred manuscript sermons, for when I began to preach I wrote out all my sermons, word for word. In those sermons that I burned up I explained all the mysteries of religion, and the doctrine of election was as clear as a Scotch mist or a San Francisco fog. As I stood by the kitchen fire where these manuscripts were burning, I really thought they threw out more warmth than they had ever thrown out before! . . .

Again, my dear people, in this decade in which it has been my happiness to administer to you, it has been my resolution to smite sin wherever I see it, reckless of the consequences. The reason sin triumphs in this country is because we do not call it by the right name. Ministers of the gospel were intended to be the Lord's artillerymen, and to fire away at iniquity wherever they see it, and let other people provide the ambulances. What has been the cause of the excitement over the sermons I have been preaching for the last three or four months? Because they were awfully true. You see a group of dogs fighting on the commons, and you throw a stone at them. Which one howls? The one that is hit. The worst sign of the times is that the public make so many ministers hush up. You might as well try to stop Asiatic cholera, or yellow fever at Grenada and New Orleans, by saying nothing about them. In order that I might take straighter aim at iniquity, I went and explored the dark places of our cities. . . . To hear some of my dear brethren talk, you would have supposed I had been the first clergyman that had ever made an exploration of underground life in our great cities. Why I could call off the names of scores of ministers and evangelists in the country who have made the same tour. The police who took me around those nights told me they had taken them around on the same rounds. I could make a big disturbance, if I had the heart, in a great many churches in Brooklyn and New York; but I never make any disturbance! The difference between my exploration and the exploration of these other dear brethren was, that they said nothing about it, except among ministerial brethren, while I uttered it in the hearing of my people, announcing the thunders of the Lord God Almighty against the crimes and warning the young men of this country to look out. The bar of God will decide which was the better plan—to look at iniquity and say nothing about it, or to look at iniquity and give the warning, not only so far as I may reach from this platform, but through these journalists, whom I shall, to the day of my death, thank for their kindness. . . .

But once more and this will close these anniversary thoughts which I have been presenting for two Sabbaths. I have tried to present to you a religion which would not leave a man in the lurch. What was the trouble with those trains that came out from Chicago, a week ago last Thursday? They started out beautifully and swiftly, but they came to the snow-banks and stopped, and the trains were disbanded. Oh! my friends, we want to get on a through train. We do not want a religion which takes us smoothly through this life, merely for a few miles on earth, and then puts us out at the snow-bank of a cheerless grave. No! You may take that train. I will not take it. I will start on a highway where the marble of the tomb is only the milestone on a road always brightening and improving. "Come with us and we will do you good; for the Lord hath promised concerning Israel." I have told the men who feel themselves to be the worst, that Christ died for them, and they have come. And now this morning, I want you all to join me on this path to heaven. It is all tracked up. Examine these tracks in the dust of the road. Ah! those are little feet that have been tracking the road. Have you lost children? They went up this way. I see their tracks on the road. But here there are larger footsteps but footsteps that were very short—very short steps, as though they were the steps of the aged. Is your father gone? Is your mother gone? They went up this way. And behold! in the track of the road I see the mark of a foot that was bare, and a scar in the hollow of the foot. Oh! it was the footstep of a wounded Christ. This is the way—walk ye in it.

D. PAINTING, CHROMOLITHOGRAPHS, SCULPTURE

When Mark Twain was in New York during the spring of 1867 as correspondent for the San Francisco *Alta California,* he reported on his visit to the exhibition of the National Academy of Design. His reactions bespeak the average intelligent but uninformed taste of the period. He begins by expressing gratitude for his ignorance of painting, "Because people who understand art find nothing in pictures but blemishes. . . . The very point in a picture which fascinates me with its beauty, is to the cultured artist a monstrous crime against the laws of coloring," just as "the very flush that charms me in a lovely face, is, to the critical surgeon, nothing but a sign hung out to advertise a decaying lung. Accursed be all such knowledge. I want none of it." And he adds: "I had no catalogue, and did not want any—because, if a picture cannot tell its own story to us uncultivated vagrants, we scorn to read it out of a book."*

The writer who would later brilliantly satirize the artistic efforts of Emmeline Grangerford was bored by

* *Mark Twain's Travels with Mr. Brown,* p. 238.

"more than half the paintings in the Academy" which were "devoted to the usual harmless subjects": "the same old pile of cats asleep in the corner, . . . the same old detachment of cows wading across a branch at sunset, . . . the everlasting farmers, gathering their eternal squashes; and a 'Girl Swinging on a Gate'; and a 'Girl Reading'; and girls performing all sorts of similar prodigies. . . ." But thirty or forty of the three hundred pictures on exhibition seemed to him "very beautiful": "I liked all the sea views, and the mountain views, and the quiet woodland scenes, with shadow-tinted lakes in the foreground, and I just revelled in the storms." He was particularly pleased by "a dreamy tropical scene—a wooded island in the centre of a glassy lake bordered by an impenetrable jungle of trees all woven together with vines and hung with drooping garlands of flowers. . . ." He also liked a genre picture representing "two libertines of quality teasing and jesting with a distressed young peasant girl, while her homely brother, (or sweetheart, may be,) sat by with the signs of a coming row overshadowing his face." On the other hand, he was repelled by a picture, "by one of the old masters, where six bearded faces without any bodies to them were glaring out of Egyptian darkness and glowering upon a naked infant that was not built like any infant ever I saw, nor colored like it, either." And he was displeased by the absence of "historical pictures" dealing with battles of the Civil War.†

In a later dispatch Mark Twain wrote at length about Albert Bierstadt's "The Domes of the Yosemite," which he considered "very beautiful." The topographical features were "correct": "they look natural; the valley is correct and natural; the pine trees clinging to the bluff on the right, and the grove on the left, and the boulders, are all like nature."‡

When one adds to these comments Walt Whitman's appreciation of John Mulvany's "Custer's Last Rally" (Document 78) one can endorse the generalization of Benjamin Rowland, Jr., that this was "an age in which taste was governed almost exclusively by the edifying

† *Ibid.*, pp. 239–41.
‡ *Ibid.*, pp. 249–50.

and pious sentiments expressed in a picture and, as a corollary, by the realistic means necessary to enhance this message and content."§

The illustrations in the following section exemplify the paintings, chromolithographs, and sculpture that appealed to the widest public during the later nineteenth century. They all have a highly representational surface in combination with an emblematic or even allegorical content; and they all appeal to strong but crude emotions: nationalism, domestic sentiment, the melodrama of physical conflict. The display might have been filled out by reproducing one of the panoramic landscapes by Bierstadt or Frederic Church (whose "The Heart of the Andes" Mark Twain also greatly admired),¶ but I have chosen to use instead works more explicitly related to the themes of popular culture discoverable in other media.

§ Introduction to James J. Jarves, *The Art-Idea* (Cambridge, Mass., 1960), p. xv.
¶ In a letter to his brother Orion (18 March 1860), in *Mark Twain's Letters*, ed. Albert B. Paine, 2 vols. (paged continuously) (New York, 1917), p. 46.

DOCUMENT 75

(PLATE 32)

Across the Continent

SOURCE: F. E. Palmer, "Across the Continent. 'Westward the Course of Empire Takes Its Way'" (Currier & Ives lithograph, 1868, from a painting by J. M. Ives). Courtesy of the Bancroft Library, Robert B. Honeyman, Jr., Collection, University of California, Berkeley.

The thousands of lithographs published by Currier & Ives during the middle and later decades of the nineteenth century constitute an almost inexhaustible source of information about the attitudes of the popular audience at which the pictures were aimed.* "Across the Continent" gathers in emblematic form the images which most Americans of the post-Civil War period associated with the West: the dramatic landscape of mountain and plains; the Indian, as a warrior on horseback or in a more pastoral role paddling his canoe along the improbable river in the middle distance; the train of covered wagons headed West into an apparently infinite expanse of desert; the decorous labor with ax and spade of the four men in lower left corner; the solid, comfortable log cabins of the village which has just sprung up on the plains, with its church and public school carefully specified; the telegraph line under construction; and the passenger train on the "Through Line—New York-San Francisco," its locomotive spouting smoke as it too heads West toward the geometrical horizon. It is a visual typology of historical stages, implying that the occupation of the continent by a healthy and virtuous people is being accomplished with breakneck speed and without suffering or hardship. The effort

* Morton Cronin, "Currier and Ives: A Content Analysis," *American Quarterly*, IV (Winter 1952), 317–38.

to render a vast historical process visually recalls Thomas Cole's series of paintings called "The Course of Empire" (1836); but this American empire can not be imagined as declining. The picture, in fact, is an iconographic counterpart of the conception of the Westward movement that underlies the references to the frontier as safety-valve in Documents 60 and 63 above.

DOCUMENT 76

(PLATE 33)

The Spirit of '76

SOURCE: Archibald M. Willard, "The Spirit of '76" (painting, 1875). Courtesy of the Western Reserve Historical Society, Cleveland, Ohio.

Willard is a prime exemplar of the American vernacular artist. The son of a Baptist minister, he grew up in a succession of small towns in Ohio, and was apprenticed to a "decorative painter" in a wagon and carriage shop. After service in the Civil War he returned to Ohio and, finding his pictures widely admired, set himself up in a studio in Cleveland. The painting now best known under the title "The Spirit of '76" was originally called "Yankee Doodle," and seems to have existed in at least two versions. It was first exhibited by a Cleveland art dealer named James F. Ryder, who in 1895 published an article describing its immense contemporary popularity. Relevant paragraphs from this article follow:

> The idea of the artist in painting the picture was to concentrate all the determination and enthusiasm possible in a few figures. No field afforded a better subject than the Revolution, with its determined old heroes and the air of "Yankee Doodle" to rouse them to the highest pitch of enthusiasm.
>
> The three chief figures meet all the requirements of the situation, and are in true keeping with the surroundings. Over them lower the clouds of smoke from a battle-field toward which they are marching. Behind them a few brave Continentals struggle up the hill, while by the side of a dismantled cannon lies a wounded soldier who raises himself on his elbow to give a last cheer to the stirring strains of

"Yankee Doodle." The lines have evidently been forced back. The dying soldier and the broken cannon show where the line has stood. The other soldiers have been retreating. But the three musicians advance, and the sound of their music thrills the retreating troops with new courage. Hats are in the air; the flag has turned; the threatened defeat is about to become a victory. The dying man raises himself to cheer. The trio of homespun musicians are discoursing with all their might that music whose shrill melody is so surcharged with patriotism. The old drummer in the centre, bareheaded, grand in his fearlessness, without coat, one sleeve rolled up as though he had turned from the plough to grasp the drumsticks, his white hair blown in the air, his eyes set close and defiant as though he saw the danger and feared it not, the sharp lines about his mouth showing a fixed determination,—all combine to make up that wonderful figure in our history which no rags could degrade nor splendor ennoble—the Continental soldier.

On the left of the brave old drummer is the fifer, who seems to have come to blow his fife, and he will do it as well here among the flying bullets as in the porch of his cottage. His eyes are fixed toward the sky as though reading the notes of his music on the clouds. Around his brow is a blood-stained handkerchief, which tells of the bullet which grazed yet spared him. His whole energy is poured into the reed at his lips, and one can almost hear the shrill notes of "Yankee Doodle" above the noise of battle.

On the right of the old man marches a boy, hardly in his teens, whose drum keeps time to the beat of the other. His face is upturned to the old man, perhaps his grandfather, as if to question perhaps the route or the danger ahead, but still with a look of rapt inspiration. No shade of fear lurks in his calm eyes, while the *"rub-a-dub"* of his little drum sounds as clear and distinct as the heavier roll of the aged drummer.

The entire group is conceived with a fervid sympathy which makes the observer concede sure victory to the combatants; victory also to the artist. The man who had carried the stars and stripes, marching under the same thrilling tune, put his heart into the picture. The work was an inspiration. Mr. Willard had no thought of depicting three generations of one family, but the inference is so natural that he has cheerfully adopted it from others.

The canvas is large and the figures are heroic in size. When finished, the picture was placed in the show window of my art store in Cleveland. The crowds which gathered about it blockaded the entrance to the gallery and obstructed the sidewalk to such an extent that it was found necessary to remove it from the window to the rear of the store, where it was on exhibition for several days, during which time all business in the store was discontinued on account of the crowds, which filled the place. The interest and enthusiasm which it created were remarkable. . . .

The painting was finally sent to the Centennial Exposition at Philadelphia and prominently placed in Memorial Hall, where it created so notable interest throughout the exposition, after which by earnest request it was taken to Boston and exhibited for several weeks in the Old South Meeting-House. From there it was taken to the Corcoran Gallery at Washington, thence to Chicago, San Francisco and other cities, always by request,—so great was the desire of the public to see the painting which had such welcome in the hearts of patriotic people.*

* James F. Ryder, "The Painter of 'Yankee Doodle,'" *New England Magazine*, 2d series, XIII (December 1895), 489–94.

DOCUMENT 77

(PLATE 34)

Custer's Last Rally

SOURCE: John Mulvany, "Custer's Last Rally" (painting, 1881, now in possession of H. J. Heinz Co., Pittsburgh; reproduced from a chromolithograph in the Library of the Kansas State Historical Society, Topeka, made probably in 1890 by D. C. Fabronius and published by the Chicago Lithographic and Engraving Company).

Robert Taft's thorough investigations led him to believe that this painting and another of the same subject, Cassilly Adams's "Custer's Last Fight," dating from the middle 1880s, are the two pictures "viewed, commented on and discussed by more people in this country than any other." (The third most popular painting in Professor Taft's ranking is Willard's "Yankee Doodle," Document 76.)*

Mulvany was born in Ireland in the 1840s but came to this country at the age of twelve. He received some training at the New York Academy of Design, served in the Union Army during the Civil War, and then studied at Düsseldorf, Munich, and Antwerp. After brief periods of residence in St. Louis and Chicago, he settled near the Iowa-Nebraska border in the early 1870s. In preparation for this painting, he visited the battlefield on the Little Bighorn and also observed Sioux Indians on a reservation. He painted the picture in Kansas City. From the first exhibition of it there in 1881, newspaper accounts were rapturous. The picture was taken East to Boston, where Mulvany revised it on the basis of suggestions by friends, and then to New

* Robert Taft, "The Pictorial Record of the Old West. IV. Custer's Last Stand—John Mulvany, Cassilly Adams, and Otto Becker," *Kansas Historical Quarterly*, XIV (November 1946), 361.

York, where Walt Whitman saw it and wrote the comment included as Document 78. Later it was shown in Louisville and Chicago, and probably in many other cities. It was bought by the Heinz Company soon after 1900. It measures 236 inches by 131 inches.

DOCUMENT 78

Mulvany's "Custer's Last Rally"

SOURCE: Walt Whitman, "Mulvany's 'Custer's Last Rally,'" first published in New York *Tribune*, 15 August 1881 (text from Walt Whitman, *Complete Prose Works* [Philadelphia, 1892], pp. 187–88).

Whitman's response to Mulvany's painting closely resembles other comments in newspapers. The slurring reference to "Messieur Crapeau" expresses the American cultural jingoism that was widespread in the 1880s and appears, for example, in Mark Twain's *A Connecticut Yankee* (1889).

When Whitman says that the painting is "all native, all our own and all a fact," he can be understood as asserting that the absence of "tricks" in its execution, the avoidance of "throwing . . . shades in masses," which makes the picture "at first painfully real," defines a native American style. Something similar seems to be intended in his further assertion that "There is an almost entire absence of the stock traits of European war pictures. The physiognomy of the work is realistic and Western." But does "physiognomy" refer to both style and subject matter, or to the emotions conveyed by the picture, or to subject matter alone? The realistic manner is solidly within the tradition of Düsseldorf, and can hardly be considered a native American technique.

Went to-day to see this just-finish'd painting by John Mulvany, who has been out in far Dakota, on the spot, at the forts, and among the frontiersmen, soldiers and Indians, for the last two years, on purpose to sketch it in from reality, or the best that could be got of it. Sat for over an hour before the picture, completely absorb'd in the first view. A vast canvas, I should say twenty or twenty-two feet by twelve, all crowded, and yet not crowded, conveying such a vivid play of color, it takes a little time to get used to it. There are no tricks; there is no throwing of shades in masses; it is all at first painfully real, overwhelming, needs good nerves to look at it. Forty or fifty figures, perhaps more, in full finish and detail in the midground, with three times that number, or more, through the rest—swarms upon swarms of savage Sioux, in their war-bonnets, frantic, mostly on ponies, driving through the background, through the smoke, like a hurricane of demons. A dozen of the figures are wonderful. Altogether a western, autochthonic phase of America, the frontiers, culminating, typical, deadly, heroic to the uttermost— nothing in the books like it, nothing in Homer, nothing in Shakspere; more grim and sublime than either, all native, all our own, and all a fact. A great lot of muscular, tan-faced men, brought to bay under terrible circumstances—death ahold of them, yet every man undaunted, not one losing his head, wringing out every cent of the pay before they sell their lives. Custer (his hair cut short) stands in the middle, with dilated eye and extended arm, aiming a huge cavalry pistol. Captain Cook is there, partially wounded, blood on the white handkerchief around his head, aiming his carbine coolly, half kneeling—(his body was afterwards found close by Custer's.) The slaughter'd or half-slaughter'd horses, for breastworks, make a peculiar feature. Two dead Indians, herculean, lie in the foreground, clutching their Winchester rifles, very characteristic. The many soldiers, their faces and attitudes, the carbines, the broad-brimm'd western hats, the powder-smoke in puffs, the dying horses with their rolling eyes almost human in their agony, the clouds of war-bonneted Sioux in the background, the figures of Custer and Cook —with indeed the whole scene, dreadful, yet with an attraction and beauty that will remain in my memory. With all its color and fierce action, a certain Greek continence pervades it. A sunny sky and clear light envelop all. There is an almost entire absence of the stock traits of European war pictures. The physiognomy of the work is realistic and Western. I only saw it for an hour or so; but it needs to be seen many times—needs to be studied over and over again. I could look on such a work at brief intervals all my life without tiring; it is very tonic to me; then it has an ethic purpose below all, as all great art must have. The artist said the sending of the picture abroad, probably to London, had been talk'd of. I advised him if it went abroad to take it to Paris. I think they might appreciate it there—nay, they certainly would. Then I would like to show Messieur Crapeau that some things can be done in America as well as others.

DOCUMENTS 79–80

(PLATES 35 AND 36)

Weighing the Baby

Checkers up at the Farm

SOURCES: John Rogers, "Weighing the Baby" (sculpture, cast plaster of Paris), March 1877. Courtesy of The New-York Historical Society, New York City.

John Rogers, "Checkers up at the Farm" (sculpture, cast plaster of Paris), December 1875. Courtesy of The New-York Historical Society, New York City.

John Rogers, born in 1829 in Salem, Massachusetts, worked as a youth in dry-goods stores and then in machine shops. His fascination with modeling as a hobby led him to spend a few months in Rome in 1858–59 studying with an English sculptor named Spence, but he was not interested in the neoclassicism he found in Rome, and returned to take a job in the city surveyor's office in Chicago. Here he achieved his first fame when he exhibited at a bazaar for the benefit of the Sanitary Commission an early version of the "Checkers up at the Farm" group (1859). Encouraged by the reception of this work, he went to New York and exhibited "The Slave Auction," which aroused the enthusiasm of abolitionists. He began producing plaster casts of his clay groups for sale, and by the later 1860s he had found a constantly increasing market for them at prices ranging from five to fifty dollars. The "Checkers" group, for example, sold for $15 (height 20 inches; base 13 by 17 inches; weight packed for shipment, 105 pounds). More than one hundred thousand copies of Rogers' sculpture groups were sold during his lifetime. His work was approved by critics as well as by the public. He was elected to the National Academy in 1863 and received a medal at the Philadelphia Centennial of 1876, where he exhibited twenty-nine groups. In 1865 Henry Ward Beecher wrote

Rogers: "I am especially gratified in the moral element that so plainly appears in all that you do. . . . You have the true and highest Artistic impulse."*

James Jackson Jarves, a pioneer critic with an expert knowledge of European painting, wrote in 1864:

> We now come to a man of a high order of ability, indeed, we may call it genius in its peculiar province, as original as he is varied and graphic, pure in sentiment, clever in execution, and thoroughly American, in the best sense of the word, in everything. If we were to compare the spirit of his compositions with foreign work, we should say that they included the finest qualities of Wilkie and Teniers. But this would not do him full justice. Beside dramatic power, picturesqueness of composition, naturalness and fidelity of detail, harmony and unity of proportions and grouping, he has a mine of humor, delicate sentiment, and elevated meaning, alike satisfying to head and heart. We know no sculptor like John Rogers, of New York, in the Old World, and he stands alone in his chosen field, heretofore in all ages appropriated by painting, a genuine production of our soil, enlivening the fancy, enkindling patriotism, and warming the affections, by his lively, well-balanced groups in plaster and bronze. Although diminutive, they possess real elements of greatness. In their execution there is no littleness, artifice, or affectation. The handling is masterly, betraying a knowledge of design and anatomy not common, and a thoroughness of work refreshing to note. His is not high art, but it is genuine art of a high naturalistic order, based on true feeling and a right appreciation of humanity. It is healthful work, and endears itself by its mute speech to all classes. The Village Post-Office, Returned Volunteer, Union Refugees, Camp-Fire, Village Schoolmaster, and Checker-Players aptly illustrate our praise. His pathos, *naïveté*, and simplicity of motive increase with his subjects, and give even to the commonplace almost the dignity of the heroic. The chief feature of his art is his power over human expression, bestowing

---

* Chetwood Smith and Mary C. Smith, *Rogers Groups: Thought and Wrought by John Rogers* (Boston, 1934), p. 97.

upon plastic material a capacity and variety of soul-action which, according to the canons of some critics, it was useless for sculpture to attempt. But he has been successful in this respect, and inaugurated a new triumph in his department. As an experiment, we should like to see the effect of one of his groups painted to life, to test the ability of color under such conditions as an auxiliary to form. At all events, John Rogers is a master of those motives which help unite mankind into one common feeling of brotherhood.†

"Weighing the Baby," one of Rogers' most popular works, shows how well he captured the essence of genre feeling. The sculpture relates a warmly humorous anecdote: the elder brother is slyly pulling on the baby's blanket to make the scales register an unbelievable weight. The clothing of all the characters and the appurtenances of the grocery store are rendered with the kind of literal realism now favored once again (with more ambiguous feeling) in "pop art."

The narrative content of "Checkers up at the Farm" is richer. A comment on the group published in 1896 shows how work of this sort was interpreted during Rogers' lifetime:

It represents a familiar New England Scene, with the city visitor at the home of the farmer. After the enjoyment and work of the day, a game of checkers is proposed. With all his ingenuity the city visitor has at last been forced by the clever Yankee into a position where he cannot "move" without being "taken." The expression on the face of the farmer, of simple childish joy at triumph over the rich and cultured city man, is excellently rendered, and his attitude is well given. The accessories are true to life; the checker-board rests on a flour barrel, and the farmer himself is sitting on a bushel basket. The face and attitude of the city man are also well expressed. He is represented as studying his position, and one sees that he is surprised and chagrined at being defeated by the farmer. Back of these two, to fill in the composition, there are the wife and child of the city visitor, the former amused and surprised

† *The Art-Idea*, pp. 220–21.

at her husband being beaten by this son of the soil, while the child amuses himself by kicking the checkers off the board. The whole group tells the story of a clean and simple New England life and of a happy democracy where the wealthy and the poor meet at intervals on a pleasant and manly footing.‡

As these comments suggest, much of Rogers' popularity was due to his ability to evoke memories of a simpler, preindustrial way of life—the emotional stock in trade of genre painting. The pastoral fantasy of harmonious social intercourse between rich and poor, even "at intervals," was especially consoling for a society torn by industrial conflict.

‡ William O. Partridge, "John Rogers, The People's Sculptor," *New England Magazine*, 2d series, XIII (February 1896), 707–8.

PART IX

Religious Revivalism

In the mainstream of religious history, the decades following the Civil War are notable for the theological controversy over Darwinism and, somewhat later, for the social gospel movement. But both these developments took place on an intellectual plane above that of popular culture. Much more conspicuous for the general public was the wave of revivalism in the 1870s and 1880s represented most characteristically by the careers of Dwight L. Moody and his musical director, Ira D. Sankey, although there were enough similar but less gifted preachers and singers to demonstrate that the movement was an outcome of social forces.

Religious revivals, of course, had been conspicuous features of American life since the Great Awakening of the second quarter of the eighteenth century, and Moody had much in common with such earlier revival preachers as George Whitfield or Charles Finney. Yet the post-Civil War wave of revivalism was different from earlier movements in several ways that clearly reveal the influence of the industrial revolution. Whereas pre-Civil War revivalism had flourished primarily in camp meetings and in small towns, Moody operated in cities—the expanding metropolises created by the centralization of industrial and financial activity. Moody displayed a remarkable power to organize his campaigns in accordance with urban conditions. It was often noted that his methods resembled those of big business. Committees of prominent ministers and laymen in the larger cities took charge of planning for the meetings; and it was the laymen, usually successful businessmen, who headed the finance and executive subcommittees, leaving to the local ministers the less vital functions. A suitable hall had to be provided, for the crowds eager to hear Moody were much too large to be accommodated by existing church auditoriums. In Philadelphia, for example, John Wanamaker offered the use of a former freight depot which he had bought with the intention of remodeling it as a warehouse. By the expenditure of $20,000 (contributed by Wanamaker) this vast structure was made into an auditorium capable of seating 11,000 persons. In New York Moody's first series of services, in 1875, was conducted in a skating rink; the following year he used Barnum's Hippodrome, remodeled at a cost of $10,000 (plus a weekly rental of $1500). Advance publicity in the form of posters and newspaper stories was systematically provided, at the expense of tens of thousands of dollars. Accommodations for reporters were arranged on the platform, and the services were reported in the press at formidable length.

Moody's attraction for business men is mentioned by Frank Norris in characterizing Curtis Jadwin, protagonist of *The Pit* (1903), an operator in Chicago real estate who eventually tries to run a corner on wheat. Describing a mission school he has organized "over on the West Side," Jadwin says to Laura Dearborn, his future wife:

". . . Moody put me up to it. He was here about five years ago, and I went to one of his big meetings, and then to all of them. And I met the fellow, too, and I tell you, Miss Dearborn, he stirred me all up. I didn't 'get religion.' No, nothing like that. But I got a notion it was time to be up and doing, and I figured it out that business principles were as good in religion as they are—well, in La Salle Street, and that if the church people—the men I mean—put as much energy, and shrewdness, and competitive spirit into the saving of souls as they did into the saving of dollars that [sic] we might get somewhere. And so I took hold of a half dozen broken down, bankrupt Sunday-school concerns over here on Archer Avenue that were fighting each other all the time, and amalgamated them all—a regular trust, just as if they were iron foundries—and turned the incompetents out and put my subordinates in, and put the thing on a business basis, and by now, I'll venture to say, there's not a better *organised* Sunday-school in all Chicago, and I'll bet if D. L. Moody were here to-day he'd say, 'Jadwin, well done, thou good and faithful servant.' "*

The list of sponsors for Moody's meetings sounds like a roster of business leaders: in Chicago, Cyrus McCormick and George Armour; in Philadelphia, Jay Cooke as well as Wanamaker; in New York, Cornelius Vanderbilt II and J. P. Morgan; in Boston, Amos A. Lawrence and Joseph Story. These men were, of course, moved in part by simple piety: Moody was a man of singularly contagious religious faith. But the business community was also uneasy about the danger to social stability from what were often called "the unchurched masses" of the rapidly growing cities. Moody's attitude toward economic and social problems was explicitly and vigorously conservative. In Great Britain, where he and Sankey had scored a sensational success before they invaded American cities of the East, the Earl of Shaftesbury had sponsored them because he feared the consequences of the broadening of the suffrage in the Reform Bill of 1867. Friedrich Engels later asserted that British conservatives had imported Moody and Sankey in order to strengthen the narcotic effect of religion on the masses.†

Yet many observers both in England and in the United States reached the conclusion that the revivalists had relatively little appeal to the urban working class. William G. McLoughlin, Jr., maintains that Moody's principal appeal was to the "country-bred, evangelically oriented, intellectually unsophisticated, and sentimentally insecure individuals" who had been uprooted by

* *The Pit* (New York, 1956), p. 123.
† William G. McLoughlin, Jr., *Modern Revivalism, Charles Grandison Finney to Billy Graham* (New York, 1959), p. 180.

the transition from an agrarian to an industrial economy.‡ Moody's message, he asserts,

> was directed toward the rural-born American, the farm boy who possessed at least a knowledge of reading, writing, and arithmetic, who was thoroughly imbued with the spirit and methods of the success myth, and who, if he were a pious evangelical church member, could easily get a white-collar job in the front office where he might put his employer under obligation to him by his push, tact, and industry.§

Young men such as these were quite distinct from the manual and unskilled laborers, who were likely to be recent immigrants from Europe and either Roman Catholics or "indifferentists"—in either case, inaccessible to a Protestant religious appeal.

Even so, the uprooted white-collar class of the cities provided a very large potential audience for the new revivalism. The lives of these people were hardly less grim than those of lower-class workers. They were confined to office or store for long hours, and came home at night to dingy boarding houses or flats. The countryside was almost inaccessible, and the commercialized amusements of the city, including the theaters, although tempting, were irredeemably wicked by the standards of the farms and villages from which the urban population was being recruited. To the lonely crowd the revival service offered a welcome release from monotony without the penalty of guilt. Mr. McLoughlin notes that

> The crowds, the hymnbook and photograph vendors, the singing, the general hubbub and excitement encouraged many to come to the warm, friendly meetings for a free evening of entertainment which bordered on the secular and yet which was good for the soul. For many regular churchgoers the meetings were social occasions for meeting friends and brightening drab lives. Moody wisely insisted that the advertisements for his meetings be placed on the amusement pages of the newspapers.¶

‡ *Ibid.*, p. 168.
§ *Ibid.*, p. 270.
¶ *Ibid.*, p. 232.

The crowds thus attracted were immense even by twentieth-century standards. Moody's associates tended toward larger estimates than did reporters for the newspapers, but there can be no doubt that at their peak in the 1870s he and Sankey regularly preached to audiences of ten thousand or more, and there were often two or even three services a day. It was claimed that at a series of Moody's meetings in Philadelphia from November 1875 to February 1876 the cumulative attendance exceeded one million, and that on one particular Sunday twenty-eight thousand different persons attended at least one of several services.

These are the outlines of a phenomenon that was novel then but has become familiar in our day. It exhibits the form imposed on the religious impulses of an uprooted Protestant population by an urban industrial society. Moody and Sankey attained a publicity comparable to that of champion athletes or television stars in the twentieth century. Everyone was familiar with their names and faces, and was continually informed of their comings and goings, their current activities, their future plans. Similar pressures would later produce the vulgarities and sensationalism of a Billy Sunday, but Moody's unblemished integrity stood the test: he remained humble and, after his fashion, austere, discouraging hysteria and doing what he could to keep attention focussed on the simple gospel that he preached.

DOCUMENT 81

(PLATE 37)

The Revivalists in Brooklyn—Opening Service of Messrs. Moody and Sankey in the Rink

SOURCE: Anonymous, "The Revivalists in Brooklyn—Opening Service of Messrs. Moody and Sankey in the Rink" (composite steel engraving and wood engraving?), *Harper's Weekly*, XIX (6 November 1875), 900–1.

Moody had attained prominence as a lay volunteer worker in home missionary activities in Chicago—in the newly organized Y.M.C.A. and in a church he founded in a slum district on the south side. He had no formal theological training, and only a few years of elementary schooling. Although he had been an itinerant revival preacher in the Middle West, his fame dated from a tour of England, Scotland, and Ireland in 1873–75 with Ira D. Sankey as his musical director. His audiences in the British Isles frequently numbered six thousand or more; two tabernacles were built in London to house his revival meetings. The service in a converted skating rink in Brooklyn depicted in the woodcut from *Harper's Weekly* was his first appearance after his return to this country. The auditorium could seat six thousand, and reporters for the newspapers estimated that five thousand more tried to enter. Streetcar companies built special tracks to the doors to accommodate the crowds.

On the platform in the foreground of the drawing are seated local ministers, the committee on arrangements, newspapermen, and an improvised choir trained by Sankey to lead the congregation in group singing. Sankey sits at the right of the preacher at the small reed organ that was the only instrumental accompaniment he used.

Mr. Moody's Work

SOURCE: Anonymous, "Mr. Moody's Work," New York *Herald*, 16 November 1875, p. 3, col. 1.

This stenographic transcript of a sermon delivered by Moody in the remodeled skating rink in Brooklyn illustrates his informal vernacular style and his ability, reminiscent of Mark Twain on the platform, to move quickly from broad humor to pathos.

MR. MOODY'S WORK

The Evangelist in Brooklyn and New York

INCREASING INTEREST DEVELOPED

Evening Meeting at the Rink

Something more than the usual crowd assembled in the Rink last evening—6,000 tickets were given out for the one meeting. The time was occupied, as is the general custom before the commencement of the meeting, in the singing of hymns by the choir. Among those on the platform were Bishop Foster and Mr. Hillman, of Troy, N.Y., compiler of the "Revivalist" and President of the Round Lake Camp Meeting Association. The meeting was opened by the singing of the 92d hymn,

Oh, think of the home over there.

Mr. Moody, after a prayer by Dr. Parmly, gave out the notices for the week and expressed his satisfaction at the new set of faces before him. Mr. Sankey then sang the 17th hymn,

Knocking, knocking, who is there?

—after which Mr. Moody read a few verses from the fourteenth chapter of Luke, then offered an earnest prayer that this week might be the mightiest of their work in Brooklyn, which petition was indorsed by hearty "Amens" all over the building. Mr. Sankey sang as a solo the eighty-first hymn. Mr. Moody surpassed any of his previous efforts last night; his earnestness was felt by every one of his hearers, and hundreds were affected to tears. He began his remarks by saying:—I want to call your attention this evening to one clause in the passage I have read to you, "I pray thee have me excused." Those three men invited to the feast wanted to be excused; it says, "They all with one consent began to make excuses." Did you ever stop to think what would take place if God should say, "I will take away all that want to be excused." If that should take place to-morrow I should have a slim audience to-morrow night. I should preach to empty chairs. "With one accord they began to make excuses," and they have kept it up pretty well ever since. They have a great many children living to-day. Bear in mind they were not invited to anything disagreeable; they were not invited to go to the Rink and hear some stammering preacher. They were invited to a royal feast. I have got a royal feast here to-night for you, and you are invited by the King of Kings. He wants you all there; He invites every one in all the universe. It is to a feast and it is a king that invites us, and He wants us to come. He don't mock you by inviting you and then not giving you the power to come. You can come if you will. But "They all, with one accord, began to make excuses." If a man prepares a feast they all hasten to come, but if God prepares a feast excuses rain in. If I should get off this pulpit and ask that lady why she don't accept God she would have an excuse

ON THE END OF HER TONGUE.

If one were not there Satan would put one there; that is what he has been doing for 6,000 years. Adam's excuse was, "It is this woman that thou gavest me"; laying the blame on God. You cannot exhaust the excuses; but let me say you can tie them all up in a bundle and label them lies. Look at these three men and see what their excuse was. The first says, "I have bought some land and must go to see it"—a good business man would say, "Why did he not see it before he bought it?" It was not that he was afraid some one would step in ahead of him, but "I must go and look at it." Strange excuse! Then supper time is no time to look at land; you want light to examine land. The second said, "Well, I have bought five yoke of oxen and I must go and prove them." Why did he not prove them when he bought them? Another downright lie. "They all with one accord began to make excuses"; they did not have them; they had to make them. The third man had married a wife and could not come. (Laughter.) Why not take the wife along—a newly married wife would like to go to a feast—or else, if she would not come, leave her at home? But you see on the face of these excuses that they were meant to ease the conscience. Some of you smile at these excuses, but have you anything better to offer? Eighteen-hundred years have rolled away; have men grown any wiser? I think not. I never have found one single excuse better than these three men gave. It is easy enough to laugh at them, but I honestly think our excuses a great deal worse than those. The greatest excuse is the Bible, and of all the sceptics and infidels there is not one who reads it through; they read a chapter here and there and say it is all dark and mysterious, and condemn the whole book. People are very guarded about giving opinions of men's books, but they are very free to condemn this book. A man must be born of God before he can understand godly things. There is one thing you understand—that you have sinned, and you know God is the friend of sinners. Take Him for a friend and you will begin to understand it. Suppose I should ask my little boy, six years old, if he had learned how to read and write and spell, and he should say, "Why, papa, I have been all day trying to learn a, b, c," and I should say, "I'll take you out of that school, you don't learn anything," you would say, "Moody, you have gone clean mad." That is about the way men reason and talk about the Bible. It will take us all eternity to know about God. Let me say, if there is any sceptic here who gives that as an excuse he will not appear at the marriage supper of the Lord, and give that as an excuse you will never give it at the throne of God. We see that it is a mighty power when men take it up with all their hearts. Some make the excuse of false professors in religion. They don't want to associate with hypocrites. What is that to you? This is an individual matter. Because there are hypocrites in the Church is no reason for your not coming. If you really do not want to associate with hypocrites you had better come to God, because they will not be at the marriage supper of the Lamb. We don't ask you to follow us; you might find a great many flaws in our characters, but you can find no flaw in our Head and Redeemer, who went up on high. God is pure and spotless, and there is no reason why you should not believe in Him. Some say it is a hard thing to be a Christian, hundreds say that the devil is an easy master and the Lord is a hard one; God commands us to do what we cannot do, and then punishes us eternally for not doing it. Do you believe that? Satan never invented such a lie as that. See what Scripture says:—"My yoke is easy and my burden is light." Scripture says:—"The way of the transgressor is hard." Do you believe the Scriptures? Don't go out of this Rink saying the devil is an easy master and God is a hard one. Ask those who have

SERVED BOTH MASTERS.

I have served both masters, and I testify that the devil has been a hard master; but I have been in the service of Christ for twenty years, and God is a delightful and easy master, and I offer Him to you to-night. Those of you who know, is God a hard master? (A unanimous "No" from the congregation.) This night change masters. This night accept the invitation. Come this night, and there is not a power on earth nor in hell that can keep you from Him. Oh! prodigal, return. Oh! wanderer, come home.

After a few seconds of silent prayer Mr. Sankey broke the intense silence by beginning to sing, in an unutterably plaintive voice, "Come Home, Come Home." After he had sung one verse Mr. Moody was obliged to stop him. The effect was so great on the audience that many sobbed aloud.

Mr. Moody then brought the meeting to an abrupt close.

DOCUMENT 83

The Prodigal Son

SOURCE: Dwight L. Moody, "The Prodigal Son," in *Moody: His Words, Work, and Workers*, ed. W. H. Daniels (New York, 1877), pp. 126–37.

This sermon was probably revised by Moody for publication from a stenographic transcript of his actual remarks, which were usually extemporized from meager notes. It was preached in the Chicago Tabernacle, probably in the autumn of 1876.

The parable of the Prodigal Son was especially relevant to the situation Moody had recently described in an appeal for funds to support the Y.M.C.A. A reporter summarized his remarks as follows:

> Its especial intent was to reach the young men of the country, to extend to them a helping, kindly hand when they come up to the city from the country. Years ago, when young men came to the cities to go into business, they lived with their employers, but now it was very different. They were obliged to live in boarding houses, and none of the attractions of a home were thrown around them. They wandered out into the streets at night, and were induced to enter the haunts of vice by the attractions and comfort which they presented. The especial aim of the Young Men's Christian Association was to reach these young men when they first came to the city, to make them feel that they were among friends.[*]

As was customary, Sankey prepared a musical setting for Moody's sermon. He sang two solos related to it in

* New York *Herald*, 19 November 1875, p. 3, col. 3.

theme: "Calling Now" and "The Ninety and Nine" (Document 86).

We have for our text to-night the man Mr. Sankey has been singing about. The trouble with him was the same as with nine tenths of the men in this city who are away from God to-night. He started out wrong. If any one had told the young man that he needed the grace of God to keep him when he was starting out to make his fortune he might have laughed at it, but we see how poorly he got along without it.

I don't know why he wanted to go away from home. Perhaps he thought his father was too strict, because he wouldn't let him stay out late at night; perhaps he couldn't get along well with his elder brother; maybe his mother had died and left him to the care of some one who didn't love him. Perhaps she had died praying for her wayward son, and he wanted to get away from the place, so as to be able to forget her prayers, that troubled him every time he thought of them.

So he goes to his father and says, "Father, I think I could get along better if you would divide your estate, and give me my share now, and let me go and begin life for myself." I suppose the old gentleman was rich, and perhaps, weak-minded; at any rate he made a very great mistake. There is nothing worse for a young man than to give him plenty of money and send him out into the world alone. People talk a great deal about self-made men, and about poor men's sons who have to struggle for their places in the world; but I tell you, I have a great deal more respect for the rich man's son who turns out well than for the poor boy who has to work his way in the world. There is nothing that puts so many temptations in a young man's way as having plenty of money.

Well, the young man took his money and went off; perhaps he went down to Egypt to get as far away from home as possible, and having plenty of money I have no doubt he was very well received, and became very popular. He was well educated and agreeable; perhaps was able to sing, and could entertain his friends with comic songs. He used to go to the opera four nights in the week, and the other three nights he spent at the theater and billiard rooms. He was certain to have plenty of friends as long as his money lasted, but after awhile he got to the end of his rope, and then his friends all deserted him; just as they did a poor fellow whom I once knew, who had plenty of friends and money, but after awhile he broke down, and got into jail, and not one of his sporting friends ever came near him. Some Christian people who were visiting at the jail went to see him in the name of the Lord, and that woke him up to understand who his real friends were.

We read that after awhile this prodigal began to be in want. His friends were gone, and he had got down very low, but I am happy to say, he didn't get down low enough to beg.

There was no meaner thing a Jew could do than to take care of swine; but it is very much to his credit that he chose to do this rather than lie around the streets loafing and begging. I had a thousand times rather be a swine-herd than a beggar.

I can see him there among the swine-troughs, ragged and hungry, the tears standing in his eyes, as he thinks of his father's well-filled table; a long table, with a good many people around it, but not long enough to reach to him in that far away country.

We find that no one gave him any thing to eat. If he had been a pig they might have fed him, but being nothing but a man he was left to take care of himself.

O, my friends, that is just the way with the devil. He will lead you away from home, and off into a far country, and into pleasure and vice, and then, when you have lost every thing in his service, he will push you down, down, down; and when he gets you into the ditch, or into the pit of ruin, instead of giving you any thing to help you he will laugh at you, and mock you for your folly.

There was another thing which the prodigal lost besides his money, and that was, his testimony. Some of those old friends of his, if they chanced to see him out there among the swine, would doubtless laugh at him, and he, perhaps, would straighten himself up and say, "You laugh at me, and call me a fool and a vagabond because I am poor, and all in rags, but you needn't be so proud. I belong to a respectable family; my father has plenty of money; he lives in a fine house, and even his servants dress better than you do." How those young fellows would laugh at that! "*Your* father rich! You look like it, don't you? *Your* father have servants! *Your* father have clothes!" And then the poor fellow, thinking of himself, couldn't answer them a word. He had lost his testimony: nobody would believe that he was the son of a great rich man, up there in Judea.

Just so every backslider from God loses his testimony when he falls into temptation, and gets away from the favor of his Lord; and if he does sometimes stand up in meeting and talk to the people about the way of life they laugh at him, and say, "You don't look or act as if you were a child of God."

Sin took this young man away from home, just as it takes us all away from God. Now the question is, How did he come to get back again?

The parable tells us, that after awhile he came to himself; that is, he woke up to the fact that he was miserable because he was away from his father. There was one thing that the prodigal never lost:—he lost his home; he lost his money; he lost his clothes; he lost his good name; he lost his respectability; he lost his testimony; but he never lost his father's love. That was his right through it all.

I find a good many men who are living in sin, who wonder why it is that God does not answer their prayers. I will tell you why it is. God loves them too much to answer their prayers while they stay away from him. Suppose the prodigal son had written his father a letter, saying: "Father, I am in want; please send me some money." Do you suppose his father would have sent it? If he had it would have been the worst thing he could have done for the boy. The proper thing for the prodigal to do was to go home; and just as long as his father kept him supplied with money off there in that foreign country there was no reason to expect him to come back. If you have gone off into sin, if you have got away from God, you must never expect him to feed you, and clothe you, and to supply all your wants, the same as if you were in his house sitting down with him and the other children at his table. What God wants of his "prodigal sons" is for them to come home, and when he gets them with him he will supply their wants and answer their prayers.

Well, I can imagine that one day a neighbor from his native town inquired after the young man, and, at last, found him down there among the swine. Of course he was greatly surprised.

"Why don't you go home to your father?" says the neighbor.

"I don't know," says the prodigal. "I am not quite sure that my father would receive me, I am such a miserable vagabond."

"Your father loves you as much as ever," says the neighbor.

"My father! Did you see him? How do you know he loves me? Does he ever speak of me?"

"Ever speak of you! He talks of you by day and dreams of you by night. I was over at his house the other day, and when I told him I was coming into this country, the old man, with tears in his eyes, begged me to look up his lost boy, and tell him to come right home, for his father was breaking his heart because he stayed so long away."

O, if there is a poor prodigal here to-night, don't go on in that terrible delusion, that your heavenly Father has forgotten you! There isn't one of God's children that is ever out of his memory.

One of the chief things in the way of this young man was his pride. I suppose he would have gone home long before he did if it hadn't been for his pride; but he said to himself, "I came away with abundance, and now I don't like to go back in rags." But at last he comes to himself, and when he finds out that his father loves him, and wants to have him back again, he makes up his mind to return.

You can see him out there in the field, as he gets down on his knees and buries his face in his hands, like Elijah upon Mount Carmel; saying to himself, "I think I had better go home; there is no one in the world that loves me as much as my father. I am surprised that he is not altogether ashamed of me, for well he might be. But I have been here as long as I can stand it, and now I will arise and go to my father!"

Then the memories of the old home come back to him. He calls to mind his childhood, and how his mother used to sing to him and pray with him, and how kind and good his father was, and how carefully they watched over him, and kept him away from harm and evil. He thinks of the tears of his mother, and remembers the day they buried her—I cannot help thinking that he had lost his mother, for there isn't any thing said about her in the story—he remembers the morning he left home, and how his old father wept over him, and how he prayed at the family altar that the Lord God of heaven would save his boy from sin, and how he asked the Lord to send his angel to watch over him. Then the prodigal opened his eyes and looked at himself; shoeless, coatless, hatless—just covered with miserable rags. "Why," he says to himself, "the very servants in my father's house are better off than I; there is bread enough and to spare in my father's house, and I am so starved that my bones almost prick through my skin: *I will arise and go to my father!*" O, that thousands here to-night would say with this prodigal, "I will arise and go to my Father." Nine tenths of the battle was won when he said those words.

And now I see him starting on his way. He goes to the man that owns the pigs and tells him he isn't going to take care of them any longer; he says he has heard from his father, who is a great and good man up there in Judea, and he is going back to him; he has been away too long already.

There is joy up in heaven now. I see the guardian angel who watches over him smiling and happy. I hear them ringing the bells of heaven because the lost one has come to himself and started for home.

It is a long journey and a hard one, but he never looks behind him: he has had too much of that far away country already, and his only thought is of his home.

I can imagine his feelings as he comes to his native land. The sky is brighter, the fields are greener, than the fields and skies in that strange country. Sometimes, as he trudges along his weary way, he wonders if his father is still living, or if he has died with a broken heart because of his wayward son.

At last he comes in sight of the old mansion. There is the old man out on the flat roof! Many a time he has been there before. Many a time his eye has been looking in the direction where his boy went.

He sees his boy afar off. He cannot tell him by any thing he has on; but love is keen. He starts for him. You can see his long white hair floating in the wind as he leaps over the highway; the spirit of youth has come back to him. The servants look at him and wonder what has come over him. It is the only time God is represented as running, and that is to meet a poor returning prodigal soul.

"But when he was yet a great way off his father saw him, and had compassion" on him. He didn't say, "He went away without cause, I will not go to meet him;" but, rushing out, he falls upon his neck, and kisses him; and the servants come running out to see what is the matter.

And now the boy begins to make his speech: "Father, I have sinned against heaven, and in thy sight, and am no more worthy to be called thy son"—and just as he is going to say, "Make me as one of thy hired servants," the father interrupts him, and says to one servant, "Go bring the best robe and put it on him!" and to another, "Go to my jewel-box and get a ring and put it on his finger!" and to another one, "Go and get him a pair of shoes!" and to another, "Go and kill the fatted calf!" What joy there was in that home!

My friend, don't you know that since that time this story has been repeated nearly every day—prodigals coming home—and I never yet heard of any one but what had a warm welcome. I have got a letter here, I think it is one of the last letters I received from England. The letter goes on to state that a son and husband had left his father's house—left his wife and children—without a cause; and now, in closing up the letter, the sister says: "He need not fear reproach, only love awaits him at home." That man may be here to-night. My words may reach him, and if so I beg him to return from his erring ways. Listen! your sister says that no reproach or harsh words will meet you on your return home; only love will welcome you when you enter the door.

The father of the prodigal did not reproach his boy: and so God does not reproach the sinner. He knows what human nature is—how liable a mortal is to go astray. He is always ready to forgive and take you back. Christ says he will forgive; he is full of love, and compassion, and tenderness. If a poor sinner comes and confesses, God is willing and ready to forgive him.

There was a lady who came down to Liverpool to see us privately; it was just before we were about to leave the city to go up to London to preach. With tears and sobs she told a very pitiful story. It was this: She said she had a boy nineteen years of age who had left her. She gave me his photograph, and said, "You stand before many and large assemblies, Mr. Moody. You may see my dear boy before you. If you do see him, tell him to come back to me. O, implore him to come to his sorrowing mother, to his deserted home! He may be in trouble; he may be suffering; tell him for his loving mother that all will be forgiven and forgotten, and that he will find comfort and peace at home." That young man may be in this hall to-night. If he is, I want to tell him that his mother loves him still.

I may not be speaking to Arthur to-night, but there may be a great many other Arthurs who have left their father's house. Let me entreat you to go home. Send a dispatch that you are coming, and start at once. And O, what joy there will be in those sorrowful homes when these long-lost prodigals return! By and by you may learn that your mother is dead, and then nothing will ever comfort you for having broken her heart. Wanderer, arise and go to thy father, who loves thee; to thy mother, who weeps over thee; and let us pray that multitudes of souls wandering from God may be this very night brought home.

Some of you say, "I don't believe God will forgive a sinner, or take him back all at once, when he has been disobeying him for so many years."

Wouldn't you do it? Come, now, if you were to find your long-lost prodigal son in the kitchen when you got home—in the kitchen because he didn't feel worthy to go into the parlor—wouldn't you forgive him, after he began to see what a sinner he had been?

I can tell you something about this out of my own experience. My father died when we were little children, and my good mother had a hard time with her large family of boys and girls. After a while one of the older boys took it into his head that he could make his fortune all alone by himself, and so he ran away.

For years and years we heard nothing of him. Sometimes it seemed as if my mother's heart would break. "O, if I could only know he was dead," she would sometimes say, "it would be better than this. Maybe he is sick and in need, or maybe he has fallen in with wicked men, who will make him as bad as themselves."

We used to sit around the fire on the stormy winter nights and listen to the stories that mother used to tell us about our father, about what he said, how he looked, how he was kind to a friend, and lost a great deal of money by him, and so our little home was mortgaged, and we were poor; but if any body happened to speak the name of that lost boy a great silence would fall upon us, the tears would come into my mother's eyes, and then we would all steal away softly to bed, whispering our good-nights, because we felt that the mention of that name was like a sword thrust to the heart of our mother.

After we got to bed we would lie awake and listen to the roaring of the wind among the mountains, thinking perhaps *he* was out in the cold somewhere. Maybe he had gone to sea, and while we were snug in bed he might be keeping watch on the wave-beaten deck; perhaps climbing the mast in just such darkness and storm. Now and then, between the gusts, a sound would be heard like the wail of the summer wind when it used to make harp-strings of the leaves and branches of the great maple-trees in the door-yard: now, soft and gentle; then, rising louder and louder. How we would hold our breath and listen! Mother was sitting up to pray for her lost boy. Next morning, perhaps, she would send one of us down to the post-office to ask for a letter—a letter from *him*, though she never said so. But no letter ever came.

Long years afterward, when our mother was growing old, and her hair was turning gray, one summer afternoon a dark sunburned man, with heavy black beard, was seen coming in at the gate.

He came up under the window first, and looked in as if he were afraid there might be strangers living in the house. He had stopped at the church-yard, on his way through the village, to see whether there were two graves instead of one where our father had been laid so many years ago, but there was only one grave there: surely his mother was not dead. But still she might have moved away. Then he went around and knocked at the door, and his mother came to open it.

Years of hardship and exposure to sun and storm had made him strange even to his mother. She invited him to come in, but he did not move or speak; he stood there humbly and penitently; and, as a sense of his ingratitude began to overwhelm him, the big tears found their way over his weather-beaten cheeks. By those tears the mother recognized her long-lost son. He had come at last. There was so much of the old home in him that he couldn't always stay away. But he would not cross its threshold until he confessed his sin against it, and heard from the same lips which had prayed so often and so long for him the sweet assurance that he was forgiven. "No, no," said he, "I cannot come in until you forgive me."

Do you suppose that mother kept her boy out there in the porch until he had gone through with a long list of apologies, done a long list of penances, and said ever so many prayers? Not a bit of it. She took him to her heart at once; she made him come right in; she forgave him all, and rejoiced over his coming more than over all the other children that hadn't ran away.

And that is just the way God forgives all the prodigal souls who come back to him. O wanderer, come home! come home!

DOCUMENT 84

The Gospel Sowers

SOURCE: Charles Nordhoff, "The Gospel Sowers," New York *Herald*, 18 November 1875, p. 4, cols. 1–3.

Like all metropolitan papers in cities where Moody and Sankey held services, the New York *Herald* reported the meetings at what would now seem astonishing length—sometimes to the extent of three or four thousand words daily, with stenographic transcripts of the sermons and prayers, and even the texts of the hymns sung. In an editorial published the day after the first revival service in Brooklyn, the *Herald* had expressed bewilderment over the popular excitement aroused by the evangelists. Moody, asserted the editorial, had nothing to say that was not said better every Sunday in any number of Brooklyn churches; he was a man of little education, and his sermons were no more than a collection of rather dull anecdotes and trite theological notions. Even Sankey's voice seemed disappointing after the immense reputation he had acquired in England. This on the whole favorable letter by Charles Nordhoff is perhaps an effort of the editors to redress the balance in the *Herald's* evaluation of the revival meetings. Particularly valuable are Nordhoff's perceptive comments on Moody's rhetoric and platform manner, placing him solidly within the vernacular tradition of campmeeting preachers rather than in the tradition of polished pulpit eloquence.

THE GOSPEL SOWERS

Mr. Moody in the Midst of His Great Work

HIS RELIGIOUS COMMON SENSE

The Proprieties of Prayer—Sankey as a Suppliant

THE SERVICES YESTERDAY

To THE EDITOR OF THE HERALD:—

I send you, at your desire, some details of the remarkable meetings held by Messrs. Moody and Sankey in Brooklyn.

Mr. Moody is a short and somewhat stout man, with a full, dark beard, rather small eyes and an active, energetic, but not nervous, habit. His manner is alert and prompt, but not graceful; his voice is unmusical, and indeed harsh; his enunciation is very clear, but somewhat too rapid, yet can be heard and understood in every part of the Tabernacle or the Rink. In the latter place he has spoken to 7,000 people. He gesticulates but little, and his gestures are evidently extremely unstudied. His style of speaking is entirely conversational, and hearing him perhaps a dozen times I have never detected him in any attempt at eloquence. He is evidently, by his pronunciation, a Yankee, clipping some of the minor words in his sentences, as the farmers in the interior of Massachusetts do; but he has no "Yankee drawl." He speaks the language of the people and has the merit of using always the commonest words; and that he had no early educational advantages is plain from his frequent use of "done" for "did" and other ungrammatical colloquialisms. In short, his appearance is not imposing; his figure is not graceful, but that of a farmer or hard-working laborer; his voice is not melodious, nor has it a great range; his language is not choice. His externals, therefore, are all against him.

HIS MAGNETISM

In spite of all these disadvantages he has succeeded in attracting in England and here vast crowds day after day, who, at some of the Brooklyn meetings at least, are composed largely of cultivated people; he has, evidently, succeeded in interesting these crowds in what he has had to say; for nothing is more remarkable at the meetings than the absolute quiet and order, the attitude of interested listeners, which prevails among the audience. He has so entirely controlled his audiences that all noisy manifestations of religious feeling have been entirely suppressed; and at the same time no one who has sat in the meetings at the Rink or the Tabernacle can have failed to see that Mr. Moody's manner of presenting his subject is to an extraordinary degree effective in moving the hearts of his hearers, in stirring devotional feelings, in producing a profound impression upon them of the importance of the message he has to deliver.

Indeed, it has been a common remark that the audiences were even more remarkable than Mr. Moody, for not only are they spontaneous gatherings; to some of the meetings admittance can be secured only by the presentation of a ticket, and these ticket meetings, where each person must be supposed at least to have had a desire to attend strong enough to induce him to take the trouble of securing a ticket, are as crowded as any others. Nor are convenient hours selected for the meetings. There is one from eight to nine in the morning, which yet has seen the Tabernacle filled with an audience at least a third of whom were men. There is another at four o'clock in the afternoon, and again not less than a third of those present have been men. After the Rink meeting in the evening there has been held a meeting in the Tabernacle for young men exclusively, beginning at nine o'clock, and this, too, I have seen crowded, the large auditorium being on several occasions incapable of holding all who came. Nor is this all. Not the least remarkable evidence of the real and profound interest excited by Mr. Moody's exhortations is seen in what are happily called the "overflow meetings," composed of persons who could not gain admission to the regular meetings where Mr. Moody exhorts and Mr. Sankey sings, and who adjourn to a neighboring church to listen to some other preacher and to sing the songs which Mr. Sankey has made familiar to them. If any considerable part of the crowds who go to the meetings were composed of the merely curious these "overflow meetings" could not exist.

Nor is even this all. Mr. Moody does not hesitate to advise people to stay away from his meetings. He has repeatedly urged that his labors are for non-church goers; that he desires room left for this class, and he has taken special means to exclude from some of his meetings all who regularly attend a church—that is to say, he does not court his audiences, but the contrary. If you go to hear him it must be because you want to; if you go the second time it must be because he interested you the first.

RELIGIOUS COMMON SENSE

I have heard him a number of times, and always with interest and gratification; and it seems to me that this arose mainly—aside from the interest which any thoughtful man may have in this subject—because he gives the impression of possessing remarkable common sense, the clear head of a business man, and a habit of attending to the one thing which he has on hand and making all parts of the audience do the same. The meetings are opened and closed promptly at the preappointed hour; there is not even a minute of time lost during the meeting by delays; his own prayers are brief, very earnest and directly to the point; and his exhortations are a running commentary on passages of Scripture which he reads rapidly, always asking the audience to turn to the passage. Indeed, so far as Mr. Moody is concerned, there is little or no "machinery." He opens a meeting as though his audience were the stockholders of a bank to whom he was about to make a report. He has the air of a business man to whom time is extremely valuable, and slow and tedious people are evidently a trial to him. In some of the prayer meetings persons in the audience take an active part; and it happened not seldom in those that I attended that some earnest but indiscreet soul made a long and rambling prayer. Mr. Moody knew how to bring back the assembly to the strict object of the hour. In one of the morning meetings a clergyman made a very long, loud and rambling prayer, full of set and stale phraseology. The moment he ceased Mr. Moody said, "Let us now have a few minutes of silent prayer; that will bring us back to ourselves, and that's where we need to get." After a brief but impressive silence Mr. Sankey spoke a few words, pertinent, pointed and forcible, of prayer, and the meeting proceeded. I hope I shall not be thought disrespectful to the clergy if I say that the prayers some of them speak at these meetings contrast unfavorably with the brief and pertinent petitions of Messrs. Moody and Sankey. The formal and threadbare phraseology of the former is strikingly inappropriate in such meetings as these, and seemed to me often to jar painfully on the feelings of the people around me.

NOT A FANATIC

Again, in one of the morning meetings prayers were asked by various individuals in the audience for people in whom they were interested. One asked the prayers of the assembly for his sister; another for her brother; one for her mother; sons for fathers; fathers for sons and daughters; wives for husbands; one for a church out of town; another for a church in New York. Finally a man shyly asked the prayers of the congregation for himself. Instantly Mr. Moody said, "That's right. I like that. I like to hear people ask prayers for themselves. That's where they are often most needed." Such an incident seems to me to show that he is not an enthusiast who has lost his self-possession; and indeed this is evident at every meeting. He is, of course, enthusiastic in his work, but with the sobriety of a business man or of a general in battle.

Again, he is never in the least afraid of his audience.

Indeed, no one can hear him without feeling that he is entirely unconscious, as much so as a child. His own personality does not trouble him. Thus at the Rink one evening, while impressing upon the assemblage the importance of immediate conversion, he said:—"I wish that friend over there would just wake up, and I'll tell him something which is important to him." And again, at another meeting, he said:—"Salvation is offered to every man in this Rink, now, to-night, at this very moment: to that man there, who is laughing and jeering—the Son of Man comes to him to-night and offers salvation."

TOO MUCH PREACHING—WORK NEEDED

Though he aims to reach more particularly the non-church going population he concerns himself also about church-goers. "The churches," he said on one occasion, "need awakening; it is too easy nowadays to be a church member. If you pay your debts and keep out of jail, that seems to be enough." At a meeting for young men, held at nine o'clock P.M. in the Tabernacle, he said, "You don't need that I should preach to you. There is too much preaching. It's preach, preach, preach all the time; and you, young men, have heard sermons enough here in Brooklyn to convert every one of you. What you need is to work among yourselves. Let the converted speak personally with the unconverted—friend to friend. Then you'll see results."

DRAMATIC UTTERANCES

He has a good deal of dramatic power, and sometimes is very effective in a natural but strong appeal or statement. "When the prisoners at Philippi with Paul cried Amen," he said, "God himself answered them Amen!" Speaking of the probability that we forget none of the events of our lives, and that this is, perhaps, to be a means of punishment in a future state, he pictured an unrepentant sinner awakening in the other world, and his misdeeds coming back upon him. "Tramp! tramp! tramp! tramp!" he said, suiting the action to the word. "Do you think that Judas, after nearly 1,900 years, has forgotten that he betrayed his Saviour for thirty pieces of silver? Do you think that Cain, after 5,000 years, has forgotten the pleading look of his brother Abel when he slew him?" he continued. In speaking of Bible incidents or parables he usually brings them in in a dramatic form—as when he remarked, "If I want to know about some man in Brooklyn I don't ask only his enemies, nor only his friends, but both. Let us ask about Christ in this way. I call first Pilate's wife"—and relating her warning to Pilate went on to call other witnesses to the character and works of Jesus.

He has made an extremely close study of the Bible, and is evidently that formidable being, a man of one book, and thus he is able to give often a novel view of a Bible passage. Thus, speaking of Jacob, he remarked that his life was a failure; pointed out that Jacob himself had complained of it, and enumerated his tribulations, which followed his misdeeds. He enforced upon the audience the necessity of reading the Bible biographies not as though they were the lives of saints, but the truthfully written lives of mortal men, in which their bad as well as their good deeds were set forth for our instruction.

EPIGRAMMATIC ELOQUENCE

He has in perfection that faculty of epigrammatic statement which one often finds among the farmers and laboring people of New England, and this has sometimes the effect of humor. Thus, preaching at the Rink from the text, "Where the treasure is, there the heart will be also," he remarked:—"If you find a man's household goods on a freight train, you may be pretty sure to find him on the next passenger train." On another occasion he told of a woman who came to him saying that she had sought Christ three years without avail. "I told her there must be some mistake about this, because an anxious sinner and an anxious Saviour could not need three years to find each other." Speaking of persons who were ambitious to make themselves prominent, he remarked:—"It does not say make your light shine, but let your light shine. You can't make a light shine. If it is really a light it will shine in spite of you—only don't hide it under a bushel. Let it shine. Confess Christ everywhere." "Satan got his match when he came across John Bunyan," he remarked. "He thought he had done a shrewd thing when he got the poor tinker stuck into Bedford Jail, but that was one of his blunders. It was there that Bunyan wrote the 'Pilgrim's Progress,' and no doubt he was more thankful for the imprisonment than for anything else in his life."

Speaking of the goodness of God and of "grace abounding," he told a striking story of a rich man who sent to a poor friend in distress $25 in an envelope, on which he wrote, "More to follow." "Now," said he, "which was the more welcome—the money or the gracious promise of further help? So it is with God's grace; there is always more to follow. Let us thank God, not only for what he gives us, but for what he promises—more to follow." Contrasting the law and the Gospel, he said, "Moses, in Egypt, turned water into blood, which is death. Christ turned water into wine, which is life, joy and gladness." Speaking of future punishment in one of his Rink sermons, he said, "God will not punish us. We shall punish ourselves. When we come before God He will turn us over to ourselves. Go and read the book of your memory, He will say." Urging the duty of immediate repentance and the joy in heaven over a repentant sinner, he said, "If the President should die to-night, or if the Governor of the State should be shot, that would make an outcry here. But perhaps even so great an event would not be mentioned in heaven at all. But," said he, raising his voice a little, "if some sinner in this assembly were just now converted, there would be a great shout of joy in heaven." Dwelling upon the certainty of future punishment, he remarked, "Some people doubt it; they think God is so loving that He will make no distinctions in another world. But do you imagine that when men had become so wicked that God sent a flood to exterminate them because they were not fit to live on earth—do you suppose that when the waters came and drowned them, He took all this wicked generation into his bosom and left poor righteous Noah to drift about in his ark? Do you suppose that when His chosen people crossed the Red Sea, and Pharaoh's host were drowned, God took those idolatrous Egyptians directly to heaven and let the children of Israel wander miserably over the desert for forty years?"

THE PROPRIETIES OF PRAYER

Speaking of the real objects to be attained by prayer, he said, "If you have a thorn in your foot, you are to pray, not that God shall relieve you of the physical pain—He can do that too—but what you are to ask Him for is grace and strength to bear the pain patiently. We should thank God for our tribulations; they are sent to us as blessings; they bring us to Him." Again, "Many things we want God knows are not good for us; if He gives them it is that we may learn through suffering; if He withholds them it is because He loves us." Again he said, "Suppose a man going from here to Chicago, who knows me and my wife. When he gets there he goes to see her, and he says, 'I saw Mr. Moody in Brooklyn.' And then, when she is naturally anxious to hear all about me, suppose he goes on to speak about himself, to tell her how he felt on the cars, and where he stopped, and what he said and did and ate. Would not she presently tell him that it was not him she wanted to hear about, but me?" Nor is he backward in impressing upon those who listen to him their own responsibility. "People attending these meetings during these two weeks," he said, "will be either better or worse. They will not go away the same men and women. If I did not want to be a Christian do you think I would ever go where the Gospel is preached? If any of you have made up your minds not to be Christians I advise you to get up and go out at once. It is not safe for you to be here."

MR. MOODY'S INFLUENCE

I do not know whether these passages which I have given from Mr. Moody's exhortations will seem to those who read them as forcible as they were to me who heard them. I took down at the time what appeared to me his most striking utterances, as the best way of showing wherein his power over his audiences consists. That he is a man of genuine power there can be no doubt. He has gathered, and held in silent attention, and deeply moved, some of the largest assemblies that any speaker has addressed in America; at least in our day. For my part I do not doubt that his words have left a lasting impression upon a great many men and women. And he has done this without frantic or passionate appeals; without the least of what we commonly call eloquence. He has none of the vehemence of Peter Cartwright or Elder Knapp, and he possesses none of the personal advantages or culture of an orator. Instead of all these he has a profound conviction of the reality of the future life; a just idea of its importance compared with this life and of the relations of the two and an unhesitating belief in the literal truth of the Bible. It is, of course, his own deep and earnest conviction which enables him to impress others.

Mr. Sankey has an effective voice, a clear pronunciation, and, I should think, a quick ear to catch simple and tender melodies. His singing was, I suspect, more effective and affecting in England than here, because the hymns he sings were not as familiar to his English hearers as they are to Americans, most of whom have been brought up in Sunday schools, or have heard their children sing Sunday school hymns at home. He is evidently a favorite with the Rink and Tabernacle audiences, and he has a pathetic and sympathetic voice. But to me the main figure is Mr. Moody. Of course a daily paper is not the place in which to discuss his theology, even if I desire to do so. Those to whom his creed is false or offensive need not go to hear him. But as to the general tendency and usefulness of his work it seems to me clear that if there is a future life it is useful to have it and its relations to the present life sometimes brought vividly before men and women actively and anxiously engaged in the daily struggle for bread. Mr. Moody addresses himself to a multitude thus absorbed; his exhortations raise them for a time out of themselves, out of sordid cares and engrossing pursuits, and present to them in a vivid, epigrammatic, often pathetic, always simple and natural way, the greatest questions and interests which can be brought to the consideration of a being gifted with immortal life. It is surely a great merit to do this, and to do it as these "evangelists" do it—calmly, without mere passionate appeals, without efforts to capture the imagination of their hearers, and without noisy or disorderly demonstrations among their hearers.

DOCUMENT 85

Moody and Sankey

SOURCE: [Arthur G. Sedgwick], "Moody and Sankey," *The Nation* (9 March 1876), 156–57.

The patronizing tone of this editorial represents the general attitude of intellectuals toward the lower middle-class phenomenon of Moody-Sankey revivalism: Sedgwick, a graduate of Harvard College and Law School, was assistant editor of *The Nation*. He records several shrewd insights into the character of the audiences and the quality of their experience. He notes the absence of "the very poor" from the services, the preacher's avoidance of the hell-fire-and-brimstone threats of old-fashioned revivalists, and the probable influence of the urban setting on this relative "mildness" and even "refinement." The observation that Sankey is essentially a "ballad-singer" who "dramatizes the sinner's or the believer's situation as he sings" is particularly significant. It does not mean that Sankey used the traditional style of ballad singing still preserved in remote rural areas, but that he sang in a direct, unornamented manner with emphasis on the literary content of the hymns. The revival service as he and Moody developed it apparently functioned as a crude art form, a kind of rudimentary music-drama.

A very short half hour spent at the Hippodrome will probably convince any one that any very subtle explanations of the success of the revival would be thrown away. When the revivalists were in England the English press (which persisted in regarding the whole movement as phenomenal and out of the course of nature) racked its brains, if the expression may be allowed, to account to an intelligent public for the extraordinary interest excited by the preaching and singing of Messrs. Moody and Sankey; and the *Saturday Review,* if we remember right, finally announced the true explanation to be that the audience were all women, and the manifestations due to hysteria caused by the overcrowding and overheating. But at the Hippodrome the building is not overcrowded or overheated, and the audience is to a great extent masculine, and yet the success of the movement is undeniable. The explanation of this success that we should be inclined to give is a very simple one, for it is nothing more nor less than that the Moody and Sankey services are an old-fashioned revival with the modern improvements. There is, we strongly suspect, no mystery whatever about the matter; and in order that we may determine whether this is so, let us examine in detail what the mystery is commonly supposed to consist of. In the first place, some people think it very inexplicable that the revival should be conducted by a plain, uneducated man like Moody. There would be far greater cause for astonishment if a revival were to be set on foot by Dr. Hall or Dr. Washburne; but that we should find Moody at the head of it is exactly what might be antecedently expected. In the second place, a good deal of surprise has been expressed at the fact that there should be so little dogmatic theology or biblical exegesis in Moody's sermons; but a revival is not the place to look for these things. A revival preacher is no pundit, but an exhorter to a new life, and he is, by the conditions under which he works, constrained to make his exhortations simple and general. He does not appeal to the select few, but to the general mass, and he must be careful—if any care were needed—never to leave their level. The crowd that goes to the Hippodrome has certain religious feelings of a very vague sort, as a common property, and it is these that must be touched. If the Hippodrome were nightly filled with thousands of people listening anxiously to an examination by Moody of Matthew Arnold's views of the Fourth Gospel, we should certainly be astonished; but that

they should go to listen to promises of happiness, of repose of conscience, and of life eternal, from a man whom
they must instinctively feel is only different from themselves by the religion which he has "got," and of which he
tells them they too may have the endless blessings for the
asking, does not strike us as strange at all.

It would certainly be singular if, as has frequently been
alleged, there were large numbers of highly educated and
critical people who were coming under the influence of
Moody and Sankey. But though this has been frequently
stated as a fact, we have seen no proof of it, and the
general character of the audience at the Hippodrome dis-
proves it. There are, it is true, in the building a large
number of such people, but most of them belong to one of
two classes, the officially religious class (of all denominations), which sees in the revival a means of bringing religious influence to bear upon people who are ordinarily
beyond their reach, or the curious. Of the latter there are
a good many, and of the former there are many more. Outside these two classes the audience is not in any way
noticeable, except from the absence of the very poor.
Roughly speaking, it looks like an audience able to pay its
way, to ride in horse-cars, or even on rapid-transit lines,
should there ever be any.

Perhaps the most noticeable thing about the Hippodrome services is the orderly simplicity which marks them.
The interior presents the appearance of a large church well
filled with regular attendants. So far from there being any
hysteria or excitement, it is difficult to detect among the
audience any trace of violent emotion. There is so little of
it, indeed, that whole rows of the audience present the
appearance that rows in the theatre or a regular church
might present. In the old-fashioned camp-meeting all sorts
of coarse devices are resorted to to induce a somewhat
hysterical condition of mind, but these are conspicuous by
their absence at the Hippodrome. It is clear at once that
you are not in the backwoods, but in a large city which has
made considerable progress in refinement, and has learned
to insist on mildness in religion. The singing, the preach-

ing, and the whole air of the place tend to a condition of sentiment somewhat akin to that which, if we may suggest such a thing, an orthodox admirer of Renan's 'Vie de Jésus' might think truly Christian, and believers of a sterner mould consider too sentimental.

It has been observed by some persons that the musical part of the Hippodrome performances is made very prominent; and so it is. But so it has also been from the beginning of time at every revival and camp-meeting in the country. At all such meetings the rebellion against the claim of the devil to "all the good tunes" has been very marked. Camp-meeting or revival music is always a protest against religious music as given in the regular churches. There are in the Moody and Sankey hymn-books a few of the old, solemn, gloomy, and grand tunes which are to be found in every Congregational hymn-book, and the contrast between these and the Moody and Sankey tunes is very noteworthy. Musically speaking, the time of the old tunes is slow and regular, and the expression in singing is of the simplest. Pure, well-trained voices are all that is needed for such music. But the Moody and Sankey hymns, while written to religious words, are made attractive by many secular contrivances. The time is now slow, now rapid, constantly changing, the notes of every variety of length, and the general effect of the whole designed to give pronounced meaning to the words. Determine the pleasure that you get from a circus quick-step, a negro-minstrel sentimental ballad, a college chorus, and a hymn all in one, and you have some gauge of the variety and contrast that may be perceived in one of these songs. Sankey's voice is a loud and distinct, though not a refined one, and he sings with expression. He is, in fact, a trained ballad-singer, and dramatizes the sinner's or the believer's situation as he sings.

Moody is a camp-meeting preacher. In his style he is perfectly straightforward and plain; he practises no arts of oratory, and even stumbles in his delivery. There is no thought, of any consequence, in what he says; it is perfectly obvious that thought is the last thing he aims at.

What he is here for is to exhort the impenitent sinner to believe and repent, and his means of convincing him that he ought to believe and repent are not those which Jonathan Edwards would have considered the most appropriate, but simply consist of exhortation and appeals.

It has been observed that revivals are apt to occur after great commercial crises: and whether this be true or not, there has not been a revival of any importance in this part of the country since that which followed the panic of 1857. During these fifteen or twenty years people have become so unfamiliar with the phenomena of revivals that they are inclined to believe there must be some mystery in the present one. The only peculiarity that we have been able to detect in it is, that in the present case the revivalists, accommodating themselves to the spirit of the times, have left out of their programme the use of the awful warnings of future damnation which used to play such a prominent part in their appeals. In the services at the Hippodrome the sinner is not frightened or browbeaten. He is affectionately entreated to enter into the kingdom of heaven. It is represented to him to be an easy matter—a matter not of ritual or works, but of exertion of the will. The revivalists' God is not the just Jehovah of the Puritans, holding the scales even and meting out rewards and punishment with an impartial and unpitying hand—a God who keeps the fires of hell constantly replenished with brimstone, and whose scheme of the universe is not complete without devils as well as angels. He is, on the contrary, a mild and loving God, forgiving and pardoning to the last; a God who cares little for correctness of dogma so that the heart be pure—the God of the ignorant no less than the wise, and who is present at the overflow meetings at the Hippodrome no less than at the churches on the Fifth Avenue corner lots.

Whether such a revival does harm or good, is one of those questions which are often put about movements on a great scale without much reflection as to what they really mean. What is meant by "good" and what by "bad" in such a connection? If we mean, Does the revival really "revive" the people affected by it? there cannot be any doubt that it does. The question in this form is very much like asking whether the women's whiskey crusade in the West in 1874 left the West at the end as drunken as at the beginning. The success of a moral or religious revival must be its own best proof. But if we ask whether the revival has, on the whole, improved the tone of those affected by it, we must ask what it attempted to do for them. Now, Messrs. Moody and Sankey's attempt has simply been to arouse an interest and belief in the efficacy of religion—not any particular kind of Christianity, but of Christianity itself; and it is utterly beyond belief that this can do any one any harm. We have no hesitation in saying that any father of a family, no matter of what sort, may risk himself, and his wife, and his children, and his maid-servant, and his man-servant, and the stranger within his gates at the Hippodrome, without fear of the result. They may not be edified, but they certainly cannot be harmed. There is only one type of person likely to be injured by Messrs. Moody and Sankey, and that is the type which from time immemorial has got little good out of any kind of religious services: we mean the character known to the religious as the "scoffer." But the scoffer will always scoff, whether there is anything to scoff at or not, and his scoffing makes but little difference in the long run.

FIVE GOSPEL HYMNS

When Moody and Sankey were making their first brilliant success in England, the London *Times* said that "The real attraction was the singing."* Although Charles G. Finney had experimented in the use of a musical director for revival services in New York as early as 1832, Sankey's function as an acknowledged colleague of the preacher was a striking innovation in the technique of religious revivals. His contribution was so great that the plan was quickly imitated; all the prominent revival preachers of the 1870s equipped themselves with professional singers and musical directors, and the practice continued into the twentieth century in Billy Sunday's reliance on Homer A. Rodeheaver and Billy Graham's on George Beverly Shea. Sankey as a singer was an almost exact analogue of Moody as a preacher. He had virtually no formal training and commanded none of the graces of operatic style. He thought of himself as preaching the gospel by means of words set to music. He emphasized careful enunciation, and in a pre-electronic era he could make

* William G. McLoughlin, Jr., *Modern Revivalism*, p. 233.

himself heard distinctly by every member of an audience of ten or twelve thousand. His solos were noted for their effect of extreme pathos. At the same time, Sankey was a gifted leader of group singing. He had first attracted Moody's attention at a Y.M.C.A. convention in 1870, when Sankey "lifted the singing from the customary slow drawl into one of his own heavenward flights of song."† Alone, if necessary, but usually with the aid of a chorus of two or three hundred singers selected from the congregations and choirs of various churches in whatever city he was working in, he could rouse a heterogeneous audience to soaring and vibrant effects. A hardened New York reporter, not particularly sympathetic with the revival services, was forced on one occasion to declare that the rendition of Philip P. Bliss's "What Shall the Harvest Be?" with Sankey singing the verses solo and the congregation, with the choir, joining in the choruses, was, "as a specimen of congregational music . . . simply magnificent."‡

But this was an unusually elaborate tune, with an antiphonal arrangement of two parts in the chorus. Most of the gospel songs for congregational singing were simpler, having a rigorously conventional melodic and harmonic structure. Anything more complex would have been ordinarily beyond the reach of a miscellaneous gathering of untrained singers. And since five or ten thousand voices could not be kept together and held up from a "slow drawl" without a vigorous, predictable beat, the most effective and popular congregational songs tended to be brisk, joyful compositions suggesting, as the editorial in *The Nation* (Document 85) notes, a "circus quick-step." Young people left the meetings singing the gospel hymns on the streets and in the cars. Given the emotional tension developed by Moody and Sankey, one is tempted to think of Negro church services in which the sermon grows rhythmic and becomes a chant, the responses of the audience fall into place as antiphonal responses, and hand clapping and even processions of singers in the aisles seem to grow in-

† W. H. Daniels, ed., *Moody: His Words, Work, and Workers* (New York, 1877), p. 483.
‡ New York *Herald*, 15 November 1875, p. 5, col. 6.

evitably out of the music. Bodily self-expression of this kind had been normal for whites as well as Negroes in camp meetings since the eighteenth century. Moody's and Sankey's audiences, however, were urban, and a sense of gentility seems to have inhibited their impulses toward physical movement. Reporters often commented with surprise on the order and decorum in the meetings. Moody sternly repressed any hint of hysteria, although he sometimes invited questions or comments from his hearers.

Even though overt physical responses to the rhythm of gospel hymns were suppressed, the congregational singing of these songs undoubtedly provided an intensely felt rhythmic experience. Here was a common denominator below the level of verbalization and thus free from the threat of doctrinal differences. Sankey's gift was to provide for each member of these vast crowds of strangers an opportunity to feel himself, by virtue of melody and rhythm, integrated with the group, accepted into a brotherhood—just as the words of the preacher and the verses of the hymns repeated over and over again the simple invitation for the lost one to come back into the security of the fold.

DOCUMENT 86

The Ninety and Nine

SOURCE: Ira D. Sankey, "The Ninety and Nine" (to words by Elizabeth C. Clephane), *Gospel Hymns Combined*, compiled by Philip P. Bliss, Ira D. Sankey, James McGranahan, and George C. Stebbins (New York, 1879), No. 6, p. 8.

This is the only tune composed by Sankey which attained wide popularity, but it was demanded of him constantly, and there are many reports of its power to bring tears to the eyes of his hearers. According to Sankey's own account, he composed the melody extempore as he sat at the organ on the platform of a meeting in Edinburgh in 1874. The words he sang were those of a poem by a Scottish woman named Elizabeth C. Clephane which he had clipped from a newspaper a couple of days before.* In the published version the song bears the stern injunction, "To be sung only as a solo"; the melody was felt to be too complex and delicate for congregational singing. The import of the words made this hymn an appropriate choice to introduce Moody's sermon on the Prodigal Son. Sankey's hearers readily interpreted the familiar scriptural imagery of shepherd and sheep as a reference to the state of the sinner lost in the desert of the industrial city.

* Ira D. Sankey, *My Life and the Story of the Gospel Hymns and of Sacred Songs and Solos* (Philadelphia, 1906), pp. 304–8.

The Ninety and Nine

"Rejoice with me, for I have found my sheep that was lost."—LUKE 15: 6.

ELIZABETH C. CLEPHANE, 1868.

TO BE SUNG ONLY AS A SOLO.

IRA D. SANKEY, by per.

1. There were nine-ty and nine that safe - ly lay In the shel-ter of the
2. "Lord, Thou hast here Thy nine-ty and nine; Are they not e - nough for

fold, But one was out on the hills a-way, Far off from the gates of
Thee?" "But the Shep-herd made an-swer: "'Tis of mine Has wan-dered a-way from

gold A - way on the moun-tains wild and bare, A-way from the ten - der
me And al-though the road be rough and steep I go to the des-ert to

Shep-herd's care, A - way from the ten - der Shep-herd's care.
find my sheep, I go to the des-ert to find my sheep."

3.
But none of the ransomed ever knew
   How deep were the waters crossed;
Nor how dark was the night that the Lord
   passed through
Ere He found His sheep that was lost.
Out in the desert He heard its cry—
Sick and helpless, and ready to die.

4.
"Lord, whence are those blood-drops all
   the way
   That mark out the mountain's track?"
"They were shed for one who had gone
   astray

Ere the Shepherd could bring him back."
"Lord, whence are Thy hands so rent and
   torn?"
"They are pierced to-night by many a
   thorn."

5.
But all thro' the mountains, thunder-riven,
   And up from the rocky steep,
There rose a cry to the gate of heaven,
   "Rejoice! I have found my sheep!"
And the angels echoed around the throne,
"Rejoice, for the Lord brings back His
   own!"

Almost Persuaded

SOURCE: Philip P. Bliss (words and music), "Almost Persuaded," *Gospel Hymns Combined*, compiled by Philip P. Bliss, Ira D. Sankey, James McGranahan, and George C. Stebbins (New York, 1879), No. 75, p. 72.

This song was used both as a solo and, especially at the end of a service, as an "invitation hymn" for congregational singing. William G. McLoughlin, Jr., remarks that songs of this type "were specifically written for the purpose of coaxing people out of their seats and into the inquiry rooms. They pleaded with the sinner, hypnotically tugging him forward by repeating over and over again the words 'come,' 'trust,' 'now' as he debated with his conscience. It was a vastly different atmosphere from Finney's righteous warning to take the anxious seat."* Here the dramatization of the lost one's situation is especially vivid. He is a wanderer, a stray from the flock, and he is invited to renounce his solitude. The decision lies within his power; if he delays, he is in mortal danger, for "doom comes at last," and his epitaph must be "Almost—*but lost!*"

The melody seems already to be mourning the fate of the wanderer who repents too late. Yet it is in ⁶/₈ time, and the sadness has a bittersweet quality, not unlike that of a slow waltz, which is emphasized by the hold in the last measure but one. This kind of pathos is capable of yielding its own sentimental pleasure.

Bliss grew up in northern Pennsylvania and Ohio with virtually no formal education, worked on farms and in lumber camps and sawmills, and then taught country schools. He had a remarkable natural bass voice.

* *Modern Revivalism*, p. 239.

After six weeks of study at a "Normal Academy of Music" in Geneseo, New York, in 1860, he became a professional music teacher, continuing to attend the Normal Academy in the summers of 1861 and 1863. In 1864 he submitted a sentimental song to Root & Cady, of Chicago, who published it. For several years he worked for this firm as traveling salesman, conductor of "musical conventions," and concert singer in small towns of the upper Middle West. He met Moody in 1870 in Chicago and through him became musical director of the First Congregational Church in that city. In 1874 he became musical director for D. W. Whittle, a friend of Moody and an itinerant evangelist, and continued in this capacity until his death in a railroad accident in 1876.†

The day after Cornelius Vanderbilt died Henry Ward Beecher devoted his remarks at a prayer meeting in Plymouth Church to a contrast between Vanderbilt's value to the world and the value of Philip P. Bliss, who had died a short time before. Bliss's life, said Beecher, was devoted to "Softening and ennobling the hearts of men."

> I don't think his hymns will last like Watts' and Wesley's [he continued], and yet they have been a power in this land. The hymns written by Mr. Bliss have been a silent influence, gentle as the rain of summer, and they have moved thousands and tens of thousands of tender roots to spring up in the hearts of men. Here is a man almost unknown, except as a "sweet singer in Israel." He held no such place as Vanderbilt, and it is not right to compare the two, except to say that it seems to me Mr. Bliss has done a far grander work, he has opened the door for souls, he has caused love to blossom, he has brought something of the spirit of heaven down to earth, he has been a tongue of the Lord. It is a noble life. . . .‡

† D. W. Whittle, ed., *Memoirs of Philip P. Bliss*, New York, 1877.
‡ New York *Herald*, 6 January 1877, p. 3, col. 5.

Almost Persuaded

"Almost Thou persuadest me to be a Christian."—Acts 26: 28.

P. P. Bliss. P. P. Bliss, by per.

1. "Al - most per - suad - ed" Now to be - lieve;
"Al - most per - suad - ed" Christ to re - ceive;
Seems now some soul to say, "Go, Spir - it, go Thy way,
Some more con - ven - ient day On Thee I'll call."

2. "Al - most per - suad - ed," Come, come to - day;
"Al - most per - suad - ed," Turn not a - way;
Je - sus in - vites you here, An - gels are lingering near,
Prayers rise from hearts so dear: O wanderer, come.

3 "Almost persuaded," harvest is past!
"Almost persuaded," doom comes at last!
"Almost" can not avail;
"Almost" is but to fail!
Sad, sad, that bitter wail—
"Almost—*but lost!*"

DOCUMENT 88

Whosoever Will

SOURCE: Philip P. Bliss (words and music), "Whosoever Will," *Gospel Hymns Combined*, compiled by Philip P. Bliss, Ira D. Sankey, James McGranahan, and George C. Stebbins (New York, 1879), No. 10, p. 12.

This vigorous tune for congregational singing, marked "Joyfully," in $\frac{4}{4}$ time, has a swinging march rhythm. One can almost hear trombones sliding upward a half-tone into the first note of the chorus. Once again the wanderer is being called home, but here he is certain to return, and the welcoming ceremony has already begun.

Sankey said that this hymn was composed in Chicago during the winter of 1869–70 after Bliss had heard Henry Moorehouse, an English evangelist, preach seven successive sermons on John 3:16.*

* *My Life and the Story of the Gospel Hymns*, pp. 344–45.

"Whosoever Will"

"Whosoever will, let him take the water of life freely."—REV. 22: 17.

P. P. BLISS.   P. P. BLISS, by per.

Joyfully

1. "Who-so-ev-er hear-eth,"shout,shout the sound! Send the bles-sed tid-ings
2. Who-so-ev-er com-eth, need not de-lay, Now the door is o-pen,
3. "Who-so-ev-er will,"the prom-ise se-cure; "Who so-ev-er will,"for

all the world a round; Spread the joy-ful news wher-ev-er man is found:
en-ter while you may; Je-sus is the true, the on-ly Liv-ing Way:
ev-er must en-dure;"Who-so-ev-er will,"'tis life for e-ver-more:

CHORUS.

"Who-so-ev-er will, may come." "Who-so-ev-er will, who-so-ev-er will,"

Send the proc-la-ma-tion o-ver vale and hill; 'Tis a lov-ing

Fa-ther calls the wand'rer home:"Who-so-ev-er will, may come."

DOCUMENT 89 (a) AND (b)

We're Marching to Zion
Shirland

SOURCES: Robert Lowry, "We're Marching to Zion" (to words by Isaac Watts), *Gospel Hymns Combined*, compiled by Philip P. Bliss, Ira D. Sankey, James McGranahan, and George C. Stebbins (New York, 1879), No. 250, p. 223.

Samuel Stanley, "Shirland", *The Congregational Hymn and Tune Book; Containing the Psalms and Hymns of the General Association of Connecticut, Adapted to Suitable Tunes* (New Haven, 1856), p. 240.

Next to Bliss, Lowry (pastor of a Baptist church in Brooklyn) and William B. Bradbury were the most successful composers of tunes for gospel songs. This hymn was composed in the 1850s but was popular in post-Civil War revivals. In it Lowry provided for an Isaac Watts hymn a new musical setting which involves the addition of a repeated line within the stanza and a chorus lacking in the original version. The drastic change in musical style represented by the gospel songs is immediately apparent if one compares Lowry's tune with "Shirland," the tune indicated for the same Watts hymn in such a standard work as *The Congregational Hymn and Tune Book* (published for the General Association of Connecticut in New Haven in 1856). Although the meter of Lowry's tune is technically ⁶⁄₈, the instruction "Spirited" suggests a tempo which would make the tune a brisk march with two strong beats per measure. Lowry also composed words and music for the march-like "Shall We Gather by the River?" (1864) and the melody for "I Need Thee Every Hour," in ¾ time, which has some of the melancholy of "Almost Persuaded."

We're Marching to Zion

"We are journeying unto the place of which the Lord said, I will give it you."—Num. 10:29.

Rev. I. Watts.

Rev. R. Lowry, by per.

Spirited

1. Come, we that love the Lord, And let our joys be known, Join in a song with sweet ac-cord, Join in a song with sweet ac-cord, And thus sur-round the throne. And thus sur-round the throne.
2. Let those re-fuse to sing Who nev-er knew our God; But chil-dren of the heav'n-ly King, But child-ren of the heav'n-ly King May speak their joys a-broad, May speak their joys a-broad.
3. The hill of Zi-on yields A thou-sand sa-cred sweets, Be-fore we reach the heav'n-ly fields, Be-fore we reach the heav'n-ly fields, Or walk the gold-en streets, Or walk the gold-en streets,
4. Then let our songs a-bound, And ev-ery tear be dry; We're march-ing thro' Immanuel's ground, We're march-ing thro' Immanuel's ground, To fair-er worlds on high, To fair-er worlds on high.

And thus sur-round the throne, And thus sur-round the throne.

CHORUS.

We're march-ing to Zi-on, Beau-ti-ful, beau-ti-ful Zi-on; We're

We're march-ing on to Zi-on,

march-ing up ward to Zi-on, The beau-ti-ful cit-y of God.

Zi-on, Zi-on,

Shirland. S.M.

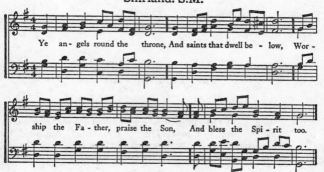

Ye an-gels round the throne, And saints that dwell be - low, Wor-

ship the Fa - ther, praise the Son, And bless the Spi - rit too.

DOCUMENT 90

Sweet Hour of Prayer

SOURCE: William B. Bradbury, "Sweet Hour of Prayer" (to words by W. W. Walford), *Gospel Hymns Combined*, compiled by Philip P. Bliss, Ira D. Sankey, James McGranahan, and George C. Stebbins (New York, 1879), No. 77, p. 74.

Bradbury, a pioneer composer of gospel songs, was also a noted compiler of hymn books from the 1850s onward. As in some other gospel hymns, there is the suggestion here of a contradiction between the meaning of the words and the emotional effect of the tune. Although the verses describe a tranquil meditation, the $\frac{6}{8}$ melody threatens to become a jig or a minstrel tap dance. The composer's indication "Slow" recognizes the need for restraint when so bouncy a tune as this was being sung by a large congregation.

Sweet Hour of Prayer

"Evening, and morning, and at noon will I pray."—Psalm 4: 17.

Rev. W. W. Walford, 1846.

Wm. B. Bradbury, 1859.

Slow.

1. Sweet hour of prayer! sweet hour of prayer! That calls me from a
world of care, And bids me at my Fa-ther's throne Make
all my wants and wish-es known: In sea - sons of distress and grief, My soul has oft - en found re - lief;

And oft es - caped the tempter's snare, By thy re - turn, sweet
hour of prayer, And oft es - caped the tempt-er's snare, By
thy re - turn, sweet hour of prayer!

FINE.

D.C.

Suggested Readings

The following twenty books are listed for the convenience of students who wish to explore various aspects of American popular culture in the later nineteenth century. Most of them have already been cited in footnotes. Roman numerals in SMALL CAPITALS refer to relevant sections of the anthology. Unless another place of publication is specified, the books were published in New York.

Carl Bode, *The Anatomy of American Popular Culture, 1840–1861* (Berkeley and Los Angeles: University of California Press, 1959). GENERAL

Paul H. Buck, *The Road to Reunion, 1865–1900* (Boston: Little, Brown, 1937). I

Wesley F. Craven, *The Legend of the Founding Fathers* (New York University Press, 1956). I

Chester M. Destler, *American Radicalism, 1865–1901: Essays and Documents* (New London: Connecticut College Bookshop, 1946). VI

Sigmund Diamond, *The Reputation of the American Businessman* (Cambridge: Harvard University Press, 1955). II

Siegfried Giedion, *Mechanization Takes Command: A Contribution to Anonymous History* (Oxford University Press, 1948). I

Thomas F. Gossett, *Race: The History of an Idea in America* (Dallas: Southern Methodist University Press, 1963). IV

Oscar Handlin, *The Uprooted: The Epic Story of the Great Migrations That Made the American People* (Boston: Atlantic Monthly Press, 1951). V

James D. Hart, *The Popular Book: A History of America's Literary Taste* (Oxford University Press, 1950).   VIII

John Higham, *Strangers in the Land: Patterns of American Nativism, 1860–1925* (New Brunswick, N.J.: Rutgers University Press, 1955).   V

Edward C. Kirkland, *Industry Comes of Age: Business, Labor and Public Policy, 1860–1897* (Vol. VI of *The Economic History of the United States*, eds. Henry David and others) (Holt, 1961).   VI, VII

Russell Lynes, *The Taste-Makers* (Harper, 1954).   VIII

William G. McLoughlin, Jr., *Modern Revivalism: Charles Grandison Finney to Billy Graham* (Ronald, 1959).   IX

Henry F. May, *Protestant Churches and Industrial America* (Harper, 1949).   IX

Perry Miller, ed., *American Thought: Civil War to World War I* (Rinehart, 1954).   GENERAL

Lewis Mumford, *The Brown Decades: A Study of the Arts in America, 1865–1895* (Harcourt, Brace, 1931).   VIII

Mary Noel, *Villains Galore: The Heyday of the Popular Story Weekly* (Macmillan, 1954).   VIII

Constance M. Rourke, *Trumpets of Jubilee: Lyman Beecher, Harriet Beecher Stowe, Henry Ward Beecher, Horace Greeley, P. T. Barnum* (Harcourt, Brace, 1927).   VIII, IX

Arthur M. Schlesinger, *The Rise of the City, 1878–1898* (Macmillan, 1933).   III

Comer Vann Woodward, *The Strange Career of Jim Crow: A Brief Account of Segregation* (Gloucester, Mass.: Peter Smith, 1957; rev. ed., 1962).   IV

ANCHOR BOOKS

AMERICAN HISTORY AND STUDIES

AMERICAN HUMOR—Constance Rourke, A12

AMERICAN LIFE IN THE 1840s—Carl Bode, ed., AD4

THE AMERICAN LITERARY REVOLUTION 1783–1837—Robert E. Spiller, ed., AD6

THE AMERICAN NOVEL AND ITS TRADITION—Richard Chase, A116

AMERICAN POETRY AND POETICS—Daniel Hoffman, ed., A304

THE AMERICAN PURITANS: THEIR PROSE AND POETRY—Perry Miller, ed., A80

AMERICAN RACE RELATIONS TODAY—Earl Raab, ed., A318

AMERICAN SOCIAL PATTERNS—William Petersen, A86

AMERICAN STRATEGY: A New Perspective—The Growth of Politico-Military Thinking in the United States—Urs Schwarz, A587

THE AMERICAN TRANSCENDENTALISTS: THEIR PROSE AND POETRY—Perry Miller, ed., A119

CAN AMERICAN DEMOCRACY SURVIVE COLD WAR?—Harry Howe Ransom, A402

CASTE AND CLASS IN A SOUTHERN TOWN—John Dollard, A95

CAVALIER AND YANKEE: The Old South and American National Character—William R. Taylor, A351

CHRISTIAN SCIENCE: Its Encounter with American Culture—Robert Peel, A446

THE CIVIL WAR IN AMERICA—Alan Barker, A274

THE COMPLETE POEMS AND SELECTED LETTERS AND PROSE OF HART CRANE—edited with an Introduction and Notes by Brom Weber, A537

CONGRESSMAN—Charles L. Clapp, A426

CONSTRAINT AND VARIETY IN AMERICAN EDUCATION—David Riesman, A135

THE DEATH PENALTY IN AMERICA, Revised Edition—Hugo Adam Bedau, ed., A387

THE EMANCIPATION PROCLAMATION—John Hope Franklin, A459

THE EXPLODING METROPOLIS—the Editors of Fortune, A146

THE FEDERALIST PAPERS, Second Edition—Roy P. Fairfield, ed., A239

THE FIRST AMENDMENT: The History of Religious Freedom in America—William H. Marnell, A472

THE FIRST NEW NATION—The United States in Historical and Comparative Perspective—Seymour Martin Lipset, A597

IDEOLOGY AND POWER IN THE AGE OF JACKSON—Edwin C. Rozwenc, ed., AD1

THE IMMEDIATE EXPERIENCE—Robert Warshaw, A410

THE INDIAN AND THE WHITE MAN—Wilcomb E. Washburn, ed., AD2

KILLERS OF THE DREAM—Lillian Smith, A339

LITERATURE AND THE AMERICAN TRADITION—Leon Howard, A329

MAN-MADE MORALS: Four Philosophies That Shaped America—William H. Marnell, A613

MARGARET FULLER: AMERICAN ROMANTIC, A Selection from Her Writings and Correspondence—Perry Miller, ed., A356

THE NATURE OF PREJUDICE—Gordon Allport, A149

THE NEGRO AND THE AMERICAN LABOR MOVEMENT—Julius Jacobson, ed., A495

ON NATIVE GROUNDS—Alfred Kazin, A69

THE ORGANIZATION MAN—William H. Whyte, Jr., A117

POLITICS IN AMERICA—D. W. Brogan, A198

POPULAR CULTURE AND INDUSTRIALISM, 1865–1890—ed. by Henry Nash Smith, AD5

THE POSITIVE THINKERS: A Study of the American Quest for Health, Wealth and Personal Power from Mary Baker Eddy to Norman Vincent Peale—Donald Meyer, A525

PROTESTANT, CATHOLIC, JEW—Will Herberg, A195

PURITAN VILLAGE: The Formation of a New England Town—Summer Chilton Powell, A441

QUEST FOR AMERICA—Charles Sanford, ed., AD3

RACE AND NATIONALITY IN AMERICAN LIFE—Oscar Handlin, A

RELIGIOUS CONFLICT IN AMERICA—Earl Raab, ed., A392

TEACHER IN AMERICA—Jacques Barzun, A25

THE THEOLOGY OF JONATHAN EDWARDS—Conrad Cherry, Introduction by Will Herberg, A542

WHITE MAN, LISTEN!—Richard Wright, A414

WHO DESIGNS AMERICA?—ed. by Laurence B. Holland, A523

ANCHOR BOOKS

HISTORY

AFRICA AND THE VICTORIANS: The Climax of Imperialism—Ronald Robinson and John Gallagher, A614

THE ANCIENT CITY—Fustel de Coulanges, A76

THE ARAB WORLD TODAY—Morroe Berger, A406

BAGEHOT'S HISTORICAL ESSAYS—Norman St. John-Stevas, ed., A451

THE BIRTH OF CIVILIZATION IN THE NEAR EAST—Henri Frankfort, A89

THE BOOK OF THE COURTIER: Baldesar Castiglione—Charles S. Singleton, trans., A186

THE BRUTAL FRIENDSHIP: Mussolini, Hitler and the Fall of Italian Fascism—F. W. Deakin, A508a

CRISIS AND COMPROMISE: Politics in the Fourth Republic—Philip M. Williams, A518

CRISIS IN EUROPE, 1560–1660—Trevor Aston, ed., A575

DARWIN, MARX, WAGNER—Jacques Barzun, A127

DISCOVERIES AND OPINIONS OF GALILEO—Stillman Drake, trans., A94

THE DISCOVERY OF INDIA—Jawaharlal Nehru, Robert I. Crane, ed., A200

THE EARLY CHRISTIAN CHURCH—J. G. Davies, A566

ENGLAND: From Pre-History to the Present—Martin J. Havran and Arvel B. Erickson, AO2

1848: THE REVOLUTION OF THE INTELLECTUALS—Lewis Namier, A385

THE ELIZABETHAN JOURNALS, Vol. I: Being a Record of Those Things Most Talked of During the Years 1591–1597—G. B. Harrison, ed., A458a

THE ELIZABETHAN JOURNALS, Vol. II: Being a Record of Those Things Most Talked of During the Years 1598–1603—G. B. Harrison, ed., A458b

THE ERA OF TYRANNIES—Elie Halévy; Robert K. Webb, trans., A463

ESSAYS ON OLD TESTAMENT HISTORY AND RELIGION—Albrecht Alt, A544

THE FALL OF PARIS—Alistair Horne, A562

FOUR STAGES OF RENAISSANCE STYLE—Wylie Sypher, A44

FROM HEGEL TO NIETZSCHE—The Revolution in Nineteenth-Century Thought—Karl Lowith; David E. Green, trans., A553

FROM THE STONE AGE TO CHRISTIANITY—W. F. Albright, A100

GATEWAY TO HISTORY—Allan Nevins, New, revised edition, A314

HISTORY BEGINS AT SUMER—Samuel Noah Kramer, A175

A HISTORY OF BOLSHEVISM—From Marx to the First Five Years' Plan, Arthur Rosenberg; translated from the German by Ian F. D. Morrow, A588

HISTORY OF ENGLAND, Vol. I—G. M. Trevelyan, A22a

HISTORY OF ENGLAND, Vol. II—G. M. Trevelyan, A22b

HISTORY OF ENGLAND, Vol. III—G. M. Trevelyan, A22c

A HISTORY OF EUROPE, Vol. 1—Henri Pirenne, A156a

A HISTORY OF EUROPE, Vol. 2—Henri Pirenne, A156b

A HISTORY OF ISLAMIC SPAIN—W. Montgomery Watt and Pierre Cachia, A601

A HISTORY OF THE ITALIAN REPUBLICS—J. C. L. Sismondi; Introduction by Wallace K. Ferguson, A520

A HISTORY OF ROME—Moses Hadas, ed., A78

A HISTORY OF WEST AFRICA—Basil Davidson, A550

HITLER'S SOCIAL REVOLUTION—Class and Status in Nazi Germany, 1933–1939—David Schoenbaum, A590

THE HOUSE OF HABSBURG—Adam Wandruszka, A453

IMPERIALISM AND SOCIAL REFORM: English Social-Imperial Thought, 1895–1914—Bernard Semmel, A618

THE INTELLECTUAL HISTORY OF EUROPE, Vol. I: The Beginnings of Western Civilization to Luther—Friedrich Heer, A610a

THE INTELLECTUAL HISTORY OF EUROPE, Vol. II: The Counter-Reformation to the 20th Century—Friedrich Heer, A610b

JOURNEYS TO ENGLAND AND IRELAND—Alexis de Tocqueville; J. P. Mayer, ed., A611

LABOURING MEN—Studies in the History of Labour—E. J. Hobsbawm, A552

MARTYRDOM AND PERSECUTION IN THE EARLY CHURCH—W. H. C. Frend, A546

MEDIEVAL CITIES—Henri Pirenne, A82

MONT-SAINT-MICHEL AND CHARTRES—Henry Adams, A166

A NEW HISTORY OF THE COLD WAR: Third edition, expanded, of A History of the Cold War—John A. Lukacs, A533

THE OLD REGIME AND THE FRENCH REVOLUTION—Alexis de Tocqueville, A60

THE PATH TO DICTATORSHIP, 1918–1933: Ten Essays by German Historians—trans. by John Conway, with an introduction by Fritz Stern, A547

THE PHILOSOPHY OF HISTORY IN OUR TIME—Hans Meyerhoff, ed., A164

THE POLITICS OF CULTURAL DESPAIR: A Study in the Rise of Germanic Ideology—Fritz Stern, A436

THE PURITAN REVOLUTION: A Documentary History—Stuart E. Prall, ed., A602

QUEEN ELIZABETH I—J. E. Neale, A105

THE RUSSIAN REVOLUTION—Leon Trotsky, F. W. Dupee, ed., A170

SEVENTEENTH CENTURY BACKGROUND—Basil Willey, A19

SEVENTEENTH CENTURY FRANCE—Geoffrey Treasure, A592

THE SIX HUNDRED DAYS OF MUSSOLINI—F. W. Deakin, A508b

THE SPLENDID CENTURY—W. H. Lewis, A122

STATES AND NATIONS—Benjamin Akzin, A493

THIRTY YEARS WAR—C. V. Wedgwood, A249

TODAY'S LATIN AMERICA—Robert J. Alexander, A327

TO THE FINLAND STATION—Edmund Wilson, A6

THE WANING OF THE MIDDLE AGES—John Huizinga, A42

THE YORKIST AGE: Daily Life During the Wars of the Roses—Paul Murray Kendall, A466